REGIME TYPE AND BEYOND

Policing is legitimized in different ways in authoritarian and democratic states. In East and Southeast Asia, different regime types to a greater or lesser extent determine the power of the police and their complex relationship with the rule of law. This volume examines the evolution of the police as a key political institution from a historical perspective and offers comparative insights into the potential of democratic policing and conversely the resilience of authoritarian policing in Asia. The case studies focus on eight jurisdictions: Singapore, Thailand, Hong Kong, Vietnam, China, Taiwan, Japan and South Korea. The theoretical chapters analyse and explain the links between policing and society, the politics of policing and recent police reforms. This volume fills a gap in the literature by exploring the nature of authoritarian policing and how it has transformed and developed the rule of law throughout East and Southeast Asia.

WEITSENG CHEN is Associate Professor at the National University of Singapore Faculty of Law and Fellow of the Institute for Advanced Study in Berlin.

HUALING FU is Professor of Law and holder of the Warren Chan Professorship in Human Rights and Responsibilities at the University of Hong Kong, and currently serves as the Dean of the Faculty of Law.

REGIME TYPE AND BEYOND

The Transformation of Police in Asia

Edited by

WEITSENG CHEN

National University of Singapore

HUALING FU

The University of Hong Kong

CAMBRIDGE
UNIVERSITY PRESS

CAMBRIDGE
UNIVERSITY PRESS

Shaftesbury Road, Cambridge CB2 8EA, United Kingdom

One Liberty Plaza, 20th Floor, New York, NY 10006, USA

477 Williamstown Road, Port Melbourne, VIC 3207, Australia

314–321, 3rd Floor, Plot 3, Splendor Forum, Jasola District Centre, New Delhi – 110025, India

103 Penang Road, #05–06/07, Visioncrest Commercial, Singapore 238467

Cambridge University Press is part of Cambridge University Press & Assessment, a department of the University of Cambridge.

We share the University's mission to contribute to society through the pursuit of education, learning and research at the highest international levels of excellence.

www.cambridge.org
Information on this title: www.cambridge.org/9781009045421

DOI: 10.1017/9781009042154

First published 2023
First paperback edition 2025

A catalogue record for this publication is available from the British Library

ISBN 978-1-316-51741-3 Hardback
ISBN 978-1-009-04542-1 Paperback

CONTENTS

FIGURES

TABLES

CONTRIBUTORS

SARAH BIDDULPH is Professor of Law at the Melbourne Law School and Director of its Asian Law Centre. Sarah's research focuses on the Chinese legal system with a particular emphasis on legal policy, law making and enforcement as they affect the administration of justice in China. Her areas of research are contemporary Chinese administrative law, criminal procedure, labor, comparative law, and the law regulating social and economic rights. In her role as Assistant Deputy Vice Chancellor International – China, she has been instrumental in developing and implementing the University of Melbourne's strategic direction for engagement with China.

WEITSENG CHEN is Associate Professor at the National University of Singapore (NUS) Faculty of Law and a fellow of the Institute for Advanced Study in Berlin (Wissenschaftskolleg zu Berlin). He specializes in comparative Chinese law within greater China as well as law and development in East Asia. Before joining the NUS Faculty of Law, he was Hewlett Fellow of the Center on Democracy, Development and the Rule of Law at Stanford University, and also practiced as a corporate lawyer at Davis Polk & Wardwell.

LOK LEE CHO is a PhD candidate in the Department of Sociology at the University of Hong Kong. Her research interests include criminology, social movement studies, policing, and political sociology. She was a visiting student researcher at the University of California, Berkeley in 2022.

JACQUES DELISLE is Stephen A. Cozen Professor of Law, Professor of Political Science, and Director of the Center for the Study of Contemporary China at the University of Pennsylvania, and Director of the Asia Program at the Foreign Policy Research Institute. His writings, on Chinese law and politics, China's engagement with the international order, legal-institutional change in China, Taiwan/cross-Strait relations, and US–China relations have appeared in *Orbis*, *Journal of Contemporary*

China, *Asia Policy*, *China Review*, *Administrative Law Review*, and other international affairs journals, law reviews, and edited volumes.

HUALING FU is Professor of Law and holder of the Warren Chan Professorship in Human Rights and Responsibilities at the University of Hong Kong, and currently serves as the Dean of the Faculty of Law. His research areas include the constitutional development and legal institutions in China.

PAUL JOOSSE is Associate Professor of Sociology at the University of Hong Kong. His work on Max Weber, political legitimation, and criminology has been published in *Social Forces*, *Sociological Theory*, and *British Journal of Criminology*, among others. He is the recipient of the American Sociological Association's Junior Theorist Award, the International Sociological Association's Junior Theorist Prize, and the ASA's Clifford Geertz Prize for best article in cultural sociology.

JEDIDIAH J. KRONCKE is Associate Professor of Law at the University of Hong Kong, having earned a doctorate in anthropology from Berkeley and a law degree from Yale. His work focuses on transnational historical and comparative approaches to cross-cultural legal analysis. His articles have addressed comparative issues relating to the US, Chinese, and Brazilian legal systems, as well as law and development, authoritarian law, comparative constitutionalism, legal education, and economic republicanism.

JEFFREY T. MARTIN is Associate Professor in the Departments of Anthropology and East Asian Languages and Cultures, at the University of Illinois, Urbana-Champaign (UIUC). He holds a PhD in sociocultural anthropology from the University of Chicago, and has spent most of his career studying similarities and differences in the way policing is organized in East Asian and Anglo-American contexts.

EUGÉNIE MÉRIEAU is an associate professor of Public Law at the University of Paris 1 Panthéon-Sorbonne, and a member of the Sorbonne Institute of Philosophical and Legal Sciences. She is the author of *Constitutional Bricolage: Thailand's Sacred Monarchy vs. the Rule of Law* (Hart, 2021).

ERIK MOBRAND is associate professor in the Graduate School of International Studies at Seoul National University. He is currently

Korea Policy Chair at the RAND Corporation. He is the author of *Top-Down Democracy in South Korea* (University of Washington Press, 2019).

KOICHI NAKANO is Professor of Political Science and former Dean of the Faculty of Liberal Arts, Sophia University in Tokyo. He specializes in the comparative politics of advanced industrial democracies and in political theory. His publications include *Party Politics and Decentralization in Japan and France: When the Opposition Governs* (Routledge, 2010).

MICHAEL NG is Associate Professor of the Faculty of Law at the University of Hong Kong. He is a legal historian focusing on the legal history of modern China and Hong Kong. He is the author of *Political Censorship in British Hong Kong – Freedom of Expression and the Law (1842–1997)* (Cambridge University Press, 2021) and *Legal Transplantation in Early 20th Century China – Practicing Law in Republican Beijing (1910s–1930s)* (Routledge, 2014), and has published in leading international refereed journals including *Law and History Review*, Modern Asia Studies, *China Quarterly*, Business History, and *Law and Literature*, among others. He held visiting positions in University of Cambridge, University of Melbourne, National University of Singapore and National Taiwan University.

TRANG (MAE) NGUYEN is an associate professor of Law at Temple University Beasley School of Law and an affiliated scholar at the US Asia Law Institute, New York University (NYU) School of Law. Her research focuses on the intersection of business law, transnational law, and comparative law. Her work has appeared in the Harvard International Law Journal, the *American Journal of International Law Unbound*, the *Stanford Law and Policy Review*, the *Harvard Human Rights Journal*, and the *New York University Law Review*, among others. Prior to entering academia, Nguyen practiced corporate law in Silicon Valley and served on the policy team of the California Office of the Attorney General. She earned a JD degree from NYU School of Law, where she was a law and business scholar and an executive editor of the *NYU Law Review*.

KEVIN Y. L. TAN specializes in constitutional and administrative law, and the legal history of Singapore and Malaysia, which he teaches at the Faculty of Law, National University of Singapore. He has written and edited over fifty books on the law, history, and politics of Singapore.

PENG WANG is an associate professor in the Department of Sociology at the University of Hong Kong. His research interests include organized crime, corruption, economic sociology, bureaucracy, and governance. He is the author of *The Chinese Mafia* (Oxford University Press, 2017).

ABBREVIATIONS

AP	authoritarian policing
ARATS	Association for Relations Across the Taiwan Straits
CCP	Chinese Communist Party
CIA	Central Intelligence Agency
CID	Criminal Intelligence Department
Comintern	Communist International
COVID-19	coronavirus disease 2019
CPM	Communist Party of Malaya
CPP	coercive political persuasion
CSOC	Communist Suppression Operations Command
CSSTA	Cross-Straits Services Trade Agreement
DP	democratic policing
DPP	Democratic Progressive Party
DRV	Democratic Republic of Vietnam
DSP	Domestic Security Protection
EIC	British East India Company
ELAB	Extradition Law Amendment Bill
HK	Hong Kong
HKPF	Hong Kong Police Force
HKSAR	Hong Kong Special Administrative Region
ICAC	Independent Commission Against Corruption
ICP	Indochinese Communist Party
ICT	information and communications technology
ISA	Internal Security Act
ISOC	Internal Security Operations Command
JPF	Justice for Peace Foundation
KMT	Kuomintang
LDP	Liberal Democratic Party
LegCo	Legislative Council
MERS	Middle East respiratory syndrome
MOFA	Ministry of Foreign Affairs
MPAJA	Malayan People's Anti-Japanese Army
MPS	Ministry of Public Security

MSS	Ministry of State Security
NGO	nongovernment organization
NPA	National Police Agency
NPC	National People's Congress
NPCSC	National People's Congress Standing Committee
NPP	Neighborhood Police Post
NSC	National Supervision Commission
OCPL	Occupy Central with Love and Peace
OSS	U.S. Office of Strategic Services
PAP	People's Action Party
PLEB	Police Law Enforcement Board
PPSO	Preservation of Public Security Ordinance
PRC	People's Republic of China
PSAPL	Public Security Administrative Punishment Law
PSB	Bureau of Public Security
RTP	Royal Thai Police
SARS	Severe acute respiratory syndrome
SBPAC	Southern Border Provinces Administrative Center
SCAP	Supreme Commander of Allied Powers
SDF	Self-Defense Forces
SEF	Straits Exchange Foundation
SHP	Special Higher Police (Tokubetsu Kōtō Keisatsu)
SIB	Special Investigation Bureau
TMPB	Tokyo Metropolitan Police Department
UK	United Kingdom
US	United States
USSR	Union of Soviet Socialist Republics
VCP	Vietnam Communist Party
VIP	very important person
VSC	Volunteer Special Constabulary

PART I

Framework

1

Mapping the Authoritarian and Democratic Divide

The Transformation of Policing in Asia

HUALING FU AND WEITSENG CHEN

1.1 Introduction

Following a previous edited volume, *Authoritarian Legality in Asia: Formation, Development, and Transition*, this book delves into a subfield of authoritarian legality by exploring the institutions of law enforcement and the concept of policing and legality in East and Southeast Asia in the context of democratic transition and authoritarian resilience. In studying constitutional transitions, scholars have invariably focused on the shifting role of the courts in limiting state power, safeguarding rights and freedoms, and sustaining the democratic agenda. Scant attention has been paid to the significant role of the police in supporting democratic transformation and maintaining authoritarian resilience in Asia. As Chen puts it in the Taiwan context, if an authoritarian state can get its police right it can get the legal system right.[1] In recent years, diminishing democratic and legal control over the police has become a global concern, epitomized by enduring police discrimination and brutality against the African American population in the US, the crackdown on dissenting voices in Hong Kong, and escalating confrontations between increasingly militarized police forces and restive communities. This edited volume is a small step toward filling a gap in the literature; it explores the nature of authoritarian policing, its transformation and resilience, and its rule of law implications. This book addresses both what Brodeur refers to as "high" policing, in other words, the policing of politics and the use of coercive state power to preempt, control, and punish political dissent and public protest, and the positioning and repositioning of regular, and "low," policing within national political structures under authoritarianism and during

[1] Chen, Chapter 8 in this volume.

transitions to democracy.[2] The discussion of the evolution of policing takes place in this book in the context of the overall development of the police, their professionalization, institutional autonomy and neutrality, legality, and credibility within the communities they control and serve.

What makes policing "democratic" is a contested concept, and the definition varies depending on the level of abstraction and the particular focus of the inquiry. While regime type, which is a contested concept itself, is a significant factor in determining the nature of the police because of the close nexus between the coercive power of the police and the state, it is never dispositive. Thus, the dichotomous categorization of authoritarian policing (AP) and democratic policing (DP), while useful as a starting point for comparative analysis, misses a large amount of nuances and often overlooks the plurality of either system, neglecting the fact that a police system could be authoritarian or democratic in multiple ways and can be both authoritarian and democratic in different aspects of policing. This volume rejects this simple binary view. It aims to untie and unpack the nexus between the police and the political system and to explore the plurality of both AP and DP. While regime type is a key variable in explaining differences in ideologies, institutional design, and operation, it is only a factor, albeit perhaps a significant one along a long spectrum of AP and DP. Other variables have exerted a powerful influence in shaping the political role of the police and their accountability.[3]

It is our intention to recognize and articulate internal variations and contradictions of both AP and DP and factors beyond regime type that shape police behavior. The political system of East and Southeast Asian states is, to a significant degree, shaped by historical development and affected by international politics and international norms, which have left deep imprints on the respective police systems. There are different levels of economic development, and state capacities also vary significantly in supporting or restraining institutional development and the level of professionalization. While Confucianism has had an impact in shaping state–society relations, reinforcing certain attitudes toward authority, elite politics, and the political culture in general, there are great variations within the region owing to differences between prevailing ideologies,

[2] Jean-Paul Brodeur, "High Policing and Low Policing: Remarks about the Policing of Political Activities," *Social Problems* 30(5) (1983): 507–520; and *The Policing Web* (Oxford: Oxford University Press, 2010).

[3] For critical analysis of regime type in the China and India comparison, see Prasenjit Dura and Elizabeth J. Perry (eds.), *Beyond Regimes: China and India Compared* (Cambridge, MA: Harvard University Asia Center, 2018).

colonial traditions, and political choices, as carefully elaborated by deLisle.[4] Accordingly, all such variations affect people's political culture, thereby constituting the sources of legitimacy of the police.

1.2 Defining Democratic Policing

There has been, in general, little academic attention paid to many aspects of AP such as its normative values, institutional blueprint, and cultural make-up. Often, AP is negatively defined, in opposition to DP. DP has received ample attention, drawing from diverse and often contradictory democratic theories developed in a specific historical context.[5] With some exceptions, theories on DP are often derivative, incoherent, or internally contradictory. They are often developed to serve a particular policy goal to respond to a unique exigency. The following section defines the core components of DP, based on the mainstream literature on DP in the US and other divided societies while taking into consideration the unique trajectory of policing in Asia.

In this part of the world, with a long history of resilient authoritarian rule under which the police served and continue to serve dictators or ruling political parties, DP hinges first and foremost on political neutrality, a high degree of institutional autonomy, and an arm's length distance from the dominant political power.[6] Political neutrality is a liberal democratic constitutional design, whereas the non-partisan police "swear allegiance to and be loyal to the Constitution and law."[7] A police force that is politically neutral would step back from political controversies and refrain from protecting any partisan interests of a government.[8] Police neutrality also serves as a shield to fend off political interference that may reduce the police to a mere instrument of political control and repression. As such, it is a strong anti-authoritarian device, together with other institutional design such as professionalism, which can be seen as necessary but not sufficient conditions for DP.[9]

4 Jacques deLisle, Chapter 14, in this volume.

5 David A. Sklansky, "Police and Democracy," *Michigan Law Review* 103(7) (2005): 1699–1830.

6 Liqun Cao, Lanying Huang, and Ivan Y. Sun, "From Authoritarian Policing to Democratic Policing: A Case Study of Taiwan," *Policing and Society* 26(6) (2016): 642–658, 647, https://doi.org/10.1080/10439463.2015.1009370.

7 Ibid., 649.

8 David H. Bayley, *Changing the Guard: Developing Democratic Police Abroad* (New York: Oxford University Press, 2006).

9 Robert Reiner, *The Politics of the Police*, 3rd ed. (New York: Oxford University Press, 2000), 54.

Political neutrality is rooted in police professionalism and institutional autonomy,[10] and relies on common professional standards, ethics, rules, and of course interests to be sustainable and legitimate. In that sense, the political neutrality of the police is a professional calling, and it is this professionalism as a shared value and identity that in turn reinforces the demand for political neutrality and institutional autonomy. While professionalism may be reduced to merely a pretext for a politicized police force that, in substance, serves partisan interests, a highly professionalized police force often shares some common core features, including education and training, centralization within a clear hierarchical bureaucratic structure, and structured bureaucratic, legal, and political accountability mechanisms. Cultivating a professional identity as a law enforcement agency offers the best antidote to politicization.

By these standards, AP is necessarily politically biased and therefore neither professional nor autonomous. Authoritarian states insist on retaining a monopoly on political power, are partisan on the grounds of class, race, religion, or politics, and are particularly repressive in silencing dissenting voices. Without exception, they use the police as the sharp edge of political control. Police in authoritarian systems are inherently politicized and loyal to their political masters, whoever they are, rather than faithful to the law.[11] They are anti-democratic in that they "take sides" in a larger political sense, as Martin pithily puts it. DP requires the police "to satisfy the divergent audience, producing representations of police power that supply plausible legitimacy on multiple and potentially contradictory grounds."[12] As he continues, "The moment police shift from the impossible aspiration of maintaining an inclusive-if-contradictory peace to a realist posture at war with some political fraction of the population under their power is the moment they cease to be democratic."[13]

While politically neutral and unbiased, DP is simultaneously subject to multifaceted democratic control and accountability mechanisms, variously defined to include "legislative authorization" and "democratically founded rules,"[14] democratic,[15] "a state–society consensus,"[16] and

[10] Herman Goldstein, *Policing a Free Society* (Cambridge, MA: Ballinger Pub. Co, 1977); ibid.

[11] Erica Marat, *The Politics of Police Reform: Society against the State in Post-Soviet Countries* (Oxford: Oxford University Press, 2018).

[12] Martin, Chapter 7 in this volume.

[13] Ibid.

[14] Barry Friedman and Maria Ponomarenko, "Democratic Policing," *New York University Law Review* 90 (2015): 1827–1907.

[15] Cao, Huang, and Sun, "From Authoritarian Policing to Democratic Policing," 648.

[16] Marat, "The Politics of Police Reform," 11.

civilian oversight and monitoring,[17] with the active participation of the communities as partners participating in policing.[18] To elaborate, while a democratic police force is apolitical and insulated from partisan interferences, they are also held accountable to external institutions and operate transparently and responsively.[19] Those accountability mechanisms are designed to prevent an autonomous police force from becoming an independent fiefdom and a law unto itself.[20] To be politically autonomous and at the same time accountable to external mechanisms is a delicate balance to strike, but both are indispensable for DP. Autonomy is often regarded as an antidote to authoritarianism to avoid state capture of a powerful force, but abundant research has shown, as highlighted by Kroncke's chapter,[21] police in democracies through well-organized unions can become a powerful interest group in their own right, highly autonomous, insulated by unionization, and effectively immune from effective external control.

While politically accountable, DP aims to treat people equally and be fair to all members of society. There is a danger, which often manifests itself forcefully, that democratic accountability of the police to majoritarian interests may turn out to be in favor of discriminative and repressive policing against minorities. Democratic police treat people with human dignity.[22] Here one sees a tension between a pretext or justification of democratic accountability and populist bias. Popular control of the police creates a well-known majoritarian difficulty, especially in highly decentralized systems such as that in the US, where the police, controlled by and accountable to the white majority, follow the majority will to the detriment of minorities, turning an otherwise democratically designed police force into a discriminatory and repressive instrument of power. Thus, DP is not a tool of particular political parties or their leaders, and

[17] Errol P. Mendes et al., *Democratic Policing and Accountability: Global Perspectives* (Aldershot: Ashgate, 1999); Andrew Goldsmith and Colleen Lewis (eds.), *Civilian Oversight of Policing: Governance, Democracy, and Human Rights* (Oxford: Hart Publishing, 2000); Andrew Goldsmith (ed.), *Complaints against the Police: The Trend to External Review* (New York: Oxford University Press, 1991).

[18] Sklansky, "Police and Democracy," 1828.

[19] Democracy is an open process and democratic police necessarily demands police transparency, especially in the age of big data and mass surveillance when the traditional accountability mechanisms are ill-fitted to control new policing technologies. Policing has to be made visible to be accountable.

[20] Matthew Light, Mariana Mota Prado, and Yuhua Wang, "Policing Following Political and Social Transitions: Russia, Brazil, and China Compared," *Theoretical Criminology* 19(2) (2015): 216–238; Marat, "The Politics of Police Reform."

[21] Kroncke, Chapter 2 in this volume.

[22] Gary T. Marx, "Police and Democracy," in Menachem Amir and Stanley Einstein (eds.), *Policing, Security and Democracy: Theory and Practice* (vol. 2) (New York: Office of Justice Program, 2001), 35–45.

it does not merely enforce the popular will. It has become axiomatic, as the painful experiences in the US and other Western democracies have demonstrated, that DP has to be impartial and fair to all members without discriminating between individuals based on grounds of status, race, or other personal attributes.[23] Democracy is thus an expansive concept that includes an element of, and aspiration for, egalitarianism, which is an enduring challenge facing the police in liberal democracies, the decentralized police system in the US being a particular case in point.[24] Otherwise, a decentralized process with democratic trappings can be captured by a populist bias that may push the police to widespread discriminatory practices. It reduces the effectiveness of accountability and authorizes or even demands hate, bigotry, discrimination, and populism of the sort that is antithetical to the rule of law.[25]

Finally, democratic police operate within the framework of the rule of law, broadly defined to include effective control of police powers by an independent judiciary. To overcome discriminative policing, the judiciary has to step in forcefully to enforce the rule of law and protect constitutional rights. In a populist society, the legislature could be biased so as to amount to part of the problem rather than part of the solution, and in this case, legislative control is remote and weak. Enhanced executive control often leads to the politicization of the police force. Ultimately, it is the rule of law, safeguarded by a powerful and independent judiciary, which offers legal remedies to correct the majoritarian bias and act fairly and proportionately for the benefit of society as a whole that sets DP apart from AP,[26] even though judicial control of the police has its inherent limitations. At a minimum, it should be borne in mind that judicial oversight, while producing significant advantages in placing police power under check, is limited in its scope, remote in its remedies, and feeble in its ability to offer a timely corrective to systemic social discrimination and political domination.[27]

There is thus no clear blueprint for DP. DP is necessarily a broad, inclusive, and frequently difficult concept that includes multiple components that can be potentially contradictory. Many nuances and a significant

[23] Sklansky, "Police and Democracy," 1815.

[24] Sklansky, "Police and Democracy," 1815–1816.

[25] Kroncke, Chapter 2

[26] Sarah A. Leo, "Democratic Policing Before the Due Process Revolution," *The Yale Law Journal* 128 (2019): 1246–1302.

[27] Gerald N. Rosenberg, *The Hollow Hope: Can Courts Bring About Social Change?* 2nd ed. (Chicago: University of Chicago Press, 2008).

degree of delicate balancing have to be put into place to realize its effect. Political neutrality is a key ingredient for DP, but neutrality alone is not sufficient and the police must be accountable legally and politically to be democratic. A police force that is politically neutral but entirely unaccountable can be highly authoritarian, with repression and brutality masquerading under the cloak of professionalism and autonomy. But democratic accountability of the police can become an enemy of its own success, whereby DP becomes self-defeating if the police are captured by a populist bias against the minority. DP thus demands a delicate balance to be struck between majority will on the one hand and equality and non-discrimination on the other hand, failing which the police become insidiously discriminative and repressive. This brings us to the role of courts against a wider rule of law backdrop in enforcing and entrenching political neutrality, autonomy, accountability, and fairness – a task that judges are not best positioned to accomplish.

1.3 Policing under Authoritarian Regimes

This book takes seriously regime type, specifically the political design of a state measured by the level of political participation and the degree of democratic accountability, and reiterates the point many have made that policing is an integral part of the overall political structure, responding to the prevailing political demand and safeguarding existing order. The nature of the political system of which the police are an integral part is a key factor in shaping the design and exercise of police power.

However, scant literature on policing has been developed in the Asian context. East and Southeastern Asian states are known for their authoritarian resilience and also a number of successful democratic transitions, where one finds the coexistence of powerful Party states and vibrant young democracies. There is a plurality of regime types that invariably exert their impact on the police. Some, such as Japan, Korea, and Taiwan, have transitioned to democracies of varying degrees of stability and maturity, demanding some democratic accountability and ensuring the police are rule-based and rule-complying. In comparison, authoritarian states rely on repressive police power to crush real or perceived challenges to maintain political order, as illustrated by such cases as China and Vietnam and in the not-so-distant past Japan, South Korea, and Taiwan.

An oft-observed starting point is political policing in highly repressive states, in which secret political police were created to serve as the core of the repressive apparatus. Police brutality and control by dictatorship offer some classic examples of what secret political police are and what can do.[28] Other cases include repressive police in highly polarized societies and occupied territories, including South Africa during apartheid,[29] and Northern Ireland during the Troubles,[30] all of which shed light on the origins of and variations among configurations of AP. A particular earlier subtype of AP is the examination of colonial policing,[31] which imposed from the outside, was often quasi-military in style and illegitimate in the eyes of the policed, and shaped policing in the colonized world in significant ways. The police system was tailor-made to suit the needs of colonialism and was often different from that in the metropoles, which were typically more "democratic."

Police in former communist states and states in transition tend to be authoritarian in the classical sense and the antithesis of DP, without democratic checks and balances and safeguards. Communist Parties in the USSR, East Germany, and China exerted absolute political control over the police force, reducing them at both the ideological and institutional levels to powerful instruments of political control and repression. In these countries, the police in particular were officially designated as part of the control apparatus created to serve the interests of the ruling party with political control and repression being primary hallmarks of Leninist policing.

However, traditional autocracy and dictatorship, with a few exceptions, have largely evolved into a new type of authoritarian regime with multiple objectives. An electoral process may have been added with some popular participation, and democratic institutions are put in place to dilute the dictatorial nature of the regime. Increasingly, legality and rule by law have also been inserted into governance structures to constrain and legitimize police power. Yet, beyond the ideological rhetoric and formal institution designs,

[28] Sheena Chestnut Greitens, *Dictators and Their Secret Police: Coercive Institutions and State Violence* (Cambridge: Cambridge University Press, 2016).

[29] Mike Brogden and Clifford D. Shearing, *Policing for a New South Africa* (Abingdon: Routledge, 1993).

[30] Aogan Mulcahy, *Policing Northern Ireland: Conflict, Legitimacy and Reform* (Abingdon: Routledge, 2013).

[31] Mike Brogden, "The Emergence of the Police – The Colonial Dimension," *The British Journal of Criminology* 27(1) (1987): 4–14; David Anderson and David Killingray, "Consent, Coercion and Colonial Control: Policing the Empire 1830–1940," in David M. Anderson and David Killingray (eds.), *Policing the Empire: Government, Authority and Control, 1830–1940* (Manchester: Manchester University Press, 1991); and Emma Bell, "Normalising the Exceptional: British Colonial Policing Cultures Come Home," *Mémoire(s), identité(s), marginalité(s) dans le monde occidental contemporain. Cahiers du MIMMOC* 10 (2013): 1–12. For a historical survey, see Caroline Elkins, *Legacy of Violence: A History of the British Empire* (New York: Alfred A. Knopf, 2022).

we know little about how the politicization of the police at ideological level is translated into institutionalized police practices in contemporary authoritarian states. We don't know whether high-profile exposures of police abuse are representative of the routine political policing on the ground. If legal reforms promoted by authoritarian states create some legal certainties to promote economic growth and improve governance, how have the police forces in those party states or other authoritarian states reconciled the conflicting imperatives between safeguarding the political order and respecting personal freedom and rights? It remains unclear how the well-disciplined, quasi-military police in Leninist states comply with legal rules.

Yet, while China and Vietnam remain hardcore communist regimes, their policing style and control strategies have evolved. Following the Tiger economies of the 1960s and 1970s, the police in both China and Vietnam have witnessed a similar pattern of changes – professionalism, institutionalization, and legalization leading to greater effectiveness and credibility for both the police and the party states. Societies in turbulent social and economic transitions call for effective leadership and guidance from the state, with the police playing an instrumental role in the maintenance of order to facilitate economic growth, social stability, and political order. Orderly development is a key feature of the East Asian model, as the Tiger Economies and the later developers have clearly demonstrated.[32] They all generated an important impact on the police and the legal system at large, softening the repressive edge of the police to place political control on a stronger legalistic footing.

Fu's chapter on the political policing of human rights lawyers in China illustrates a new style of authoritarian high policing in China with a humane touch.[33] Instead of the intimidation, torture, and unlawful detention that often capture the popular imagination of China's political police, the Chinese security police have adopted a process that the author refers to as coercive political persuasion. The police routinely engage key members of the community of human rights lawyers by inviting them for tea and meals and exerting pressure through persuasion and influence. When persuasion fails to work, the police resort to relational violence, by mobilizing relatives, family members, employers, and other "significant others" to amplify the pressure to comply. To effectively "disappear" dissident lawyers on sensitive dates, the police invite them to tour China's

[32] Randall Peerenboom, *China Modernizes: Threat to the West or Model for the Rest?* (Oxford: Oxford University Press, 2007).

[33] Fu, Chapter 3 in this volume.

scenic places at the cost of the state. The security police have preferred to absorb and soften resistance from lawyers through soft violence, all done with a thin veil of legality.

Biddulph's chapter offers an incisive study of the continuing evolution of police administrative power to punish minor crimes, posing a question whether legal reforms have improved the protection of rights and enhanced police accountability. Or in her words, "What do these reforms say, if anything, about the particular character of authoritarianism and authoritarian legality in policing in this field?" There is a clear trend in the direction of the legalization of police administrative power consistent with the wider trend toward enhanced legality that many have observed, but the critical point that Biddulph makes is that with some exceptions legalization has not resulted in greater accountability of the police in China in their exercise of administrative power. Judging from the outcome of a series of reforms coupled with the massive use of surveillance technology and a refocus on social control, the author points out that the reform presents not a story of straightforward progress toward limiting police power, but one "that reorganised police powers rather than significantly disempowering the police."[34] Shedding light on the nature of authoritarian legality, Biddulph concludes:

> While we can trace the development of a legal field, the mere increasing importance of legality does not determine what mix of values will be produced by the contests that build the legal field. Also, the state-centred model of legality remains vulnerable to political intervention, being circumvented and being weakened when political imperatives do violence to the fundamental principles of legality enacted in the law.[35]

Nguyen's chapter similarly presents a particular strategy of political persuasion by the Vietnamese police in preempting and controlling political dissent.[36] By controlling discourse power, or managing the narrative, the police shape and reinforce public opinions so that citizens would think and act as the party state demands with the aim of forestalling "a peaceful evolution and self-evolution," a deep-felt concern that has strong resonances in China.[37] Echoing other research on China and similar political systems,

[34] Biddulph, Chapter 4 in this volume.
[35] Ibid.
[36] Nguyen, Chapter 5 in this volume.
[37] Hualing Fu, "China's Imperatives for National Security Legislation," in Cora Chan and Fiona De Londras (eds.), *China's National Security: Endangering Hong Kong's Rule of Law?* (Oxford: Hart Publishing, 2020), 41–60.

Nguyen's chapter demonstrates the close link between thoughts and action and their mutual reinforcement; authoritarian regimes demand rigid conformity in thought and belief, and have a propensity to extensively use spies to uncover heretic thoughts and aggressively deploy propaganda to achieve uniformity.[38] Thought policing becomes a necessity contributing significantly to the making of a police state. As Nguyen's chapter powerfully illustrates, the battle against the enemy starts in the mind and persists.[39]

1.4 Democratic Transition and Authoritarian Resilience

Political change – democratization – often leaves deep footprints on political policing by triggering changes in the status, power, and accountability of the police, as observed in contemporary Taiwan, South Korea, and Japan. As new democracies wrestle themselves out of their authoritarian shackles, past abuses perpetrated by the police are often made public, leading to nearly universal demand for structural reforms to hold the police accountable. Political changes often lead to meaningful changes in political policing in terms of the narrative, institutional design, and practices. As has been observed, at the moment when an authoritarian state transitions to democracy, the locus of power in the legal system shifts from the police to the courts. The kind of repressive and intrusive high policing that was epitomized by the Garrison police in Taiwan, the national security establishment in South Korea, and the Interior Ministry in Japan all experienced transformative changes during periods of democratic transition. Formal accountability mechanisms, American in style and compatible with democracy, are in place in all three jurisdictions, setting them apart from their neighbors.

It is less well known whether those institutional changes have been effective in achieving police accountability on the ground, just as it is unclear whether the democratic transition has made a real difference in making the police more accountable or less repressive. Given the peaceful democratic transition in South Korea and Taiwan in particular, how have the police, often a key supporter of the old order,

38 David H. Bayley, *Patterns of Policing: A Comparative International Analysis*. Crime, Law, and Deviance Series (New Brunswick, NJ: Rutgers University Press, 1985), 207–208.

39 For the Chinese case, see Suzanne E. Scoggins "Propaganda and the Police: The Softer Side of State Control in China," *Europe-Asia Studies* 73(1) (2021): 200–220, https://doi.org/10.1080/09668136.2020.1850644.

responded to new accountability mechanisms? Does this response undergird or undermine the emerging democratic system that chips away at their powers slowly but decisively? Given the resilience of institutions, does the authoritarian legacy retain a strong hold on police and policing in a democratic setting? Constitutional convergence in the region notwithstanding,[40] historical inertia is surprisingly difficult to overcome in shaping the exercise of police power and promoting a culture of accountability.[41] Several contributors aim to illuminate these dynamic changes through case studies of transition in their respective jurisdictions.

Nakano offers a striking example of the revolving door phenomena in that senior police officers in the *ancien régime* were first removed and then moved to other key state or non-state sectors.[42] Tracing closely the career path and retirement patterns of elite police officers in postwar Japan, Nakano provides powerful evidence of political continuity amid unprecedented democratic change, showing not only a clear cultural and institutional resilience but also laying bare the close, unbroken ties between the former police and national political and business elites. The US Occupied Forces abolished the Ministry of Interior, which was dominated by the police, in the aftermath of the war, only to find senior officers resurfacing in other ministries, continuing to exert an influence and shape postwar Japanese policies in the areas of defense and public order.[43] Japanese politics seems to be defined not by the contours of its constitutional straightjacket on full public display but by the subtle maneuvering in the shadows that kept Japanese conservatism intact.

While Nakano focuses on the continuity of individual senior police officers, Chen examines the survival of norms and culture of policing in Taiwan.[44] As Chen puts it, while the democratic transition has successfully put an end to the repressive political police, the "bad cops" and the institutions of high policing, the regular police, the "good cops" trained during the authoritarian era, have remained largely intact after

[40] Po Jen Yap and Chien-Chih Lin, *Constitutional Convergence in East Asia*. Comparative Constitutional Law and Policy (Cambridge: Cambridge University Press, 2021).

[41] For the authoritarian resilience of the police in the post-Soviet Countries, see Marat, *The Politics of Police Reform*.

[42] Nagano, Chapter 9 in this volume.

[43] For a study of the institutional crossover in the context of political policing in Norther Ireland, see Kevin Hearty, *Critical Engagement: Irish Republicanism, Memory Politics and Policing* (Liverpool: Liverpool University Press, 2017).

[44] Chen, Chapter 8.

the democratic transition, allowing authoritarian features to creep in or to continue. The process of politicization, depoliticization, and repoliticization is an interesting one. Before the democratic transition, the Taiwanese police were placed under the tight, centralized political control of the ruling party, the Nationalist Party, Kuomingtang (KMT), as pointed out clearly by Chen and others. In the wake of the democratic transition, policing was decentralized to dilute political control as a gesture by the KMT, which remained in power in the initial years following democratization; moreover, the police were made directly accountable to the democratically created local governments. It transpires that decentralization may have made the police more democratically accountable, but this did not depoliticize the police. Instead, the democratic process is such that decentralization creates opportunities and incentives for capture by local political forces, leading to a repoliticization of the police. In the context of Taiwan's fragmented political system with protracted partisan political fights after democratization, sometimes police made decisions in the course of several political incidents according to their unique partisan views. As Chen points out, democratization opens up new corruptive opportunities and can breed its own anti-democratic practices at microlevel.

The police system may be immune from political change notwithstanding the democratization of the larger political system. This continuity thesis is most forcefully argued in Mérieau's chapter in relation to the lack of any meaningful democratic impact on Thai political policing. While in both Taiwan and South Korea regime change did induce a corresponding institutional change in the high policing, Mérieau makes the argument that AP persists in Thailand following the country's political democratization. Open repression of political dissent and blunt disregard for legal rules on the part of the police and security forces have continued. What then explains the Thai exception that proves the rule? Relying on Fraenkel's dual state conceptualization, Mérieau explains that a prerogative state, or the deep state, has persisted in Thailand, which is centered on the police and the military. The deep state is highly autonomous of the political process, and largely a power unto itself unaccountable to democratic processes. Thus, despite democratization, with newly designed legal and political accountability mechanisms, the prerogative state "continues to function according to fully fledged authoritarianism and to its own set of norms and hierarchies."[45]

[45] Mérieau, Chapter 10 in this volume.

1.5 DP in the Shadow of Authoritarianism

There is thus a need to pluralize regime types, both authoritarian and democratic, and to unpack the respective policing so as to identify their multifaceted and multidimensional nature. Police could be politically repressive in silencing political dissents but at the same time radically communitarian in partnering with communities to address local issues. While police could be racially discriminatory or religiously repressive but at the same time democratically accountable, they might leave political dissidents entirely alone to their oppositional politics but at the same time be abusive and violent toward suspects and the public at large and corrupt to the root.

The line between AP and DP is even more fluid and fuzzy. Any single standard, as discussed earlier, either neutrality, professionalism, autonomy, external accountability, decentralization, or the rule of law, will not be able to set DP apart from the autocratic counterpart and proves to be ill-founded. The attributes of DP are inherently contentious. All designs may have their strong democratic potentials, but placed in different political circumstances, they either reinforce the authoritarian style of the police or are too weak or remote to offer an effective corrective to the authoritarian propensity.

While regime type matters in one dimension in locating a country's place along with the democracy to authoritarianism spectrum, it may matter less or differently in other dimensions. Beyond regime type, chapters in this book consider police-community relations, public order maintenance, social services, and police discipline, all of which are also universal functions of police across all regime types, to rediscover democratic practices and potential in otherwise authoritarian political systems.[46] Beyond the repressive and preventive high policing that was often the mirror image of authoritarian politics, there is a service-oriented, people-friendly, and well-disciplined police force that reinforces a paternalistic government.

Against this backdrop, this book unveils the very diverse roles of the police in authoritarian and semi-authoritarian states. It attempts to unpack and disentangle what is dictated by politics and the characteristics that may transcend regime type. In South Korea under colonial and authoritarian rule, for example, the police were particularly brutal and repressive in serving the regimes and crushing any sign of dissent and resistance, yet they continued to manage the mundane tasks of people registration, maintaining sanitation, assisting and controlling vagrants, the homeless, and prostitutes, and creating peace and order so as to facilitate the social

[46] Reiner, *The Politics of the Police*.

and economic transformation of South Korean society, as Mobrand in this volume and others have observed.[47] While high policing was largely an assertion of violence from the state, the welfare-oriented low policing was embedded in the local communities, tied to social structures, and accountable to the people it served through informal (rarely rule-based) and occasional illegal mechanisms (e.g. through working with secret societies). It was through this contradictory process, working with and against criminal organizations at the same time, simultaneously helping and exploiting the poor, thereby undergirding and undermining the state that the police muddled through the period of transformation and managed to build their credibility as an effective and legitimate force. The embedded nature of the police reduced regularity and increased discretion, although ironically this very arbitrariness blunted the harshness of the authoritarian state.

In Taiwan, the police developed a long-lasting relationship of mutual support and respect with their local communities, instilling high levels of credibility and deference. Chen links the extensive administrative role of the police directly to the Japanese colonial legacy.[48] Following systematic reforms to centralize and streamline political policing by the KMT government in the early 1950s to create pervasive and intensive political control embedded in the society,[49] and with the control of the police by military officers who were parachuted into senior positions where they remained until the end of martial law,[50] low policing was allowed to remain separate from political policing in its organizational identity and its relationship to the community. In this way, the police management of household registration, coupled with other administrative duties and powers, allowed the police to become deeply rooted in their communities, extending state control into the very fabric of society across a wide range of political and social matters.

Similarly, the Japanese police are well known for their intimate and reciprocal relations with the communities they served, as Kroncke points out,[51] both during the authoritarian period and after the transition to democracy; police service to the communities is exemplary in Singapore, and, similarly, police in China and Vietnam under the one-party rule are duty-bound to

47 Mobrand, Chapter 6 in this volume; Byongook Moon, "The Politicization of Police in South Korea: A Critical Review," *Policing: An International Journal of Police Strategies & Management* 27(1) (2004): 128–136; Vincent J. Hoffman, "The Development of Modern Police Agencies in the Republic of Korea and Japan: A Paradox," *Police Studies* 5(3) (1982): 3–16.

48 Chen, Chapter 8.

49 Greitens, "Organizing Coercion in Taiwan," in *Dictators and Their Secret Police*, 75–111.

50 Liqun Cao, Lanying Huang, and Ivan Y. Sun, *Policing in Taiwan: From Authoritarianism to Democracy* (Abingdon: Routledge, 2014).

51 Kroncke, Chapter 2.

serve the public. The strong bonds between the police and the community are an enduring feature of police in societies of this region, providing a façade of avuncular benevolence notwithstanding the repressive nature of the regime writ large. Police in authoritarian regimes, while harshly treating enemies of the state, thus create an image of being people-friendly, community-based, service/welfare-oriented, and in this way even democratic.

Democracy per se does not ensure accountability and it is well documented that democracies face their own disciplinary difficulties in dealing with police violence.[52] Kroncke's chapter forcefully rebuts the often reflexive assumption that democratic regimes are more accountable and less violent than authoritarian regimes in terms of policing practices. Narrowing the scope of inquiry to the use of force by the police, it becomes clear, though often ignored, that regime type has little if any impact on the persistence and the level of police violence. Police may be insulated from and are beyond the reach of mechanisms of democratic accountability in otherwise democratic states. In her chapter on Thailand, Mérieau makes the argument that police violence and brutality have persisted in spite of democratic reforms.[53] In Kroncke's chapter, it is noted that police violence was aggravated and amplified in the Philippines' populist democracy under Duterte; and, in the Japanese case, the fact that "near unrestrained authoritarianism" has persisted in the formal criminal justice system in Japan could be interpreted as a forceful illustration of Kanoki's continuation thesis on the persistence of the Japanese national security state.[54] Behind the smiling face of the Koban officers, there is a repressive system that exists independently of the larger democratic political system. Seen in that light, the Thai deep state wielding excessive political power is hardly surprising. Democracy, hollowed of it its liberal core, may camouflage, energize, and indeed necessitate repressive policing. The persistent racist policing throughout US history and its contemporary practices is a direct consequence of the highly decentralized police structure, in which policing minorities reflects the majoritarian views of the white population.

What makes police in this region accountable is their embeddedness in the community, their interaction with local residents in friendly terms, and their service orientation. Something that is short of what Marat calls "a state–society consensus,"[55] but community-oriented and people-based,

52 Marat, *The Politics of Police Reform*.
53 Mérieau, Chapter 10.
54 Kroncke, Chapter 2.
55 Marat, *The Politics of Police Reform*, 11.

nonetheless, and with a strong dose of paternalism. The police also actively engage local communities to secure cooperation, incentivize compliance with the law, and facilitate the implementation of public policy in sharp contrast to the colonial police who were inserted from the outside as strangers. In addition to top-down policy implementation, the police also support residential organizations, respond to local initiatives where possible, and help solve local problems. The police in those circumstances often serve as an indispensable intermediary between the people and authoritarian states, creating a conduit or node in communications that became a functional substitute for democratic procedures designed to facilitate similar dialogue in lieu of improving local accountability.[56] Community police of this sort maintain local order relying on discretion, individual qualities of the police officers on the ground, and informal accountability.

Community policing in this region is an organic and deeply entrenched practice. The paternalistic role of the police and the embedding of policing into welfare provision has much to do with the prevailing cultural propensity resulting from institutional designs that embed the state in local neighborhoods. The chapters here on China, Japan, Singapore, South Korea, and Taiwan all touch upon special police-in-community features with the effect of inducing localized police accountability in the larger authoritarian context. The embeddedness of the police makes them partially accountable to the people they serve, and potentially democratic in this unique sense.

1.6 The Exceptional Hybridity of Hong Kong and Singapore

Singapore and Hong Kong are often regarded as the exception that proves the rule, characterized as hybrid regimes with freedom, high income, and a strong rule of law without "genuine" democracy. Hong Kong and Singapore were former British colonies, both exemplary in embracing and practicing the English rule of law in a largely benign but strict authoritarian political system. There was shared history between the two cities in the development of the colonial police, forming a particular DNA that was subsequently confirmed and reinforced by subsequent development. Police were ostensibly political in safeguarding the colonial order; they

[56] For studies of the interaction between the state and the society at the neighborhood level, see Benjamin L. Read, *Roots of the State: Neighborhood Organization and Social Networks in Beijing and Taipei* (Redwood City, CA: Stanford University Press, 2012); and Luigi Tomba, *The Government Next Door: Neighborhood Politics in Urban China* (Ithaca, NY: Cornell University Press, 2014).

were racist in their composition and in targeting the native population,[57] "policing by strangers" in design.[58] They focused on monitoring ethnic communities and were repressive in cracking down on any political mobilization. Given their colonial nature, the police were quasi-military in their command structure, organization, and ethos.

Policing in the earlier stage of nation-building was often political and repressive. In the earlier decades of the police development in Singapore, as Tan points out,[59] a weak state was confronted with an organized, secretive, and often subversive society; therefore, the colonial government and the government led by the People's Action Party (PAP) following it had to invest heavily in political monitoring and control and enhance political repression so as to establish a normal political order. What is needed in any failed states is an effective central government to restore stability, and Singapore proves to be a successful example. To achieve the goal, policing was necessarily politicized and biased against political opposition, serving as an effective instrument against enemies of the emerging state, whoever they were. It was only after the establishment of a stable political order and after the enemy was kept at bay that the scale started to tip toward low policing. There seems a more symbiotic relationship of sorts between political policing and routine policing. Arguably, the authoritarian practices contributed to community-friendly policing in both symbolic and utilitarian ways. Tan's chapter on DP in Singapore makes the argument explicitly. Under the PAP government, the police have been professionalized and become more rule-bound and legally accountable, not in spite of the Internal Security Act regime but because of it.

Those authoritarian features that were developed during the formative years full of crisis and uncertainty were subsequently institutionalized during normal times. Sporadic reforms and changes notwithstanding, police in Hong Kong and Singapore remained a sharp instrument of the colonial state, with a fragile institutional autonomy, endemic corruption, and politically repressive targeting of pro-communist activities. In pointed contrast to Singapore, Hong Kong never experienced a period of protracted nation-building thus setting the two apart, as Tan's chapter demonstrates.

[57] Peter Wesley-Smith, "Anti-Chinese Legislation in Hong Kong," in Ming K. Chan and John D. Young (eds.), *Precarious Balance: Hong Kong Between China and Britain, 1984–1992* (Hong Kong: Hong Kong University Press, 1994); Carol A. G. Jones with Jon Vagg, "The Hong Kong Police," in *Criminal Justice in Hong Kong* (Abingdon: Routledge-Cavendish, 2007), 45–96.

[58] Jones with Vagg, "The Hong Kong Police," 56.

[59] Tan, Chapter 11.

Hong Kong presents an intriguing case study of the rise, fall, and rise again of political policing. Owing to the nature of colonial policing and Hong Kong's geopolitical delicacy, the city remained a politically contentious place as a former British colony in East Asia. Moreover, rivaling political forces, either pro- or anti-communists waged their overt or covert battles to gain influence in Hong Kong and beyond. The primary task of the police was political until the Sino-British political settlement reached in the early 1980s. Contrary to the popular myth of Hong Kongers' legendary political apathy, Hong Kong has always been a place of political contention and resistance; furthermore, political censorship, surveillance, and punishment were far more prevalent and repressive than what was doctrinally presented.[60] The political freedom and rule of law that the colony offered, all in relative terms, attracted political dissidents of different sorts to Hong Kong who used Hong Kong as a base to support different political organizations and ideas. The Communist Party was not the first to use Hong Kong to subvert the authorities on the mainland when the former was under siege on the mainland and is not the first to highlight Hong Kong's role as a subversive base when it controlled the mainland. In addition, all governments in the Mainland since the Qing and multiple foreign powers, including Japan and the US, have pressurized the government of Hong Kong at various stages of its colonial history and in one way or another prohibited and suppressed political speech and activities that were regarded as offensive. The colonial police played a highly politicized role in maintaining a delicate balance of political tranquility in the territory with the Special Branch, the political police unit, playing an instrumental role in keeping agitation and mobilization at bay. Ng's historical analysis of political censorship and repression in relation to the charge of seditious libel demonstrates the intensive attention the Special Branch paid to political expression and agitation.[61]

Political stability in the region since the mid-1950s and the consequent social and economic take-off that made Hong Kong one of the Asian Tigers also transformed the police. The end of the wars and revolutions in China and reestablishment of political order created a peaceful environment for social and economic development in Hong Kong, and without

[60] Michael Ng, *Political Censorship in British Hong Kong: Freedom of Expression and the Law (1842–1997)* (Cambridge: Cambridge University Press, 2022); Hualing Fu, "Past and Future Offences of Sedition in Hong Kong," in Hualing Fu, Carole Peterson and Simon Young (eds.), *National Security and Fundamental Freedoms: Hong Kong's Article 23 Under Scrutiny* (Hong Kong: Hong Kong University Press, 2005).

[61] Ng, Chapter 12.

existential threats, the colonial government could divert resources to building institutions and improving governance. In the following three decades, Hong Kong developed a political system that King famously referred to as "administrative absorption of politics,"[62] whereas legality, promoted in the form of "legal fetishism" to use Martin's term, served as an alternative to democratization. Facing a turbulent society in social and economic transition in the postwar era, the colonial government effectively used good governance to build legitimacy, which allowed the police to conflate legality with consent. Facing the imminent reunification with China and the uncertainties and anxieties it brought about, the rule of law slowly became the focal point of Hong Kong's identity, which could be used to assert and defend itself in sharp contrast with the Mainland, commonly perceived in Hong Kong as lawless. The rule of law, which was later on referred to as a core value, sustained Hong Kong's transition to Chinese rule. While a colony without any prospect of meaningful democratic participation, people were content with the rule of law system that was underwritten indirectly by the political system in Britain. There was a strong consensus within Hong Kong that peace, order, good government with abundant social and economic rights, and freedom guaranteed by the rule of law was the endgame.

To keep pace with the social and economic developments in the postwar era, the police sloughed off the vestiges of corruption, improved their relationship with communities, became well disciplined, legally accountable, and above all politically neutral as a law enforcement agency to serve and protect Hong Kong. Their professionalism, effectiveness, and accountability brought them credibility in the eyes of the people of Hong Kong. The residents of Hong Kong were well known for being rule-abiding, and the police were effective in enforcing rules, forming a symbiotic circle in constructing an exemplary free and orderly society.

While politics was absorbed, it never disappeared. Democracy, which was a marginal pursuit in Hong Kong prior to the 1980s, became a dominant concern in the following three decades once the prospect of Hong Kong's reunification with China arrived on the horizon. The formula of peace, order, and good government without democracy, which sustained

[62] Ambrose Y. C. King, "Administrative Absorption of Politics in Hong Kong: Emphasis on the Grass Roots Level," in Ambrose Y. C. King and Rance P. L. Lee (eds.), *Social Life and Development in Hong Kong* (Hong Kong: Chinese University Press, 1981); and Carol A. G. Jones, *Lost in China? Law, Culture and Identity in Post-1997 Hong Kong* (Cambridge: Cambridge University Press, 2015).

British rule in Hong Kong, was no longer regarded as feasible under Chinese rule. It was said that the rule of law could no longer be sustained without democratic participation to give oxygen to it. Nevertheless, the constitutional structure that China designed for Hong Kong makes it impossible to seek "genuine" democratization as Hong Kong demands through institutional means, forcing the population in general and the younger generations in particular onto the streets to exercise popular constitutionalism through civil disobedience. While Beijing may have preferred not to disturb the colonial equilibrium in retaining good governance without thorough democratization, it could not convince Hong Kong people of the feasibility of this bargain. Hong Kong, determined to achieve full or genuine democracy as it defines was set on a collision path. The democratic contention in the post-transition era in Hong Kong was such that the rule of law in Hong Kong could no longer tame and control the democratic impulse. By 2014, Hong Kong's democratic frustrations and energies accumulated and evolved onto a massive scale of civil disobedience following the eruption of the Occupy Central Movement, together with the rise of a violent independence movement. When political tensions resurfaced on the streets and morphed into violent confrontations, police neutrality was no longer possible, and at that moment police had to take a side, using Martin's term. For the protesters, the rule of law was no longer an asset. The public order laws as enforced by the police and upheld by the courts have become a liability and a formidable barrier to the path to democracy. In 2019, the youth fighting for democratic governance and the police trying to maintain law and order clashed violently on Hong Kong's streets.

Wang, Joosse, and Cho capture the moment when the rule of law was no longer able to contain the demand for democratization.[63] Triggered by an anti-extradition Bill that set to create a mechanism for formal repatriation of fugitive offenders between Mainland China and Hong Kong, the political energies coalesced and then erupted into an unprecedented level of violence between the police and the protesters. In late 2019, Hong Kong became uncharacteristically confrontational and violent, with the city literally being set on fire. The conflict between police and the community intensified quickly and their relationship deteriorated sharply. To the protesters and their supporters, the police were brutal, violent, and repressive, but the police felt they were merely pushed to the front to hold a thin blue line between chaos and order as they are duty-bound to do.

[63] Wang, Joosse, and Cho, Chapter 13 in this volume.

The sudden turn of the Hong Kong police from the "soft" to "hard" model of protest policing and from DP to AP cannot be explained effectively by looking only at the police operations at street level or at any "police-centric" models, according to Wang and his co-authors. The rise of AP in Hong Kong can only be explained by embedding the police in the larger geopolitical context. By 2019, and forcing the relentless forces demanding democratic changes in society at large, the police no longer had the capacity to facilitate protest demands and channel their aspiration through communications and negotiation as they used to do. The authors identified the changes in the larger society that were detrimental to DP in Hong Kong as a legitimacy crisis of governance at a macrolevel factor, the erosion of police authority within the local political culture at a mesolevel, and tactical changes in police–protester interactions, involving the increased use of masks and collective action frames of identification as victims of police as microlevel factors. Together, these have inaugurated reaction spirals that have led to Hong Kong's unprecedented state of social fission, where "soft" policing is now all but impossible, and where the police force is beset by a widely subscribed demand for its outright disbandment.

In response to sustained protestor violence, China enacted a National Security Law and extended it to Hong Kong. A key feature of this law is a massive buildup of the national security police and a determination to securitize all of Hong Kong society. The Special Branch, the political police that reigned in Hong Kong before 1997, returned with a vengeance, and Hong Kong is set to repeat the similar censorship and prosecution that Ng vividly describes in his chapter, except that the tables have been turned and those deemed as anti-communist agitators are at the receiving end.[64]

1.7 Conclusion

This book explores diverse aspects of policing in a range of Asian jurisdictions, providing case studies that illustrate the impact of a political system on the roles and functions of the police. This book also aims to go beyond regime type and the simplistic dichotomy between democracy and authoritarianism in examining the police. Through studying policing in authoritarian states, hybrid states, and democratic states in Asia, the contributors offer nuanced, critical analyses of that transformation and the resilience of authoritarian states.

[64] Hualing Fu and Michael Hor (eds.), *Hong Kong's National Security Law: Restoration and Transformation* (Hong Kong: Hong Kong University Press, 2022).

This region is a patchwork of different regime types that have left deep imprints on the policing of their respective jurisdictions: North Korea and Taiwan can be tentatively located at the opposite ends of a long spectrum between autocracy and democracy. Authoritarian states tend to maintain a separate and powerful branch of political police that they are invariably ready to use in order to safeguard the existing political order. As such, they are oppressive when punishing dissenting forces and voices and intrusive when monitoring society. Democracies hold a strong discipline of political neutrality, and the police effectively refrain from intruding into the realm of political rights and freedom. Regime type clearly matters in how security and freedom are defined and how different balances are struck between them.

That being said, once we evaluate police and policing from a functionalist perspective, with broader benchmarks to include the equal treatment of individuals and responsiveness and accountability to communities, the explanatory power of regime type diminishes quickly. The Singaporean police force would rank highly on both scales, and hence can be characterized as democratic in spite of, if not because of, a highly authoritarian internal security regime. Similar cases can be made in relation he community-centered, service-oriented policing in a wide variety of jurisdictions regardless of their political nature. By the same token, police in democracies can be highly discriminatory, repressive, and authoritarian when it comes to policing certain minority groups. This is because the police can adapt and respond to particular political dynamics. With populist or discriminatory sociopolitical conditions at the local level, decentralized democracies can become breeding grounds for police bigotry and abusive police practices. There is clearly an endogeneity factor as Kroncke reminds us in his chapter, which argues that police monopolize the use of violence, and, as such, authoritarianism is in the institutional DNA of all police, which necessarily must be controlled closely.

2

Discipline or Democracy

The Endogeneity of Police Accountability

JEDIDIAH J. KRONCKE

2.1 Introduction

2.1.1 The Uncertain Democratic Payoffs of Policing Scholarship

As Durkheim famously described, criminality is an integral, not antagonistic, component of all known human societies.[1] The deviant defines the normal, and serves to reinforce the normal through its suppression. As such, mechanisms meant to suppress criminality are universal. The Durkheimian vision thus posits that even the most pragmatically constructed of these conceivable mechanisms forever chases its symbolic tail. This sets up an inescapable dilemma for those tasked with reducing crime. Attempts to reduce crime, a category itself forever in reformulation, have an intention that can never fully come to fruition. Whether recognized or not, those given the formal social role of policing crime are caught juggling an objective, statistical task that can never be completely satisfied and is subject to constant moralistic scrutiny.

Wherever in time and geography one places its starting point, the systemic empirical study of policing is a relatively new phenomenon. In the contemporary era, bureaucratic and technological changes have given heretofore unavailable access to the day-to-day activities of police across the globe, which can be quantified and compared to a degree that is truly global. At the same time, these new images of police conduct – most controversially as full video renderings – are subject to quite stridently divergent interpretations by competing social actors. The fact that police violence, though long acknowledged as an inherent part of policing, is no longer invisible either statistically or visually means that anxiety over its legitimate use grips democratic and nondemocratic regimes alike. In premodern societies the lack of statistical data about policing left only general

[1] Emile Durkheim, *The Division of Labor in Society* (New York: The Free Press, 1997[1893]).

moralism as the grounds for evaluation, and while the allure of such moralism persists, modern policing faces technical, empirical scrutiny over its methods and goal. Yet this has in some ways increased the politicization of policing, in which the interpretation of policing statistics has become a routine aspect of political competition. All of this reciprocally agitates moral evaluations of policing and leaves actual changes in policing behavior resistant to any durable progressive scientific development.

Thus, while there are heated debates over policing techniques and criminological theories in academic, public and professional settings, it is not surprising that there appears to be little settled as to objectively good practices to reduce crime through policing. Moreover, the very expertise that academic studies of policing in the past half-century have developed still rarely serves as the basis of actual systemic policy reform. In a flurry of arguments about statistically significant impacts or trends, few case studies exist where anything but wholesale institutional reform (itself often the result of external sociopolitical change) has led to a measurable long-term decrease in police violence.[2]

Further complicating the field, while policing has grown more visible, the empirical study of policing has not necessarily become easier, as police themselves understand the stakes of their public representation and the deeply affective nature of their violence. Democratic and authoritarian regimes alike produce statistical data about crime and policing through a variety of means, and third-party access to policing and other arenas of criminal justice are often highly guarded. The development of police monitoring technology – most notably body camera devices – has shown the interest and effectiveness of policing entities in producing publicly available statistics and proactively generating their own interpretations of recorded violence.[3] Policing is thus not simply regulated by social institutions; they iteratively react to their own regulation and intervene in the politics that produce such regulation.

The technical empiricism that has arisen over police practices and violence reflects the perceived importance of fair policing, even for

[2] In the United States (US), the complete disbanding of the Camden, New Jersey police department has been evaluated by many as an example of the type of radical reform required to change policing outcomes. Subsequent evaluations have rendered these conclusions more tentative, with some arguing that even in a wealthy democracy disbanding the entire local polity would be required. Anthony O'Rourke, Rick Su, and Guyora Binder, "Disbanding Police Agencies," *Columbia Law Review* 121 (2021): 1327.

[3] Nathaniel Bronstein, "Police Management and Quotas: Governance in the CompStat Era," *Columbia Journal of Law and Social Problems* 48(4) (2015): 543.

authoritarian regimes. Yet most publics still resist accepting the obvious sociological factors that have been shown historically – time and time again – to cause relative increases and decreases in crime rates. Most glaringly, simple economic indicators are far more reliable than any modulation in technical police practices in tracking and predicting changes in crime over time. Such public resistance helps explain why scholarship on policing often acknowledges these realities, but still pursues scientific knowledge that aims to improve crime reduction as a policy objective. The dissonance between sociological and technical discourses on crime is well on display in an increasingly interconnected, global professional discourse on police discretion across regime types. Sociological perspectives that posit the relative impossibility of crime prevention render the intransigent focus of professional policing discourse on "discretion." Analytically fetishizing the individual actions of police officers in highly charged, if statistically exceptional, circumstances give rise to a hypermoralism through which police subjectively view and rationalize their use of violence and resonate with public moralism about police violence.[4] This resonance between narratives about "discretion" and social moralism reinforces their elevated status in political competitions. In the end, technical studies of policing practices validate discretion as an important professional virtue that policing reform dare not compromise; not because of the actually established impacts on the rate of crime, but because to do otherwise is to return to the far less comfortable, and often politically treacherous, critiques of the core social values that Durkheim posited crime exists to reinforce.

In this context, discussions over "democracy" as a value internal or external to policing regimes take on a slippery quality. The idea that police should be accountable for the illegitimate use of violence is taken as the premise for a wide range of current or proposed accountability mechanisms. Outside the most repressive, personalistic authoritarian regimes, most nations have practices of political and legal accountability for policing that are derived from some combinations of constitutional, statutory and any other number of regulatory sources. These systems range from centralized oversight run by legislative bodies to decentralized oversight through private rights of actions granted to aggrieved citizens in judicial contexts. Most countries subject police to some sort of formal training

[4] Steve Herbert, "Morality in Police Enforcement," *Law and Society Review* 30(4) (1996): 799. Herbert's ethnographic study of the Los Angeles Police Department was pioneering in its focus on the professional moralistic ethos of policing as driven by the impossibility of crime reduction.

or educational requirement – though still far from uniform in federal democracies such as the US. The recruitment and training of police is also embedded in formal means of discipline, both external and self-regulatory in nature, alongside often powerful informal norms derived from institutional relationships within the larger criminal justice system and the existential realities of on-the-job anxieties. Beyond these formal sources of accountability is the rise of direct citizen oversight bodies and private media scrutiny. And for each of these varying sources of accountability there is now a scholarship that examines their impact and efficacy – all of which still hunt for points of scientific consensus on what can be done to better regulate police misconduct and reduce police violence. Yet the hope among potential reformers that greater visibility would prompt an easier path to reform has yet to lead to greater restraint on police violence, even based on well-established empirical studies.[5]

Even formally democratic societies hew to the Durkheimian mold by accepting varying levels of collateral injustice – most recurrently on socially stigmatized populations – to pursue what is deemed socially desirable policing practices. The intractably cultural and moralistic views of crime across human societies are most overtly on display in the near-universal sanction and cooperation among democratic and nondemocratic regimes over actions to combat nonstate violence as "terrorism" rather than crime.[6] Even policing reform, rare itself, is more often only enabled by strong swings in partisan politics for democratic regimes or from a sense of performative crisis among relatively stable authoritarian regimes. The fact that authoritarian regimes have sought to professionalize and rationalize their police while many democratic countries still bear the mark of feudal legacies in their policing structures muddies the distinction between authoritarian and democratic policing reform.

[5] Following the viral recording of the 2020 murder of George Floyd by a police officer, the US has become a global flash point for discussions concerning reforming police violence, and the complicated politics of such reform even in the context of a new generation of more sophisticated empirical studies of policing. See Jessica Eaglin, "To 'Defund' the Police," *Stanford Law Review* 72 (2021): 122. Prior to this, "broken windows policing" was also pioneered in the US before reaching international circulation and influence. It similarly has had much greater political popularity than its empirical track-record has ever justified. Bernard Harcourt and Jens Ludwig, "Broken Windows: New Evidence from New York City and a Five-City Social Experiment," *University of Chicago Law Review* 73(1) (2006): 271.

[6] The shifting line around "crime" and "terrorism" has a long twentieth century history intimately tied up with colonialism. For a cogent review of anthropological analyses of this dynamic, see Edmund R. Leach, *Custom, Law and Terrorist Violence* (Edinburgh: Edinburgh University Press, 1977).

What is "modern" about policing is difficult to discern when policing institutions can survive large-scale political transitions, or – such as in the case of the medieval English sheriff – centuries of political turmoil. In some cases, modern authoritarian has been more active in "reforming" their basic policing institutions than democracies given less direct need to respond to social moralism. As a summary result, an internationalized discourse on policing has emerged across regime-types that prioritizes nonsociological approaches with the aim to improve policing as a matter of technical rather than a particularly democratic practice.[7] While this literature has become more robust and expansive, best practices remain elusive though ever desired.

The fundamental argument advanced in this chapter is that policing is in effect endogenous, and cannot be effectively reformed except at the margins through technical reform. Historical and cultural factors, unless themselves subject to transformation, drive the reality of policing – especially police violence – in a matter that defies the relevance of even the basic distinction between democratic and authoritarian regimes. The growing comparative turn in policing underscores this trend. The growing professionalization of policing in authoritarian regimes and the continued intensity of police lethality in many democratic regimes lays bare this reality. It appears that if any comparative lesson is to be drawn, it is that a highly disciplined and professionalized police force, whatever its political context, is preferable to one that is not – regardless of the normative quality or character of a regime. To the extent that the collateral violence of policing can be reduced, this seems to hold across all regime types. This chapter explores this dynamic in the modern Asian context in Japan, China and the Philippines.[8]

[7] One of the newest arenas in this global trend is "predictive policing." It has similarly resisted acknowledging sociogenic drivers, and also failed to find empirical validation as a technical modulation capable of reducing crime. Albert Meijer and Martijn Wessels, "Predictive Policing, Review of Benefits and Drawbacks," *International Journal of Public Administration* 42(12) (2019): 1031.

[8] A notable recent study compares Russian policing with practices in China and Brazil and comes to a parallel conclusion that regime type is not a useful explanatory frame. After differentiating political "repression" and social "abuse" to label police violence, it notes that "By postulate, these features of democratic policing should be relatively likely to accompany democratic political institutions, and relatively unlikely to accompany nondemocratic ones. Through our empirical investigation, we partially refute this assumption. Indeed, our findings are somewhat counterintuitive." See Matthew Light, Mariana Mota Prado, and Yuhua Wang, "Policing Following Political and Social Transitions," *Theoretical Criminology* 19(2) (2015): 216–238, https://doi.org/10.1177/1362480614568742.

2.1.2 Transnationalizing the Professional Discourse

In recent decades the rise of transnational networks of policing practices and institutions has further strengthened shared professionalized discourses on policing. Police organizations, commonly public sector police unions, have generated regional patterns of leadership and collective identity formation.[9] Some of this transnational networking is incident to the globalization of crime itself and the collaborative regimes generated to achieve enforcement goals.[10] At the same time, case-specific information sharing has evolved into more systematic patterns of professional networking among national and subnational agencies and individuals, again across political regime type.[11]

Some may point to the positive fruits of this sharing at the policy level. The spread of the Swedish ombudsman system as a means of facilitating police accountability is a classic forerunner of this new global trend.[12] Perhaps the most dramatic development has been the near universalization of the ideal of "democratic" or "community" policing that posits police-community engagement as an important driver of policing outcomes. As with many areas of regulation, the 1990s witnessed a surge in programs sponsored by the US that had the objective of reforming foreign policing practices in the service of political democratization, even though such programs were formally abolished in the 1970s.[13]

Thus, even in authoritarian regimes, policing discourse selectively adopts new terms such as "problem-oriented" or "value-based" policing, and even in formally democratic countries the need to develop new "human rights" policing is portrayed as a universal need. What is rarely addressed is whether such practices can be solely technical in nature – changing police tactics and procedure – and how they should be judged and by what measured outputs. As a result these practices remain shrouded in the same empirical murkiness as to whether they can systemically and durably reduce crime or reduce police violence. Study of and collaboration

9 Monique Marks and Jenny Fleming, "Police as Workers: Police Labour Rights in Southern Africa and Beyond," *South African Crime Quarterly* 19 (2007): 13.

10 Giulio Calcara, "A Transnational Police Network Co-operating Up to The Limits of the Law: Examination of the Origin of INTERPOL," *Transnational Legal Theory* 11(4) (2020): 521.

11 Michael Walton, "Informal Transnational Police-to-Police Information Sharing: Its Structure and Reform" (LLM Thesis, Osgoode Hall Law School, 2014).

12 Alison Brysk, *Global Good Samaritans: Human Rights as Foreign Policy* (New York: Oxford University Press, 2009), 32.

13 David Bayley, *Democratizing the Police Abroad: What to Do and How to Do It* (Washington, DC: US Department of Justice, 2001), 35.

with policing institutions under authoritarian regimes leads to an ethical quagmires about whether "improved" policing shores up a regime's legitimacy or is an effective way to protect citizens from state coercion.[14]

2.1.3 Discipline or Democracy for Police Accountability

The tension between empowering police to fight crime and punishing police for misconduct was recognized even in premodern societies.[15] The general global twentieth-century transition to democratization has done little to decisively resolve this tension. The US, perhaps plainly now more than ever, is a primary example of an intensely scrutinized regime of policing within a democratic regime where empirical data production has had little impact on resolving deeply partisan views of the sources of crime and the role of police.[16] Structurally, the US has a policing system that is structurally highly democratic given its decentralized nature and emphasis on direct local mechanisms of accountability.[17] Although often lost in international discourse, the majority of American geographical space is policed by nonprofessional sheriffs who are locally elected, and whose actions are, in the first instance, regulated by locally elected judges and prosecutors.[18] In urban settings, policing is carried out by unionized professionals who enjoy a highly-localized electoral union structure that is more formally democratic than in any other country.[19] As such, centralized top-down policing of police misconduct is incredibly difficult,[20] and American labor scholars remain conflicted about the impact that police unions have on the officials who are supposed to regulate them,[21] even

[14] Johannes Gerschewski, "Legitimacy in Autocracies: Oxymoron or Essential Feature?" *Perspectives on Politics* 16(3) (2018): 652.

[15] Defining the precise and comparative premodern history of "policing" is a fraught and conceptual muddy comparative exercise. See F. M. Dodsworth, "The Idea of Police in Eighteenth-Century England: Discipline, Reformation, Superintendence, c. 1780–1800," *Journal of the History of Ideas* 69(4) (2008): 583.

[16] Nirej Sekhon, "Police and the Limit of Law," *Columbia Law Review* 119(6) (2019): 1711.

[17] Samuel Walker, "Governing the American Police: Wrestling with the Problems of Democracy," *University of Chicago Legal Forum* 2016 (2016): 615.

[18] Ibid.

[19] Margaret Levi, *Bureaucratic Insurgency: The Case of Police Unions* (Lexington, MA: Lexington Books, 1977).

[20] Gilbert Rivera, "Armed Not Militarized: Achieving Real Police Militarization," *Berkeley Journal of Criminal Law* 20(2) (2015): 227.

[21] Catherine Fisk and Song Richardson, "Police Unions," *George Washington Law Review* 85(3) (2017): 712; Melissa Morabito, "American Police Unions: A Hindrance or Help to Innovation," *International Journal of Public Administration* 37(11) (2014): 773.

though criminologists are much less sanguine given police unions' effective frustration of external accountability.[22]

The debates on American policing thus make clear that while a decentralized and unionized police could be categorized as hyperdemocratic, this says little about functional accountability. The sociolegal scholarship on American policing further demonstrates how these democratic structures do not deprive police of near-impenetrable recourse to hypermoralism to justify their use of violence within local communities, and display the same characteristics found elsewhere about resistance to reforming even routine policing habits,[23] and violent spillovers into their domestic lives.[24] Moreover, the local, democratic nature of American policing means that limited functional accountability for misconduct is acute for nonlocals and for minoritized groups.[25]

The traditional American critical reaction to this condition has been to promote the external discipline of police by removing police employment protections, prohibiting unionization or centralizing their administration.[26] It does seem clear that unionization may facilitate police misconduct to varying degrees,[27] but if such is the case why hasn't there been reform in the face of this clarion empirical record? What seems clear is that even in highly partisan municipal settings, popular dissatisfaction with policing is far less than reformers and scholars would hope for. Not only have some American states further strengthened statutory rights for police facing misconduct charges in recent years,[28] but also,

22 Stephen Rushin, "Police Union Contracts," *Duke Law Journal* 66(6) (2017): 1191; Also see Jonathan Abel, "Cops and Pleas: Police Officers' Influence on Plea Bargaining," *Yale Law Journal* 126(6) (2017): 1600.

23 Kim Loyens, "Law Enforcement and Policy Alienation: Coping by Labour Inspectors and Federal Police Officers," in Peter Hupe, Michael Hill, and Aurélien Buffat (eds.), *Understanding Street-Level Bureaucracy* (Bristol: Policy Press, 2015), 99.

24 Robert Sgambelluri, "Police Culture, Police Training, and Police Administration: Their Impact on Violence in Police Families," in Donald Sheehan (ed.), *Domestic Violence by Police Officers* (Washington, DC: US Department of Justice, 2000), 309.

25 Stephen Schulhofer, "Criminal Justice, Local Democracy, and Constitutional Rights," *Michigan Law Review* 111(6) (2013): 1045.

26 Leo Troy, "Are Municipal Collective Bargaining and Municipal Governance Compatible?" *Journal of Business Law* 5(3) (2003): 453.

27 Dhammnike Dharmapala, Richard H. McAdams, John Rappaport, "Collective Bargaining Rights and Police Misconduct: Evidence from Florida," *The Journal of Law, Economics, and Organization* 38 (1)(2022): 1–41, https://doi.org/10.1093/jleo/ewaa025.

28 Kevin Kennan and Samuel Walker, "An Impediment to Police Accountability?: An Analysis of Statutory Law Enforcement Officers' Bills of Rights," *Public Interest Law Journal* 14(2) (2005): 185.

when centralized federal oversight has been enacted it has been weakly enforced, in large part because of the fear of political backlash.[29] The very fact that American police unions have survived the larger assault on public sector unions in the US points to the fact that these features of the system are not so much pure accidents of history as they are the product of the same intransigent Durkheimian moralism that resists technical revision.[30] Furthermore, this dynamic is found in virtually every country that has allowed collective bargaining for police,[31] or which faces endemically high rates of police violence.[32] "Democratic police" in any straightforward sense appear to be nonviolent or easily held to account for their violence.

Whatever sociological factors may drive cultural attitudes about crime, the question remains then of what particular use is the frame of authoritarianism and democracy in the study of policing, especially given the burgeoning transnational professionalized discourse of technical reform. Are their techniques of discipline themselves not simply products of more basic social conditions or adjuncts to historical changes, especially those that are powerful enough to transcend other endemic factors such as wealth or social homogeneity?

2.2 Police Accountability in Asia

An attempt to explore these dualisms of democracy/discipline and moralism/technocracy in the context of Asian policing offers stark variations to test their utility. Many democratic regimes in the region have had colonial or noncolonial experiences with authoritarian regimes,[33] and have been impacted by the transnationalization of policing discourse to varying degrees. In contrast to other regions of the world, there are few regional treaties or conventions to address policing, though all share the globally common prohibition on police unionization.[34]

[29] Stephen Rustin, "Federal Enforcement of Police Reform," *Fordham Law Review* 82(6) (2014): 3189.

[30] Richard Freeman and Eunice Han, "The War against Public Sector Collective Bargaining in the US," *Journal of Industrial Relations* 54(3) (2012): 386.

[31] Mark Finnane, *When Police Unionise: The Politics of Law and Order in Australia* (Sydney: Hawkins Press, 2002).

[32] Jan French, "Rethinking Police Violence in Brazil: Unmasking the Public Secret of Race," *Latin American Politics and Society* 55(4) (2014): 161.

[33] For one survey of such diversity, see Maya Tudor and Dan Slate, "*Nationalism, Authoritarianism, and Democracy: Historical Lessons from South and Southeast Asia*," *Perspectives on Politics* 19 (3) (2021): 706.

[34] Monique Marks and Jenny Fleming, "The Right to Unionize, the Right to Bargain, and the Right to Democratic Policing," *Annals of AAPSS* 605 (2006): 178, 187.

Here we will consider three countries that offer key variations on these dualisms: Japan, the Philippines and China. Japan represents a stable, wealthy and institutionalized democracy, which has a highly professionalized and centralized policing regime. The Philippines represents a less stable democracy with fewer economic resources, and which has a more formally decentralized system of policing. China is a rapidly developing and more populous authoritarian regime, which has a policing regime that is under stress as it seeks to professionalize while existing within a more formally centralized but functionally decentralized system.

2.2.1 Democratically Authoritarian Police in Japan

The system of Japanese policing was reconfigured as part of the many reforms started during the American occupation following World War II.[35] As with many of these reforms, the changes insisted on by American actors, even large legal transplants, were quickly remodeled by Japanese actors and dynamics. Notably, policing was one area where American reformers did little to try to replicate actual American practices given their highly informal and localized nature. By contrast, from the outset modern Japanese policing was highly centralized,[36] with the 1954 Police Law enshrining many extant practices and formally outlining the still basic structure of how powers to regulate police were to be distributed.[37] In brief, a National Public Safety Commission directly oversees the National Police Agency, which in turn appoints other national and prefectural level officials. At the local level, police stations are overseen by prefectural officials, which display great variation in practices based on their urban versus rural placement given the sharp differences these divisions mark in Japanese life.[38]

This top-down system of control is also reflected in the highly professionalized and routinized structure of police recruitment, training and discipline. The major centers of policing education, such as the International Research and Training Institute for Criminal Investigation and the Tokyo Police Academy, emphasize both an academic and a militaristic approach

[35] Rande Kostal, *Laying Down the Law: The American Legal Revolutions in Occupied Germany and Japan* (Cambridge, MA: Harvard University Press, 2019).

[36] Christopher Aldous and Frank Leishman, "Policing in Post-War Japan: Reform, Reversion and Reinvention," *International Journal of the Sociology of Law* 25(3) (1997): 135.

[37] D. C. S. Sissons, "The Dispute Over Japan's Police Law," *Pacific Affairs* 32(1) (1959): 34.

[38] Frank Leishman, "Koban: Neighborhood Policing in Contemporary Japan," *Policing* 1 (2007): 196.

to instruction and socialization.[39] The internal bureaucratic capacity of these policing institutions – especially in data collection and analysis – has made the influence of Japanese academics on policing behavior and reform much less than in most other developed democracies.[40]

While the centralized regulation of Japanese policing gives officials strong top-down disciplinary powers, Japanese policing is intensely community-oriented at the local level.[41] Local police spend a great deal of their time engaged with local constituents and provide high levels of informal dispute resolution that are one of the now traditional explanations for Japan's low per capita number of private lawyers.[42] Coupled with Japan's comparatively low levels of defined crime, the investigation of serious crimes primarily falls to regional police authorities. Much of the literature on Japanese policing revolves around this community focus, as well as the active participation of lay citizens through various volunteer organizations.[43]

The most notable recent reforms in Japanese policing followed the increase in crime after the Japanese economy's downturn in the 1990s.[44] Following the same moralism found elsewhere, simply acknowledging that crime and economic performance are inherently correlated was not seen as a politically satisfactory response by the government. Instead, the response to this relative increase was a national action plan developed in 2002, which led to a massive increase in the resources committed to minor crime enforcement and a tenfold increase in the use of local koban volunteer patrols increasingly staffed by retired police officers.[45] In contrast to

[39] The funding and capacity of the Japanese police is often cited as favorable by researchers who favor technocratic solutions to policing issues. See, for example, Andrew Millie and D. K. Das, "Education and Training in Four Countries: Getting Rule of Law Messages Across," in Kauko Aromaa and Slawomir Redo (eds.), *For the Rule of Law: Criminal Justice Training and Teaching Across the World* (Helsinki: HEUNI (The European Institute for Crime Prevention and Control), 2008), 184.

[40] Ryuji Okabe, "Police Innovation Paradigm in the US and Japan," *Police Practice and Research* 15(3) (2014): 192.

[41] Leishman, "Koban."

[42] For a survey of the long-standing comparative debate on the low levels of Japanese litigation, see Tom Ginsburg and Glenn Hoetker, "The Unreluctant Litigant? An Empirical Analysis of Japan's Turn to Litigation," *The Journal of Legal Studies* 35(1) (2006): 31.

[43] L. Craig Parker, *The Japanese Police System Today: A Comparative Study* (Armonk, NY: M. E. Sharpe, 2001), 210.

[44] For an example of the professionalized production of policing research in Japan, see Taisuke Kanayama and Arichika Eguchi, *Japan's Challenge on the Increase in Crime in the New Century* (Police Policy Research Center, National Police Agency of Japan).

[45] Ibid.

the fairly common resistance of rank-and-file officers to top-down policy shifts in other unionized contexts, Japan was able to implement these changes with relatively little resistance, as had been the case in other policing policy changes.[46]

At first blush then, it would seem that Japanese policing combines elements of centralization and community policing that are often held as at odds in other contexts. The surge in police resources following the 2002 reforms has led to a popular trope that there are too many police without enough crime to occupy their time.[47] Yet foreign observers frequently point to a lack of transparency and accountability in Japanese policing, as well as the open informal acceptance of spheres of social influence for organized crime.[48] Others note that while Japanese crime statistics paint a picture of overall low incidence, the lack of externally produced empirical data makes comparative claims difficult and also masks areas of massive under-enforcement such as sexual and domestic violence.[49]

This locally engaged but authoritarian policing structure points to the fact that the dualities of democracy/discipline and moralism/technocracy found in many Western sociolegal studies of policing are far from universal. It further suggests that the general Japanese view of crime follows the Durkheimian mold by forming its own categories of criminality, and is premised on a powerful popular bifurcation of the citizen/criminal divide.

Japanese police engage in forms of highly localized community policing, with a low incidence of police violence. Social media sites contain widely circulated images of Japanese police using a wide range of near-pacifistic techniques to subdue lawbreakers, and again retell the trope of the Japanese police officer as social worker. Yet Japanese policing reflects a highly charged version of Durkheimian morality when it comes to criminality. Accountability for actual misconduct is much weaker and those deemed criminal are granted few liberties. With some recent international notice, the harsh treatment of criminal suspects is intense, and there are many established critiques of the use of forced confessions to sustain

46 Okabe, "Police Innovation Paradigm in the US and Japan."

47 Such claims take current policing priorities as a given, see Rob Fahey, "The Myth of Japan's Bored Police," *Tokyo Review*, August 25, 2017, www.tokyoreview.net/2017/08/myth-japans-bored-police/.

48 David Johnson, "Above the Law? Police Integrity in Japan," *Social Science Japan Journal* 6(1) (2003): 19.

49 Kazumi Ogaswara, "Current Status of Sex Crimes and Measures for the Victims in Japan," *Japan Medical Association Journal* 54(3) (2011): 164.

Japan's near 90 percent criminal conviction rates.[50] While the outward appearance of Japan as an ethnically homogeneous society might seem to explain generally low levels of police violence, once one crosses over from citizen to criminal, there is little built into the Japanese system to restrain police violence.

Moreover, if one is from a traditional minoritized group, or a foreign citizen, then popular concern with police violence seems near absent. Thus, while before one crosses the citizen/criminal divide Japanese policing has a quite democratic and prosocial face, the comparative intensity of this leniency is matched by the near unrestrained authoritarian face that exists on the other side.

Japanese policing is thus both highly democratic and authoritarian because popular views of crime produce these same patterns. The recent uptick in the targeting of foreign citizens, primarily for violating labor market restrictions, in national political discourse has led little protest and any notion of abuse was successfully waved away by police leaders, citing infringement on the professionalized integrity of police institutions.[51] Thus, we have a highly moralistic and technocratic discourse on policing that can sustain hyperprofessionalism with few real mechanisms for accountability.

2.2.2 *The Ravages of Presidentialism on Philippine Police Violence*

While of comparable populations, the cultural diversity of the Philippines stands in stark contrast to the relative homogeneity of Japanese society. With the Philippines itself, regional variations both ethnically and religiously generate quite different perceptions of criminality, which is most notable in the characterization of Filipino Muslims as terrorists and their treatment as domestic insurgents.[52] This social diversity reflects the complicated colonial history of the Philippines, with both Spanish

[50] The issue of Japan's treatment of the accused has flared up again recently, and drawn several competent defenders. See Bruce Aronson, "Carlos Ghosn and Japan's '99% Conviction Rate,'" *The Diplomat*, March 31, 2020, https://thediplomat.com/2020/03/carlos-ghosn-and-japans-99-conviction-rate/.

[51] For an extensive, if now potentially dated, study, see Wolfgang Herbert, *Foreign Workers and Law Enforcement in Japan* (London: Kegan Paul International, 1996). Yet ever since, English-language newspapers on Japan affairs recurrently mention raids on foreign "illegal" workers.

[52] Steffen Jensen and Karl Hapal, "Police Violence and Corruption in the Philippines: Violent Exchange and the War on Drugs," *Journal of Current Southeast Asian Affairs* 37(2) (2018): 39.

and American occupations having built up repressive police institutions whose legacies persist after several regime changes.[53]

The renewal of Filipino democracy in 1987 has thus left unresolved the authoritarian legacy of these foreign occupations and the twenty-year dictatorship of Ferdinand Marcos. This authoritarian legacy is well evidenced in the realm of policing. The actual institutions of policing from these colonial and authoritarian eras, notably the Philippine Constabulary, have never been fully revolutionized – though reformed in 1990 following democratization and formally reorganized in 1998.[54] Filipino policing is now theoretically under civilian control, but in structure and personnel it is still marked by a militaristic culture sustained in part by its responsibility for suppressing domestic unrest following the imprint of the Cold War and religious strife.[55] What seems most challenging for outside observers of modern policing in the Philippines, as well as for many domestic reformers, is that extreme police violence has emerged through continued majoritarian democratic consent.[56]

Beyond its democratic character, this level of violence exists even though police in the Philippines are formally disciplined and governed by a wide array of accountability mechanisms. Many of these mechanisms would appear to be world-leading in their progressive character. Following such international norms, there is a police ombudsman, a specialized department to receive citizen complaints, and both anti-corruption and human rights agencies focused on regulating police misconduct.[57] Moreover, quotas exist for the participation of women, alongside special processes for reporting domestic violence.[58]

[53] Cicero Campos, "Law Enforcement Policy Strategy in the Republic of the Philippines," *Police Studies: The International Review of Police Development* 14 (1991): 76; Julian Go, "The Imperial Origins of American Policing: Militarization and Imperial Feedback in the Early 20th Century," *American Journal of Sociology* 125(5) (2020): 1193.

[54] Walter Ladwig, "When the Police Are the Problem: The Philippine Constabulary and the Hukbalahap Rebellion," in Christine Fair and Sumit Ganguly (eds.), *Policing Insurgencies: Cops as Counterinsurgents* (New Delhi: Oxford University Press, 2014), 19.

[55] Alfred McCoy, *Policing America's Empire: The United States, the Philippines, and the Rise of the Surveillance State* (Madison, WI: University of Wisconsin Press, 2009) and Jeremy Kuzmarov, *Modernizing Repression: Police Training and Nation-Building in the American Century* (Amherst, MA: University of Massachusetts Press, 2012).

[56] Catherine Valente, "Duterte Maintains High Approval, Trust Ratings," *The Manila Times*, April 8, 2021, www.manilatimes.net/2021/04/08/news/national/duterte-maintains-high-approval-trust-ratings/861230.

[57] Melchor de Guzman and Flocergine de Guzman, "Civilian Review and the Police," *Journal of Ethnicity in Criminal Justice* 8(1) (2010): 18.

[58] Laura Serquina-Ramiro, Bernadette J. Madrid, and Ma. Lourdes E. Amarillo, "Domestic Violence in Urban Filipino Families," *Asian Journal of Women's Studies* 10(2) (2004): 97–119, https://doi.org/10.1080/12259276.2004.11665971.

While these formal mechanisms exist, the regulation of Filipino policing is most directly structured by two institutional factors: 1) a decentralized devolution of police disciplinary powers to local political representatives, and 2) the disproportionate influence of the executive branch following the Philippine importation of the American presidentialist model. As such, the National Police Commission, which sits at the top of the police institutional hierarchy, is composed of senior appointments made by the president, starting with its director-general.[59] Thus while local police officials hold the most immediate disciplinary powers, policy is set in a top-down fashion. Continuity with past authoritarian norms is in part facilitated by the fact that the director-general is almost exclusively appointed from the graduates of the Philippine Military Academy.[60] This combination of decentralized discipline and top-down policymaking has led to a heavy emphasis on patronage politics for internal promotion that limits the incentives of both mayors and governors to carry out discipline in practice, and rank and file hesitancy to report colleague misconduct.[61]

These larger structural realities have stymied the efficacy of reforms aimed to rationalize and lessen police violence. In international comparisons, the citizen oversight mechanism created in 1998 – the Police Law Enforcement Boards – is often cited as an example of functional accountability.[62] These boards are required to have one woman and one practicing lawyer (with some substitutions) among its members and they have the power to suspend police. Yet in operation the functional independence of these boards is quite weak, as local chiefs of police can limit the outcome of almost any civilian complaint to a two-week suspension, and cases can linger unresolved for years.[63]

While the general structure of policing in the Philippines is well known, more specific empirical studies of policing in action are highly underdeveloped.[64] Much less is known about the internal procedures of the

[59] Glenn Varona, "Politics and Policing in the Philippines," *Flinders Journal of History and Politics* 26 (2010): 101.

[60] In this way, the Philippines shares many of the policing pathologies evident in Brazil, where the effects of colonialism and postcolonial dictatorships are strongly felt in the present, especially in the impact and popularity of the military. See Light et al., "Policing Following Political and Social Transitions."

[61] Varona, "Politics and Policing in the Philippines."

[62] Melchor de Guzman, "Integrity of Civilian Review: A Contemporary Analysis of Complainants' and Police Officers' Views in the Philippines," *Police Practice and Research* 8(1) (2007): 31.

[63] Ibid.

[64] Varona, "Politics and Policing in the Philippines."

Public Safety College and other sites of police training.[65] In contrast to the Japanese example, where statistical data is produced and molded by an active bureaucracy, in the Philippines little investment has been made in public accounting, and policing institutions have been able to block a great deal of even local research.[66]

What is clear is that while this system may seem to give police a great deal of impunity in practice, this impunity has not led to either high morale or a sense of personal empowerment. Local police face recurrent budget shortfalls, to the extent that in 2003 there was even an attempt to supplement low salaries by allowing the use of police infrastructure and time to engage in side-businesses within their communities.[67] Thus low public perceptions of the police are matched by similar low self-perceptions of work conditions and performance.[68]

If the weakness of this system was generally acknowledged before, the massive campaign of police violence and repression following the election of Rodrigo Duterte as president in 2016 cemented the notion. Duterte's political campaign was grounded in a hypermoralistic condemnation of drug trafficking, which has been buoyed by what some have called "penal populism."[69] While the levels of extrajudicial killings openly acknowledged by the Duterte regime have shocked many outside the Philippines, others have noted his campaign's consonance with historical practices,[70] and his success in using his normal powers over the police to institute "re-education" programs and to quickly rearrange resistant personnel.[71] Following this dramatic increase in police violence, little has been said of the many formal accountability mechanisms put in place over the past two decades.[72] Moreover, it is far from clear that Duterte's tactics deviate

[65] Mayra Tulauan, *Perceived Effectiveness of the Recruitment and Selection Process for Uniformed Personnel of the Philippine National Police* (MA Thesis, Ritsumeikan Asia Pacific University, 2014).

[66] Glenn Varona, *Police Ethics and Governance: Challenging Police and Social Corruption in the Philippines* (Saarbrucken: Lambert Academic Publishing, 2012).

[67] Varona, "Politics and Policing in the Philippines," 116.

[68] Tulauan, *Perceived Effectiveness of the Recruitment and Selection Process.*

[69] David Johnson and Jon Fernquest, "Governing through Killing: The War on Drugs in the Philippines," *Asian Journal of Law and Society* 5(2) (2018): 359.

[70] Peter Kreuzer, "Police Use of Deadly Force in the Philippines," *Austrian Journal of South-East Asian Studies* 12(2) (2018): 149.

[71] Jensen and Hapal, "Police Violence and Corruption in the Philippines."

[72] Ibid.; ethnographic study of the recent increase in violence shows an intensification of the local negotiations between police and citizens, rather than a sharp distinction from previous eras.

from popular will, and there is certainly a marked difference in the domestic and foreign media coverage of the killings.[73]

Here we have a structure of policing in a democracy that contrasts sharply with that of Japan, being both decentralized and furnished with low levels of professionalization. But it is unclear that if Japanese institutions were to be transplanted to the Philippines the outcome would be any different given that the implementation of democratic will seems to have been achieved in both instances. Clearly, Japanese ethnic homogeneity and greater social wealth are key attributes to lower overall levels of criminality – even if such also make the citizen/criminal dividing line so harsh. But to the extent that such social factors are relevant, it seems that while a wider and more diverse swath of Philippines society is deemed by many as "criminal," it is all the more unsurprising that the greater formal accountability innovations in the Philippines have not been able to reduce police violence.

Here it seems clear that in each country shifts in popular moral reasoning about who is deserving of police violence is more determinative of who receives such violence than any formal institutional configuration. If Filipino politics reflects its greater cultural diversity than that of Japan, it appears that the consequence of moralistic targeting of minoritized groups is one of degree and extent rather than institutional design.

2.2.3 Democratic Policing in Authoritarian China?

That two democracies such as Japan and the Philippines demonstrate such high levels of variability in policing cultures is far from empirically controversial. What if we compare these democracies with the policing culture of a formally illiberal and authoritarian regime such as China? China is vastly larger in population and size, and has elements of both cultural homogeneity but also pronounced regional variations in ethnic and religious traits. Would it be possible to say that policing in China is in any way more "democratic" than in formally democratic regimes, either at the level of community engagement or accountability? If the outcomes of policing in Japan and the Philippines are so different, yet largely democratically driven, what is the exact remaining impact of regime type for understanding policing structures and outcomes?

To start, we see a range of analogous developments and drivers in modern Chinese policing as in many other countries. Since 1978, the entire

[73] Mark Thompson, "Duterte's Violent Populism: Mass Murder, Political Legitimacy and the 'Death of Development' in the Philippines," *Journal of Contemporary Asia* 52 (3)(2021): 403.

system of governance in China has been transformed, and an overt concern with policing reform therein has been consistent. Comparing levels of crime and police violence over time in China can be challenging, and until 1986 such data was officially considered a state secret. Yet current attempts to compare police in China to democracies such as the US have consistently failed to show that Chinese policing is more violent in the experiences of the vast majority of its citizens. Where there are no (immediate) contemporary comparable incidents of overt state violence in many developed democracies – such as those undertaken during the Tiananmen Massacre or consistent state violence in Xinjiang – the same cannot be said of democracies at the same income level as China's. And it only takes a few decades in the past to see large-scale acts of police violence against minorities and dissident political groups in many, if not all, of the world's democracies. What seems clear is that just as in many other areas of law, the idea that authoritarian regimes always favor pure caprice and a lack of internal restraint does not hold in the Chinese context, if at all more globally.[74] Policing is seen as both an instrument of direct state power and simultaneously as a forum for improving social service provision. Police accountability, whatever its normative foundations, is seen as part of a social legitimacy that still has to be courted rather than enforced.[75]

Structurally, the legacy of the pre-1978 Maoist state makes any clear institutional comparisons between Chinese policing and other countries difficult in a post-Soviet world. Formally, the Ministry of Public Security oversees provincial-level security bureaus, as well as those for large cities and autonomous regions.[76] The lower per capita number of professional police, generally set at just above 2 million, does not represent the wide distribution of policing power to any number of state agents. Almost every legal and political unit in China can have a set of enforcement agents attached to it, including the judiciary and procuratorate.[77] The vast system of urban/rural registration requires a massive amount of

[74] For a review of the growing recognition that authoritarian regimes have a vested interest in producing some forms of credible, routine restraints through law, see Tamir Moustafa, "Law and Courts in Authoritarian Regimes," *Annual Review of Law and Social Sciences* 10(1) (2014): 281.

[75] Jinghan Zeng, "The Debate on Regime Legitimacy in China: Bridging the Wide Gulf Between Western and Chinese Scholarship," *Journal of Contemporary China* 23(88) (2014): 612.

[76] Kam Wong, "Policing in the People's Republic of China: The Road to Reform in the 1990s," *The British Journal of Criminology* 42(2) (2002): 281.

[77] Lena Zhong and Peter Grabosky, "The Pluralization of Policing and the Rise of Private Policing in China," *Crime Law and Social Change* 52(5) (2009): 433.

manpower to monitor, and administrative policing bodies are on the rise systematically.[78] While formal accountability mechanisms are primarily administrative rather than legal in nature, concerns about the actions of these agents are expressed in the same gamut of mechanisms, formal and informal, by which Chinese citizens launch their many complaints.[79]

Yet the policing capacity of the Chinese state is still one of its major challenges.[80] The multiplicity of policing actors has not stopped the growth of private security forces, and many local governments rely on unregulated informal agents to supplement their police force.[81] Professionalization and more direct disciplinary control of police have thus been ongoing concerns. As with so many areas of Chinese legal reform, the Police Law of 1995 began an iterative process by which police professionalization was seen by the central government as both a strategy to promote social legitimacy and to improve its control over local agents.[82] To make the claim that police serve the interests of the Chinese state is to invite the difficult question of defining who the Chinese state is in any particular matter, as local–central government tensions are a core area of contest in Chinese governance for which centralization of police discipline is one index of success.[83]

As with Japan, the low relative rates of crime in China have been subject to fluctuation based on issues of economic and social distress.[84] In 2003, a new Minister of Public Security used local corruption as a rationale for a reform campaign that purged many police officers while attempting to centralize initial recruitment.[85] Part of this campaign emphasized that

[78] Fei-Ling Wang, "Reformed Migration Control and New Targeted People: China's Hukou System in the 2000s," *The China Quarterly* 177 (2004): 115.

[79] Michael Palmer, "Changing Policing in the People's Republic of China," *Taiwan in Comparative Perspective* 3 (2011): 66. It is a long-standing, but thoroughly incorrect presumption by many outside China that Chinese citizens are passive or reluctant to litigate their rights.

[80] Guangzhen Wu, David A. Makin, Yongtao Li, Francis D. Boateng, and Gassan Abess, "Policing Integrity in China," *Policing: An International Journal of Police Strategies & Management* 41(5) (2018): 563, https://doi.org/10.1108/PIJPSM-01-2017-0008.

[81] Zhong and Grabosky, "The Pluralization of Policing."

[82] Jianhua Xu, "Authoritarian Policing with Chinese Characteristics: A Case Study of Motorcycle Bans in the Pearl River Delta," *Crime, Law and Social Change* 61(4) (2014): 439.

[83] Murray Tanner and Eric Green, "Principals and Secret Agents: Central versus Local Control Over Policing and Obstacles to 'Rule of Law' in China," *The China Quarterly* 191 (2007): 644.

[84] Borge Bakken, "Moral Panics, Crime Rates and Harsh Punishment in China," *Journal of Criminology* 37(4) (2004): 69.

[85] Ivan Sun and Yuning Wu, "Chinese Policing in a Time of Transition, 1978–2008," *Journal of Contemporary Criminal Justice* 26(1) (2010): 20.

police should engage in greater "community policing" in terms that both reflected "mass line" policies of the past but also the infiltration of international policing discourse.[86] As with many other areas of reform, this push was later reconsidered when it became linked to decreasing professionalism among police.[87] If we move even closer to the day-to-day lives of Chinese police, we can see a range of community expectations that stimulate police practices resembling those in Japan,[88] though with vastly different resources.[89] Yet while the sources of this community policing may be different, the net effect is the same: community-engagement reduces police brutality for the majority of the population even as it offers up the prospects of even greater police surveillance of minoritized groups.[90]

While the policing of public protest draws the most attention internationally,[91] there are many other much more mundane areas where budgetary shortfalls and increasingly heavy reporting requirements lead to shirking and other behaviors tied to low morale.[92] While investments by the state in training, salaries and equipment have increased, Chinese police often feel highly restrained in both their formal duties and in their ability to resist local interests.[93] Public security chiefs have been brought into party leadership positions in part to strengthen central disciplinary power, but also to give them a better bargaining position for budgetary negotiations.[94] As younger, more professionalized and better educated police come into power, there is evidence that they will be better able to

[86] Lena Zhong, "Community Policing in China: Old Wine in New Bottles," *Police Practice and Research* 10(2) (2009): 157.

[87] Sun and Wu, "Chinese Policing in a Time of Transition."

[88] Xiaohai Wang and Dennis Wong, "Police Social Service Work in China: Community Policing with Chinese Characteristics," *Asia Pacific Journal of Police & Criminal Justice* 9(1) (2012): 34.

[89] Xiaoming Chen, "Community and Policing Strategies: A Chinese Approach to Crime Control," *Policing and Society* 12(1) (2010): 1.

[90] The use by the Chinese state of new surveillance technologies – both in general and specifically for minoritized groups – has been a flashpoint for larger debates over such police powers and global democracy. Richard Van Noorden, "The Ethical Questions That Haunt Facial-Recognition Research," *Nature*, November 18, 2020, www.nature.com/articles/d41586-020-03187-3.

[91] Suzanne Scoggins, *Policing China: Street-Level Cops in the Shadow of Protest* (Ithaca, NY: Cornell University Press, 2021).

[92] Suzanne Scoggins and Kevin O'Brien, "China's Unhappy Police," *Asian Survey* 56(2) (2016): 225.

[93] Hualing Fu, "Zhou Yongkang and the Recent Police Reform in China," *Australian and New Zealand Journal of Criminology* 38(2) (2005): 241.

[94] Yuhua Wang, "Empowering the Police: How the Chinese Communist Party Manages Its Coercive Leaders," *The China Quarterly* 219 (2014): 625.

manage these challenges, as savvy police use of social media platforms such as Douyin indicate.[95] And for particular areas of enforcement, even outside critics of the regime place their hope in the creation of professionalized police bodies to enact their favored policies.[96] Still, as elsewhere, local police are subject to top-down campaigns whose symbolic impetus leaves them open to criticism from both state agents and the public at large, with the composition of local public security committees often the result of limited electoral processes.[97] In summary, the sources of job satisfaction for local Chinese police have many of the same sources as in other jurisdictions, and are subject to praise and blame most often driven by external social phenomena.[98]

The Xi regime's recent massive uptick in direct repression of social protest and the wholesale attempt to violently reorganize Uighur society makes it difficult to advance any broadly positive normative assessment of Chinese policing in action. The growth of professionalization, however seriously contemplated by the central administration, is still restrained by the particular ideological legacy of Maoism, which – even in more overly social theoretical terms – saw crime as moralistically sourced in political questions.[99] Objective empirical studies of Chinese policing will likely become increasingly difficult for outsiders, and will remain underdeveloped as an academic field of inquiry domestically.[100] If concerns about the effectiveness and aims of policing are still primarily grounded in promoting regime-supportive social stability, there will likely be few developed forms of legal accountability created under current authoritarian rule.[101]

But is this an issue of degree or nature with the policing examples explored in this chapter? If Chinese police stations had the same level of training and funding as those in Japan, would their day-to-day practices of community policing vary so much? Save as a harbinger of total regime destabilization, would existing modes of social accountability be sufficient to deter the type of systemic extrajudicial police violence that is now an everyday occurrence in the Philippines? Is it authoritarianism that

95 Scoggins and O' Brien, "China's Unhappy Police."

96 Michael Wunerlich, "Structure and Law Enforcement of Environmental Police in China," *Cambridge Journal of China Studies* 12(4) (2017): 33.

97 Jianhua Xu, "Drive-Away Policing and Situational Crime Prevention in China," *Australian and New Zealand Journal of Criminology* 37 (2012): 77.

98 Jonathan Walton, *Intensifying Contradictions: Chinese Policing Enters the 21st Century* (Seattle, WA: National Bureau of Asian Research, 2013).

99 Ibid.

100 Kam Wong, "Police Scholarship in China," *Police Practice and Research* 10 (2009): 503.

101 Fu, "Zhou Yongkang and the Recent Police Reform in China."

drives the behaviors we see among Chinese police or the almost universal authoritarian human views of crime – and which are consistently on display in democratic regimes across the globe?

2.3 Endogeneity and Police Studies

The late twentieth-century faith in the progress of liberal democracy has been broken by both the durability of authoritarian regimes and the backtracking of democratic consolidation in many new and old democracies alike.[102] This teleological faith allowed many unpleasant social practices to be accepted as inherently temporary and perhaps as acceptable costs of transitions to a better world, of which police violence against socially disfavored groups was a recurrent example.[103] While there has been a secular global decrease in crime in the latter half of the twentieth century, the flagging of democracy has renewed concern among an increase in illegitimate state violence and the renewed vulnerability of minority populations to majoritarian repression.[104] In this context, is it giving up even more discursive ground to claim that what can be made better about policing as a technical practice is both universal and limited in democratic and authoritarian regimes alike? Is a highly professionalized police force subject to centralized control in a capable authoritarian regime better than an informal and decentralized system in a weakly democratic regime? Do we lose transformative possibilities or moral coherence to promote a technically-oriented discourse on the seemingly intractably moralistic cultural terrain of crime reduction?

These are difficult questions, but it seems clear that while any "ideal" model of policing would exist under a democratic regime, it is hard to say anything other than that the existence of a formally authoritarian regime puts some sort of ill-defined ceiling on the quality of police accountability. Certainly, competent political scientists could subdivide democratic regimes into new and more diverse subtypes, or fashion "democracy" as a

[102] While this trend is now almost completely uncontroversial, a great deal of controversial territory remains on the consequences of this shift for undermining traditional theories of law and democracy. Kim Scheppele, "Autocratic Legalism," *University of Chicago Law Review* 85(2) (2018): 545.

[103] Jeremy Kuzmarov, "Modernizing Repression: Police Training, Political Violence, and Nation-Building in the 'American Century,'" *Diplomatic History* 33(2) (2009): 191.

[104] The idea of "punitive penalism" has recently gained favor as a vehicle for expressing the lack of any limiting principle for the political popularity of stigmatizing groups as beyond the respect of the rule. Michelle Bonner, *Tough on Crime: The Rise of Punitive Populism in Latin American* (Pittsburgh, PA: University of Pittsburgh Press, 2019).

statistical isolate, but such work would only recur back to the wide-variety of democracy regimes and the overall weakening of democracy itself as the most important variable in analysis of police violence. As our short case-studies have shown, mechanisms for police accountability seem to be both highly path-dependent and driven by social visions of crime, and are intransigently resistant to systemic reform without social crises. All of which helps explain why attempts to improve police systems by foreign nations or international agencies have given notably few, if any, encouraging examples for outside interventions, even by well-funded governments.[105]

Ultimately it appears difficult to tie regime type to either technical police effectiveness in consistently reducing crime or in explaining levels of police lethality. Democratization itself has proven limited in making policing more democratic,[106] and the most lethal police forces in the world exist among the oldest and youngest of the world democracies.[107] Even defining democratic policing would require disaggregating aspects of policing that look more democratic in China than they do in the Philippines, or more coherently authoritarian in Japan than traditionally so in Northern Europe. If what one hopes for is a simple statistical reduction in police violence and effective accountability for police misconduct by social minorities, then few countries seem to satisfy both conditions. The policy conclusions of sociogenic theories of crime have only made some inroads in small, highly homogeneous democratic countries, and Japan serves as a clear counterexample. The focus on purely procedural notions of policing legitimacy also seems only able to yield improvements at the margins of existing substantive cultural baselines.[108]

Once you look to policing in practice, further examples such as Brazil and its globally-leading levels of police lethality,[109] or comparatively tranquil Singapore,[110] all resolve into broader sociological factors or traditional

105 Bayley, *Democratizing the Police Abroad.*

106 Jianhua Xu, "Authoritarian Policing with Chinese Characteristics," 441.

107 Mahesh Nalla and Chae Mamayek, "Democratic Policing, Police Accountability, and Citizen Oversight in Asia: An Exploratory Study," *Police Practice and Research* 14(2) (2013): 117.

108 Dietrich Oberwittler and Sebastian Roché (eds.), *Police–Citizen Relations Across the World: Comparing Sources and Contexts of Trust and Legitimacy* (New York: Routledge, 2018).

109 French, "Rethinking Police Violence in Brazil."

110 Though no police force can fully transcend the cultural biases of its population, it does seem that Singapore policing has avoided systemic police violence and been able to adapt to past critiques – such as its engagement with domestic violence. Jon Quah, "Curbing Police Corruption in Singapore: Lessons for Other Asian Countries," *Asian Education and Development Studies* 3(3) (2014): 186.

Durheimian line-drawing around who is and is not criminal – where ultimately even levels of overall police violence gave way to legitimate normative concerns about the distribution of such violence.

As a result, if mirroring local political will is the test of democracy, then police violence is highly democratic in many countries. The level of police violence in the US has led some to argue that local democracy is the enemy of the rule of law; but if not democracy then what would be the rule of law's ally?[111]

Thus the appeal of the technocratic discourse on policing remains. There do appear to be empirical lessons from the more technical study of policing, if only as enabling conditions. Internal self-regulation is almost never a good mechanism for promoting police accountability, nor necessary to promote professionalization. Police unions exist where the populace deems them legitimate, but even here they can gain enough independence to resist more democratic reforms – as recently seen in Tunisia.[112] Independent monitoring and transparency can lead to better empirical understandings of policing, but this does not itself lead to political movements for better policing. Decentralization is, as it is generally in politics, sometimes resistant to top-down change but susceptible to local majoritarian capture.[113] That a highly professionalized, well-resourced and centrally disciplined policing system comes across as the best institutional framework for policing across regime-type only opens up the possibility that a policing system will most directly express whatever dominant political will it responds to – for better or for worse.

It is hard not to be outraged at police misconduct and fall prey to a reverse moralism that prioritizes holding individual police officers accountable for their actions. Dissatisfaction with the apparent endogeneity of police accountability leaves the scholar of policing in a difficult position of speaking truth to power, when that power is often itself democratic will. Moreover, it seems we are still far away from a schematic understanding of the full institutional patterns of policing in different societies, so perhaps simply improving the empirical comprehensiveness

111 Walker, "Governing the American Police."

112 Sharan Grewal, "Time to Rein in Tunisia's Police Unions," *Project on Middle East Democracy*, March 29, 2018, https://pomed.org/wp-content/uploads/2018/03/Grewal_FINAL_180329.pdf.

113 Mark Ungar and Antony Pereira, "The Persistence of the Mano Dura: Authoritarian Legacies and Policing in Brazil and the Southern Cone," in Katherine Hite and Paola Cesarini (eds.), *Authoritarian Legacies and Democracy in Latin America and Southern Europe* (Notre Dame, IN: University of Notre Dame Press, 2004), 26.

of policing studies is hopeful enough. If political authoritarianism is here to stay, again across regime-type, then holistic studies of policing may be able to leverage the appearance of technocratic sophistication toward more humanist policing when a political aperture presents itself in any particular country.[114]

In sum, however one may feel about the broader institutional design issues, the wide variance among Asian nations does not provide any clear indication as to what a commitment to the analytic rubric of authoritarianism genuinely provides for policing.

[114] Colleen Kadleck and Lawrence Travis, *Police Department and Police Officer Association Leaders' Perceptions of Community Policing* (Washington, DC: US National Institute of Justice, 2004), 140–141; and Jenny Fleming and H. R. Hall, "Police Leadership in Australia: Managing Networks," in Paul Hart and John Uhr (eds.), *Public Leadership: Perspectives and Practices* (Canberra: Australian National University Press, 2008), 165.

PART II

Authoritarian Policing: Past and Present

3

High Policing and Human Rights Lawyering in China

HUALING FU*

3.1 Introduction

This chapter studies the interaction between human rights lawyers and activists and political policing in China. It is well known that police in authoritarian states, in general, suppress political dissents, broadly defined to include speeches, associations, or acts that are regarded as posing challenges to the political authority and the political order it represents.[1] Commentators associate political policing with those harsh tools from the conventional repression toolkits often seen in brutal regimes – kidnapping, torture, and arbitrary detention, and characterize it as mostly sham legality, defined by trumped-up charges, public confessions, and show trials.[2] While coercion is key to authoritarian governance, coercive and repressive measures in and of themselves do not produce regime resilience and deliver the order, compliance, and effective governance that are commonly observed in China. Beyond high-profile episodes of political repression, how is political policing routinely done?

Increasingly, commentators have documented the systemic use of "soft repression," which is preventive and preemptive in nature, characterized

* The author would like to thank Sarah Biddulph, Chen Weitseng, Hilary Josephs, Grace Mou, and Michael West for their comments on the earlier versions of the chapter, Chloe Tang for her research assistance, and friends in Mainland China for sharing their views.

1 Sheena Chestnut Greitens, *Dictators and Their Secret Police: Coercive Institutions and State Violence* (Cambridge: Cambridge University Press, 2016). For the study of political police in China, see Michael Dutton, *Policing Chinese Politics: A History* (Durham, NC: Duke University Press, 2005); and Suzanne E. Scoggins, *Policing China: Street-Level Cops in the Shadow of Protest* (Ithaca, NY: Cornell University Press, 2021).

2 Michael Caster, *The People's Republic of the Disappeared: Stories from inside China's System from Enforced Disappearance* (Safeguard Defenders, 2017); Eva Pils, *China's Human Rights Lawyers: Advocacy and Resistance* (London: Routledge, 2014); Flora Sapio, *Sovereign Power and the Law in China* (The Netherlands: Brill, 2010); and Hualing Fu and Michael Dowdle, "The Concept of Authoritarian Legality: The Chinese Case," in Chen Weitseng and Hualing Fu (eds.), *Authoritarian Legality in Asia* (Cambridge: Cambridge University Press, 2020).

by surveillance, early intervention, and political persuasion.[3] The process is informal and interactive, in which the Chinese political policing systems bring government pressure and other nonstate forces to bear on target groups and individuals to achieve compliance. Subtle intimidation, consent under duress, relational repression, and voluntary detention, all hallmarks of China's political policing, have worked to constrain legitimate advocacy without frequently resorting to direct violence or blatant violence of legal rules. I call the process coercive political persuasion (CPP) because at the heart of the process are the persistent efforts on the part of the national security police to bring changes in ideological positions and political activities on the part of specific individuals in particular communities through a wide range of formal and informal and legal and extralegal means with varying degrees of coercion.

Using the interaction between police and human rights lawyers and activists who have been at the receiving end of state repression in the past two decades as a case study,[4] this chapter aims to shed light on a neglected aspect of political policing in China by offering an integrated conceptual framework for understanding CPP in China. Other research has analyzed the process by which human rights lawyers have advocated for social change through legal education, litigation, and legislative lobbying. Lawyers, together with their partners in the media and nongovernmental organization (NGO) sectors through a unique "rights complex" have made a collective effort to chart a liberal course through legal mobilization.[5] This chapter shifts the focus from lawyers' resistance through human rights lawyering to political policing, thereby highlighting the use of CPP by the political police to constrain lawyers' activism to a narrow political and legal space. CPP is more than repressive. It is also interactive, communicative, and constitutive in that through police and lawyer

[3] Yanhua Deng and Kevin J. O'Brien, "Relational Repression in China: Using Social Ties to Demobilize Protesters," *The China Quarterly* 215 (2013): 533–552, at 534; Rui Hou, "Maintaining Social Stability without Solving Problems: Emotional Repression in the Chinese Petition System," *The China Quarterly* 243 (2020): 635–645; and Kevin J. O'Brien and Yanhua Deng, "The Reach of the State: Work Unit, Family Ties and 'Harmonious Demolition'," *The China Journal* 74 (2015): 1–17.

[4] Pils, *China's Human Rights Lawyers*.

[5] Hualing Fu, "Social Organization of Rights: From Rhetoric to Reality," *UCLA Pacific Basin Law Journal* 36(1) (2019): 1–33; Siodhbhra Parkin, "LGBT Rights-Focused Legal Advocacy in China: The Promise, and Limits, of Litigation," *Fordham International Law Journal* 41 (2018): 1243–1262. For legal advocacy and resistance in the criminal law field, see Sida Liu and Terence C. Halliday, *Criminal Defense in China: The Politics of Lawyers at Work* (Cambridge: Cambridge University Press, 2016).

interaction boundaries of legality and permissible space are confirmed, sometimes negotiated and agreed upon, rules amplified and enforced, and order and stability achieved. Most lawyers are managed and constrained through the CPP process, but for those who risk escalating their social-legal activism, the force of the repressive apparatus would apply directly.

3.2 High Policing and Policification of Law

Political policing, or "high policing" as originally framed by Brodeur, remains a prevailing paradigm in academic research of political policing in liberal democracies.[6] High policing concerns the protection of a political regime and aims at the prevention of broadly framed political crime,[7] whereas low policing concerns the protection of individual victims and public order maintenance.[8] High policing targets activities that challenge the political authorities and the established constitutional order with regime change as the ultimate agenda.[9] In relation to political crimes that high policing aims at preventing, the state is depicted as the victim.

To maintain political order, high policing needs to collect and assess the widest possible range of information to identify, assess, and remove risks. In its original formulation, high policing is therefore "absorbent policing," meaning that it "aims to control by storing intelligence" and "[t]his intelligence gathering is all-encompassing: it extends to any domain that may further the implementation of state policies."[10] It "emphasizes intelligence gathering, information storage, and police access to interconnected data banks."[11] To gather information on its real or potential enemies, high policing "makes extensive use of undercover agents and paid informers," and "acknowledges its willingness to do so."[12] The nature of

6 Jean-Paul Brodeur, "High Policing and Low Policing: Remarks about the Policing of Political Activities," *Social Problems* 30 (1982): 507–520; *The Policing Web* (Oxford: Oxford University Press, 2010); and Gary T. Marx, "High Policing," *Encyclopedia of Criminology and Criminal Justice, Springer*, para. 34, https://web.mit.edu/gtmarx/www/highpolicing.html.

7 Marx, "High Policing."

8 Alex Luscombe and Kevin Walby, "High Policing and Access to Information" 16 *Police Practice and Research* 16, (2015): 485–498.

9 Andrea Mateus-Rugeles and Paula C Arias, "Narcotraffic as Connected Political Crime in Colombia: The FARC Case" *University of Miami Inter-American Law Review* 51 (2) (2020): 1–62, at 26.

10 Brodeur, "High Policing and Low Policing," 513.

11 Greg Martin and Rebecca Scott Bray, "Discolouring Democracy – Policing, Sensitive Evidence, and Contentious Deaths in the United Kingdom," *Journal of Law and Society* 40 (2013): 624–656, at 632.

12 Brodeur, "High Policing and Low Policing," 514.

high policing is such that it often involves secrecy and deceit to cover up "practices that would be considered improper in a democratic society," and "contradict the spirit of constitutional government."[13] High policing, for example, "does not support the respect of basic human rights,"[14] and involves extralegality; that is, "policing that clearly falls outside the statutory powers of agencies conducting those practices or that otherwise violate laws of a country."[15]

The preventive nature of high policing shifts the focus of attention from act to actors, and from punishing past wrongs to managing future risks. Thus, "individuals are punished not on account of the harm they have actually caused, but because of the threat that they represent by virtue of their actual or perceived belonging to a group designated as an enemy of the state."[16] The actor-based aspect forms part of the state's "political strategy of social control, focusing on risks emanating from collective structures rather than on individual conduct."[17] In the end, criminal punishment and police preemptive measures are based on an individual's association with a particular political ideology.[18]

Given the main task is to remove any risks that may threaten regime safety, the preemptive mandate becomes predominant and the control net is necessarily cast as wide as necessary. Traditional criminal law, based on subsequent punishment, is deemed as inadequate to cope with political threats, and the imperative to control the enemy demands the "policification" of criminal law, shifting the gravitas of the criminal process from prosecution and trial to investigative and preventive measures, with the police enjoying extensive legislative, judicial, and executive powers in the process.[19] The police are politically mandated

[13] Ben Bowling and James Sheptycki, "Global Policing and Transnational Rule with Law," *Transnational Legal Theory* 6 (2015): 141–173, at 166.

[14] Jean-Paul Brodeur, "Trotsky in Blue: Permanent Policing Reform," *Australia & New Zealand Journal of Criminology* 28 (2005): 254–267, at 265.

[15] Luscombe and Walby, "High Policing and Access to Information," 485, 487.

[16] Henri Decœur, "The Criminalisation of Armed Jihad under French Law: Guilt by Association in the Age of Enemy Criminal Law," *European Journal of Crime, Criminal Law and Criminal Justice* 25 (2017): 299–326, at 324–325.

[17] Decœur, "The Criminalisation of Armed Jihad under French Law," 325.

[18] I Decœur, "The Criminalisation of Armed Jihad under French Law," 325.

[19] Günther Jokobs, "On the Theory of Enemy Criminal Law," in M. D. Dubber (ed.), *Foundational Texts in Modern Criminal Law* (Oxford: Oxford University Press, 2014), 415–424; Markus D. Dubber, *The Dual Penal State: The Crisis of Criminal Law in Comparative-Historical Perspective* (Oxford: Oxford University Press, 2018), 169–174; and Luscombe and Walby, "High Policing and Access to Information," 485, 486.

and legally empowered to perform an interventionist function; that is, to proactively detect, sort out and remove any risk factors with few if any legal and moral constraints.

High policing is common in contemporary societies and elements of high policing are found in all types of states.[20] Every regime creates its particular enemy and has to face its unique challengers – it is always a crime to use violence or foreign collaboration to overthrow a regime and subvert the political order that the regime establishes – and high policing is put in place to monitor and preempt those challenges. Yet regime type still matters tremendously in shaping police.[21] High policing in liberal democracies operates according to a high degree of democratic and legal accountabilities, with the boundaries of high policing defined with relative clarity and maintained with rigor. The treatment of enemies, however defined, is more restrained, operating under the same constitutional framework and subject to meaningful legal control. Because of the public accountability mechanisms, high policing in liberal democracies tends to be less visible.[22] On the contrary, high policing in authoritarian states, shaped by their cultural tradition and history, develops a sharper distinction between the people and their enemies and creates a dual system for the differentiated treatments, with preemptive high policing operating in the open not concerned with legal and political accountability. Let us turn to enemies and high policing in the Chinese system and the degree to which the Chinese case may depart from the prevailing liberal paradigm.

3.3 The Construction of Enemies and Chinese High Policing

China defines itself as a constitutional party-state that practices "democratic dictatorship." The Chinese Communist Party (CCP) is the leading party that monopolizes all political powers; its leadership is the core of Chinese socialism and as such is not challengeable.[23] Political challenges, defined as attempts to change, undermine, or overthrow the constitutional order, in any form and through any means, are subversive. Legitimate dissent and

[20] Marx, "High Policing."

[21] Ibid.; Greitens *Dictators and Their Secret Police*; David H. Bayley, *Patterns of Policing: A Comparative International Analysis* (New Brunswick, NJ: Rutgers University Press, 1985).

[22] Jokobs, "On the Theory of Enemy Criminal Law."

[23] For a review of the Party's role in the constitutional order, see Hualing Fu and Zhai Xiaobo, "What Makes the Chinese Constitution Socialist?" *International Journal of Constitutional Law* 16 (2018): 655–663; and Biddulph, Chapter 4 in this volume.

lawful opposition are not really viable concepts in this political design. In a system where the monopoly of power is hardwired into the constitution, police power is necessarily politicized to serve the principal function of safeguarding the constitutional order.[24] It is a trite observation that authoritarians prohibit dissenting political views and place dissidents, broadly and fluidly defined to fit the prevailing political needs, under tight legal and, more often than not, extralegal or illegal control.[25] Regime type matters significantly in relation to the political position of the police force and the repressive use of police power to serve a particular political ideology.

Police in China serve the interests of the Party. At its core, the relationship between the Party and its police has remained unchanged since the establishment of the party-state notwithstanding the fundamental social and economic changes in China. In essence, the police are under the total control of the Party and indeed exist mainly to safeguard the leadership role of the Party and prevent and punish any activities that may undermine the Party's leadership position. A discourse of absolute control by the Party is express, direct, and overwhelming.[26] The Party's control over the police is thus plenary, and a key point to reiterate is that the Party is ultimately in charge of the police, whether high or low, whether targeting the enemy or citizens, and whether preventing political dissidents or investigating common crimes.[27]

"The Enemy" is a familiar concept in Chinese political and legal discourses and is embedded in the Chinese constitutional structure.[28] In spite of reforms since the 1980s, the divide in the constitution between people and their enemies, antagonistic contradictions between them based on the fundamentally different interests, and the use of the people's dictatorship to suppress enemy individuals or groups remain a live dogma and surfaces forcefully from time to time, in particular in moments of crisis, real or perceived.[29] Enemies are subject to the dictatorial power of the

[24] Dutton, *Policing Chinese Politics*; Scoggins, *Policing China*.

[25] Greitens, *Dictators and Their Secret Police*.

[26] Scoggins, *Policing China*; Hualing Fu, "A Bird in the Cage: Police and Political Leadership in PRC," *Policing and Society* 4 (1994): 277–291.

[27] Biddulph, Chapter 4.

[28] Fu and Dowdle, "The Concept of Authoritarian Legality."

[29] Hualing Fu, "China's Imperatives for National Security Legislation," in Cora Chan and Fiona De Londras (eds.), *China's National Security: Endangering Hong Kong's Rule of Law?* (Oxford: Hart Publishing, 2020); Jialin Zhang, *China's Response to the Downfall of Communism in Eastern Europe and the Soviet Union* (Stanford, CA: Hoover Press, 1994); M. E. Sarotte, "China's Fear of Contagion: Tiananmen Square and the Power of the European Example," *International Security* 37 (2) (2012): 156–182.

party-state; law, in the words of a foreign ministry spokesperson, will not be able to shield those who are politically ill-motivated.[30]

Who the enemies are then becomes a vexing question. Revolutions against enemies have a violent and tortured history. The source and identity of enemies have also evolved and have, in the reform era in particular, moved beyond the traditional class-based classification to more politically or ideologically driven categorizations. While market reforms promoted by the Party have witnessed the vanishing of the old "Black Five Categories,"such as landlords and capitalists of the exploiting class, they have been quickly replaced by a "new-Black Five Categories," implicating moderate social forces that are perceived to pose political and ideological challenges, including NGO leaders, social media activists, religious believers, and, of course, some human rights lawyers.[31]

"Color revolution" is a primal fear of the CCP and is a perennial issue of concern in contemporary China.[32] Any regime change risk to foreign countries would, without exception, heighten the attention of the party-state, which then designs domestic responses sharply and forcefully. Domestically, color revolution is broadly defined to include any foreign-supported programs and activities that may be regarded as challenging the constitutional order and domestic political authorities. Acts that are regarded as sedition, subversion, infiltration, and sabotage have allegedly happened in the fields of religion, education, media, NGOs, and of course law,[33] mostly supported by allegedly suspicious if not hostile overseas forces.[34] While the Party initiated and continues to support economic liberalization, it remains highly vigilant in fending off any possible regime change risks.

Legal mobilization and resistance have become a perceived front for a color revolution and as such a central concern in China. China's political system is not open to free political participation, and there is no electoral politics or alternative mechanisms to channel grievances and conflicts into a political process for effective resolution. Legal reform, with its

[30] Kai Wen, "Southern Weekend Speaks to the Foreign Ministry to Defend the Rule of Law" [為捍衛法治向外交部嗆聲], *Southern Weekly* [《南方周末》], March 17, 2011.

[31] Fu and Dowdle, "The Concept of Authoritarian Legality."

[32] Sarotte, "China's Fear of Contagion."

[33] Fu, "China's Imperatives for National Security Legislation."

[34] Thomas E. Kellogg, "The Foreign NGO Law and the Closing of China," in Chen and Fu, *Authoritarian Legality in Asia*; Heike Holbig and Bertram Lang, "China's Overseas NGO Law and the Future of International Civil Society," *Journal of Contemporary Asia* 52 (4) (2022): 574–601.

promotion of legal rights and law-based dispute resolution, channels problems, some deeply political, into the legal system, giving lawyers the opportunities and incentives to play a role in providing political representation and a bridging, and from time to time organizing, function.[35] When that happens, the line between legal advocacy and political representation becomes blurred.[36]

Human lawyers aspire for liberal values and have been a leading force in organizing a rights-based legal mobilization. Halliday and others have pointed out that the legal profession is inherently liberal in nature, destined to strive for political liberalism – defined as individual rights, political freedoms, and accountable government.[37] There has been a persistent rights mobilization in China since the early 1990s, and lawyers have played a central role in coordination and leadership in that emerging rights movement in the wide-ranging fields of labor, gender, sexual orientation, environment, education, and religious and criminal justice. A small group of human rights lawyers was particularly active, well-organized, and networked, taking on a firm liberal political stance and often with close foreign connections. Human rights lawyers, for what they do and for what they are, have been subject to tight political monitoring and control at the receiving end of the CPP, subject to close scrutiny particularly as to whether and how they may be implicated in an international conspiracy to undermine the Party's rule and legitimacy. The enemy is an enduring concept in a system with a political monopoly of power and the Party is constantly searching for an enemy to struggle with. Rights lawyers became a new target of Chinese high policing in the context of a renewed concern over color revolution risks that aggressive lawyering might bring about.[38]

The Ministry of Public Security (MPS) is the principal department in charge of domestic political policing, with the first bureau, Domestic Security Protection (DSP), serving as the headquarters of a nationwide

[35] Pils, *China's Human Rights Lawyers*. Hualing Fu and Richard Cullen, "Weiquan (Rights Protection) Lawyering in an Authoritarian State: Building a Culture of Public Interest Lawyering," *The China Journal* 59 (2008):111–127.

[36] Sida Liu and Terence C. Halliday, *Criminal Defense in China: The Politics of Lawyers at Work* (Cambridge: Cambridge University Press, 2016).

[37] Lucien Karpik and Terence Halliday, "Legal Complex," *Annual Review of Law and Social Science* 7 (2011): 217–236.

[38] Hualing Fu, "The July 9th (709) Crackdown on Human Rights Lawyers: Legal Advocacy in an Authoritarian State," *Journal of Contemporary China* 27(112) (2018): 554–568; Hualing Fu and Han Zhu, "After the July 9 (709) Crackdown: The Future of Human Rights Lawyering," *Fordham International Law Journal* 41 (2018): 1135–1164.

system. There is a DSP at every Bureau of Public Security (PSB) at county and district levels. While the DSP does not have a physical presence at community police stations (paichu'suo), the latter have the function of political monitoring and work closely with the DSP.[39] The MPS shares those responsibilities with the Ministry of State Security (MSS) and other security forces, such as military intelligence. The MSS, set up in 1983, has a focus on anti-espionage and anti-intelligence with foreign sources, although the division of labor between the two agencies has never been clear.

The DSP has jurisdictions broadly defined as gathering enemy intelligence and political trends in society and monitoring, studying, and investigating cases endangering national security and activities in relation to cults and unlawful organizations, unlawful publication, infiltration activities by international terrorist groups, hostile forces, and criminal activities, separatist activities and the unspecified sabotaging "psychological warfare". Functions and jurisdictions at local level are more specific. The DSP in Kaihua County of Zhejiang offers a detailed list, including the prevention of interference by "hostile forces" in significant events that may have a bearing on social and political stability, investigation of cases that endanger social and political stability, national unity, ethnic harmony, and basic political principles as established by the Constitution, and, interestingly, the development of "hidden forces" of informants and their "professionalization" and "socialization."[40]

Chinese high policing is organized under a highly centralized and hierarchical system. While police in its ordinary meaning, under the framework of fragmented authoritarianism, is largely a local matter belonging principally to local government, with the central authority, the MPS, playing a secondary role, political policing is decisively a central matter in policymaking, agenda-setting, and action taken on individual cases.[41] The discretion that a PSB and individual officers may have in handling ordinary criminal cases diminishes significantly when it comes to managing suspicious political matters. National security is mostly a nationwide concern, and there is a clear national pattern. Agencies throughout the country act in sync, demonstrating a high degree of uniformity, consistency, and deference to superior departments.

[39] See Biddulph, Chapter 4.

[40] Internal security of Kaihua County of Zhejiang Province (浙江省衢州市开化县国内安全保卫大队), www.kaihua.gov.cn/art/2020/11/16/art_1229090959_103559.html.

[41] Scoggins, *Policing China*.

High policing enjoys a number of special legal powers in investigating political cases that are otherwise not available. Political offences in China are listed in the criminal code under the chapter of offences endangering national security, such as treason, secession, and subversion.[42] In the Chinese case, they also include *de facto* national security offenses. Thus, unauthorized public protest could be regarded as a national security offense *de facto*, even though the charge is an ordinary public order offense under Article 293 of the criminal law. The special powers to investigate political offenses, *de jure* and *de facto*, include a prolonged interrogative detention, *ex incommunicado*, and no access to lawyers without special approval of the police in charge.[43] The exceptional police power forms the backdrop of the preemptive CPP.

3.4 "Drinking Tea": Coercion Embedded

While Chinese high policing is often called secret police, the operation does not operate in great secrecy with respect to their endeavors to nip dissent in the bud. On the contrary, they reach out in the open and have institutionalized preemptive and preventive practices – a key difference from the high policing practice in democracies. In addition to relying on covert surveillance through phone-tapping or infiltration and building a professional "hidden force," they also use open, face-to-face, and interactive meetings with target individuals of a certain status, position, or influence, with varying degrees of formality, frequency, and coerciveness. Civil society activists, including human rights lawyers, once they have attracted security attention, may be invited to meetings, a process that is commonly referred to as "drinking tea."

Being invited to tea is political policing with a light touch, a euphemism for a police encounter that serves a wide range of purposes. The first meeting has a powerful symbolical significance, signaling that the individual concerned is officially on the security radar and that a record has been entered in the dossier of political control; the individual concerned

[42] Hualing Fu "Counter-Revolutionaries, Subversives, and Terrorists: China's Evolving National Security Law," in Hualing Fu, Carole Peterson, and Simon Young (eds.), *National Security and Fundamental Freedoms: Hong Kong's Article 23 Under Scrutiny* (Hong Kong: Hong Kong University Press, 2005).

[43] Joshua Rosenzweig, "Disappearing Justice: Public Opinion, Secret Arrest and Criminal Procedure Reform in China," *The China Journal* 70 (2013): 73–97; Zunyou Zhou, "Residential Surveillance at a Designated Residence: A Special Form of Pre-Trial Detention in China's Criminal Procedure," *Journal of Contemporary China* 30 (2021): 102–117.

is likely to have been assessed, categorized, and labeled according to the perceived risk. It is worth reiterating that all high policing geared to risk assessment and prevention, and meeting for tea has little, if anything, to do with any criminal investigation. Individuals invited to tea are wide-ranging, including activists for rights advocacy, human rights lawyers, civil society organizers and leaders, academics, journalists, grantees of foreign-sponsored projects, or veteran and hardcore dissidents. Having a tea meeting is the most common police encounter, regularized and taken for granted by both sides. For veteran human rights lawyers, avoiding and managing liability is part of the professional risk that is taken.

Tea meetings have a short history in Chinese high policing. Political policing used to operate in the dark and was an invisible force defined mostly by covert operations and secretive control. Chinese high policing was a mysterious force, like its foreign counterparts, exerting control by pulling strings in the shadows. This could be explained in part by the type of threats that the security force was facing. Put simply, the enemy of the old-style conspired and then acted in the dark, and high policing responded through covert operations. Meetings for tea are likely a product of the rights protection (*weiquan*) movement in China that appeared as part of the stability maintenance (*weiwen*) politics after 2003, when civil society forces made their powerful debut and soon developed their own momentum in creating a force independent of the party-state.[44] As mentioned earlier, legal mobilization and resistance were well accepted and practiced, with lawyers becoming key catalysts and organizers in an emerging rights-based, lawcentric movement, which was often foreign-funded. In response, the security police started to target human rights lawyers for enhanced scrutiny, realizing with shock that somehow some of them had become a driving force in the potentially hostile color revolution conspiracy.[45] In general, the new enemy, now aiming at changing the system through the system, operated in the open mostly through legal and legitimate means. High policing, in response, has also opened up its

44 Susan Trevaskes, Elisa Nesossi, Flora Sapio, and Sarah Biddulph (eds.), *The Politics of Law and Stability in China* (Cheltenham: Edward Elgar, 2014); Sarah Biddulph, *The Stability Imperative: Human Rights and Law in China* (Vancouver: UBC Press, 2015). In some of the Internal Security's websites, *weiquan* is specifically mentioned as a security target. Internal security of Heng County, Guangxi (广西南宁横州市横县国内安全保卫大队), www.gxhx.gov.cn/hxgaj/nsjgsz_18249/t1415150.html.

45 Hualing Fu, "The July 9th (709) Crackdown on Human Rights Lawyers"; Eva Pils, "The Party's Turn to Public Repression: An Analysis of the '709' Crackdown on Human Rights Lawyers in China," *China Law and Society Review* 3(1) (2018): 1–48.

operations and started to engage with potential risk factors directly and through open channels. In Chinese practices, once an individual appears on the horizon of high policing and becomes a security target, an agent is assigned to manage the file and maintain contact with the target. The monitoring is based on the place of registration of a lawyer's legal practice. The monitoring and interaction continue until the lawyer withdraws from his or her activism that is regarded as risky, moves to another jurisdiction, in which case another minder takes the file over, or escalates the action and takes the matter to a new level.

The institutional and personnel arrangement in high policing is stable, and human rights lawyers often maintain regular contact with the same security officers for a long period of time. Regularity also reduces the level of fear and concerns on the part of lawyers, and repeated interactions often produce better understanding between the two parties and some respect for each other at a personal level. To a degree, the state has assigned the duty of high policing to a team of officers who have personal responsibilities over the lawyers' compliance. The relationship is thus personal in part at least, and tension may arise from time to time if the police demand is deemed excessive or lawyers are regarded as uncooperative. There have been many examples of unhappy episodes resulting in pushing and shoving. Between maximizing control as high policing demands, and minimizing interference as the human rights lawyers prefer, the two sides have to reach a tacit understanding as to how best to achieve the optimal result. Many do cooperate with each other most of the time. As several lawyers conceded, most of the officers were decent people who were just doing their jobs and following orders, and were able to show understanding and even respect for what the lawyers did and the clients they represented.[46] Police officers were no longer from privileged backgrounds as they used to be prior to the market reform, and, being mostly from a working-class background, they could understand the grievances and hardship underpinning some of the politicized cases.

The police invite lawyers for tea to ask specific questions or to address particular issues, often in relation to certain actions or events, such as an online posting, a meeting, a dinner gathering, or an open letter. Some of the meetings are for fact-finding, with the police interested primarily in the particulars of certain events. Lawyer G was invited for a meeting after she

[46] Xie Yanyi, "Over Tea Sessions I Advised Security Officer: We Are All Slaves and Should Work Together to Solve the Problem of Slave Owners" (喝茶时我劝国保：大家都是奴隶，应该一起解决奴隶主问题), September 20, 2017, *Aboluowang*, www.aboluowang.com/2017/0920/996599.html.

joined other lawyers to petition the National People's Congress to pass legislation for better protection of the rights of lawyers. During the interview, the officers asked who drafted the letter and who the organizer was, and then implored G to act with caution in the future. G was also invited to another meeting to explain her joining the legal team to defend the Feminist Five.[47] A group of lawyers had issued an open letter calling for the immediate withdrawal of the charges against these five activists, with a legal opinion on the case attached. During the meeting, the police again asked which lawyer had led the action, what the motivations were, and who the recipients of the legal opinions were.[48] Lawyer L was invited to a meeting over a petition cosigned by ten lawyers in 2017, concerning the safety of vaccines in China. That petition was made in response to a massive vaccine scandal the previous year, which led to multiple deaths of children. There was no criticism nor censure in relation to the petition and the police just wanted to have background details. Lawyer L explained to the police that there was no political motivation and asked the police not to be too sensitive.[49]

The meetings have become first-hand sources of information for the police. Typically, upon meeting with foreign consular officials or returning from attending overseas workshops or conferences, lawyers are invited to share the substance of their meetings and inform on the identities of other participants.[50] The police are also keen to know the operation of certain foreign NGOs, funding sources, project activities, and the link to foreign individuals. They are also interested in lawyers' dissenting views on certain policy issues.[51] Some lawyers and NGO staff have said that the security police are interested in gathering different views to inform decisions and policies. Throughout the CPP process, the identity of lawyers as a resource for information and as a target to control becomes blurred, and the information gathering nature of these meetings makes some lawyers vulnerable to the accusation of being police informants. Lawyers have to make a judgment as to what information to share. Some offer information that they think is harmless, such as the venue, host, and the content of a meeting; while other more cautious lawyers choose not to say anything during the entire meeting.

[47] Lawyer G's social media post on September 21, 2016. Quoted with permission.

[48] "Chinese Women's Rights Activists Suppressed by Government Around March 8 International Women's Day" (中国女权人士在三八国际妇女节前后受到政府打压), March 11, 2016, *Radio Free Asia*, www.rfa.org/mandarin/zhuanlan/fuyouluntan/women-03112016162513.html

[49] Lawyer L's post on WeChat on March 7, 2017. Quoted with permission.

[50] Communications with a lawyer, 2021.

[51] Communications with a former foreign NGO employee, 2019.

Some lawyers and particular NGO leaders are of the view that a meeting with the police is important to find out that what they are doing is within the boundaries of lawful advocacy and therefore safe. No one wants to go to a detention center for their work and few can be confident that they know where the precise lines in the sand are drawn. To proceed with caution, as all want to do, a meeting with the police can actually help to clarify doubts and better assess risks. As Franceschini puts it, through meetings for tea, "the Party-state gets to remind labour activists that they are under surveillance, while activists benefit from a direct line to the authorities and are able to avoid unnecessary risks if their activities are too close to the limits of what is allowed."[52] Through repeated interaction and negotiations, boundaries of permissible rights lawyering become clearer. In the "policified" world,[53] criminal law rules do not offer useful guidance and court decisions often add little comfort for lawyers. Security officers ironically have, in some circumstances, played the occasional role of risk analysis consultants, guiding human rights lawyers and NGOs in navigating the turbulent waters while constraining them from developing their full potential.[54]

Depending on the circumstances, a meeting for tea can appear to be a "friendly" encounter.[55] Some meetings take place in relaxing social settings and informally with a human touch, with the police inviting targets to meals in restaurants or tea in cafés; occasionally they shower lawyers with small gifts or even red packets (containing "lucky money") on special occasions such as Chinese New Year. The exchange can be open and friendly, with the police showing a high level of tolerance and understanding.

[52] Ivan Franceschini, "Meet the State Security: Labour Activists and Their Control," in Jane Golley, Linda Jaivin, and Luigi Tomba (eds.), *Control: China Story Yearbook 2016* (Canberra: ANU Press, 2016), 67–73.

[53] Jokobs, "On the Theory of Enemy Criminal Law."

[54] This room of symbiotic maneuvering vanishes quickly at a repressive turn against NGOs. See Ivan Franceschini and Elisa Nesossi, "State Repression of Chinese Labor NGOs: A Chilling Effect?" *The China Journal* 80 (2018): 111–129.

[55] Zha used the following words to describe the security teams who were the minder of her brother, a veteran dissident jailed for his participation in the CDP: "They were unfailingly polite, even solicitous, bargaining on his behalf at shops and carrying heavy bags for him. One hot afternoon, they helped install an air-conditioner in his apartment." See Zha Jianying, "China's Bizarre Program to Keep Activists in Check," December 17, 2018, *New Yorker*, www.newyorker.com/magazine/2018/12/24/chinas-bizarre-program-to-keep-activists-in-check. Although the helping hand offered by the security force was offered in the particular case of post-imprisonment monitoring, many lawyers noted the friendliness and politeness in their dealings.

Beyond information gathering, a meeting often serves the purpose of giving a warning to lawyers about refraining from doing something in the future. Earlier meetings for tea involved the signatories of Charter 08 and happened immediately before and after the arrest of Liu Xiaobo.[56] For many lawyers, this was their first encounter with high policing. Most of the meetings, as some of the lawyers recalled, were low key and respectful, with polite officers asking quick questions. Police asked for details about the drafting process and the signature campaigns, and cautioned lawyers not to take further action in support of the charter.[57]

Another important thread that triggers frequent meetings relates to lawyers' participation in legal mobilization supporting certain cases that are branded as politically sensitive. Invariably, police have requested lawyers either to withdraw from certain support groups or to refrain from participating in further activities. In the immediate aftermath of the 709 crackdowns on human rights lawyers, over 200 lawyers who participated in or associated with human rights lawyering were invited to tea on an urgent basis and demanded not to give support to lawyers who were under arrest.[58]

Guo Wengui's initial public exposé of corruption scandals in China[59] seems to have gone viral on China's social media and caused a shock wave in the security establishment, which rushed to meet lawyers and warn them to withdraw from some WeChat groups on the matter, and not to give support to Guo's allegations. Again, this was a nationally coordinated action and the questions that police asked in different parts of China

[56] In December 2008 a group of Chinese intellectuals published a manifesto, referred to as Charter 08, calling for political reform in China. Liu was one of the organizers of manifesto and was later charged with the offence of subverting state power. See Jean-Philippe Beja, Hualing Fu, and Eva Pils, Liu Xiaobo, Charter 08 and the Challenges of political Reform in China (Hong Kong, Hong Kong University Press, 2012).

[57] Jiang Tianyong, "I Was Invited to Tea by Internal Security because of the Charter 08" (我因08宪章被国保约谈), January 8, 2009, *Boxun.com*, www.boxun.com/cgi-bin/news/gb_display/print_versiOn.cgi?art=/gb/china/2009/01&link=200901080013.shtml&__cf_chl_jschl_tk__=pmd_56e1686435836538279bd73b8edc3db60e8dc811-1628483638-0-gqNtZGzNAjijcnBszQgi; Liu Shihui, "I Am Emotionally Stable After Being Invited to Tea by Internal Security" (我被国保约谈情绪很稳定), February 17, 2009, *Boxun.com*, https://news.boxun.com/news/gb/china/2009/02/200902171408.shtml.

[58] "Lawyer Wang Cheng Releases Record of Meeting to Tea by Security Police" (王成律师公布被国保警方约谈记录), July 13, 2015, *Civil Rights and Livelihood Watch*, https://msguancha.com/a/lanmu4/2015/0713/12794.html. For the background, see Fu, "The July 9th (709) Crackdown on Human Rights Lawyers," and Pils, "The Party's Turn to Public Repression."

[59] Lauren Hilgers, "The Mystery of the Exiled Billionaire Whistleblower," *The New York Times Magazine*, January 10, 2018, www.nytimes.com/2018/01/10/magazine/the-mystery-of-the-exiled-billionaire-whistleblower.html.

were the same: Did you see Guo's videos? Did you forward them? What were your views on them? What social media do you use?[60] Invariably, the police insisted on checking cell phones on the spot or taking them away for examination. Some lawyers submitted but others declined, without incurring consequences. The message from the police was often well-received and acted upon.

If repeated police warnings fail to persuade or deter, the police escalate their action. A sign of police escalation is the change of venue from a relaxing restaurant or café to a police station or a lawyer's residence. Once this happens, the atmosphere changes and the meeting becomes more formal and bureaucratic, with an invitation to tea being hardly distinguishable from a police interrogation – some meetings even take place in an interrogation room, though without invoking interrogation rules and measures. Upon finishing one meeting, an angry lawyer protested that he would not attend any future meetings with the police unless they could provide a legal document to compel him to do so.[61]

During the meetings, the police often take notes of the conversations, and upon finishing, may ask the lawyer to confirm the accuracy of these notes and put their signature to them. Some agree to do so while others refuse; there are no standard practices. During one meeting, the police even insisted on videotaping the conversation. Unable to stop the police from doing so, the lawyer took out his cell phone and insisted on taping the conversation as well.[62] There are often tensions, and no tea is served during these meetings, as one lawyer lamented.[63]

This is the time when voices are raised and threats are made to achieve compliance or express frustration. The line between persuasion, warning, and intimidation starts to fade, and the coercive elements of the CPP loom larger. Here is an example that borders on abuse from a police officer to a lawyer:

> I told you not to mingle with sensitive people. You never listened, and now you even took a photo with xxx, who had the photo published overseas. We just wrote a report and were preparing to communicate with the Bureau of

[60] "Four Lawyers Summoned for Watching Guo Wengui's Revelations" (因涉观看郭文贵爆料 四律师遭传唤), September 30, 2017, https://lvshiquanyiguanzhu.blogspot.com/2017/09/blog-post_34.html?m=1.

[61] Lawyer Wen Donghai, "Harassed Three Times, Summons Continue" (三次被骚扰 传唤仍继续), July 13, 2015, *NTDTV*, www.ntdtv.com/gb/2015/07/13/a1210077.html.

[62] Lawyer L's social media post on February 25, 2018. Quoted with permission.

[63] Lawyer P's social media post on November 7, 2017. Quoted with permission.

> Justice to have your practicing certificate restored. Now our superior had named you by name in an official circular and you brought trouble onto yourself again.[64]

Here is another example:

> We have told you many times not to run around that country, but you never listened to us. Now it has become a big issue. A task force has been formed in the city under the direct order of the Ministry in Beijing and the province. So many of us have to work overtime because of you, aren't you ashamed of yourself? You have given us so much trouble and you should confess your problems immediately.[65]

While there are no legal or regulatory rules to require lawyers to attend these meetings, all attend as asked with little resistance, if any. Many lawyers have tried, in one way or another, to avoid a meeting with the police. Some pretend to be on business away from the city, others intentionally stay away from their office upon discovering a meeting has been requested, and still others ask to talk over the phone in lieu of a physical meeting. One NGO staff member said that she was able to reduce the frequency of meetings by insisting on having meetings only in expensive places.

The police are often persistent and know where to reach the lawyers. They make requests repeatedly, and they reach out to lawyers via a third party, such as law firm partners or community police. They are also patient, diligent, and often polite. In order not to cause any inconvenience for lawyers, they pick them up from home for meetings or escort them to train stations afterwards, allowing lawyers to maintain their schedule. Some lawyers make the argument that whatever they did was misunderstood by the police and should not be a subject of political monitoring. Lawyers may be able to get away with matters that are not regarded as important, and the security police may allow them to let meetings slip away. But if the matter is of urgency, either ordered from above or as a part of coordinated action, such as during the 709 crackdowns on human rights, lawyers will know it is time to comply.

Lawyers know well what is in store if they refuse to cooperate in matters that are important high policing matters. There are two escalation options for police when they are facing a noncomplying lawyer: one is extralegal

64 Lawyer W's social media post on December 8, 2017. Quoted with permission.

65 Xu Juan, "The 25 Hours I Was Kidnapped by Security Officer" (我被国宝绑架的25小时), August 4, 2014, *China Citizens Movement*, https://cmcn.org/archives/6079.

and the other legal. The extralegal measure is the use of "relational repression," while the legal process is invocation of formal criminal law power. Both prove to be effective.

3.5 Relational Repression

If direct meetings, soft and hard, fail to achieve compliance from lawyers, the police may turn to their loved ones and leverage social and institutional ties to exert pressure. Traditionally, the police seek help from family members, school teachers, and community leaders to persuade delinquent youths to return to normal society, a process that Braithwaite calls integrative shaming.[66] China has been a faithful subscriber to restorative justice for community correction, with a cultural propensity for preemptive, extralegal dispute resolution and strong moral persuasion and education. Extending the preemptive, corrective, and integrative concept of intervention to political offenders, the party-state has used relational repression, making the family bond and social ties the pressure point, persuading human rights lawyers and others who are on a dissidence path to return to the normal political community and into compliance.

Deng and O'Brien have defined relational repression in China, in the context of protest demobilization, as "a control technique that uses social ties to demobilize protests." Their research has shown that repression with a human touch, in a Chinese style, has evolved into a core, though contentious, crisis management strategy.[67] In policing lawyers, the political police use kinship and social and professional ties to bring pressure to bear: it is common to mobilize fathers, mothers, wives, siblings, relatives, friends, and other significant parties to do thought work on lawyers so that they comply with political instructions. In Chinese high policing, social power is often tapped into by the powerful security police to achieve what they cannot otherwise achieve short of using direct force – a unique feature of the Chinese national security state is that it is able to mobilize informal social pressures to support its national security agenda.

China is of course not alone in mobilizing third parties to enforce political control. Many have observed the common practice in authoritarian states of an indirect application of coercive state power through third

[66] John Braithwaite, *Crime, Shame and Reintegration* (Cambridge: Cambridge University Press, 1989). For a similar observation on Taiwan, see Chen, Chapter 8 in this volume.

[67] Yanhua Deng and Kevin J. O'Brien, "Relational Repression in China: Using Social Ties to Demobilize Protesters," *The China Quarterly* 215 (2013): 533–552, at 534.

parties, such as requiring hotels to cancel bookings for events, tax authorities to audit entities, or landlords to evict tenants, all new control tactics for neo-authoritarian leaders in the age of authoritarian legalism.[68] However, China's high policing proves more able to secure the compliance of any such third parties and is effective in conquering resistance or hesitation. Moreover and key to the argument in this chapter, China has developed an additional human touch, using human vulnerability to generate "an irreducible amount of pressure" and "emotional blackmail,"[69] which strikes where it is soft and vulnerable, and is hence more painful and effective.[70]

To resort to kinship and social ties is effective, but this has its limits and even risks. It only works when ties are strong enough to have a mutual impact: a lawyer who is a young father may be willing to give in if his son's interest is "casually" brought into the conversation during a chat over tea. For the same reason, a father's wrath or a mother's tears may soften the resolve of a lawyer to resist police pressure. The discourse that a lawyer may be endangering national security could be empty rhetoric and a shallow threat, but may be taken more seriously by family members and others in social circles that are new to the discourse. The closer the ties are, the more impactful the relational repression can be. High school classmates or fellow lawyers who convey a message to the police may be too distant to be effective and persuasive, but a message from a tearful mother carries a different weight.

Involving people with strong ties carries its own risk, however. Loved ones, wives in particular, have shown a tendency to side with their husbands instead. Wives of leading lawyers prosecuted in the 709 crackdowns decisively showed their loyalty to their husbands, and their action, legal or extralegal, to rescue their husbands caused much embarrassment to political policing in China.[71] As many parents have informed the police,

68 Kim Lane Scheppele, "Autocratic Legalism," *The University of Chicago Law Review* 85(2) (2018): 545–583.

69 Deng and O'Brien, "Relational Repression in China."

70 Wu Gan, "The Bible of 'Having Tea'" ("喝茶"宝典), May 3, 2012, *Human Rights in China*, http://biweeklyarchive.hrichina.org/article/1539.html.

71 The police were forced to negotiate with the wives to reduce or silence their advocacies. A typical exchange is a written message or a video recording from the detained husband in exchange for dropping the lawyer that the wife has retained for the husband or not to make a protest on social media. Lawyer Sui Muqing's Wife, "Rights Lawyer Sui Muqing Under Secret Surveillance, World Seeks" (维权律师隋牧青被秘密监视居住，全世界在寻找), July 30, 2015, *Boxun.com*, https://boxun.com/news/gb/china/2015/07/201507301755.shtml?__cf_chl_jschl_tk__=pmd_0ddae55dcb807050ba1eeaf9d1e64e322353d51b-1628497793-0-gqNtZGzNAfijcnBszQbO.

"our children have grown up and are beyond our control," While they may not know what their children are doing, they have faith that they will be doing the right thing.[72]

3.6 The Twilight of Authoritarian Legalism

How to assess the legality of Chinese high policing in triggering CPP? How do the surveillance, meetings under duress, and application of relational repression square with the police claims of legality? From China's turning away from law under President Hu Jintao[73] and the purported return to the law under President Xi Jinping,[74] how to legally justify the preemptive and, from time to time, aggressive CPP and open interference in the personal and professional lives of many rights lawyers? After all, the targets in this study are mostly experienced, die-hard human rights lawyers who are well known for their courage and fighting spirit.

First of all, blatant violations of legal rules have been well documented by scholars and NGOs, ranging from house confinement, extralegal detention, and other types of illegality. Some of the abuses may be seen as innovative and bordering on absurdity, especially in dealing with lawyers from outside jurisdictions who are handling sensitive local cases that local lawyers are unwilling to take on.[75] How seriously should we take the claim that the Chinese political police make their work conform to the requirements of legality? A healthy dose of cynicism is necessary to believe this claim because authoritarian legality has such a low threshold that police frequently pass rules of law, that is the existence of an enabling rule, for the rule of law. China's reliance on legality is consistent with and part of the authoritarian legality that has been on the rise globally,

[72] Wu Yutong and Cheng Wen, "Police Induced Jiang Tianyong's Parents to Record a Video Persuading Their Son to Confess to the Crime" (警方誘江天勇父母錄製勸兒認罪視頻), March 31, 2017, *RFA*, www.rfa.org/cantonese/news/lawyer-03312017092502.html.

[73] Carl Minzner, "China's Turn against Law," *The American Journal of Comparative Law* 59(4) (2011) 935–984.

[74] Albert H Y Chen, "China's Long March towards Rule of Law or China's Turn against Law?" *The Chinese Journal of Comparative Law* 4(1) (2016):1–35; Taisu Zhang and Tom Ginsburg, "China's Turn toward Law," *Virginia Journal of International Law* 59(2) (2019): 306–389.

[75] In one particular case, upon knowing a human right lawyer was coming to the city to handle a sensitive case, the police intercepted the lawyer in the airport; took him to and confined him in a hotel, grabbed his ID card from his wallet, and bought a one-way ticket for him. They literally pushed him into the airplane to send him back to his home city. See Liu Shihui, "How I Was Kidnapped and Deported in Shanghai" (我在上海被绑架遣送经过), January 21, 2016, *WQW*, https://wqw2010.blogspot.com/2016/01/blog-post_32.html.

where neo-autocrats, backed by electoral legitimacy, use constitutional means to practice "constitutional malice" to defeat both democracy and constitutionalism.[76]

Nevertheless, authoritarian legality covers a wide spectrum of meaning, and our analysis needs to be nuanced to capture and differentiate diverse shades. At one end of the spectrum, legality is a sham that does little more than empower the police to take certain actions without meaningful accountability, such as the notorious secretive detention of some human rights lawyers and political dissidents. In the case of the power to detain, the law authorizes trap-door legality that triggers a lengthy pretrial *ex incommunicado* detention – disappearing a suspect into a black hole once the legal rule is triggered.[77] At the other end of the scale, the demand for legality makes a difference in constraining police and in softening the hard edge of Chinese high policing. Law has also become a weapon of the weak.

In the context of the CPP, the demand for legality sometimes makes police repression subtler and more indirect, and the police find it necessary to sugarcoat otherwise repressive measures. For instance, does a lawyer have to open the door when the security police come to issue an invitation for tea? It turns out that, for all their aggressiveness, forced entry into homes in political cases, while existing to facilitate a formal criminal process, especially criminal detention, is unheard of in the CPP context. Indeed, such open demonstration of force is regarded unnecessary and indeed counterproductive given the nature of the CPP.

Legality is a fuzzy concept in political policing, and fine legal analysis, even if possible, is not often applied by lawyers in the CPP context. Most police targets, including lawyers, allow police to enter their apartments voluntarily. The police have also developed a strategy to avoid confrontation that may put the question of legality to the forefront. For example, when the security police approach human rights lawyers, they are mostly accompanied by community police officers with whom the lawyer is familiar – the institution of the neighborhood in China has a long history, and community police, embedded in the neighborhood, enjoy a high degree of trust. Those community officers are often the ones who knock on the door,

[76] Scheppele, "Autocratic Legalism." See also David Landau, "Abusive Constitutionalism," *U.C. Davis Law Review* 47 (2013): 189. For a thick study of the rise of an illiberal legalism in Hungary and Poland, see Timea Drinoczi and Agnieszka Bien-Kacala, "Illiberal Constitutionalism: The Case of Hungary and Poland," *German Law Journal* 20 (2019): 1140–1166.

[77] Rosenzweig, "Disappearing Justice."

introduce themselves, and initiate the conversation. They play an important role in reducing the level of suspicion and tension. In any event, given the routinized surveillance and the overwhelming authority of the security police over their target population, Chinese high policing, focusing on routine surveillance and regular intervention, operates in a slow-paced and incremental fashion with little excitement. There is indeed no need for rushed action.

Not every lawyer would open the door to the police, especially for a meeting in the middle of the night. But to stall the police at the door is to challenge the skill of the lawyers and test the patience of the police. Many lawyers have reported successfully frustrating the police's attempt to enter. In one case, police first knocked on the door between 1 and 2 am and were found still waiting outside the door at 6.30 am, according to a lawyer.[78] Lawyers often have time to send messages to alert others before they open the door to let the police in.

The police are also tactical in deciding when to invite a lawyer for a chat and when to compel questioning. What is initially an invitation may quickly be switched to legal compulsion if the circumstance so demands. The merging of consent and voluntariness with compulsion and coercion creates a fuzzy zone in which vaguely provided powers are exerted and fragilely protected rights are asserted. The case of lawyer P who posted online that "Legally speaking, Falun Gong is not an evil cult in Chinese law" is illustrative of the CPP process at the harsh end of the spectrum. In that case, the security police asked the lawyer for a meeting at the police station, but initially sent two community officers to the lawyer's home to fetch the lawyer.

The following extracted dialogue records what happened subsequently between the police officers (P) and the lawyer (L):

P: Our leaders wanted to talk to you at the station.
L: What to talk about?
P: Our leaders will talk to you about the details. We are not quite sure about what and we are here just to send the message.
L: Since it is just a talk, your leaders could come here to talk to me…
P: (after reporting back to leaders through phone) If that's your attitude, then we are here to summon you for an investigation.
L: Then please show me the summons and your work ID.
P: I am Officer XXX and there is my work ID. I am here to give you an oral summons and to investigate your positing on Falun Gong.

78 Lawyer C's social media post on July 14, 2015. Quoted with permission.

L: Oral summons is limited to the investigation of an administrative offense while it is being committed. So you are in my house to discover me committing an administrative offense. Am I committing an offense?
P: (after making another call) Let's wait for the leaders.
S1: (after thirty minutes) Who do you think you are and we could not even invite you over for a chat? We have to come over to your place in person!
L: So what is the matter? Whatever you want to know we can talk about it here and now.
S1: It is you who posted that "Falong Gong his not a cult in the legal sense," isn't it? You wanted to be unconventional! I am giving you the summons.
L: Where is the summons in writing?
S1: This is an oral summons and I just discovered the posting you had posted online.
S2: Don't waste words with him. (and starts to push the lawyer)
L: What are you doing?
S2: Since you are not cooperating, we have to summon you by force.
L: (after a minor push and shove) OK, OK, I will go with you after changing my shoes…[79]

Law is what the police interpret it is. Lawyers normally don't see the need or the necessity to resist a meeting, and comply to avoid any confrontation. The lawyer P was released after a two-hour long session.

Ultimately, the police can make a threat to lawyers that they will impose harsher criminal measures if needed. Once the CPP fails to work and lawyers continue to resist, the threat is open and direct: either a lawyer cooperates in this informal setting or is forced to "walk through another door" and to continue the conversation "in alternative ways." The police have different tools in their toolkit and have in their possession all "the eighteen martial arts," as they claim, which allow them to manage lawyers in "a comprehensive way." But the option is entirely that of the lawyers', as they often say, and of course the police prefer a friendly chat over tea, but they are ready to use an alternative way to achieve the same. The cruelty of the interrogation in the black-hole of *ex incommunicado* detention is a familiar story among human rights lawyers, and few want to experience it if they have a choice. They comply in the shadow of harsh penalties.[80]

3.7 Supervised Tours: Alternative to Coercion

The Chinese political police try to avoid direct confrontation and the imposition of harsh measures as much as possible – they are innovative

[79] Lawyer P's social media post on November 7, 2017. Quoted with permission.
[80] Caster, *The People's Republic of the Disappeared.*

in their control tactics not least because harsh measures are costly and could be counterproductive – and prefer to maximize their control and at the same time minimize lawyers' resistance. Zha's documentation of her brother's encounter with the police well captures the essence of China's high policing: "The Chinese police state can be at once harsh and accommodating, insidious and absurd." It was 1984 with a significant Chinese twist.[81]

The supervised tour is illustrative of the contention and possible compromise in Chinese high policing to suit a special purpose. The police may request human rights lawyers not to leave the cities of their residence during "sensitive periods," fearing they may travel to Beijing in particular to cause trouble. Other more "sensitive" human rights lawyers may not even be allowed to leave their residence – effectively imposing a house arrest – for fear that associating with dubious characters may lead to troubles during a sensitive period. After all, the best-organized movement since 1989 – the New Citizens Movement – developed its momentum through gatherings at dinners.[82] A mere physical presence in a sensitive place on a sensitive date, such as a stroll of a known dissident in Tiananmen Square on June 4 is both a symbolic protest and a security risk if uncontrolled. And they have been effectively controlled.

Without activating the power to detain, it is costly to prevent wayward lawyers and activists from making public appearances, which is regarded as a risk in itself.[83] The police try different ways to force those lawyers to stay at home. When sensitive dates approach, police cars are parked near the residence of known targets, with security officers, supported by others in the pervasive surveillance system, literally guarding the gates of residential compounds, corridors of a building, and even stationed at the doors of an apartment to stop lawyers from leaving their homes. The tension is high and the process is tense, costly, and exhausting for the police and their targets. As it happens, on special dates, the police are

[81] Zha Jianying, "China's Bizarre Program to Keep Activists in Check," December 17, 2018, *New Yorker*, www.newyorker.com/magazine/2018/12/24/chinas-bizarre-program-to-keep-activists-in-check.

[82] Eva Pils, "From Independent Lawyer Groups to Civic Opposition: The Case of China's New Citizen Movement," *Asian-Pacific Law & Policy Journal* 19 (2018): 110–152.

[83] It is difficulty to come up with the exact number of lawyers who may be subject to intensive political control. But lawyers who were invited for tea are likely to be in the hundreds and those invited to tour are likely to be in the dozens.

fully mobilized and watch their numerous targets twenty-four hours a day for days or even weeks, literally struggling to push those who disobey the order back to their apartments, all carried out under political orders but without any legal authorization.

Facing an often irreconcilable conflict between the legal imperative to control lawyers through legal means and the stability imperative to prevent any risk that lawyers may pose, the police become creative in designing soft repressive measures to induce compliance. One key innovative tactic is to persuade lawyers to make a tour within the province, nationwide, or even abroad if a foreign element is involved, temporarily removing risk from the home jurisdiction during a sensitive period. This tour is made at the request of the police, at police expense, and of course accompanied by police. The Chinese state has had a separate budget line for stability, which in certain years may have surpassed the defense budget. Money for order has had a unique meaning in China, achieving the dual purpose of legality and stability.

Lawyers call these events "forced tours," and police call them "stability maintenance tours." While the lawyer is not dragged on a tour, the police often don't take no for an answer, although negotiation is possible on details and particulars. It is a real tour because lawyers, and their minders, travel to and stay at popular tourist sites as tourists, dining at regular restaurants and checking in at regular hotels. The point is not only that the lawyer is touring outside their residential area, but also that they are "happily" under police supervision. In one case, upon discovering a target lawyer was already on a tour in a coastal city with his family during a sensitive period, his minder nevertheless immediately flew to the city to join the tour.

The rationale for the popularity of the supervised tour as a popular tool of political policing is clear. These lawyers don't present an immediate danger and are mostly a liberal pain in China's authoritarian neck, with perhaps some remote potential to symbolically insult the party-state and cause some minor political embarrassment in a sensitive period – for example, by being involved in some form of memorial for June 4 or making a petition to dignitaries from foreign nations who are on state visits. In the eyes of the state, they are more a hassle than a threat – yet it is well known how the Party treats a real threat.

Supervised tours offer a solution to clumsy and difficult operations to stop lawyers leaving their homes and spare the embarrassment of justifying something that is impossible to justify. Many lawyers often accept the offer with reluctance and some bargaining on routes and duration, while a few decline to cooperate on principles and prefer to stay at home to fight the police.[84] On the other hand, police are willing to play the tour guide role, enjoying themselves in the course of sightseeing while placing their target under tight control. Indeed, officers also use the opportunity to tour new places and happily enjoy the benefits that this particular work brings to them.

The need for a forced tour is situational and its duration is flexible. Lawyer Zhang was a repeat guest for the supervised tour. In 2006, the police sent him on a nearly one-month tour to stop him from attending the trial of another well-known activist. Under the watchful eyes of three officers, he toured multiple scenic sites in two provinces.[85] In 2007, he was again forced on a tour, staying at a leisure site between June 2 and June 5, to prevent him from making comments to commemorate June 4.[86] In 2010, to prevent a possible gathering to celebrate Liu Xiaobo's receiving the Nobel Peace Prize, lawyer Zhang was sent away for a twelve-day tour to a southern island. Another lawyer was made to stay in the magnificent autonomous prefecture of Sipsong Panna for two months.[87] As sensitive dates continue to increase, more tours are being imposed on lawyers: Lawyer Pu was taken to tour historic sites in two Eastern provinces to avoid the 2015 National Day in Beijing;[88] a number of activists, including lawyers, were requested to leave Beijing for tours in 2018 so as not to disturb a conference attended by visiting African dignitaries;[89]

[84] One lawyer openly challenged those who enjoyed free meals in those tea sessions or benefited from supervised tours, asking them to think hard about the morality of complying with the Party's soft repression. Lawyer's posting, quoted with permission.

[85] Lin Huixin, "Lawyer Zhang Jiankang Talks About His House Arrest and Gao Zhisheng's Case" (张鉴康律师谈软禁经过及高智晟案), October 13, 2006, *Epochtimes*, www.epochtimes.com/gb/6/10/13/n1485688.htm.

[86] Guo Ruo, "Zhang Jiankang Was Forced to Travel for Four Days" (张鉴康被强制旅游四天), June 6, 2007, *Epochtimes*, www.epochtimes.com/gb/7/6/6/n1735626.htm.

[87] "Human Rights Lawyer Jiankang Zhang Returns to Xi'an After 'Being Traveled'" (维权律师张鉴康"被旅游"后回到西安), December 20, 2010, *Boxun.com*, https://news.boxun.com/news/gb/china/2010/12/201012201519.shtml?__cf_chl_jschl_tk__=pmd_5c86487f3d7503292ba8bce51e00ea9050574262-1628502539-0-gqNtZGzNAfijcnBszQii.

[88] Jiang Xue, "The Torturous 17 Months of Pu Zhiqiang's Wife Meng Qun" (浦志强妻子孟群17个月煎熬), October 5, 2015, *RFI*, www.rfi.fr/cn/%E9%A6%96%E9%A1%B5/20151005-%E6%B5%A6%E5%BF%97%E5%BC%BA%E5%A6%BB%E5%AD%90%E5%AD%9F%E7%BE%A417%E4%B8%AA%E6%9C%88%E7%85%8E%E7%86%AC.

[89] Zha Jianying, "China's Bizarre Program to Keep Activists in Check," December 17, 2018, *New Yorker*, www.newyorker.com/magazine/2018/12/24/chinas-bizarre-program-to-keep-activists-in-check.

and others were forced to take a tour because the government was holding a key national meeting.[90]

There are restrictions and bargains at every stage of the process. To avoid the sensitivity of June 4, police requested Lawyer Sun to depart for a tour on May 26, claiming that May 26 was a good day to travel, Sun counteroffered June 3, and they finally settled on May 27.[91] During his near one-month tour, lawyer Zhang insisted on making a detour to a city to handle a prearranged criminal case. The three officers agreed and traveled to a new destination so that the lawyer could attend to his affairs, and once he had finished his work, the team continued their tour.[92] Some lawyers also have a say in where to travel and what sights to visit. There are reports from activists that they have bargained for a single room, instead of sharing one with a minder,[93] and that they have been allowed to use their phones to take photos and even write their daily tweets on Weibo;[94] but others were not allowed these privileges. In general, tours are well supervised but within certain confines, and the police are flexible and willing to meet the demands of their targets; the relationship is strangely amicable under the circumstances.

3.8 CPP at Work

"Thought work" is a key, and also unique, component in China's high policing.[95] Lawyers' advocacy is seen as posing some color revolution risks and an ideological battleground that the Party is not prepared to surrender. Historically, part of the mission in China's political policing, as it was preached if not fully practiced, was not merely to discover

[90] Christian Shepherd, "For Some Chinese Dissidents, Party Congress Means a Paid 'Vacation'," October 22, 2017, *Reuters*, www.reuters.com/article/us-china-congress-rights-insight-idUSKBN1CR01T.

[91] Sun Wenguang, "Supervised Tour on June 4th" (六四"被旅游"纪), June 10, 2014, *Boxun .com*, https://bnn.co/news/gb/pubvp/2014/06/201406101123.shtml.

[92] Lin Huixin, "Lawyer Zhang Jiankang Talks About His House Arrest and Zhisheng Gao's Case" (张鉴康律师谈软禁经过及高智晟案), October 13, 2006, *Epochtimes*, www .epochtimes.com/gb/6/10/13/n1485688.htm

[93] Jianying Zha, "China's Bizarre Program to Keep Activists in Check," December 17, 2018, *New Yorker*, www.newyorker.com/magazine/2018/12/24/chinas-bizarre-program-to-keep-activists-in-check.

[94] Hua Yong, "Half of Freedom Left" (剩下半个自由), May 31, 2016, *CDT*, https:// chinadigitaltimes.net/chinese/516591.html.

[95] Nguyen, "Chapter 5."

antirevolutionary facts, not even merely to force a confession in public, but also to convince the enemy, and through the enemy the people, that the Party was right and had the truth in its hands.[96]

The need to convince human rights lawyers that what they have done is wrong and dangerous to the country and that the state intervention, as unpleasant as it is, is necessary and justifiable has continued. What do police officers say to the often well-educated lawyers about political stability, national security, regime legitimacy, and even democracy during their lengthy conversation? Beyond making specific inquiries and demands, what grand narratives do security officers use in asserting their authority? There are three types.

The first is one of national security and patriotism. China's political police, despite their openly avowed and well-understood politicization, often try to avoid the political nature of the CPP process. Rather, they claim a surprising degree of political detachment and neutrality, projecting an image that they are national security professionals rather than political henchmen, and take pride in putting themselves among the rank and file of the Western national security establishment. The CCP is one thing – a reality to accept – but the security of the nation is another. They may guard the constitution with the Party at the center, not because the Party is infallible but because it is the only viable choice.[97] In essence, they often insist that what they do is not different from political policing in other countries, in particular the United States (US). In the following extract, the tone and language used against a lawyer who posted a prodemocracy message online is illustrative:

> You should know that no country, even the capitalist US, allows a subversive organization to exist; your grievance with the Bureau of Justice is none of our business, but do you really want to return the power to the people? Is that something that you should be thinking about? What are you capable of? What can you change? We will let you go today but I sincerely advise

[96] W. Allyn Rickett, "Voluntary Surrender and Confession in Chinese Law: The Problem of Continuity," *The Journal of Asian Studies* 30 (4) (1971): 797–814; Hong Lu and Terance Miethe, "Confessions and Criminal Case Disposition in China," *Law & Society Review* 37(3) (2003): 549–578. For the return of show-trials since 2013, see Magnus Fiskesjö, "The Return of the Show Trial: China's Televised 'Confessions," *Asia-Pacific Journal: Japan Focus* 15(13.1) (2017), http://apjjf.org/2017/13/Fiskesjo.html; and Yuanyuan Liu, "Staging Repentance: A Discourse Analysis of Mediated Confession in Xi Jinping's First Five-Year Term," *Journal of Current Chinese Affairs* 47 (3): 17–45.

[97] Huang, Haifeng, "Propaganda as Signaling," *Comparative Politics* 47(4) (2015): 419–444.

> you not to circulate that information any longer and not to think it is nothing if it happens in virtual space. A network is a public place - do you dare to hoist a banner and make a similar speech in the People's Square? … I advise you again to return to reality and take care of the interests of your wife and kids. Don't post those again or we will punish you once we find it out.[98]

Then they admonished lawyers for being pawns of hostile foreign forces and made mockery of the lawyers' argument about the relevance of their work to democracy, the rule of law, and the protection of human rights in China. In the police narratives, whatever advocacy human rights lawyers may have engaged in and regardless of their immediate contributions, often as grantees of foreign donors, their actions must be placed in the larger context of international politics, examined under the national security microscope, and seen through the particular lens of a color revolution risk. When faced with the legality challenge, the security police often retreat to the narratives of an international conspiracy against China in which foreign-sponsored color revolutions are conveniently used as the underpinning concerns. Foreign support allows foreign forces a foothold in the Chinese legal system, bringing human rights lawyering to a heightened level of political concern. Officials often name names, telling the lawyers having teas with who may be foreign agents and deeply involved anti-China conspiracies. "The water is deep," as they often say.[99] When further pushed, frustrated officers raise their voices and make accusations that the lawyer has committed great sins and damaged the national interests in ways that they were unaware of themselves. The following conversations between a rights activist (X) and a team of police (P) about the former's networking with other activists is representative. The activist was intercepted by the police on the streets after a meeting with another police target and refused a police invitation to have a talk in a police station. She then was dragged into a station after a standoff on the street that had attracted public attention.

X: Who are you, and on what basis do you detain me [at a local police station]?

P: "Who am I? You don't know me but you know this uniform that I am wearing. Don't you know what the police uniform is for?"

X: "Police summons require a police ID and summons certificate. Do you have them?" …

[98] Lawyer P's social media post on November 7, 2017. Quoted with permission.

[99] Wu Gan, "The Bible of 'Having Tea'."

P: (banging the table) We are the national security police of N city. X, you have no idea how serious your matter has become. You are out of your mind! Look at you, every day you wandered around and get so excited about it. You are so naive. You should confess everything to us quickly.[100]

The logic is clear: a matter in the hands of the national security police necessarily becomes a potential national security risk, involving hostile foreign forces, and the security police are best-positioned to assess the risk and prevent the harm. As the police told X, we are here to save you and you better put aside legal procedure and rights.[101] You are near the edge of a cliff and we are here to pull you back so that you don't fall over.[102]

The second narrative is to admit the malfunctions of the government and the wrongs that may have been done to lawyers or their clients in the past, such as misappropriation of land, wrongful action in the criminal process, or irregular disciplinary actions. It is composed of the following statements: 1) the government is not perfect and it makes many mistakes, even serious ones; 2) the government is willing to learn lessons and to change, but change requires time and patience. Lawyers should make constructive criticisms and channel their criticisms directly to the government rather than airing them in the media, especially foreign media, as that can be weaponized by China's enemies; and 3) human rights lawyers have made contributions to the improvement of rights and freedoms of the people, but their legal actions cannot be carried out in a way that may pose a national security threat.

While presenting itself as the guardian of China's national security, taking care of China's overarching interests, the security police claim to transcend any local or sectorial interests, and often distance themselves from any disputes that lawyers and others may have with a government department or any particular government policy, and even express sympathy if not support for the position that a lawyer may take on a particular issue of contention. On many occasions, they have sided with lawyers in criticizing the enforcement of certain government policies, and even express their willingness and ability to help out lawyers in managing their relationship with the government regulator, such as restoring a practicing certificate that was suspended, and so on. But they insist that whatever actions a lawyer is to take cannot become a national security risk, and,

100 Xu, "The 25 Hours I Was Kidnapped by Security Officer."

101 When Xu demanded to see a lawyer before answering any questions, the police laughed back that "you must have watched too much movies from Hong Kong." Ibid.

102 Ibid.

as national security specialists, their job is to assess risks and remove risk factors; the work is politically neutral and nearly actuarial in nature, reinforcing the first narrative.

The third narrative is one of detachment, in which security police show little interest in values, international politics, or patriotism. The officers claim they are just doing their jobs without even pretending to understand the nature of the matter. The conversation can be long or short, and the tone can be cold and curt or warm and friendly, all depending on the personality and circumstances. They may admire the passion of a lawyer and the talents of a dissenting artist, but their personal views do not affect their professional work. In justifying their intervention, the police just simply say: "Look, we have never met before and we don't know each other and I am here just to execute an order."When prompted by lawyers, they may make a crisp response to criticisms and comments: "Yes, China is a one-party dictatorship, but what is your point?" In responding to a lawyer's call for democracy in China, they may quickly reply: "Do you really think China can be a democracy?" or "Can you really return the power to the people?" They often follow some of these questions by advising lawyers to "go back to your wife and child," to "find a way to make some money," or to "lead a peaceful life."

Many lawyers use these opportunities to explain to officers the meanings of their actions and the significance of the rule of law and democratic values that they promote through their actions. According to lawyer G, during the meeting on the Feminist Five, the lawyers lectured the police on gender equality and police responsibilities in combating sexual harassment.[103] In explaining what motivated their participation in Charter 08, lawyers invariably let the interviewing officers know their view on the democratic values that Charter 08 embodied.[104] At dinner, Lawyer X was invited by the police (who had taken him to dinner to prevent him from joining another dinner gathering of dissidents), he tried to convey to the police the message that lawyers, however radical they may appear, still try to bring the social conflict to courts for legal resolution, effectively

[103] Lawyer G's post on WeChat on September 21, 2016.

[104] Jiang Tianyong, "I Was Invited to Tea by an Internal Security Officer for Charter 08," (我因08宪章被国保约谈), January 8, 2009, *Boxun.com*, www.boxun.com/cgi-bin/news/gb_display/print_versiOn.cgi?art=/gb/china/2009/01&link=200901080013.shtml&__cf_chl_jschl_tk__=pmd_56e1686435836538279bd73b8edc3db60e8dc811-1628483638-0-gqNtZGzNAjijcnBszQgi; Liu Shihui, "I Am Emotionally Stable After Being Invited to Tea By an Internal Security Officer" (我被国保约谈情绪很稳定), February 17, 2009, *Boxun.com*, https://news.boxun.com/news/gb/china/2009/02/200902171408.shtml.

reducing the risk of street action. Thus they were at the end of the day on the side of the government, and should be tolerated.[105] But no lawyers had any hope that their conversations would have an impact on officers. They fell on deaf ears, one lawyer insisted.

3.9 Conclusion

The constitutional endorsement of the CCP's monopoly of political power effectively outlaws any political opposition and dissidents. It also justifies and indeed demands preemptive and preventive high policing action in the broad sphere of speech and associations. Thus, regime type matters in determining the threshold question. Admittedly, the line is fuzzy even in democracies between legitimate dissent without fear and challenging political advocacy that may trigger high policing intervention. But, in general terms, mere political agitation for change, without more, does not activate directly the deployment of repressive measures by the state, and the constitutional protection of individual rights and freedom remains rigorous so as to constrain open and blunt interference. With a high threshold, early intervention into mere political advocacy is less likely to occur, and when it happens, it has to operate in secrecy. In democracies in general, liberal institutions have by and large worked effectively to ensure the constitutional accountability of security agencies and their preemptive and clandestine investigations into political and ideological expressions.

On the contrary, while authoritarian states openly constitutionalize the dichotomy between their enemies and the people, the line between legitimate dissent and criticism and a perceived national security threat is blurred and often reduced to invisibility. A fuzzy line may remain in the constitutional abstract, but the nature of the state is such that the state can legitimately intervene in legal and political advocacies at the earliest possible moment. With a low threshold, a wide range of political speeches and activities would become police property and subject to police monitoring and intervention. For that reason, human rights lawyering has attracted immense national security attention; indeed, it has become a primary target owing to its legal contestation with the state on some cutting-edge issues, its network building, extralegal social mobilization,

105 Sui Muqing, "The First Meeting for Tea on New Year's Eve" (阳历除夕夜遭遇第一次喝茶), January 2, 2013, *Boxun.com*, https://boxun.com/news/gb/china/2013/01/201301022125.shtml?__cf_chl_jschl_tk__=pmd_e1581949caf8995da9fee82867369d5c5f0a70c5-1628586797-0-gqNtZGzNAfijcnBszQgO.

and the support, financial or otherwise, that it receives from foreign government and organizations.

Instead of a sharp line between active lawyering, legitimate dissent, and political subversion, there is a large gray area in which these three concepts may dangerously overlap. As a result, most human rights lawyering would become problematic, offensive, and ultimately dangerous to the security of the party-state. Of course, as is often the case, whether and where a human rights lawyer has crossed the Rubicon and a qualitative change has taken place is context-driven and situational. It is not the quality of the act but the totality of the circumstances that matter. Few, if any, have committed a political offense out of the blue. Human rights lawyers, like other fellow dissident suspects, become the enemy of the state only after repeated interactions, including a long series of chats over tea, persuasion by families, friends and other third parties, multiple supervised tours, and harassment and intimidation of various kinds. Eventually, the wider political atmosphere changes, and some individuals can no longer be tolerated. Properly understood, political offenses, given their nature, often involve a series of interactions, negotiations, and compromises between the actor and the authority in a wider domestic and international context.

In China's national security state, the political control of lawyering is a state project of total social mobilization, with participation of multiple institutions including professional regulators, law firms, family members, and many significant others. Occupying the commanding heights, the security police can strategically deploy forces to suit what circumstances and situations demand. The house of justice of Chinese high policing has many rooms, each equipped with different software and hardware to handle different exigencies. They have mastered the eighteen types of martial arts and are well equipped to manage the potential enemy within the legal profession with optimal force and effectiveness.

Yet Chinese high policing, following the global trend, has tried to avoid open coercion and blatant violence against legal rules. In this new model, the Chinese national security state is not defined primarily by repression and punishment as old-fashioned autocratic states were. Its preemptive and preventive strategies to monitor and remove risk factors are also different from modern democratic states. A key feature of Chinese high policing is the will and capacity to engage and persuade, through the interactive CPP process, individuals whose acts may be regarded as a potential national security concern.

Preemptive policing does not constitute a strike as a preemptive strike ordinarily connotes. It is neither swift, brutal, nor bureaucratic. Rather, force is subtly applied through an indirect, informal, and even communicative process. As lawyers proceed with their legal advocacy or extralegal mobilization, police calibrate their countermeasures to constrain, limit, and moderate using tools ranging from subtle warning and direct intimidation to legal compulsion. For the political police, those lawyers are treading on a dangerous path and need to be prevented from falling off a cliff into a criminal abyss. The key point is not just that legitimate dissent is not a viable concept in China, or that the police can and do monitor human rights lawyers at key junctures, but that the police actively use instruments of communications, persuasion, and negotiation, in a coercive institutional setting, of course, to achieve their goals, reflecting the Chinese model of earlier intervention in disputes and preemptive governance.[106]

Political persuasion is not empty talk. It is backed up by the power to punish and repress, as has been amply demonstrated and is well known to be consequential. CPP is functionally efficacious because it operates in the long shadow of state repression. It does not necessarily imply that political policing is less repressive, less coercive, or even benevolent. On the contrary, the coercive state has widened its net of control and become more intrusive, inclusive, and expansive, leaving little room to hide and escape. In the national security state, control can be friendly, but is nevertheless forceful and even total.

[106] Victor H. Li, *Law without Lawyers: A Comparative View of Law in China and the United States* (Stanford, CA: Stanford Alumni Association, 1977); Hualing Fu and Michael Jackson, "Protest, Law and Regime Type," in Brian Christopher Jones (ed.), *Democracy and Rule of Law in China's Shadow* (Oxford: Hart, 2021), 11–32.

4

Transformation in Policing Minor Offending in China

SARAH BIDDULPH

4.1 Introduction

Each of the contributors to this volume has been asked to explore the character of law, legality and authoritarianism in policing in jurisdictions of the Asian region. This chapter focuses on the policing of minor offending in China. In contrast with political policing, legal regulation has become increasingly important in defining and regulating the policing of minor offending. In this chapter I explore what these reforms might tell us, if anything, about the particular character of authoritarianism and authoritarian legality in this sphere.

While this chapter primarily focuses on minor offending, it is important not to lose sight of its location in the broader field of policing in China, where a more varied picture emerges. We see that there is not a consistent move toward legally defined and constrained police power in the broader field of policing in China, particularly in policing political security, national security, terrorism, and extremism, where political imperatives are ascendant. This chapter thus explores how we might understand legal reforms both in the area of minor offending and within broader exercise of police power. It asks how divergences in legality across different spheres of policing challenges our understanding of the idea of legality.

To address these questions, we are faced with two questions of interpretation. The first is to examine our expectations about the significance of legalisation of police powers in the context of authoritarian governance. The rhetoric of legalisation, even in China, has been redolent with ideas of regularisation of police power by law, transparency and accountability in the exercise of power, protection of citizens' lawful rights, substantive

The research for this chapter was supported by a grant from the Australian Research Council [FT130100412].

and procedural justice. This language holds out the tantalising prospect that legalisation will strengthen the reciprocity between governors and the governed and facilitate a move from state-centred governance to more people-centred governance. This chapter engages with this question in its examination of legalisation of policing administrative powers to address minor offending.[1]

The second, related, question of interpretation is the place of legality in a context of radically divergent modes of policing within China. In Chapter 3 in this volume, Hualing Fu discusses this issue by reference to the divergence between high policing (political policing) and low policing (for individual victims and public order maintenance)[2]. Another influential conceptual framework of authoritarian legality in China (for examining the relevance of law in certain areas of policing and its irrelevance in others) draws on the conceptual dichotomy drawn between ordinary and exceptional (or political) justice of the dual state.[3] As Fu demonstrates in his analysis of the political policing of lawyers in this volume, law and legality may be present in political or high policing, but it is not essential. Elsewhere, Fu and Dowdle have argued that 'a defining characteristic of authoritarian legality is the existence of a dual system- the coexistence of a normative state where legal rules matter and a prerogative state where politics trumps', noting that in China the sphere of political repression is poorly separated from the normal system.[4] In the sphere of the exception, administration of justice and the exercise of coercive power are determined politically. Even if law is technically present, in enforcement the exception is essentially a lawless space. According to this conceptual framing, the sphere of ordinary justice is where principles and practices of legality are able to operate relatively unfettered. According to Fu and Dowdle, 'the normal legal

[1] Discussion of other administrative detention powers that are not related to minor offending, for example for people who are mentally ill, is outside the scope of this chapter.

[2] Fu, "Chapter 3."

[3] Ernst Fraenkel, *The Dual State: A Contribution to the Theory of Dictatorship* (New York: Oxford University Press, 2017); Carl Schmitt, *Political Theology: Four Chapters on the Concept of Sovereignty* (Chicago: University of Chicago Press, 2005); Mary Gallagher, *Authoritarian Legality in China: Law, Workers, and the State* (Cambridge: Cambridge University Press, 2017); Eva Pils, "The Global Consequences of China's Dual State," Unpublished Conference Paper (2019).

[4] Hualing Fu and Michael Dowdle, "The Concept of Authoritarian Legality: The Chinese Case," in Chen Weitseng and Hualing Fu (eds.), *Authoritarian Legality in Asia: Formation, Development and Transition* (Cambridge: Cambridge University Press, 2020), 63–89, at 67.

system [is] rule-based, institutionalised, and semi-autonomous'.[5] Fu has argued that the concept of authoritarian legality embodies a tension between normal law (where the normal legal system largely functions such as in the area of private law) and that of the extra-legal or prerogative state.[6]

But, as ideal types, the spheres of the norm and the exception do not map well onto identifiable areas of policing.[7] In the area of political policing, law is not absent, though it exists as one of a suite of available policing strategies. In the area of minor or ordinary offences, we would expect the normal legal system to function more completely, or with less political interference. But here, as well, we see the intervention of political and ideological factors that both structure and disrupt legality in policing.

One aim of this chapter is to explore the explanatory value and limits of this conceptual dichotomy in relation to ordinary and political policing. The core argument of this chapter is that principles of legality are structured by the particular way leadership by the Chinese Communist Party (CCP or Party) is conceived and given form (this has changed over time), ideological commitments and the pragmatic objectives and realities of governance of social order and maintaining political and social control. This chapter explores the relationship between professionalisation of the police force and legality in policing minor offending and the ways in which politics and ideology both underpin and permeate the structuring and functioning of this field of policing.

In relation to the first question of interpretation, the significance of legalisation, it argues that legalisation of policing has indeed led to development of a semi-autonomous legal field comprised of legal specialists

[5] Ibid., 82.

[6] Hualing Fu, "Duality and China's Struggle for Legal Autonomy," *China Perspectives* 1(116) (2019): 6–7.

[7] The use of ideal type here draws on Weber's discussion in *Economy and Society*. See Max Weber, *Economy and Society: An Outline of Interpretive Sociology*, trans. Ephraim Fischoff (Berkeley, CA: University of California Press, 1978), 19–22. See also discussion in Richard Swedberg, "How to Use Max Weber's Ideal Type in Sociological Analysis," *Journal of Classical Sociology* 18(3) (2018): 181–196. Its objective is heuristic; to devise a special type of conceptual construct that facilitates comparison and analysis of the ideal type against the empirical facts being observed. The point of the claim that the concepts of 'norm and exception' and, below, 'friend and enemy' should best be understood as ideal types is to distinguish these terms as analytical constructs (grounded in reality but not completely reflecting reality) from a pure description of empirical fact.

and the increasing relevance of legal authorisation and legal reasoning in defining and protecting police power.[8] But the existence of a legal field does not at the same time determine its fundamental principles or values and so does not inevitably move legal regulation toward more people-centred principles that emphasise protection of citizens' lawful rights over the state-centric preference for police empowerment and flexibility in enforcement.

In relation to the second question of interpretation, this chapter's working hypothesis is that 'ordinary' policing is not a space where principles of legality can operate relatively unfettered. As Fu's chapter demonstrates, political policing is not an entirely lawless space. Ordinary policing, similarly, is not entirely a space of legality. Instead, legality is permeated by and supports (rather than contests) fundamental principles of Party leadership and ideological commitment to the people's democratic dictatorship and democratic centralism. The focus of this chapter on the way politics and ideology both structure and disrupt the administration of justice in ordinary policing directs attention to the highly politicised nature of legality and away from the conceptual duality of the norm and the exception (and the prerogative state).

Policing powers are scattered across a range of functions and controlled by a range of different ministries including state security, people's armed police, judicial police, transport police, forestry police, public security, auxiliary police and local government enforcement officials (*chengguan*). This chapter focuses on the public security police (*gong'an*) under the control of the Ministry of Public Security (MPS) who continue to exercise primary power in relation to minor offending, including administrative measures and sanctions and criminal investigation police. For convenience, in this chapter, I refer to these public security forces as 'police'.

The chapter first describes the framework of policing of social order and some of the significant changes since the beginning of the reform era (here from 1979) with its focus on the reforms of police administrative powers. It then goes on to add the layers of context that structure the meanings and function of principles of legality in policing minor offending, starting with Party leadership, then ideology and finally principles of legality themselves.

[8] An argument made in Sarah Biddulph, *Legal Reform and Administrative Detention Powers in China* (Cambridge: Cambridge University Press, 2007).

4.2 Policing Social Order: Social Order and Social Control

4.2.1 Comprehensive Management of Public Order

At the end of the Cultural Revolution, systems for regularised governance of social order and crime were re-established under the umbrella of the Comprehensive Management of Public Order.[9] This policy incorporated formal and informal techniques of social control[10] including education and persuasion, administrative measures and dictatorship through severe punishment of serious crime.[11] This comprehensive approach to social management was retained and reformulated at the Third Plenum of the 18th Party Congress with a call to improve social governance: 'adhere to systematic governance, strengthen leadership of the Party Committee, give play to the leading role of government, encourage and support participation by all sectors of society, realise government management and society self-regulation and resident self-governance'.[12]

As part of the process of reinstitutionalisation and professionalisation of police powers in the early 1980s, the division between administrative and criminal powers and punishments was reinstated. Criminal law and procedure were codified (initially at least) in the 1979 *Criminal*

[9] The CCP Central Committee on June 14, 1981 approved and issued the Central Political-Legal Committee *Summary of the Public Order Meeting of the Five Major Cities of Beijing, Tianjin, Shanghai, Guangzhou and Wuhan*, where the policy was set out. It was endorsed in the Central Committee's *Directive on Strengthening Political-Legal Work*, January13, 1982.

[10] Yingyi Situ and Weizhang Liu, "Comprehensive Treatment to Social Order: A Chinese Approach against Crime," *International Journal of Comparative and Applied Criminal Justice* 20(1) (1996): 101–102.

[11] Biddulph, *Legal Reform and Administrative Detention Powers in China*.

[12] 坚持系统治理，加强党委领导，发挥政府主导作用，鼓励和支持社会各方面参与，实现政府治理和社会自我调节、居民自治良性互动 (at paragraph 47). The Communique of the Third Plenary Session of the 18th Central Committee of the Communist Party of China, Decision on Several Major Issues on Comprehensively Deepening Reform was adopted on November 12, 2013. There have been various formulations of this method of social management. The slogan 'The Party leads, the government takes responsibility, society cooperates, and the public participates' was first articulated at the fourth Plenum of the 16th Central Committee in 2004 and has been restated in several forms since. In 2012 the 18th National Congress of the Communist Party reiterated the demand with an additional prescription that the rule of law protects the social management system (党委领导、政府负责、社会协同、公众参与、法治保障的社会管理体制) On October 31, 2019 the fourth Plenum of the 19th Central Committee adopted the Decision on Some Major Issues Concerning How to Uphold and Improve the System of Socialism with Chinese Characteristics and Advance the Modernization of China's Governance System and Capacity for Governance, which further articulated these principles.

Law and *Criminal Procedure Law*. Administrative powers remained poorly supported by law. These divisions mapped (albeit imperfectly) onto the strategies adopted to prevent and control crime adopted within the framework of the Comprehensive Management of Public Order. The framework was formulated as three escalating lines of defence against crime and social disorder. The first line of defence encompasses community-based strategies such as education, persuasion, regulation and mediation of disputes in the local community (the latter as part of the mass line of policing).[13] Regulation in this category includes registration by the local police of people considered politically suspect or likely to harm social order, known as the focal population (重点人口).[14] This register continues to be very important in targeting and monitoring these groups. The second line of defence employs more coercive administrative sanctions or measures when a person has committed more serious offending or refuses to reform after repeated education. Finally, the third line of defence is criminal sanctions, to be used against the small number of most serious offenders.

Of course, these distinctions between rehabilitative and punitive powers do not map neatly onto the messiness of the real world where rehabilitative powers are often punitive in fact and the development of police powers was influenced by power struggles between agencies, personality politics, responses to scandals and even humanitarian impulses. Enforcement practices similarly have been influenced by security panics, resource limitations, the intensity and reasons for confrontational protests and disruptive conduct, amongst others.

Generally, the first and second line of defence corresponded conceptually with administrative powers exercised by the police and community organisations such as the neighbourhood and street committees. They were considered appropriate to be used to address non-antagonistic contradictions, where people could be educated and

[13] The mass line of policing required the police to rely on the masses, wholeheartedly serve and work in close association with them. Zhansheng Song, Zhimin Wang, Wannian Song, Wenqing Zhang, Yongzhi Song, and Yilin Liu (eds.), *Zhongguo Gong'an Dabaike Quanshu (Encyclopedia of China's Public Security)*, vol. 2 (Changchun: Jilin Renmin Chubanshe (Jilin People's Press), 2000), 24–30.

[14] Michael Dutton and Tianfu Lee, "Missing the Target? Policing Strategies in the Period of Economic Reform," *Crime and Delinquency, Special Issue: Crime and Justice in China and Japan* 39(3) (1993): 326–330; Jinsheng Tian, "Dui Woxian Zhongdian Renkou Guanli Gongzuo de Diaocha Yu Sikao" (An Investigation and Reflections on My County's Focal Population Management Work), *Beijing Renmin Jingcha Xueyuan Xuebao (Journal of the Beijing People's Police Academy)* 3(59) (1999): 27–30.

persuaded to be good citizens. Criminal justice was located at the punitive end of the spectrum to deal with antagonistic contradictions that warranted the full force of the state's punitive powers. A view at the time was that the range of antagonistic contradictions was small and the range of non-antagonistic contradictions broad.[15] According to this logic, the scope of administrative law should be very broad and the scope of criminal law small.[16]

The structure of Comprehensive Management of Public Order thus never completely ceased to reflect the influence of Mao's theory of contradictions with its division between antagonistic and non-antagonistic contradictions and the corresponding distinction drawn between the people and the enemy, even though use of this conceptual framework was largely confined to the political-legal organs.[17] This changed in 2019 when differentiation between the treatment of people who are part of the masses and those who are not was expanded to local governance nationwide.[18]

As the discussion that follows will show, changes in the economic base and the subsequent proliferation of minor property-related offending

[15] Xiao Yang, *Zhongguo Xingshi Zhengce he Celue Wenti* (*Problems of China's Criminal Policy and Tactics*) (Beijing: Falu Chubanshe (Law Press) 1996), 96.

[16] Dong Wei (魏东), "Reform of the Security Punishment after China's Abolition of Re-Education through Labour" (我国废止劳教以后的保安处分改革), *Journal of Sichuan University* (*四川大学学报*) 1 (2015): 81–88.

[17] Mao Zedong divided contradictions into antagonistic contradictions, those between enemies and the people and non-antagonistic contradictions, those amongst the people. Contradictions amongst the people were seen as non-fundamental and might be caused by mistaken views or conflicts over material resources. They could be resolved by education, persuasion, or the use of coercive administrative measures. Non-antagonistic contradictions, are to be solved by 'the democratic method, the method of discussion, of criticism, of persuasion and education…' Contradictions between the people and the enemy on the other hand were fundamental and could not be resolved by non-coercive means. They could only be resolved through the use of violent coercion and suppression. Mao Zedong, "On the Correct Handling of Contradictions Among the People," in Foreign Languages Press (ed.), *Quotations from Chairman Mao Tsetung* (Beijing: Foreign Languages Press, 1972), 45–57. In the reform era, the emphasis on stability preservation, coupled with institutional pressures on local agencies to ensure social stability has, perversely, led to increasing abuse of punitive powers such by local governments and officials: Qinqin Ren, Jianhua Wang, and Zhao Jia, "Shiying Minzhu fazhi jinchang gaige laojiao zhidu" (Adapt to the Evolution of Democracy and the Rule of Law: Reform Re-Education through Labour), *Xinhua net*, January 9, 2013, http://news.xinhuanet.com/legal/2013-01/09/c_114312339.htm; Sarah Biddulph, *The Stability Imperative: Human Rights and Law in China* (Vancouver: UBC Press, 2015).

[18] Massimo Introvigne, "Fengqiao Experience: The CCP Revives a Maoist Terror Strategy," *Bitter Winter*, August 13, 2020, https://bitterwinter.org/fengqiao-experience-the-ccp-revives-a-maoist-terror-strategy/.

have undermined the idea that the scope of criminal justice (and so harsh punishment) should be small. The discussion on Ideology further shows that reinvigoration of the people's democratic dictatorship as a framing device for political-legal work from January 2019 has further eroded the mapping of legal categories of administrative and criminal onto the political categories of the people and the enemy.

4.2.2 Police Administrative Powers – Rationalising and Transforming Punishment of Minor Offending

Fu and Dowdle rightly point to broad and unaccountable police power as one of the core institutional supports that sustains authoritarian repression. They point particularly to the large suite of administrative sanctions exercised by the police in China as an archetype of authoritarian policing both because of their open-ended scope and because of a lack of meaningful oversight.[19] An account of the transformation of police administrative powers thus provides an avenue to explore the changing shape of authoritarian policing in the context of social order policing and the role of law in that.

At the beginning of the 1980s, the police exercised a wide range of administrative powers that enabled them to register, detain, interrogate and coercively repatriate on a vast scale. Administrative powers developed as ad hoc and fragmented responses to political needs and emerging social and political problems. They were poorly defined by law, if at all, and as construction of the legal system progressed, they became increasingly targeted for criticism not only because of their widespread abuse but also because of their illegality. They were attractive to the police in that they gave flexibility in responding to political directives and priorities, and were able to transform in response to emerging social order problems arising from social and economic dislocation and the breakdown of existing social control mechanisms. One illustration is the power of the police to detain sex workers and their clients for between six months and two years under detention for education (收容教育 *shourong jiaoyu*), which was revived in 1985 during a hard strike campaign to eradicate prostitution.[20]

[19] Fu and Dowdle, "The Concept of Authoritarian Legality: The Chinese Case," 76, 78–80.

[20] Eradication of prostitution was included in each of the three annual 'battles' of the 1983–1986 Hard Strike against Serious Crime. It was also targeted in the concerted action against the Six Evils from 1989–1990. See discussion in Biddulph, *Legal Reform and Administrative Detention Powers in China*, 157–162.

Administrative powers were also attractive to the police because the overlap between them gave police broad enforcement discretion. One example was the power to impose an administrative fine and administrative detention of up to 30 days (行政拘留 *xingzheng juliu*) under the Public Security Administrative Punishment Law (PSAPL) for sex workers and their clients either instead of or in conjunction with a term of *shourong jiaoyu*. The power to impose a sanction, to detain and to administer the detention centres in which these people were held were all concentrated in the hands of the police and poorly controlled.[21] As the police also had primary responsibility for maintaining social order and attacking crime, but little capacity to prevent socially disruptive conduct, rampant overuse and abuse of administrative powers such as these was inevitable.

From the mid-1990s, there has been a substantial reorganisation of police administrative powers; preserved and expanded, abolished, converted into a 'welfare measure' or transformed into criminal powers.[22] Increasingly, the lack of an adequate, or any, legal basis for many of these administrative powers, systematic and severe abuse and police impunity combined to erode political support for these powers to continue, at least in their current form.

Some significant police administrative powers were reconfigured and retained. The 2007 NPC *Drug Prohibition Law* consolidated a number of administrative powers for managing and punishing drug-dependent people, including those targeted originally for *laodong jiaoyang*. These include registration of drug users (and so flagging their resident identity card so that can be subjected to ongoing surveillance and 'dynamic management' 动态管理) (Article 36), two years' administrative detention in coercive quarantine for drug rehabilitation, with a possible extension of one year (Articles 38, 47), and the addition of two new administrative compulsory orders imposed by the police but administered by the local street committee (together with the justice department). The first of these, for three years, is served in the community under supervision (Community Rehabilitation; Article 33). The second may be imposed after a period of coercive quarantine for drug rehabilitation and may be served in the community or in a closed setting (Giving up Drugs and Recovering Health,

[21] Sarah Biddulph, "Justice at the Margins: Notions of Justice in the Punishment of Prostitution," in Flora Sapio, Susan Trevaskes, Sarah Biddulph, and Elisa Nesossi (eds.), *Justice: The China Experience* (Cambridge: Cambridge University Press, 2017), 321–323.

[22] A comprehensive account is found in Sarah Biddulph, Elisa Nesossi, Flora Sapio, and Susan Trevaskes, "Detention and Its Reforms in the PRC," *China Law and Society Review* 2 (2017): 1–62.

Article 48). While some power has been transferred to the local community and justice agencies, perceptions about the intractable nature of drug dependency and its related social harms have resulted in police administrative power in this area being consolidated.

The police continue to exercise extensive administrative powers to manage public order and punish minor public order infringements under the Public Security Administrative Punishments Law (PSAPL) and People's Police Law.[23] Even where the power to impose an administrative sanction remains in the hands of the police, there has also been a gradual move to transfer management of detention centres to the justice department, thus breaking the monopoly held by the police over decision-making and enforcement in administrative cases.

Administrative detention powers such as detention for education (*shourong jiaoyu*) were first allowed to attrite and then, when detention centres had been nearly emptied, abolished.[24] Coercive testing for STIs and treatment were retained. The power to detain and repatriate unauthorised entrants into major cities under the power of detention for repatriation (*shourong qiansong*) were converted into purported 'welfare' measures.[25]

[23] Police retain coercive powers in relation to public order infringements under the including fines, warnings and imposing administrative detention of up to 30 days. Policing urban areas including street vendors is now the responsibility of *chengguan*, who are employed by municipal governments. Police retain coercive powers in relation to public order infringements under the PSAPL to exercise coercive measures including move on powers, powers to detain drunks, clearing a public place and imposing administrative detention of up to 20 days. Police also retain the power to detain (*liuzhi panwen*) in the police station under the 1995 People's Police Law (as amended in 2012), for an initial period of twenty-four hours and no more than forty-eight hours in the police station for interrogation in relation to suspected offenses. The power to detain juvenile offenders under detention for re-education (*shourong jiaoyang*) remains scantly examined, and to date appears not to have been reformed.

[24] *Shourong jiaoyu* could be imposed for between six months and two years for education of sex workers and their clients under the Decision on Strictly Prohibiting Prostitution and Using Prostitutes (which also allows coercive testing and treatment for sexually transmitted infections (STIs), and coercive treatment). This power was abolished in law on December 28, 2019. It was abolished in a manner reminiscent of the process of abolishing *laojiao*, that is it was gradually abolished in practice because people were no longer sent to detention centres. Police powers to compel testing and treatment such as *qiangzhi yiliao, feiziyuan zhuyuan zhiliao* remain extensive and are exercised in conjunction with powers relating to drug use and dependency, mental illness and sex work.

[25] *Shourong qiansong* (detention for repatriation) of unauthorised rural migrants into cities was abolished in 2003 and replaced by an allegedly non-coercive welfare power by the State Council *Measures on Aiding Vagrants and Beggars Having No Means of Livelihood in Cities*

The powers of *shourong shencha* (收容审查 detention for investigation) and portions of *laodong jiaoyang* (劳动教养 re-education through labour) have been moved into the criminal justice system.[26] *Shourong shencha* enabled the police to detain for interrogation people whose identity could not be established, who were suspected of gang crimes or were floating from place to place committing crimes. This detention power was commonly used as a substitute for the more restrictive criminal investigation power of criminal detention.[27] In the 1996 amendment to the Criminal Procedure Law it was added as a criminal coercive measure.

As the scope of *laodong jiaoyang* was so broad, only the most serious of transgressions targeted for punishment under this power, including dangerous or drunk driving, fraud and counterfeiting, minor property offences such as theft and extortion, were criminalised by amendments to the Criminal Law in 2011 (Amendment 8) and 2015 (Amendment 9), where the threshold for a range of crimes was lowered. Existing public order offences were expanded, including the offence of 'picking quarrels and causing trouble' (Article 293) turning it into a very flexible pocket

which in theory allocated management power to the Civil Affairs Administration. Police lost the unlimited power they exercised under *shourong qiansong* to sweep up persons in public places such as beggars, vagrants, mentally ill people, unauthorised street vendors, undocumented migrant workers, petitioners and others considered to be 'untidy' or unsightly during major events. In theory, accommodation is provided for free to vagrants and places of accommodation, administered by the civil affairs department, and is open so that people are permitted, in theory, to come and go as they please. See discussion of the reform process in Keith Hand, "Using Law for a Righteous Purpose: The Sun Zhigang Incident and Evolving Forms of Citizen Action in the People's Republic of China," *Columbia Journal of Transnational Law* 45 (July 2006): 114–195.

26 *Laodong jiaoyang* enabled police to impose a period of administrative detention for between one and three years with a possible extension of one year. *Laodong jiaoyang* was used for a wide and from the 1980s, ever-expanding range of minor offending including general trouble-making conduct (including repeat and nuisance petitioners) and political dissent. It was abolished on December 28, 2013 by the NPC Standing Committee *Resolution on Abolishing Laws and Regulations on Re-Education through Labour* (*Quanguo Renda Changweihui Guanyu Feichu Laodong Jiaoyang Falü Guiding De Jueding*).

27 Under *shourong shencha*, a suspect could be detained for one month with a possible extension up to three months. The power was described in the 1980 *Notice On Supporting the Unification of the Two Measures of Forced Labour and Detention for Investigation with RETL*, but arguably this was not a proper legal basis as required by the Administrative Punishments Law, or later the Legislation Law. By the time it was reformed, it was one of the worst abused of police administrative powers. Biddulph, *Legal Reform and Administrative Detention Powers in China*, 10–11; Sarah Biddulph, "What to Make of the Abolition of Re-Education Through Labour?" in Elisa Nesossi, Sarah Biddulph, Flora Sapio, Susan Trevaskes (eds.), *Legal Reforms and Deprivation of Liberty in Contemporary China* (Abingdon and New York: Routledge, 2016), 23–42.

offense (so called because it is so large that a wide range of conduct can be stuffed in).[28] It is probably more accurate to say that *laodong jiaoyang* was dismembered, with some transgressions no longer punishable, some transferred to alternative administrative mechanisms and a portion transferred to the criminal justice system. Although systemic and serious abuse of it was one motivation to abolish this much maligned power, it was also seen as anachronistic, no longer accurately targeting the types of conduct most damaging to social order and losing its effectiveness as a tool of social control.[29]

In administration of criminal justice, the police, procuratorate and courts often cooperate, but the ways in which powers are divided between the agencies does in fact constrain police autonomy. Police now at least must demonstrate to the procuratorate that they have evidence of a crime and that the prosecution is viable in ordinary cases. The changing nature of crime and inclusion of administrative transgressions into the criminal law has also prodded change. Alongside economic reform, the volume and scope of minor offending in areas such as public order, property, traffic and economic crimes has increased to make up approximately 70 per cent of all crime.[30] Some Chinese commentators have continued to resist the expansion of the number of criminal offences at the bottom end of the scale, arguing that the proper scope of Chinese criminal justice should remain narrow according to the policy of 'small criminal law' (*xiao xingfa guannian*).[31] But arguably it is far too late for that argument to be successfully made in view of the range of new criminal offences already created.[32]

In theory, administrative powers continued to be conceived as tools to resolve non-antagonistic contradictions and so associated with less stigma and less violently repressive than criminal powers. Throughout the

[28] Qianfan Zhang (张千帆), "Extending 'picking Quarrels and Causing Trouble' to Internet Speech" (延伸到网络言论的'寻衅滋事'), *FT Chinese Web*, February 4, 2015, www.ftchinese.com/story/001060493?full=y.

[29] Biddulph, "What to Make of the Abolition of Re–Education Through Labour?"

[30] Huawei Gong (贡华维), "A Study of the Criminal Policy of Minor Crime" (轻罪刑事政策研究), *Journal of Tianjin Administrative College of Politics and Law (天津市政法管理干部学院学报)* 89(3) (2006): 8–12.

[31] Wei, "Reform of the Security Punishment after China's Abolition of Re-Education through Labour", 82.

[32] Sarah Biddulph, "Punishments in the Post Re-Education through Labour World: Questions about Minor Crime in China," in Yun Zhao and Michael Ng (eds.), *Chinese Legal Reform and the Global Legal Order: Adoption and Adaptation* (Cambridge: Cambridge University Press, 2018), 15–43.

reform era, police analyses of administrative powers and the conduct they targeted has consistently been framed in terms of non-antagonistic contradictions.[33] While the relationship between criminal justice and antagonistic contradictions was reaffirmed at the beginning of the Hard Strike against Serious Crime (the *Yanda*) in August 1983 when Deng Xiaoping clearly identified crimes that undermined the success of the newly initiated reforms as struggles against the 'enemy',[34] the alignment between criminal justice and antagonistic contradictions has eroded over the reform era. This is so particularly since the partial retreat from the Hard Strike with adoption of the criminal justice policy of Balancing Leniency and Severity, expansion of the scope of criminal offences at the minor end of the scale and transfer of some administrative powers into the criminal justice system.[35]

4.2.3 Implications

How do we evaluate these reforms in terms of legality and their impact on authoritarian policing?

The account given here shows that reforms have responded to practical changes in the social order environment and changing evaluations of the efficacy of the powers to preserve social order, including whether serious abuse of the power itself exacerbates social instability. These were clearly considerations in abolishing *laodong jiaoyang* and *shourong jiaoyu*.

In part, reforms are also responsive to claims that these powers are illegal, and so abolition has given the authorities an opportunity to respond to pressure for reform in the name of promoting governance according to law, without significantly reducing the power of the coercive apparatus (including but not limited to the police) for social control.[36]

33 Official interpretations of mass incidents sparked by conflicts over material interests and livelihood are characterised as 'contradictions amongst the people' unless they become particularly large and violent: Hongjie Ren, *Shehui Wending Wenti Qianyan Tansuo* (*A Preliminary Exploration of Problems of Social Stability*) (Beijing: Chinese People's Public Security University Press (Zhongguo Renmin Gong'an Daxue Chubanshe), 2005), 49, 259).

34 Xiaoping Deng, "Uphold the Four Cardinal Principles, 30 March 1979," in Lenin Bureau for the Compilation and Translation of Works of Marx Engels and Stalin under the Central Committee of the Communist Party of China (ed.), *Selected Works of Deng Xiaoping (1975–1982)*, vol. 2 (Beijing: Foreign Languages Press, 1993), 176–177.

35 Susan Trevaskes, "The Shifting Sands of Punishment in China in the Era of the 'Harmonious Society,'" *Law & Policy* 32(3) (2010): 332–334. Supreme People's Court, *Opinion on Implementing the Criminal Justice Policy of Balancing Leniency and Severity*, February 8, 2010.

36 Biddulph, "What to Make of the Abolition of Re-Education Through Labour?"

There have also been unintended consequences that both exacerbate and mitigate illegality and injustice. On the one hand, removing the power to detain and repatriate repeat petitioners (under *shourong qiansong*) has not improved their situation but seen establishment of illegal, secret detention facilities by private companies contracted to seize and repatriate petitioners (black gaols) and establishment by local governments of illegal detention facilities such as Education and Reprimand Centres (*xunjie zhongxin* 训诫中心) and Legal Education Bases (*fazhi jiaoyu jidi* 法制教育基地) for purported education of petitioners upon their repatriation.[37]

On the other hand, in addition to the already increasing number of minor offences, expansion of the criminal justice system to absorb some conduct previously punished administratively has seen detention houses (*kanshousuo*) filled with people who have committed minor offences and who, upon conviction, may have been eligible for a non-custodial sentence. This has driven efforts to process these types of cases quickly and to increase the proportion of people released on bail. Many of the discussions about criminal justice reform since the Chief Justice, Zhou Qiang, launched the fourth five-year court reform plan at the end of 2013 have been around improving the speed and efficiency of handling of criminal cases at the minor end of the scale.[38] The 2018 amendment to the Criminal

[37] Human Rights Watch, "We Could Disappear at Any Time: Retaliation and Abuses Against Chinese Petitioners," *Human Rights Watch* 17(11) © (December 2005): 46–49; Human Rights Watch, "An Alleyway in Hell: China's Abusive 'Black Jails'," *Human Rights Watch* (2009): 1–51; Renwen Liu, "CASS Expert: Re-Education through Labour or Its Reincarnation as Admonition Centres and the Like" (Sheke Yuan Zhuanjia: Laojiao Huoyi Xunjie Zhongxin De Xingshi Fusheng) (社科院专家：劳教或以训诫中心等形式复生), Ifeng.com, May 12, 2014, http://news.ifeng.com/a/20140512/40253643_0.shtml.

[38] Two sets of pilot reforms to speed up the process and improve efficiency of pre-trial criminal processes are well known. The first is the pilot for expedited handling of criminal cases (*sucai chengxu*). This pilot sought to further expedite summary procedure by imposing tighter time limits and going some way in simplifying (or truncating) the procedures for investigating, prosecuting, and trying cases. The other reform is *renzui renfa*, which was incorporated into the *Criminal Procedure Law* in its 2018 amendment as *Procedures for Public Prosecution Cases where Parties have Reached a Settlement* in Section V Chapter II (articles 288–290). This procedure applies where an accused acknowledges the main criminal facts, accepts the charges and agrees with the procuratorate's sentencing recommendation. This trial is sometimes referred to as plea bargaining, but it more closely resembles a form of expedited sentencing following a guilty plea. Efficiency here is achieved at the expense of procedural safeguards, with duty lawyers not authorised to represent the accused, just to educate them. The reform where the police continue to play a more significant, though not monopoly, role is in administration of the process of criminal reconciliation (*xingshi hejie*) where the police (and other actors in the criminal justice system)

Procedure Law to include an expedited sentencing procedure reflects the outcome of these pilot reforms. The outcomes in terms of legality are mixed. Timely access to justice supports legality, but these gains are undermined if speed comes at the expense of procedural fairness and protections against undue pressure to confess and accept whatever punishment the procuratorate offers.

4.2.4 *Changing Technologies of Social Control*

Another change has been in the technologies of social control at the local level with an emphasis on strengthening local governance and social control at the grass roots, so marking a shift away from reliance on police administrative detention powers in maintaining social control. Revamped policies for the comprehensive management of public order have now focused on strengthening and systematising localised forms of governance and control that were weakened by the breakdown in the early reform period of the Maoist systems of social control predicated on a static population.[39]

The Third Plenum of the 18th Party Congress in 2013 called for strengthening of the grass roots comprehensive management of public order model with establishment of a 'three dimensional public security prevention and control system'.[40] In line with this priority, policing of social order has included widespread deployment of closed-circuit television and big data processing capabilities under the Multi-Dimensional System for Crime Prevention and Control (立体化治安防控体系). It builds on grid-based management (网络化治理) at local levels in China, developed following the Party's call in 2004 to build a new social management system (社会管理创新). The grid model of comprehensive governance based on the locality brings together the neighbourhood and resident committee, police and social services within a geographically defined grid.[41] Finally, police are called on to intervene proactively to carry out

engage in a form of mediation under which the victim (or their family) forgive the accused, receive agreed compensation and in exchange the accused will either be charged with a lesser offence or given mitigated punishment.

39 Biddulph, *Legal Reform and Administrative Detention Powers in China*.

40 Qi Wang and Jing Sun, "Research on Constitution and Innovation of County-Wide Three Dimensional Society Security Prevention and Control System," *Journal of Guangxi Police College* 33(6) (2020): 65–73.

41 Beibei Tang, "Grid Governance in China's Urban Middle-Class Neighbourhoods," *The China Quarterly* 241 (2020): 43–61.

education and resolve disputes in the community (the mass line) through the Safe Community Construction programme.[42] In addition, police have increased their capacity for localised control through administrative powers such as registration, testing, licensing and inspection.

The discriminatory and repressive potential of this increased technological capacity is highlighted by the revitalisation of local governance and policing priorities that distinguishes between governance of the people and the enemy, under the rubric of implementing the 'Fengqiao Experience' (枫桥经验) (discussed further in Section 4.4 on ideology). Its political significance is that it requires governance and enforcement to be carried out on the basis of 'correctly applying the theory of contradictions'. That is, distinguishing between the people and the enemy.

China's effective emergency response to the COVID-19 pandemic to prevent population mobility, enforce lockdown, testing, quarantine and implement social welfare measures, has built upon and helped to improve the efficacy of grid-based management.[43] During the emergency COVID-19 pandemic response in early 2020, local officials were supported by private security, police, organised volunteers and government officials. Special police units were responsible for conducting a strike hard campaign against pandemic related crimes such as spreading rumours, online fraud, price gouging and selling wildlife.[44]

One significant change to the overall comprehensive management of public order, highlighted during the emergency COVID-19 response, has been the expansion of comprehensive surveillance and big data gathering and tracking to render the population transparent once again (this transparency was dramatically eroded in the early reform period when a housing market was introduced and population mobility increased). During the pandemic, grid management, expanded use of electronic surveillance and big data went a long way to eliminating individual anonymity.[45]

[42] Feng Jiang and Chuanyu Xie, "Roles of Chinese Police Amidst the COVID-19 Pandemic," *Policing: A Journal of Policy and Practice* 14(4) (2021): 1127–1137.

[43] Chunling Xiang, "Prevention and Control of the Pandemic Must Make Good Use of Community Grid Management," *Cpc News (Reproduced from Study Times)*, February 10, 2020, http://theory.people.com.cn/n1/2020/0210/c40531-31578754.html. The cpc news site describes grid management as a 'new type of urban governance model, based on grid work units, with information technology as the core, with meticulous management the objective and socialisation as the means' (社区网格化管理是一种以网格单位为基础，以信息技术为核心、以精细化管理为目标和以社会化为手段的新型城市治理模式).

[44] Jiang and Xie, "Roles of Chinese Police Amidst the COVID-19 Pandemic."

[45] Ibid.

4.3 Party Leadership

4.3.1 Party and Law

Much has been made of the centralisation of power by Xi Jinping and the use of legality as one of the weapons to build and buttress the leadership of the Party over everything. This provides an important context for any contemporary exploration of the nature of authoritarianism in policing in China and the role of legality in shaping the ways this authoritarianism is given form. While the way in which the Party has exercised leadership has changed over time,[46] the process of strengthening Party control over all aspects of the legal system has been ongoing since Xi Jinping became General Secretary of the Party at the end of 2012.

The Decision issued by the Fourth Plenary session of the Party's 18th Central Committee in 2014 on Some Major Questions in Comprehensively Promoting Governing the Country According to Law (the 'Fourth Plenum Decision'),[47] to build a 'socialist rule of law system with Chinese characteristics' asserts that Party leadership must be exercised over all aspects of 'governance according to law',[48] thus firmly locating law and legality as tools for strengthening Party leadership and for achieving Party goals including strengthening governance capacity. It states that Party leadership will be implemented 'through the rule of law'. Governance according to law has been elevated to a place of political centrality by its inclusion as one of the Party's 'Four Comprehensives' strategic objectives alongside strengthening Party discipline.[49] Party leadership over law was constitutionally entrenched in the March 2018 amendments to the Constitution, where a sentence added to Article 1 elevated Party leadership from the Preamble to the body of the Constitution. It provides that: 'The leadership of the Chinese

[46] In Lin Feng's terms, 'ruling style'. Feng Lin, "The 2018 Constitutional Amendments: Significance and Impact on the Theories of Party–State Relationship in China," *China Perspectives* 19(1) (2019): 11–21.

[47] *Some Major Questions on Comprehensively Promoting Governing the Country According to Law* (Fourth Plenum Decision).

[48] See discussion in Susan Trevaskes, "A Law unto Itself: Chinese Communist Party Leadership and Yifa Zhiguo in the Xi Era," *Modern China* 44(4) (2018): 347–373.

[49] Each of the comprehensives was announced incrementally from November 2012 (Comprehensively: building a moderately prosperous society (2012), deepening reform (2013), strictly governing the Party (October 2014), governing according to law (October 2014)) before being announced as an official Party and national strategy in February 2015.

Communist Party is the most essential characteristic of Socialism with Chinese characteristics.'[50]

Governance according to law is directed toward improving governance capacity and ensuring agencies such as the police act as better tools to implement Party policies (certainly never to act as an institutional check on Party power). In his address at the National Conference on Political-Legal Work in 2014, Xi Jinping referred to political legal organs as the 'dagger handle of the Party', re-emphasising the primary obligation owed by these agencies to the Party. This point was reiterated in the Central Committee's Regulation on Party Political Legal Work issued on January 18, 2019. This document affirms the absolute leadership of the Party over political-legal work. It also requires political-legal organs to distinguish between, and handle correctly, contradictions between the people and the enemy and those amongst the people. It requires the accurate exercise of the functions of the people's democratic dictatorship.[51]

At the top political levels, these statements show a retreat from discourse that emphasises the identity of the police described in functional institutional terms defined by law, to re-emphasising the identity of the police as a component of the political category of the political-legal organs whose role is to implement the people's democratic dictatorship, which requires differential treatment of the people and the enemies over whom dictatorship shall be exercised.

The move back to emphasising the priority of political work and the people's democratic dictatorship in directing police work has quickened. This impact has been felt explicitly in local policing and governance of local communities. In his address at the Central Political-Legal Commission meeting in December 2019, Chen Yixin, its Secretary General, emphasised the need for political legal work to focus on modernising and strengthening comprehensive social governance at the community level.[52] Chen called for 'resolutely developing the "Fengqiao Experience" and speeding up modernisation

[50] Trevaskes, "A Law unto Itself: Chinese Communist Party Leadership and Yifa Zhiguo in the Xi Era," argues that governance according to law might now be seen as a core political platform.

[51] 严格区分和正确处理敌我矛盾和人民内部矛盾这两类不同性质的矛盾，准确行使人民民主专政职能

[52] Yixin Chen, "Chen Yixin: Thoughts for Planning Next Year's Work Must Accuately Identify the Focus for 'Governing China'" (陈一新：谋划明年工作思路要找准助推'中国之治'着力点), *Weixin* (blog), December 9, 2019, https://mp.weixin.qq.com/s/8JUpWuOJIGM7-kMN5gq5mg. A partial translation of this speech is contained in Bill Bishop, *Sinocism Newsletter,* December 10, 2019, https://sinocism.com/p/politburo-meeting-the-fengqiao-experience

of local governance', including resolving local disputes locally.[53] The *People's Daily* published an article on 12 August 2020 in which it affirmed the 'Fengqiao Experience' as a form of 'new thinking in resolving contradictions' and a 'monument of grassroots governance in New China'.[54]

Calls to learn from the 'Fengqiao Experience' explicitly reinsert politicised forms of social mobilisation into local governance and policing. The 'Fengqiao Experience' refers to the methods used in Fengqiao, Jiangsu province, in 1963 to implement the Four Cleanups Movement (四清运动).[55] In Fengqiao, the local community mobilised to take matters into their own hands to identify reactionary elements and to carry out denunciation rallies against them to achieve transformation through education, persuasion and monitoring. Targets were, in practice, subjected to relentless persecution and public humiliation as part of the purge. From 2019, the police have been asked to implement the 'Fengqiao Experience' in local community policing, by strengthening their role in identifying potential troublemakers and carrying out education, persuasion and surveillance.[56]

Professionalism and rule of law are now clearly located as tools of politics and serve to strengthen governance capacity of the Party. The turn to politics described here might readily be interpreted as a turn away from law and legality. But, contrary to the period of the Cultural Revolution, when law and politics, revolutionary credentials and professionalism were seen as antithetical, the new formulation places law and professionalism in the service of politics, Party leadership and the implementation of the people's democratic dictatorship. So the formulation of the relationship between Party leadership and law described in this section renders this explicit embrace of political categories as the basis for exercise of coercive power entirely consistent with China's version of governance according to law.

Xi Jinping's reference to political-legal organs being the 'dagger handle of the Party' raises two issues relevant to understanding the character of authoritarian policing; ensuring control over the dagger and the way in which the dagger is used. While the focus of this chapter is on the way in which the

53 Ibid.

54 *People's Daily*, "Building a Dream of Peace Together (The Chinese System Face to Face # 10): How to Build a Social Governance System of Co-Construction, Co-Governance and Sharing" (同心共筑平安梦（中国制度面对面⑩）——共建共治共享的社会治理制度如何搭建), *People's Daily (Renmin Ribao 人民日报)*, August 12, 2020.

55 The term the 'Fengqiao Experience' was resurrected by Xi Jinping in 2013 when he called for study and 'Fengqiao Experience' People's Daily reproduced at https://chinamediaproject.org/2013/10/17/xi-jinping-playing-with-fire/, David Bandurski, October 17, 2013.

56 Jiang and Xie, "Roles of Chinese Police amidst the COVIC-19 Pandemic."

dagger is wielded – that is, the exercise of police power – some brief comment on how the Party controls the police is warranted, as campaigns and law are used both by and against the police and so illustrate another dimension of authoritarian legality; that exercised by the Party over the police.

4.3.2 Party and Police: Ensuring Police Fidelity to the Party

Central Party leadership has used a comprehensive range of political, administrative and legal measures to ensure its control of the police. Some are straightforward purges of the top ranks of the police for real or imagined disloyalty, including the arrest and conviction of the Vice Minister of Public Security, Sun Lijun.[57] The arrest and prosecution of Zhou Yongkang was also understood to be a purge of a factional rival to Xi Jinping.[58] In a similar vein, the transfer of the People's Armed Police back to the sole control of the Central Military Commission and removing shared control by the Ministry of Public Security placed this armed force more directly under Xi Jinping's control.[59]

Control is exercised through routinised administrative mechanisms such as performance evaluation, Party control over appointment and promotion,[60] and legal and disciplinary oversight.[61] In addition, positive

[57] Joyce Huang, "China's Vice Minister of Public Security Arrested in Corruption Probe," *VOA News*, April 20, 2020, www.voanews.com/east-asia-pacific/chinas-vice-minister-public-security-arrested-corruption-probe. Sun was arrested in early 2020, after having overseen a series of crackdowns on various groups seen as opposing or challenging Party leadership including Falungong and rights lawyers. Sun was arrested ostensibly for corruption-related offenses, but the arrest was widely seen as a political purge to protect Xi Jinping from a challenge from high up within the Public Security apparatus.

[58] Kerry Brown, "Xi Jinping vs Zhou Yongkang: Xi Jinping's Anti-Corruption Forces Are Closing in on Zhou Yongkang in a Sensational Example of Chinese Politics," *The Diplomat*, March 17, 2014, https://thediplomat.com/2014/03/xi-jinping-vs-zhou-yongkang/.

[59] Viola Zhou, "Why China's Armed Police Will Now Only Take Orders from Xi and His Generals," *South China Morning Post*, December 28, 2017, www.scmp.com/news/china/policies-politics/article/2126039/reason-why-chinas-armed-police-will-now-only-take; Suzanne Scoggins, "Policing Modern China," *China Law and Society Review* 3 (2018): 79–117, at 95, https://doi.org/10.1163/25427466-00302001.

[60] Yuhua Wang, "Empowering the Police: How the Chinese Communist Party Manages Its Coercive Leaders," *China Quarterly* 219 (2014): 625–648, at 630, 645, doi:10.1017/S0305741014000769.

[61] Legal oversight and discipline mechanisms include legal regulations such as the *Public Security Organ Inspection Regulations* (*gong'an jiguan ducha tiaoli*) and the *Public Security, Police and Law Enforcement Responsibility and Accountability Provisions* (*gong'an jiguan renmin jingcha zhifa guocuo zeren zhuijiu guiding*). See also discussion in Scoggins, "Policing Modern China," 89.

incentives such as placing public security (police) chiefs into local government positions and into the Party's leadership teams strengthens institutional control at the local level by both strengthening police chiefs' bargaining power in relation to police funding,[62] and embedding police more firmly within local governance structures at a time when the focus of social control is shifting to local communities.

The National Supervision Commission (NSC), established by constitutional amendment at the March 2018 meeting of the National People's Congress, is another powerful institutional mechanism for supervising the police. The NSC is generously empowered under the Supervision Law (SL), to exercise expanded investigation and enforcement powers to pursue corrupt Party members and government officials. The scope of supervision has been expanded inter alia to 'strengthening the supervision of all public officials exercising public power' (公职人员) for a wide range of criminal, administrative and disciplinary breaches including suspected corruption, bribery, neglect of duty, malfeasance in office or any other duty-related violation or crime (SL Article 34).[63] The NSC's jurisdiction reaches to lazy or poor governance (懒政怠政) and in this respect facilitates increased micro-management of the exercise of police functions. An illustration from early 2020 was the threat made to local officials (subsequently made good for the leadership of Wuhan) that failure actively to take all necessary measures to wage the 'People's War' on COVID-19, or diverting materials or resources from their intended recipients, would be treated as a severe disciplinary offence.[64]

The broad remit of the NSC has turbocharged a range of campaigns directed against official misconduct. One illustration is the use of the

[62] Wang, "Empowering the Police: How the Chinese Communist Party Manages Its Coercive Leaders."

[63] Ling Li, "Politics of Anticorruption in China: Paradigm Change of the Party's Disciplinary Regime 2012–2017," *Journal of Contemporary China* 28(115) (2019): 47–63.

[64] Michael Smith, "China Will 'Punish' Officials Who Cover Up Virus," *AFR online*, February 4, 2020, www.afr.com/world/asia/china-will-punish-officials-who-cover-up-virus-20200204-p53xiv; Josephine Ma and Mimi Lau, "Xi Jinping 'Put China's Top Echelon on Notice' in Early Days of Coronavirus Outbreak," *South China Morning Post* (online edition), February 15, 2020, www.scmp.com/news/china/politics/article/3050815/xi-jinping-put-chinas-top-echelon-notice-early-days-coronavirus, referring to Xi's speech in a special meeting of the Politburo Standing Committee on February 3, 2020. This is a persistent feature of supervision and discipline of state officials where failure to implement a campaign sufficiently and vigorously will result in punishment. See, for example, Biddulph, *Legal Reform and Administrative Detention Powers in China*, 286.

Saohei Chu'e specialist struggle (扫黑除恶专项斗争), waged as a three-year nationwide campaign from 2018.[65] Its targets in the first year were local tyrants and criminal gangs. In the second year, it was local officials providing protective umbrellas for these activities. This campaign is clearly understood by local officials as seeking to make the existing anti-corruption campaign more effective and extending its scope to strengthen discipline at local levels. It is a mechanism to extend the anti-corruption campaign to capture those local officials who were seen as resistant to attempts by the central authorities to strengthen discipline and rectitude at the local level (through such mechanisms as the Eight Regulations 八项规定). Local police are a clear target.

4.4 Ideology – the People's Democratic Dictatorship and Creation of the People and the Enemy

As the discussion in Section 4.2 demonstrates, reforms of police powers disrupted the easy equivalence between administrative and criminal and people and enemy. But tracing reforms of police powers from administrative to legal and administrative to criminal is inadequate on its own to support an argument that the authoritarian nature of policing is changing or moderating. These changes have taken place in the presence of ongoing, even strengthened, engagement with the ideological categories of the people's democratic dictatorship and the distinctions in policing to be drawn between the people and the enemy. This section focuses on the reinvigoration of these political categories and their impact on policing.

4.4.1 Impacts on Policing

At the beginning of the reform era, the Party determined to retreat from what it identified as the leftist error of pursuing 'class struggle as the key link'. Instead, it identified the key contradiction as being between 'the ever-growing material and cultural needs of the people and backward social production'.[66] As a consequence, from 1978 the public security

[65] "中共中央，国务院发出《关于开展扫黑除恶专项斗争的通知》," *Xinhua (新华社)*, January 24, 2018, www.xinhuanet.com/legal/2018-01/24/c_1122309773.htm.

[66] Harro von Senger, "Ideology and Law-Making," in Jan Michiel Otto, Maurice V. Polak, Chen Jianfu, and Li Yuwen (eds.), *Law Making in the People's Republic of China* (The Hague: Kluwer Law International 2000), 41–54. This decision adopted the resolution of the Eighth CCP Congress in 1956 and ended the 'two line struggle' (between modernisation

forces were required to transform from acting as a purely political weapon of Communist Party dictatorship to a more professional force with their own institutional interests.[67] Law has been one important way to achieve this – by entrenching their powers and building and protecting institutional autonomy.[68]

The change of fundamental policy direction in 1979 had profound implications for the police force, which, as one of the political-legal organs, had focused on acting as 'a sharpened weapon for suppression of class enemies'.[69] From 1979, the National Conference of Public Security Office and Bureau Chiefs determined that the tasks of the police were to 'conscientiously transform [themselves] from taking class struggle as the key link and serving political movements, to taking the path of protecting the four modernisations and serving economic construction….'.[70] Police responsibility was now to protect the successful implementation of the four modernisations and economic construction and to administer the Party line and the law as one.

Still, the Maoist understanding of the need to identify, classify and punish socially disruptive conduct and crime on the basis of distinguishing between the people and the enemy has continued to inform choices about the appropriate approach to deal with transgressions. Despite

and class struggle) that had ensued since then. See also discussion in James P. Brady, "The Transformation of Justice under Socialism: The Contrasting Experiences of Cuba and China," *The Insurgent Sociologist* 10(4) (1981): 5–24; Michael Dutton, *Policing Chinese Politics: A History* (Durham: Duke University Press, 2005).

[67] Michael Dutton, "The End of the (Mass) Line? Chinese Policing in the Era of Contract," *Social Justice* 27(2) (2000): 69–70; Harold Tanner, *Strike Hard! Anti-Crime Campaigns and Chinese Criminal Justice, 1979–1985*, Cornell East Asia Series, vol. 104, (Ithaca, NY: Cornell, 1999), 32–35.

[68] Biddulph, *Legal Reform and Administrative Detention Powers in China.*

[69] Harro von Senger, "Recent Developments in the Relations between State and Party Norms in the People's Republic of China," in S. R. Schram (ed.), *The Scope of Power in China* (Hong Kong: The Chinese University Press, 1985), 171–207; and Wang Fang, *Mao Zedong Gong'an Gongzuo Lilun (Mao Zedong Public Security Work Theory)* (Beijing: Qunzhong Chubanshe (Masses Press), 1993). Zhengci Falu Jiaoyanshi (ed.), *Gong'an Gongzuo Gailun (Introduction to Public Security Work)* (Beijing: Zhongguo Xingshi Jingcha Xueyuan Chuanshe (China Criminal Police Institute Press), 1983), cites Lenin in support of the proposition that as an instrument of class rule, the police are an instrument of violence to carry out the dictatorship of the proletariat.

[70] The *Key Points of Public Security Work* were adopted in January 1979 at a national conference of public security department and bureau heads: Guoguang Xi and Lei Yu (eds.), *Zhongguo Renmin Gong'an Shigao (Draft History of the Chinese People's Public Security)* (Beijing: Jingguan Jiaoyu Chubanshe (Police Officers' Education Press), 1996), 367; Gao, 1994: 326–7.

having disappeared from public discourse until its re-emergence in 2019 in the Central Committee's Political-Legal Work Directive, the distinction between non-antagonistic contradictions (those amongst the people) and antagonistic contradictions (those between the people and the enemy) has remained a central organising theme in policing strategies and enforcement choices throughout the entire reform period.

4.4.2 Constituting the People and the Enemy

In practice, the boundary between the different types of contradictions has always been unstable and the definition of the enemy plastic. The definition of the enemy has changed alongside the change in the Party's 'key contradiction'. So, at the beginning of the reform period in 1983 enemies became those whose conduct undermined economic reform. After forty years of economic reform, economic crime is less of a fundamental threat to the overall economic reform project and, by extension, political stability. It is both natural and inevitable that the focus of political policing has shifted to address the most current threats as determined by the new definition of the primary contradiction. In his report to the 19th National Party Congress in October 2018, Xi Jinping indicated that the primary contradiction had evolved to be the 'contradiction between unbalanced and inadequate development and the people's ever-growing needs for a better life' enabled by China's rise. Achieving Xi Jinping's call for the great rejuvenation of the Chinese nation; China's rise and security, is now a political priority that needs to be protected at all costs.[71]

The new areas of political threat (and so new 'enemies of the people') reflect this shift, and include terrorism, extremism, subverting state power, undermining the Party's monopoly on power and serious breaches of Party discipline. It extends to damaging core institutional frameworks, including challenging official meanings of core concepts such as rule of law. These new enemies are identified by Fu and Dowdle as the "'5 elements' of human rights lawyers, house churches, political dissidents, opinion leaders and economically disadvantaged groups"'.[72] The focuses of state terror and law have also moved to reflect these priorities.

[71] *Xi Jinping's Thoughts on Socialisms with Chinese Characteristics for a New Era*, first delivered in the opening speech at the 19th Party Congress in October 2017. It was added to the Preamble of the Constitution at the March 2018 meeting of the National People's Congress.

[72] Fu and Dowdle, "The Concept of Authoritarian Legality: The Chinese Case," 70–71.

The distinction between friend and enemy suggests an exercise in categorisation that is achieved by working out who falls into one category or the other. But seeking to categorise purely by considering conduct assumes an objective, bright line distinction that does not exist and underestimates the shifting and personal dimensions of being an enemy. In his chapter in this volume, Hualing Fu discusses how rights lawyers, depending on the character of their ongoing engagement with the political police, might 'become the enemy of the state only after repeated interactions'.[73]

The same considerations apply to being a member of the people. Being a good citizen, having high quality (suzhi 素质) and demonstrating accepted standards of civility is an ongoing process of engagement with Party-state programmes, policies and priorities, and emulation of models.[74] As a vanguard, the Party has asserted both the right and the responsibility for shaping the moral life of citizens.[75] This is reflected in the ongoing commitment to constructing 'socialist spiritual civilisation' as a key element of political and ideological work.

4.4.3 Legal Accommodation of the Friend/Enemy Distinction

As Hualing Fu's chapter in this volume documents, policing of rights lawyers combines a range of legal, extra-legal and illegal measures. Even within the scope of legal measures, law enacts the elasticity that enables differential handling of enemies of the people.

Some parts of the criminal law and procedure are facilitative of differential treatment of people classified as the enemy in that they enable prosecution and punishment on political grounds. They include 'pocket offences' such as causing trouble and disturbing social order, subverting state power and offences of revealing state secrets. The 2012 Criminal Procedure Law legalised the coercive power of residential surveillance at a designated location (Article 73), enabling those suspected of harming national security, major corruption or terrorism to be detained

[73] Hualing Fu, "High Policing and Human Rights Lawyering in China" in this volume.

[74] On the significance of emulation see Borge Bakken, *The Exemplary Society, Human Improvement, Social Control and the Dangers of Modernity in China*, Studies in Contemporary China Series (New York: Oxford University Press, 2000).

[75] Harry Harding, *China's Second Revolution: Reform after Mao* (Sydney: Allen & Unwin, 1987), 173; Biddulph, *Legal Reform and Administrative Detention Powers in China*, 105–107.

incommunicado outside formally established and administered detention facilities for six months.[76]

An increasing number of coercive powers relating to detention and punishment of people outside the scope of 'ordinary' crime, in the political areas of national security, terrorism and extremism, are exercised by other state agencies where professionalism and legal restrictions on how these powers may be used are largely absent. Unlawful powers such as *shuanggui*, previously exercised by the Party's Discipline Inspection Commission, were used to detain and interrogate Party officials suspected of corruption offences incommunicado for six months. This power has now been given a clear legal basis and its scope expanded. The 2018 Supervision Law (Article 22) now empowers detention (*liuzhi*) by the supervision organs for investigation of a person suspected of corruption, bribery, neglect of duty, malfeasance in office or any other serious duty-related violation or duty-related crime. Article 43 enables them to be detained for a total of six months, an initial period of three months with a three-month extension. These people are commonly denied access to legal counsel and their families not notified. The Criminal Procedure Law makes provision for people to be transferred into criminal detention if the supervisory organ obtains evidence to support a criminal prosecution (CPL Article 170).

For those people convicted of a terrorism or (religious) extremism offences, the Counterterrorism Law, Article 30 enables a person considered to be socially dangerous (有社会危险性), to be subjected to 'settlement and education' (安置教育) after release. This power has echoes of the power of retention for in-camp employment (留场就业), under which a person could be retained indefinitely after their prison term expired. That power fell into disuse after passage of the Prison Law in 1994.[77]

In other cases, coercive and punitive measures are imposed without any clear legal authorisation. The large-scale detention of Muslims in Xinjiang is an illustration.[78] The concept of the 'people's enemy' and state terror

[76] Joshua Rosenzweig, "Residential Surveillance: Evolution of a Janus-Faced Measure," *SSRN*, October 12, 2013, http://ssrn.com/abstract=2641010; Fu and Dowdle, "The Concept of Authoritarian Legality: The Chinese Case," 70.

[77] Biddulph et al., "Detention and Its Reforms in the PRC," 16; Sarah Biddulph, "Arbitrary Detention," in Sarah Biddulph and Joshua Rosenzweig (eds.), *Handbook of Human Rights in China*, Handbooks of Research on Contemporary China Series (Cheltenham and Northampton: Edward Elgar Publishing, 2019), 371–396.

[78] Adrian Zenz, "'Thoroughly Reforming Them toward a Healthy Heart Attitude' – China's Political Re-Education Campaign in Xinjiang," Academia.com, May 15, 2018.

consequent upon it, acts as a type of meta-concept that transgresses the boundaries of legal/illegal and the institutional mapping of jurisdiction and powers of state agencies set out by law.

4.5 Principles of Legality

In this section, I focus on the roles of legality in shaping the authoritarian character of policing minor offences.

Over the reform era there has been a decisive embrace of construction of a comprehensive legal system to underpin governance. Starting from the beginning of the reform era in the early 1980s, law has served to institutionalise state power and the power of the police, both to authorise and constrain, to allocate powers and responsibilities between agencies of state. The passage of legislative instruments that established increasingly demanding standards of lawfulness against which police powers and enforcement practices were judged made continuing to use administrative detention powers that were illegal – at least in their existing form – and untenable.[79] These requirements of legality provided an opportunity and a legal vocabulary for advocates of reform to participate in discussions about practical problems and reform of police powers.[80] A legal field has thus gradually emerged as an arena where competing institutional interests are fought and resolved and where basic principles of governance are given specific legal balance and form. The MPS has participated actively in processes of law reform and legislative drafting, seeking to shape, authorise and protect its own powers and delineate its roles and responsibilities in relation to other political legal-agencies. It has had varying degrees of success.[81]

Emerging principles of legality have provided reasons (and possibly drivers) for change, particularly for police administrative powers. But legal reasons were probably never going to be enough to warrant the abolition of administrative detention powers. Pragmatic calculations such as whether the powers continued to be effective in maintaining social stability (*laojiao* and *shoujiao* are two examples), whether the calculation

[79] Amongst these reforms, the *Administrative Litigation Law* introduced a question of lawfulness to which the police needed to respond, mandatory procedural rules became significant with passage of the *Administrative Punishments Law*, and the *Legislation Law* imposed standards for legality and constitutionality of police powers.

[80] Biddulph, *Legal Reform and Administrative Detention Powers in China*.

[81] Ibid.

about degree of social harm caused by the targets of these powers had changed, costs and alternative methods for social control have also been significant factors.[82]

Beyond the role of legality in evaluating specific police powers, law has been a useful mechanism in enabling key political projects such as strengthening Party leadership and governance capacity. Law supports Party control over the police by establishing boundaries for police power and a standard against which to judge police conduct. Despite rhetorical commitments to people-centred governance, which gives priority or value to protecting individual rights and freedoms, the account of administrative powers in this chapter points to a framework that reflects state-centred approaches to governance. State-centred governance is more interested in responding to Party-state interests in effective governance, strengthening what He Xin has called 'political controls' by higher level agencies over lower level agencies, and ensuring proper empowerment of the police to better attain overarching objectives of political stability and social control.[83]

One of the justifications for strengthening legality in police powers has been that the law 'provides a precise measure' for judging police conduct and so becomes one of the tools for the Party to use in exercising control over the police.[84] Arguably, providing a more detailed legal basis for police powers and strengthening accountability mechanisms has rationalised the structure of police power and strengthened political control over policing. Citizens have enthusiastically taken up the opportunities they have been given to complain about police decision-making, to the chagrin of local social order police who now claim to be a 'vulnerable group', beset on all sides.[85] But overall, legal reforms have not significantly increased

[82] Biddulph, "What to Make of the Abolition of Re–Education through Labour?"

[83] Xin He, "Administrative Law as a Mechanism for Political Control in Contemporary China," in Stephanie Balme and Michael Dowdle (ed.), *Building Constitutionalism in China* (New York: Palgrave Macmillan, 2009), 143–161, makes this argument about the role of administrative litigation in facilitating central control over local decision-making, a form of political control.

[84] MPS 2000 *Notice on Implementing the 'State Council Decision on Comprehensively Carrying Forward Administration According to Law'* 2000 required police to:

> …fundamentally transform traditional concepts of administrative enforcement, work habits and work methods that have become inappropriate. Acquire a firm grasp of legal system concepts in both thought and action, use law as the accurate measure, study how to be good at using legal methods to manage state administration work and to carry out management functions.

[85] Suzanne Scoggins and Kevin O'Brien, "China's Unhappy Police," *Asian Survey* 56(2) (2016): 225–242.

the capacity of citizens to use the law to protect their own rights and interests against the police across the board. Increasingly stringent legal constraints on some substantive and procedural aspects of police power, but not others (such as detention of drug-dependent people), can also be understood as part of the agenda to 'strengthen governance capacity', by carving off from reform those powers where there is little political will to constrain police power.

In addition to the purely instrumental uses of law to empower or constrain, the Party has sought to shape a growing ideology of governance according to law (rule of law to some) as well as incorporating values such as openness, proportionality, timeliness and fairness into specific regulations governing police work (such as 2012's MPS *Regulations on the Procedures for Handling Administrative Cases by Public Security Organs* revised in August 2020). In many respects, legality serves Party interests well; improving professionalisation and efficiency of governance, providing systematic mechanisms for oversight and control of police power, and controlling arbitrary and abusive use of power that might alienate the people from the police and ultimately the Party-state.

But, as the legal regulation of police powers has increasingly, albeit unevenly, articulated basic principles of legality –including equality before the law, transparency and substantive and procedural justice, there is an inevitable tension with accommodating the distinction between the people and the enemy. At one level, there is no simple way to map police power defined in legal terms with its distinction between legal/illegal onto this political terrain. Even though legislation can be facilitative of the use of relatively uncontrolled force, or be ignored, the fixed nature of law corresponds poorly in many respects to the flexibility required for political approaches to policing.

The pervasiveness of the people's democratic dictatorship and the increasing importance of categories of people and enemy that it establishes across spheres of ordinary policing (at the community level and in areas of administrative regulation and minor crime), as well as political policing,[86] pose challenges to the integrity of the very concept and implementation of law-based governance in policing. Viewed from a legal standpoint, administrative and criminal punishments should be directed to unlawful conduct rather than being determined by the political character of the person; that is what they have done, not who they are. However,

[86] See also Fu, Chapter 3 in this volume.

when police administrative and criminal justice powers are defined vaguely, overlap or enact political concepts, either explicitly or implicitly (extremism being one and pocket offences such as picking quarrels and causing trouble is another), spaces are then created within the law itself for the operation of the friend/enemy distinction.

Governance and policing at the local level are an example where implementing the people's democratic dictatorship already corresponds reasonably well with existing powers. The existing police power to register and monitor the *zhongdian renkou* corresponds readily with conduct targeted for enhanced monitoring under the 'Fengqiao Experience'; troublemakers, repeat petitioners or politically unreliable people. Similarly, police responsibility to educate, persuade and mediate local disputes allows a large measure of freedom to target these groups.

The political determination of who falls into the category of the people and who is the enemy weakens the capacity of law to define its own boundaries, that is to act as a semi-autonomous system. It is very easy for people to fall outside the political category of the 'people' if they assert their rights too persistently or disruptively. For example, disruptive petitioners may move quickly beyond being seen as rightful resisters to being characterised as undermining social order or worse.[87]

4.6 Conclusion

I return now to the questions and two issues of interpretation set out in the introduction.

The first is the significance of legalisation of police powers in the context of policing administrative powers to address minor offending. The account of transformation of police administrative powers in Section 4.2 affirms the importance of law and conformity with principles of legality in shaping how administrative powers have been transformed and even in playing a role in their ultimate fate. But the outcome of these reforms, with limited exceptions, has not been to deprive the police of their substantive power. In relation to punishment and management of drug-dependent people, a police-centric model of administrative powers has been enacted in law, with the police responsible for registration and detention decisions, and other agencies such as the justice departments and local resident committees taking on responsibility with the police

[87] Biddulph, *The Stability Imperative: Human Rights and Law in China.*

for the ongoing monitoring and support of recovering drug addicts. In relation to police investigation powers, the criminal coercive power of criminal detention replaced an unlimited detention power in *shourong shencha*, but the police managed to extract other concessions in the scope of criminal coercive powers in the Criminal Procedure Law. *Laodong jiaoyang* was a bitter loss but compensated in part by transfer of the power to punish drug-dependent people away from *laodong jiaoyang* and offset in part by increasing in the scope of minor offending punishable under the Criminal Law. In relation to the detention of sex workers and their clients, the police lost a detention power that gave them great opportunity to extract payments, but which did not otherwise give them a great deal of power. Ultimately detention of sex workers was a power the police were increasingly unwilling to exercise. The story of legalisation told in Section 4.2 is one of reorganisation of police powers rather than one of constraining or disempowering the police.

It is also clear that reforms to these powers in the name of legality were supported by a range of other factors, including changing views about the seriousness of the harm to social order posed by these transgressions, the effectiveness of these powers to protect social order, the availability of alternative regulatory powers and the weight of negative public sentiment. The growing importance of other forms of social control including new technologies such as blanket surveillance, increasingly interconnected big data capacity and multi-institutional social management policies focused on the local community have gained importance in the overall mix of comprehensive governance measures.

While we can trace development of a legal field, the increasing importance of legality says nothing about the values these laws promote and protect. The discussion of legal reforms of administrative powers shows that a state-centred model of legality continues, which privileges police demands for empowerment and efficiency. A state-centred model, which does not go far to entrench citizen rights or capacity to hold police accountable in the exercise of coercive power, remains vulnerable to political intervention, being circumvented and weakened when political imperatives run counter to the fundamental principles of legality enacted in the law.

The second question of interpretation is to consider how we might understand these legal reforms within the broader context of policing in China where we see divergences between operation of principles of legality in different spheres of policing. What is the explanatory value of the conceptual dichotomy between ordinary and exceptional justice, in which ordinary justice should generally operate according to law? In examining how principles of legality function in policing of ordinary offences, the analysis in this chapter supports the working hypothesis that 'ordinary' policing is not a space where principles of legality can operate relatively unfettered. Ultimately, the picture painted is even more complex than this working hypothesis suggests. In the sphere of ordinary policing there are at least two ways in which this complexity challenges both the integrity of the concept of ordinary and a neatly drawn conceptual dichotomy between norm and the exception. First, principles of legality are enacted differently across the field of ordinary policing. Second, the relation between law and politics may be both constitutive and conflictual.

On the first point, the state-centred conception of legality documented in relation to administrative powers, enacts power and accountability unevenly. The administrative powers enacted in the Drug Prohibition Law, for example, have been rendered lawful in a narrow constitutional sense (that is, in conformity with the Legislation Law) but decision-making remains highly discretionary and accountability for decision-making remains ephemeral. Combined, the three coercive orders that may be imposed by the police on drug-dependent people add up to eight years, with a possible extension up to nine years. On the other hand, detailed procedural requirements have been specified for the exercise of other powers to impose administrative punishments including those under the PSAPL. Abolition of *shourong jiaoyu* removes an unconstrained detention power from the police, but leaves police with powers to fine and impose short periods of detention under the PSAPL.

On the second point, the discussion in this chapter of Party leadership and the impact of ideology on the institutional structure and principles of legality demonstrates that the very concept of legality is enlivened by and entirely permeated by shifting notions of Party leadership and Party ideology. It is still possible to judge police conduct against the criteria of legal/illegal/extra-legal. But the significance of those distinctions is arguably eroded where the concept of legality itself incorporates political concepts such as the people's democratic dictatorship and where the law continues to enact offences that are inherently political. Reinvigoration of the people's democratic dictatorship with its assertion that drawing the proper distinction between antagonistic and non-antagonistic contradictions as the core task of the political-legal organs of state and local public order management raises the real prospect that the question of who you are, as opposed to what you have done, will be of first importance in application of legal powers by the police.

Another caution against conceiving the exception and the norm as a dichotomy or as a dual system, rather than as ideal types, is that the key concepts of the people and the enemy are also best understood as ideal types. This chapter shows that people may not fall neatly into the category of people and enemy and that these categories may not always make explanatory sense. The erosion of the correlation between administrative sanctions to be applied to the people and criminal sanctions to the enemy documented in this chapter is one example. What is a drug-dependent person? What is a person who has committed a minor criminal offence? Another caution when using the categories of the people and enemy as explanatory tools is that the category boundaries are fluid and being a member of the people is precarious. People become the people only through their ongoing engagement and compliance with Party policies, programmes and campaigns to be civilised, of high quality, to emulate models and to demonstrate subordination to Party leadership. People become the enemy through their ongoing engagements with the police where they resist or refuse to be a model socialist citizen, for example by engaging in persistent petitioning or engaging in confrontational protest. Hualing Fu also makes this point in relation to enemies in his discussion of political policing and lawyers.

5

From Revolutions to COVID-19

Policing Narratives in Vietnam

TRANG (MAE) NGUYEN

5.1 Introduction

"Nations carve their police system in their own likeness," wrote police scholar Philip John Stead in reflecting on how policing institutions are an expression of the political, cultural, and ideological traditions of a particular time and space.[1] Following Stead's observation, this chapter examines one function of the police in Vietnam – narrative management – and how it evolved as an expression of the nondemocratic regime's politics and ideologies. Narrative management here refers to efforts by policing institutions to enforce public opinion in accordance with the vision set forth by the party-state – a practice of thought work that has a long tradition in socialist countries.[2] Narrative management can be done through both hard and soft measures. Reports on authoritarian policing have shed light on the hard practices of coercion, crackdowns, and punishment for those deemed subversive to the national narrative. While coercion remains a key feature of authoritarian policing (and, arguably, of all policing),[3] the soft practice of public opinion manipulation plays a sizable role in the work of Vietnamese policing institutions. Some have even argued that

[1] Wilbur R. Miller, "Police and the State: A Comparative Perspective," *American Bar Foundation Research Journal* 11(2) (1986): 339–348, at 339 (quoting Stead).

[2] The Chinese Ministry of Public Security, for example, engages in extensive ideological campaigns as part of a multipronged strategy to reinforce regime stability – an extension of its long history of "mass line" (*qunzhong luxian*), which emphasizes the strategy of reaching out to and co-opting the public into police work. See Suzanne Scoggins, "Propaganda and the Police: The Softer Side of State Control in China," *Europe-Asia Studies* (2020), https://doi.org/10.1080/09668136.2020.1850644.

[3] The distinguishing feature between democratic and authoritarian policing, according to criminal law scholar Jerome Hall, is not coercion but the rule of law: "[I]t is a startling fact that there is hardly a single physical brutality inflicted by the Gestapo and the NKVD [Russian Commissariat] which American policemen have not at some time perpetrated."

this emphasis on narrative management and, beyond that, psychological manipulation is what distinguishes the police culture of Vietnam, China, and North Korea from their noncommunist counterparts.[4]

Though thought work may no be an obvious police function, Vietnamese Public Security forces have a long history of engaging in public relations campaigns. As detailed herein, this strategic function hearkens back to the Vietnamese communist leadership's deep reliance on public intelligence and support to consolidate power during the colonial eras, reaching new heights in the postwar era with the proliferation of mass organizations that reached into all aspects of civilian lives. The police's role as public educators is recognized in Vietnam's official socialist ideologies and law. As the country transitioned from war to a nation-building era to unprecedented economic leaps, police work on ideology control remained laser-focused on buttressing regime legitimacy, even as the core narratives shifted from nationalism to economic development to public health in the wake of the COVID-19 pandemic. Rising wealth, strength against China, and increased international integration are all important metrics for the monopolized leadership of the Vietnamese Communist Party (VCP). At the same time, the party-state has also tied its economic and technological upward mobility to what it deems an ideological warfare that has spread unchecked through the Internet. Warnings against the dangers of "peaceful evolution" and "self-evolution," which once dominated Vietnam's war slogans, continue to pepper recent news and political speeches and are explicitly linked to the Internet's outsize reach. As detailed later, the Vietnamese police's thought work was accordingly expanded, culminating in the controversial 2018 Cybersecurity Law. The roles of authoritarian policing institutions, however, are complex. While this chapter highlights the Vietnamese police's

But the police in dictatorships exert "domination by sheer physical force unlimited by law," which is "the antithesis of the rule of law" found in democratic societies. Jerome Hall, "Police and Law in a Democratic Society," *Indiana Law Journal* 28 (1953): 133–177, at 138, 143; see also Sarah A. Seo, "Democratic Policing Before the Due Process Revolution," *Yale Law Journal* 128: 1246–1302 (2019). However, scholars have argued that, at least in the United States, the police lack adequate oversight. See Barry Friedman and Maria Ponomarenko, "Democratic Policing," *New York University Law Review* 90 (2015): 1827–1907, at 1827 (arguing that policing institutions in the US suffer from a lack of democratic foundation because they are mostly regulated by post hoc judicial adjudication rather than ex ante governing rules like other administrative institutions).

[4] Christopher Goscha, "Intelligence in a Time of Decolonization: The Case of the Democratic Republic of Vietnam at War (1945–50)," *Intelligence and National Security* 22(1) (2007): 100–138, at 132.

strong grip on a vibrant society, Vietnam's experience with the COVID-19 pandemic also points to the productive side of a close state–society relationship: when the party-state acted legitimately and transparently, its workers – the police included – were able to gain public trust, mobilize society, and induce compliance with restrictive measures, enabling the nation to avert the worst of a deadly crisis.

The chapter proceeds in three parts. Section 5.2 sketches a brief history of the modern Vietnamese police as it emerged during the colonial war, focusing on its intimate linkage with the VCP from the very start. Section 5.3 discusses the role of the police in narrative control and traces how this function evolved in three instances: (1) the warnings against peaceful evolution and self-evolution that persisted into Vietnam's postwar reform era, (2) the combating of ideological counternarratives on the Internet, and (3) most recently, the Public Security's narrative-shaping roles in grassroots responses to the COVID-19 pandemic. Section 5.4 draws some broad conclusions on authoritarian policing through the experience of Vietnam.

5.2 Brief History of the Modern Vietnamese Police

Vietnam's Public Security force officially emerged in 1946 at the tail end of World War II, shortly after Ho Chi Minh declared the formation of the Democratic Republic of Vietnam (DRV), or North Vietnam, in September 1945.[5] By then, the North Vietnam that Ho's young government took over was a deeply wounded land, still in the midst of territorial contest. The people of Tonkin had lived through France's colonial rule, a brief but brutal Fascist Japan takeover, and a devastating famine that claimed as many as 2 million Vietnamese lives.[6] But unlike the Bolsheviks, whose negative attitude toward law manifested soon after the 1918 revolution,[7] Ho Chi Minh appeared to regard legality as a central instrument for state-building efforts.[8] The young government had not been recognized

[5] I primarily trace the history of the Public Security force as it formed in North Vietnam as that entity is the predecessor of Vietnam's Ministry of Public Security. Another police force, the National Police, also existed in South Vietnam in service of the Republic of Vietnam.

[6] R. B. Smith, "The Work of the Provisional Government of Vietnam, August–December 1945," *Modern Asian Studies* 12(4) (1978): 571–609.

[7] See generally Vladimir Gsovski, "The Soviet Concept of Law," *Fordham Law Review* 7 (1938): 1.

[8] See Truong Trong Nghia, "The Rule of Law in Vietnam: Theory and Practice," in *The Rule of Law: Perspectives from the Pacific Rim* (Missoula, MT: Mansfield Center for Pacific Affairs, 2000): 123–141; Pip Nicholson, "Vietnamese Jurisprudence: Informing Court Reforms," in Pip Nicholson and John Gillespie (eds.), *Asian Socialism and Legal Change: The Dynamics of Vietnamese and Chinese Reform* (Canberra: Australian University Press, 2005).

by any other nations, and its leadership was concerned that the nascent state would not be legitimized without a constitution or legal system.[9] In the ten months following the proclamation of independence, while on-the-ground warfare raged on, Ho issued a series of presidential decrees to commission the drafting of Vietnam's first constitution, create essential governmental bodies including the National Assembly and the Ministry of Justice, and declare universal suffrage.[10] Vietnam's first constitution, adopted in 1946, was a remarkable mix of liberal and socialist values, offering, for example, both the abolition of private ownership and separation-of-power mechanisms.[11] Communist control was far from consolidated at this point, and the DRV continued to battle French troops and vied for civilian support against not only the French but also competing non-communist nationalist groups.[12] This pluralistic political environment, as reflected in the lively debates among the various constitutional schools of thought during the drafting process, led to the many progressive features of an otherwise socialist constitution.[13]

It was in this chaos that the DRV's Public Security Department was created, charged with the paramount mission of maintaining order and keeping the newborn state alive.[14] Like other Vietnamese institutions,[15] its beginning was rooted in colonial continuity and international expertise, particularly from France, the Soviet Union (USSR), and China.[16] First modeled after the French colonial police (la Sûreté générale indochinoise), the Bureau of Security Forces for Northern Vietnam (So Liem Phong Bac Bo) gained access to French police files stored in abandoned archives, enabling the new Vietnamese leadership, once subjects of

9 Ibid.

10 "He Thong Sac Lenh – Nguon Luat Chu Yeu Cua Nha Nuoc Viet Nam Dan Chu Cong Hoa [Presidential Decrees – The Main Source of Law of the Democratic Republic of Vietnam], 1945–1946," *Nhan Dan (People)*, May 4, 2017.

11 Giao Cong Vu and Kien Tran, "Constitutional Debate and Development on Human Rights in Vietnam," *Asian Journal of Comparative Law* 11 (2016): 235–262.

12 Christopher Goscha, "The Creation of a Vietnamese Intelligence Service, 1945–50," in R. Gerald Hughes, Peter Jackson, and Len Scott (eds.), *Exploring Intelligence Archives: Enquiries into the Secret State* (London: Routledge, 2008): 103, 105.

13 Vu and Tran, "Constitutional Debate and Development on Human Rights in Vietnam," 239–241.

14 Goscha, Marr, and Pribbenow, "The Creation of a Vietnamese Intelligence Service," 104.

15 For a study on how Vietnamese courts borrowed the structures of the Soviet courts system but diverged in their operations, see Pip Nicholson, *Borrowing Court Systems: The Experience of Socialist Vietnam* (Leiden: Martinus Nijhoff, 2007).

16 Christopher Goscha, *The Penguin History of Modern Vietnam* (London: Allen Lane), 104–105.

French repression, to glean intelligence and techniques from its former colonial master.[17] The first heads of the new security department were part of a group of Vietnamese nationalists that had traveled to communist bases in the USSR, China, and Madagascar, among other outposts.[18] Ironically, French colonial prisons, where captured Vietnamese revolutionaries from Moscow, Guangzhou, and elsewhere served time together, had become fertile grounds for knowledge transfers, intelligence sharing, and radicalization.[19] Soviet methods and knowledge further made their way to Vietnam through southern China, where the USSR had helped create the first modern Chinese military academy.[20] Colonial continuity expanded beyond paper files and colonial prisons to human resources. While the DRV's Public Security Bureau carefully weeded out colonial spies, its leadership deliberately retained Vietnamese civil servants who had served in the notorious Sûreté, recognizing that their knowledge and expertise were an "invaluable resource which the revolution had to know how to use."[21]

From the beginning, the Indochinese Communist Party (ICP) – the VCP's predecessor – had sought to gain direct control over the DRV's security forces.[22] In 1946, as the war with France intensified, Ho Chi Minh issued Decree 23 to unify the various civilian-militia groups and the Bureau of Security Forces into a centralized department, the Vietnamese Public

[17] Ibid.

[18] Goscha, *Penguin History*, 104.

[19] For a riveting analysis of the colonial prisons and the communist bonds forged within, see Peter Zinoman, *The Colonial Bastille: A History of Imprisonment in Vietnam (1862–1940)* (Berkeley: University of California Press, 2001).

[20] Goscha, *Penguin History*, 104. Vietnam nationalists had first turned to Japan as a model after the Meiji Japanese army defeated the Russians in 1905 – a first Asian military victory over a Western power. The Dong Du (Go East) movement to study the Japanese model was short-lived, as Japan itself adopted the Western colonial model and turned Korea into a colony of its own. For a history of intra-Asia military knowledge transfer, see Christopher Goscha, "Building Force: Asian Origins of Twentieth-Century Military Science in Vietnam (1905–1954)," *Journal of Southeast Asian Studies* 34(3) (2003).

[21] Goscha, *Penguin History*, 105 (quoting Nguyen Van Ngoc, a former DRV deputy minister of Public Security). Colonial elites were also retained in other technical fields including law, agriculture, and medicine. See Tuong Vu, "The Revolutionary Path to State Formation in Vietnam: Opportunities, Conundrums, and Legacies," *Journal of Vietnamese Studies* 11(3/4) (2016): 267–297, at 281, www.jstor.org/stable/26377924 (arguing that the early DRV government's retention policy was motivated by the desire to restore order to gain international recognition).

[22] The Indochinese Communist Party (1930–1951) became the Vietnamese Workers' Party (1951–1976). Since 1976, it has been known as the Vietnamese Communist Party.

Security Department (Viet Nam Cong An Vu).[23] While officially located within the Ministry of the Interior, unofficially the head of the Public Security Department reported directly to the ICP's Central Committee – the party's internal legislative organ.[24] The party's firm control over its security force was made official in 1950 with the Central Committee's issuance of Directive 10/CT/TW, titled "The Party Leads the Police."[25] The document instructed party branches at all levels to gain better management over police affairs, pointing out that party bureaucrats had failed to realize the importance of the police in state-building: "In the people's democratic state machine led by our party, Public Security is an instrument of struggle against the reactionary forces inside and outside the country and [vital to the] protection of the people's interests." Party branches had not adequately coordinated with the police, and the apparatus had lost its prestige owing to "many regrettable incidents." Going forward, party leaders from villages to provinces were to gain better leadership over the police units at their respective levels: "Each level must delegate a party cadre to lead the police. Select a member with good ability to strengthen the implementation of party policies and guidance (*nam vung duong loi, chinh sach cua Dang*)."[26]

The 1950s also marked a starting period of institutionalization of the Vietnamese police. In August 1953, six months after the Public Security Department was elevated to subministry level, the Government Council (now the Office of the Government, headed by the prime minister) upgraded it to ministry level.[27] By that time, the DRV had been unseated

[23] Office of the President of the Democratic Republic of Vietnam, Decree 23 on Establishing the Public Security Department, as Part of the Ministry of Interior, February 21, 1946, https://perma.cc/T6CM-BRA4.

[24] Political scientists studying Vietnam and China have argued that the Central Committee in Vietnam's political apparatus "has more institutionalized presence and plays a far more decisive role" in setting policies than its Chinese counterpart. Edmund Malesky, Regina Abrami, and Yu Zheng, "Accountability and Inequality in Single-Party Regimes: A Comparative Analysis of Vietnam and China," *Comparative Politics*, 43(4) (2011): 401–419.

[25] While the actual text of Directive 10/CT/TW is not publicly available, its content has been detailed in both the Ministry of Public Security's documents and academic sources. See, for example, Office of the Minister of Public Security, "Dang Lanh Dao – Nhan To Quyet Dinh Thang Loi Cong Tac, Chien Dau Cua Cong An Nhan Dan" (Party Leadership – The Deciding Factor for the Victory of the People's Police), February 2, 2018, https://perma.cc/J3FP-PUPN; Goscha, "Intelligence in a Time of Decolonization," 117–118.

[26] Goscha, "Intelligence in a Time of Decolonization," 117–118.

[27] Office of the President of the Democratic Republic of Vietnam, Decree 141, February 16, 1953, https://perma.cc/B978-XJDP (elevating the Public Security Department to subministry level); Ministry of Public Security of Socialist Republic of Vietnam, "History of People's Public Security Forces in Vietnam," January 9, 2018, https://perma.cc/F4XK-8L8M.

from the capital and was deep in guerrilla warfare with France from its makeshift headquarters in the northwest mountains.[28] Across the border, Mao Zedong was in the midst of a massive land reform and land collectivization process, and Vietnam would soon kickstart its own land reform campaign.[29] With military draft and mobilization laws on the books, the police and the army accompanied VCP cadres to towns and villages to organize local mass organizations, launch "new heroes" campaigns, and mobilize civilians to join the war and reform efforts.[30] The role of the Ministry of Public Security (MPS) in narrative management was thus part of the DRV's larger campaign to "mobilize civilians and convert enemy soldiers" (*dan van, binh-dich van*). Mass mobilization (*dan van*) referred to efforts to recruit civilians in contested areas to support the communist cause; conversion of enemy soldiers (*binh-dich van*) referred to efforts to encourage troop defections.[31] For example, to encourage desertion among French troops, the DRV changed its narrative from "inevitable victory against French colonizer" to "peace and repatriation" (*paix et rapatriement*), which it believed would better resonate with soldiers in the left-behind French Expeditionary Corps, the majority of whom were non-French nationals from colonies in Algeria, Morocco, Senegal, and elsewhere.[32] To enlist civilian support against anticommunist raids, Public Security and military personnel launched the Three Nots campaign: civilians "do not know, do not see, do not hear" about DRV troops' movements, and they "do not work for, do not sell food to, and do not aid" the enemies.[33] To guard against espionage,

[28] Goscha, *Penguin History*, 278.

[29] For a detailed comparative account of land reforms in both countries, see Edwin Moise, *Land Reform in China and North Vietnam: Consolidating the Revolution at the Village Level* (Chapel Hill, NC: University of North Carolina Press, 1983).

[30] Goscha, *Penguin History*, 278–282. For a careful account of the so-called new heroes campaign to reconstruct a Vietnamese national identity based on Socialist patriotic ideals, see Benoît de Tréglodé, *Heroes and Revolutions in Vietnam, 1948–1964* (Singapore: NUS Press, 2012).

[31] Le Van Cu, "Chinh Sach Doi Xu Cua Viet Nam Voi Tu, Hang Binh Au-Phi Trong Khang Chien Chong Thuc Dan Phap" (Vietnam's Policy Towards Imprisoned and Defected Troops from Europe and Africa during the Anti-Colonial War against France), *Tap Chi Nghien Cuu Lich Su (History Review)* (2012): 33–44.

[32] Christopher Goscha, *Historical Dictionary of the Indochina War (1945–1954): An International and Interdisciplinary Approach* (Copenhagen: NIAS Press, 2011), 177.

[33] People's Police Academy, "Phong Trao Toan Dan Bao Ve ANTQ Qua Cac Thoi Ky Va Kinh Nghiem Rut Ra Doi Voi Cong Tac Van Dong Cua Luc Luong Cong An Nhan Dan Trong Giai Doan Hien Nay" (The Campaign to Protect National Security and Experiences Learned from the People's Public Security on Mobilization in the Current Period), December 5, 2017, https://perma.cc/3HXC-R5RA.

Public Security further directed a campaign to "guard secrets" and "prevent leaks" (*bao mat, phong gian*) in hamlets, villages, and collectives to weed out counterrevolutionaries.[34]

After reunification in 1975, VCP leadership cemented narrative management as a "critical task" for the police through an administrative document issued by its highest political body, the politburo.[35] Underscoring the importance of popular support, former MPS minister and prime minister Pham Hung, charged with implementing the politburo's policy, noted in his instruction to the MPS, "The work of the police is political." Mass support, he reminded them, would activate a network of informants to aid with police work and, furthermore, would "empower the people to stand up themselves" against criminals and counterrevolutionaries. Of special importance was sustaining the faith of religious and ethnic minorities from the central highlands – the site of a separatist militant movement that had caused friction for nearly three decades alongside Vietnam's international and civil conflicts.[36] The problem, diagnosed Pham Hung, was not of might but of legitimacy. "Mobilizing ethnic minorities is the biggest, most difficult, and most complicated task," he noted. "It requires patience, concrete plans, and deep understanding [of the political, socioeconomic, and cultural factors] to solve issues about their needs, culture, education, medical care. Persuasion is not about force, though force has its usefulness."[37]

Today, the MPS's emblem depicts a sword and a shield, a symbol of the police's roles as "a sharp weapon and a pillar of the Party."[38] The

[34] People's Police Academy, "Phong Trao Toan Dan Bao Ve An Ninh To Quoc Va Kinh Nghiem Rut Ra Doi Voi Cong Tac Van Dong Cua Luc Luong Cong An Nhan Dan" (The History of the Campaigns to Mobilize All Citizens to Protect National Security and Lessons for the People's Police on Mass Mobilization), December 4, 2017, https://perma.cc/8UJE-3D3H.

[35] *Biographies of Vietnam's Party and State Leaders: Pham Hung* (Hanoi: National Political Publishing House, 2007), 220 (citing the VCP politburo's Decision 31-NQ/TW (issued on December 2, 1980), On the Duty to Protect Political Stability, Maintaining Order, and Ensuring Public Safety in Changed Circumstances).

[36] The central highlands' separatist movement *Front unifié de lutte des races opprimées*, or FULRO, translated as the United Liberation Front for the Oppressed Races, comprised a diverse group of Christian montagnards, Muslim Chams, and Hindu Khmer, united by a desire to drive Vietnamese, whether North or South, out of their lands. Stan B-H Tan, "Swiddens, Resettlements, Sedentarizations, and Villages: State Formation among the Central Highlanders of Vietnam under the First Republic, 1955–1961," *Journal of Vietnamese Studies* 1 (2006): 210–252.

[37] *Pham Hung*, 221–222.

[38] Martin Grossheim, "The 'Sword and Shield of the Party': How the Vietnamese People's Public Security Forces Portray Themselves," *Intelligence and National Security* 33(3) (2018): 439–458, at 440 (quoting former VCP general secretary Le Duan).

MPS Central Party Committee (Dang Uy Cong An Trung Uong) – the VCP's unit located within the MPS – is appointed by the politburo and includes both the general secretary of the VCP (who currently also holds the position of state president) and the prime minister. The Central Party Committee, which has vertical units mirroring the MPS at central and local levels, directly oversees the MPS's efforts to promote party policies and ideologies within the agency and to the wider public.[39] As reflected in the VCP's internal rules and in the Law on the People's Public Security, party leadership over the MPS is "absolute and direct on all fronts."[40]

Much remains unknown about the Vietnamese police today, including the number of people on the force. One well-cited estimate puts the number at 1.2 million officers nationwide, with an additional 5 million local self-defense and militia forces overseen by the People's Army of Vietnam.[41] In a major reorganization, the 2018 Law on the People's Public Security sought to professionalize the commune police, who, while largely responsible for law enforcement in rural hamlets and villages, were not deemed official government agents.[42] Faced with increasing complaints about rights violations at rural levels, lawmakers officially placed these semiprofessional groups under the MPS's aegis.

5.3 Narrative Management as a Core Policing Function

This part examines narrative management as a core function of the Vietnamese police in three instances: (1) the warnings against peaceful evolution and self-evolution that were rooted in wartime atmospheres but continue to pervade today's political slogans, (2) the Internet as new ground for ideological policing, and (3) most recently, the Public Security's narrative-shaping roles in grassroots responses to the COVID-19 pandemic. While the first two case studies highlight the

[39] Vietnamese Communist Party Constitution (Dieu Le Dang), Article 25, https://perma.cc/D2M4-K6CF.

[40] Ibid.; Law on the People's Public Security, Article 4, https://perma.cc/5SG2-4JVU.

[41] Carl Thayer, "The Apparatus of Authoritarian Rule in Vietnam," in Jonathan London (ed.), *Politics in Contemporary Vietnam: Party, State and Authority Relations* (London: Palgrave Macmillan, 2010), 135–161, at 137. By comparison, Vietnam employs about 2.5 million people in its public sector. Historian Olga Dror has challenged Thayer's estimates, noting the lack of official sources. See Olga Dror, review of "The 'Sword and Shield of the Party': How the Vietnamese People's Public Security Forces Portray Themselves," by Martin Grossheim, H-Diplo, September 14, 2018, https://perma.cc/9CHZ-MP7E.

[42] Law on the People's Public Security, Articles 17, 45.

MPS's strong grip on ideological control, the third showcases the productive side of a close state–society relationship: when the party-state apparatus acted legitimately and gained public trust, its mobilization workers – the police included – were able to induce high compliance with restrictive public health measures, enabling the nation to avert the worst of a deadly crisis.

5.3.1 *Peaceful Evolution and Self-Evolution*

Throughout Vietnam's history, one potent narrative has been the need to guard against ideological threats from both external enemies and internal institutional weakness. Warnings against the danger of peaceful evolution and self-evolution, which once dominated Vietnam's war slogans, continue to appear in recent political speeches and are explicitly linked to the Internet's outsize reach. As early as the 1970s, VCP leadership had identified peaceful evolution as a principal threat to the DRV's political and national interests. First developed in the 1940s to counterbalance Soviet expansion during the Cold War, the concept referred to a process of gradual regime change through cultural and political influence rather than through force.[43] United States Secretary of State John Forster Dulles employed the phrase in a series of speeches describing strategy against Red China,[44] prompting Mao Zedong to denounce it as a deceptive Western tactic to destroy Socialist achievements.[45] In the 1980s, translated Chinese books and Vietnamese writings that circulated internally among Vietnamese party members, police, and military bureaucrats credited peaceful evolution as the invisible weapon that fell on the USSR's empire, pointing out the corrosive power of ideals such as freedom, democracy, and political pluralism where containment and military force had failed.[46] According to these writings, Khrushchev's policy of peaceful coexistence with the West was evidence that the USSR had been infected by "bourgeois liberation" and strayed from Marxist-Leninist ideologies, leading to its inevitable demise.[47]

[43] Anne-Marie Brady, "Regimenting the Public Mind: The Modernization of Propaganda in the PRC," *International Journal* 57(4) (2002): 565–566.

[44] Ibid.

[45] Chih-Yu Shih, "China's Socialist Law under Reform: The Class Nature Reconsidered," *American Journal of Comparative Law* 44 (1996): 627–646, at 641.

[46] Tuong Vu, *Vietnam's Communist Revolution: The Power and Limit of Ideology* (Cambridge: Cambridge University Press, 2017), 210–215.

[47] Ibid.

The linkage between peaceful evolution and Khrushchev's peaceful coexistence policy resonated with the DRV's own ideological purge in the late 1960s.[48] During this time, as China was amid the fever of its Cultural Revolution, Vietnam launched a campaign against an opposing group within the VCP who had advocated for a more "humanist" approach toward the ongoing civil war against South Vietnam.[49] Known as the Anti-Party Revisionist Affair of 1967, the hunt to investigate and weed out revisionist factions was jointly headed by the MPS and the military. The investigation first turned inward to review and screen all security cadres who were studying and working abroad, resulting in the recall and dismissal of high-ranking officials trained in the USSR who might have been exposed to erroneous Soviet revisionist ideals.[50] The MPS's investigation of civilian cases employed informants and surveillance to identify those with connections or contact with foreigners, resulting in the arrests of hundreds of party cadres and intellectuals, many of whom subsequently underwent reeducation.[51]

Hard crackdowns aside, former Public Security director Tran Quoc Hoan emphasized political education (*tuyen huan*) as a main way to combat ideological threats. From artistic activities such as singing and dance shows (*hoat dong van nghe*) to news, films, and television programs, each represented an opportunity to improve morals within the security force and build up the image of the police as an embodiment of Socialist virtues in public consciousness.[52] Director Hoan instructed that it was no longer sufficient to outsource these public relations functions; the MPS was to build its own in-house public outreach capabilities. In 1964, the MPS published the first issue of its theory-oriented *People's Police Review*, dedicated to its antiespionage missions.[53] In 1967, around the same time that

[48] Martin Grossheim, "The Lao Động Party, Culture and the Campaign against Modern Revisionism: The Democratic Republic of Vietnam Before the Second Indochina War," *Journal of Vietnamese Studies* 8(1) (2013): 80–129.

[49] Lien-Hang T. Nguyen, "Vietnam's Anti-War Movement," *New York Times*, August 25, 2017.

[50] Lien-Hang Nguyen, *Hanoi's War: An International History of the War for Peace in Vietnam* (Chapel Hill, NC: University of North Carolina Press, 2012), 69.

[51] Ibid.; Grossheim, "The Lao Động Party," 98–100.

[52] "Cong Tac Tuyen Huan Trong Tam Nhien Chien Luoc Cua Bo Truong Tran Quoc Hoan" (Propaganda as a Strategy of Minister Tran Quoc Hoan), *People's Police Magazine*, January 13, 2016.

[53] "Tap Chi Cong An Nhan Dan Phan Dau De Xung Dang La Co Quan Ly Luan Chinh Tri, Nghiep Vu Cua Dang Uy Cong An Trung Uong Va Bo Cong An" (The *People's Police Magazine* Strives to Become the Political, Ideological Arm of the MPS and Its Central Party Committee), *People's Police Magazine*, June 25, 2009.

the Anti-Party Revisionist Affairs were underway, the MPS created the Department of Political Affairs, with goals to strengthen its curriculum on VCP ideologies. Today, the MPS oversees multiple public engagement outlets, including two print mediums, a publishing house, a television network, and a museum. As reported in the state-run *Nhan Dan* (*People*) magazine, these departments employ nearly 1,300 personnel, 800 of whom are card-carrying journalists.[54]

The focus on ideology intensified during Vietnam's reform era. In 1986, following a decade of severe economic hardship, the VCP's Sixth National Congress launched *doi moi* ("renovation") – a comprehensive reform program to overhaul its economy and administrative state. The goal of *doi moi* was to liberate the country's "productive forces" in order to increase national production "while remaining within the orbit of socialism."[55] The politburo had made clear that, to renovate the economy, the focus on war and struggle must give way to an emphasis on "peace and international cooperation." Now that Vietnam had unified, it was no longer foreign invasions but "economic weaknesses, political isolation, and economic blockade [that were] major threats to [the] country's security and independence."[56]

The narrative of a young nation under threats remained salient and ran concurrent to the emphasis on economic development. The VCP's 1994 Party Congress named peaceful evolution one of four threats against national security (albeit the last), following, in order, economic backwardness (*tut hau*), the loss of Socialist orientations, and corruption.[57] Reports of the VCP's Tenth Party Congress in 2006 repeated this list of concerns even as they reaffirmed the policy of "proactive, active international economic integration" and "international cooperation in all fields."[58] In 2016, official VCP documents added "self-evolution" and "self-transformation" to the list of perceived threats. If peaceful evolution is about external influence, then self-evolution refers to internal weaknesses in party cadres' ideologies, which in turn lead to decaying morals. A think piece published in the *Communist Review* identified three main reasons for self-evolution: (1) globalization and capitalism, which have imported hostile values, especially through the Internet; (2) continued efforts by capitalist nations to

54 Ibid.

55 Nguyen Manh Hung, *New Context of Vietnam's National Security Challenges* (Singapore: ISEAS Publishing, 2016), 6.

56 Ibid., 6–7.

57 Ibid., 10–11.

58 Ibid., 7.

denigrate socialist values through concepts such as democracy, human rights, and multiparty systems; and (3) weaknesses in the existing system of ideological education, which lead to corruption, decaying morals, and loss of legitimacy.[59] Security forces were themselves susceptible to these personal failings; to boost their "immunization," policemen and woman, starting with the rank and file, had to strengthen their own ideology and retrue their moral compass.[60]

Thought work against these threats intensified during the period leading up to the amendments to the Vietnamese Constitution in 2013. During the public comment period, various groups, including legal academics, former party officials, and religious leaders, submitted comments on the draft constitution. A group of seventy-two prominent Vietnamese intellectuals, led by constitutional law scholar and former minister of justice Dr. Nguyen Dinh Loc, published a petition, now known as Petition 72, advocating for, among other items, the abolishment of the VCP's exclusive leadership over the administrative state, depoliticization of the military and the police, a constitutional court, and universal human rights.[61] Anchoring itself to Vietnam's first constitution, the group advocated for an embrace of liberal values alongside Socialist ones, as Ho Chi Minh did in 1946.[62] In return, army and MPS-affiliated journals and publications labeled the petition a product of outside influence aiming to delegitimize the armed forces by decoupling them from the party's moral leadership.[63]

5.3.2 Ideological Threats in the Internet Era

The rapid, exponential expansion of the Internet in Vietnam complicated the VCP's fixation on narrative control. A latecomer to the Internet – its public did not have online access until 1997 – Vietnam now boasts one

[59] "Chong Dien Bien Hoa Binh, Tu Dien Bien, Tu Chuyen Hoa Trong Noi Bo – Mot So Van De Dat Ra Doi Voi Luc Luong Cong An Nhan Dan Giai Doan Hien Nay" (Peaceful Evolution, Self Evolution, Self Transformation in Party Cadres – Some Issues with the People's Police Today), *Communist Review*, September 10, 2019.

[60] "Phong Ngua Tu Dien Bien, Tu Chuyen Hoa Trong Cong An Nhan Dan" (Preventing Self Evolution, Self Transformation in the People's Police), *People's Police Magazine*, October 26, 2017.

[61] Bui Ngoc Son and Pip Nicholson, "Activism and Popular Constitutionalism in Contemporary Vietnam," *Law and Social Inquiry* 42(3) (2017): 677–710.

[62] Ibid.

[63] "Phong, Chong Khuynh Huong 'Phi Chinh Tri Hoa Luc Luong Vu Trang' O Nuoc Ta Hien Nay" (Prevent, Combat Calls for Depoliticization of Armed Forces in Our Country), *Ministry of Public Security Gazette*, December 27, 2016.

of the highest Internet penetration rates worldwide.[64] Today, over half of its nearly 100 million people are on the Internet, and it is ranked seventh among countries with the highest number of Facebook users.[65] Very early on, the VCP was confronted with the question of how to both facilitate and constrain access to the Internet, which it recognized as essential to attract commercial and investment activities. Of great concern was access to discourse by Vietnamese expatriates in the US and elsewhere, many of whom had supported the Republic of Vietnam and fled as refugees after the DRV took over the South in 1975. VCP leaders debated these concerns at the Eighth Party Congress in 1996, characterizing information control as a twin goal of economic development: "Development must couple with good management of mass communications. … Internet access can improve international connection; at the same time it needs to be limited to prevent negative activities occurring through the network."[66] Following this formulation, subsequent legal documents granting permits to Internet infrastructure construction included broad statements that Internet growth in Vietnam must follow the principle of "matching management to development … to prevent activities that use the Internet to negatively affect national security, ethics, and cultural norms."[67] During this period, as Vietnam started to vie for membership in the World Trade Organization, the VCP further made clear that rapid development of information infrastructure was a top priority.[68]

The MPS's role was accordingly expanded. While earlier legal documents had delegated licensing and technological gatekeeping responsibilities to organs such as the Department of Post and Services and the Ministry of Information and Communication, Decree 55, issued in

64 Freedom House, Freedom on the Net 2020, Vietnam Country Profile, https://perma.cc/65KQ-LBXC.

65 Statista, "Leading Countries Based on Number of Facebook Users as of October 2020 (in Millions)," https://perma.cc/WFR7-K2GH; Statista, "Number of Facebook Users in Vietnam from 2017 to 2023 (in Millions)," June 5, 2020, https://perma.cc/2CZ8-WJGS.

66 Office of the Government of the Socialist Republic of Vietnam, Report of the Central Committee, Eighth Party Congress (Bao Cao Chinh Tri Cua Ban Chap Hanh Trung Uong Dang), *Phat Huy Suc Manh Toan Dan Toc, Tiep Tuc Doi Moi, Day Manh Cong Nghiep Hoa, Hien Dai Hoa, Xay Dung Va Bao Ve To Quoc Viet Nam Xa Hoi Chu Nghia* (*Promote National Strength, Innovation, Industrialization, Modernization, Build and Protect the Socialist Vietnam's Motherland*).

67 Office of the Government of the Socialist Republic of Vietnam, Decree No. 55/2001/ND-CP on the Management, Provision and Use of Internet Services, August 23, 2001, Article 3.

68 Vietnam Communist Party Politburo, Directive No. 58-CT/TW on Stepping Up the Application and Development of Information Technologies in the Cause of Industrialization and Modernization in the 2001–2005 period, October 17, 2000.

2001, officially named the MPS as the main agency to "maintain national security with regards to internet activities."[69] Subsequent decrees reaffirmed the MPS's role on Internet censorship, with an increasing focus on blogs and social media sites.[70] Police responsibility was expanded to include the authority to "organize, direct, and guide the collection, discovery, investigation, and analysis of information, documents, and activities" occurring online to the extent that they could be deemed subversive to national security.[71] This expansion in responsibility was further reflected in the MPS's human resources. As it gained jurisdiction over the Internet, the MPS created two specialized units to deal with online threats. The Department of High-tech Crime Prevention, established in 2010, focuses on illicit cyberactivity, including online gambling, fraud, and financial crime; the Department of Internet Security, established in 2014, manages and censors online content deemed harmful to the VCP and to national interests.[72] The 2018 Law on Cybersecurity merged these two units into a cybersecurity department, with a direct reporting line to MPS leadership.[73]

The 2018 Cybersecurity Law places the MPS at the center of the VCP's Internet management efforts. With a mission to "protect national security and social order in cyberspace," the new law defines cybersecurity as "online activities that do not cause harm to national security, social orders, and the rights and legal privileges of organizations and individuals."[74] Unlike the 2015 Law on Cyberinformation Security, which focuses on breach of data privacy, data theft, and infringement of intellectual property, the 2018 Cybersecurity Law legalizes a stronghold on content management. Pursuant to the new law, foreign companies that "provide services on the telecommunication network, internet, and other value-added services on the Internet in Vietnam" are required to maintain a data presence as well as a physical presence in Vietnam,

[69] Office of the Government of the Socialist Republic of Vietnam, Decree No. 55/2001/ND-CP on the Management, Provision and Use of Internet Services, August 23, 2001, Article 33.

[70] Office of the Government of the Socialist Republic of Vietnam, Decree No. 97/2008/ND-CP on the Management, Provision and Use of Internet Services and Electronic Information on the Internet, August 28, 2008; Office of the Government of the Socialist Republic of Vietnam, Decree No. 72/2013/ND-CP on Management, Provision, and Use of Internet Services and Information Content Online, July 15, 2013.

[71] Decree No. 72/2013/ND-CP, Article 39(2).

[72] BBC Vietnam, "Viet Nam Thanh Lap Cuc An Ninh Mang" [Vietnam Creates a Department of Internet Security], August 29, 2014, https://perma.cc/MGC7-EW4R.

[73] National Assembly on Cyber Security, Law on Cybersecurity, 24/2018/QH14, June 12, 2018.

[74] Ibid., Articles 1, 2.

either in the form of a branch or a representative.[75] Critically, wherever they are located, companies must also cooperate with the authorities to provide information on their users when a user is investigated or deemed in breach of Vietnamese laws.[76] While the law appears to most clearly target Internet provider platforms such as Facebook and YouTube, its broad language has caused concerns among nontech companies who provide online services to clients in Vietnam (e.g. banks, airlines, and hotels).[77]

As with most laws in Vietnam, clarification of ambiguities will come in the form of implementation decrees prepared by the MPS. No drafts have yet been made public as of this writing in December 2020, and little is known about the MPS's approaches on how to interpret and implement the new law. There is little doubt, however, that the MPS's ownership of the implementation process signifies a marked expansion of its jurisdiction and power over Vietnam's highly contested cyberspace.[78]

5.3.3 COVID-19 and Grassroots Policing

While the examples given so far focus on the extent to which the VCP and the MPS exercise various forms of ideological control, the following discussion highlights the productive roles that the police can play in a close-knit state–society relationship when the state acts with transparency and accountability. The COVID-19 pandemic hit Vietnam earlier than most other countries, with the first cases discovered just before the Lunar New Year, at around the same time as the first lockdown in Wuhan.[79]

75 Ibid., Article 1.

76 Ibid., Article 26.

77 Timothy McLaughlin, "Under Vietnam's New Cybersecurity Law, U.S. Tech Giants Face Stricter Censorship," *Washington Post*, March 16, 2019.

78 The MPS is not the only agency tasked with monitoring online content. In January 2018, the Ministry of Defense announced the creation of its cyberspace unit to "protect Vietnam's sovereignty on the internet," citing as a factor risks related to the South China Sea dispute. Just a month before, a general in the People's Army had announced the operation of a "public opinion brigade," known colloquially as Force 47, comprising 10,000 individuals. Little public information exists on how these various entities overlap in their functions and jurisdictions. See "Hon 10000 Nguoi Trong Luc Luong 47 Dau Tranh Tren Mang" (Over 10,000 Individuals Are Part of Force 47's Online Combat Group), *Tuoi Tre News*, December 25, 2017; "Bo Quoc Phong Cong Bo Quyet Dinh Thanh Lap Bo Tu Len Tac Chien Khong Gian Mang" (The Ministry of Defense Announced the Creation of a Command on Online Warfare), *People's Army Online*, January 8, 2018.

79 Letter to the Editors, "Importation and Human-to-Human Transmission of a Novel Coronavirus in Vietnam," *New England Journal of Medicine* 382 (2020): 872–874.

At the time of this writing (December 2020), Vietnam has registered just above 1,400 confirmed cases and thirty-five deaths, making it the third-safest country in the world, about 2,500 times less deadly than the United States.[80] Having experienced SARS and MERS, and forecasting an inevitable spread owing to its numerous geographical, economic, and migration ties with China, the Vietnamese government swiftly implemented restrictive measures, including border closures, extensive contact tracing, and forced mass quarantine.[81] The MPS played and continues to play a critical role in the government's COVID-19 response – one that evoked wartime exigencies, characterized the virus as a "foreign enemy," and sought to revive a mass mobilization campaign to induce compliance with restrictive measures.[82]

From the very start, the MPS was a key part of the Vietnamese government's COVID-19 efforts. Established in January 2020, the national COVID-19 steering committee included high-ranking officials across ministries, mass organizations, the army, and the police, as well as representatives from the media and information technology companies.[83] The MPS established its own steering committee, headed by the deputy minister. Subsequently, police officers at all levels of government were directed to actively participate in disease prevention and control, including following public health leaders' mandates. While the army was tasked with refitting military bases into quarantine camps for inbound travelers, Public Security forces were in charge of grassroots surveillance and mobilization to identify and isolate local outbreaks (*di tung ngo, go tung nha, ra tung truong hop*: "visit each alley, knock on each door, go over each case").[84] In addition to enforcing face-covering and quarantine rules,

[80] Johns Hopkins University & Medicine, Coronavirus Resource Center, "Mortality Analysis," https://coronavirus.jhu.edu/data/mortality (accessed December 24, 2020). Mortality rates are calculated per 100,000 people.

[81] Trang (Mae) Nguyen and Edmund Malesky, "Reopening Vietnam: How the Country's Improving Governance Helped It Weather the COVID-19 Pandemic," Brookings Institution, May 20, 2020, www.brookings.edu/blog/order-from-chaos/2020/05/20/reopening-vietnam-how-the-countrys-improving-governance-helped-it-weather-the-covid-19-pandemic/.

[82] Ibid.

[83] Office of the Government of the Socialist Republic of Vietnam, Decree No. 170/QD-Ttg on the Creation of the National Steering Committee to Prevent, Manage a Respiratory Infection Disease Caused by a New Coronavirus, January 30, 2020.

[84] Ministry of Public Security News, "Bo Cong An So Ket Cong Tac Phong, Chong Dich COVID-19 Trong Luc Luong Cong An Nhan Dan Nam 2020" (The Ministry of Public Security Reviews 2020 Tasks on COVID-19 Preventions and Management), December 21, 2020.

local police officers, together with medical personnel and neighborhood committee members, participated in grassroots efforts to publicize top-down COVID-19 policies, often by knocking on doors and talking face to face with the citizens in their allocated jurisdictions. They also distributed face masks, hand wash and sanitizers, even food and essential items to communities under temporary mass quarantine. It helps that grassroots mobilization is already a part of the responsibilities of frontline community policing, where officers are tasked with visiting homes and getting to know the identities and circumstances of people in their administrative units – a way of intelligence gathering that became critical for contact tracing efforts.[85] As one ward police officer described, "In Vietnam we consider the relationship between the police and the community the most important, so we only use the law if needed."[86]

Narrative management, as mentioned before, is an important component of grassroot policing. In the context of COVID-19, delivering public services and protecting public health directly impact the legitimacy of the VCP. In August 2020, the MPS's Central Party Committee issued a directive reiterating the MPS's roles within the larger national public health response.[87] Education through communication, noted the directive, "is a major battleground to motivate the entire people, in order to maintain social stability and security as we fight the disease."[88] This directive was implemented through two prongs in narrative management. First, in line with frontline policing as described earlier, security forces were mobilized to provide information to the community on the VCP's rapidly changing COVID-19 directives and policies, thereby enabling better transparency. In providing essential public services and public health messaging, police officers relayed these actions within the narrative of a determined leadership, which, against all odds, was able to protect and provide for its populace when more prosperous nations have failed. Second, the MPS actively investigated crimes associated with the pandemic, including the spread of misinformation on patients or with

[85] For an insightful description of the roles of the local police in response to another epidemic (HIV prevention), see Melissa Jardine, Nick Crofts, Geoff Monaghan, and Martha Morrow, "Harm Reduction and Law Enforcement in Vietnam: Influences on Street Policing," *Harm Reduction Journal* 9 (2012): 1–10, at 2, https://doi.org/10.1186/1477-7517-9-27.

[86] Ibid., 6.

[87] Ministry of Public Security, Central Party Committee, Directive 04-CT/DUCA on Increasing Preventive Measures against the COVID-19 Pandemic in New Circumstances, August 8, 2020.

[88] Ibid.

respect to the party-state's national response. As a pun on COVID-19, official news started analogizing the threat of peaceful evolution to a virus that "attacks each organization, work unit, and individual, to weaken ideological beliefs and convictions, sow chaos to our lives and emotions, leading to doubts with regards to the Party's leadership."[89] The best vaccine against this ideological virus was to strengthen supervision and control at the local levels to ensure that local bureaucrats act with morality, not only with law and logic but also with "sentiment" (*hop tinh hop ly*) to rebuild popular trust and support. The news report concluded, "The success of our fight against COVID-19 can be applied in the continued fight against the ideological virus."[90]

Vietnam's experience with the COVID-19 pandemic highlights the achievement of a close state–society relationship when the party-state acts with transparency and legitimacy, which has, in turn, boosted trust and confidence from the public. Public Security forces play a critical role in the party-state's COVID-19 success, both in the hard measures of quarantine enforcement and punishment and in the soft measures of grassroots mobilization. At the same time that the Vietnamese government prioritizes strategic transparency with regard to its COVID-19 policies, it continues to advance ideological narratives and heavily punish criticisms of government actions. While Vietnam's improving governance has helped it weather the COVID-19 pandemic and enabled the reopening of its society and economy ahead of most peers, continued transparency and public support for bureaucratic work, including police work, will remain critical as Vietnamese leaders continue to grapple with balancing the core pillars of its legitimacy, which now includes public health in addition to economic growth and social stability.

5.4 Conclusion

Patrolling at the frontier of state–society relations with deep roots extending into each, Vietnam's Public Security typifies some of the key themes of authoritarian policing astutely drawn out by the diverse chapters in this book. First, the Vietnamese police is entwined with Vietnam's single ruling party institutionally, functionally, and ideologically. The

[89] Vietnam Fatherland Front, "Fight the Peaceful Evolution Virus: Boost Immunization, Prevent a Toxic Virus" (Chong Virus Dien Bien Hoa Binh: Tang Cuong Suc De Khang, Dap Tat Virus Doc Hai), April 6, 2020, https://perma.cc/GEC4-RF6R.

[90] Ibid.

VCP's unit located within the MPS includes the party's highest-ranking leaders, and likewise the head of Public Security is a member of the VCP's highest political unit. The VCP's leadership over the MPS is institutionalized in Vietnam's constitution, the MPS's organic law, and the VCP's internal rules. The police's legitimacy and that of the party-state are mutually reinforcing, and the police's thought work against real and perceived ideological threats can cut both ways on legitimation. Second, like other authoritarian policing institutions, the MPS is tasked with powers and obligations that extend well beyond conventional policing. In addition to ordinary police functions, the MPS carries out a wide range of mandates that reflect the VCP's priorities, including regime survival (by recruiting members to the communist cause), evolving perception of threats (e.g. the recent Cybersecurity Law), and social change (saliently shown through the COVID-19 pandemic). Finally, the police's extensive penetration into society – a form of grassroots policing – can be both productive and uneasy. The police's presence at each administrative level of society facilitated surveillance and control that can, and have, turned repressive. Yet Vietnam's experience with the COVID-19 pandemic also demonstrates that a close relationship between state agents and society is critical for effective mobilization and compliance. The key variable is public trust, gained through transparency and responsive governance – values not often associated with a nondemocratic regime. Improving governance, transparency, and public support for bureaucratic work, including police work, will remain critical as Vietnam charts its way through a shifting global order.

6

Unrestrained but Limited

Policing Vagrancy in Authoritarian Seoul

ERIK MOBRAND

A feature of authoritarian regimes is that police roles can sprawl. A regime with strong control over coercive forces – and few restraints on how those forces are used – may deploy police to accomplish a range of tasks. These tasks may include dealing with dissent, as well as more mundane aspects of rule. Police stand, after all, on the front line of relations between the state and society. How do police cope with expanding responsibilities? Are police effective agents of social transformation in authoritarian settings?

South Korea's past offers an example of an authoritarian context in which police roles proliferated. Besides maintaining order, police officers were deployed for all sorts of purposes. They kept tabs on the opposition and on activists. They broke protests. When housing was to be cleared, police were called in to assist with demolition. They checked the prices of goods in markets in order to ensure that price policies were being followed. Police were positioned as representatives of a state that had, in the 1960s and 1970s, ambitious plans for remaking society. Police were backed by extensive coercive forces, including the intelligence agency and one of the world's largest standing armies.

While the police role in suppressing dissent is well documented, in part because it sparked such outrage, less attention has been given to the ways police managed other aspects of state–society relations on an everyday basis. This chapter uses the policing of vagrancy in authoritarian Seoul as a lens through which to view this subject. Police assumed responsibility for the main areas of administration of the city's large underclass. In fighting crime and working to modernize the city, police took on the task of providing for the welfare of the city's most desperate residents. To prevent petty crime organizations, police established job centers for youths. To fight prostitution, police managed facilities where young women could learn trades. Providing rudimentary forms of welfare became tasks for police, a point that has largely gone unnoticed in studies of welfare in South Korea.

The expansion of police responsibilities, though, stretched police resources. In order to attend to their many tasks, police relied on delegates with no formal authority and on irregular procedures. Massive queues in summary courts meant insufficient space in police cells. Police turned to campaign-like crackdowns in which many suspects were rounded up at once, then a few charged. Measures such as these contributed to maintaining social order but avoided regular legal procedures. Given numerous, complex tasks, police struggled as agents of the state's social engineering initiatives. These observations point to a situation of unrestrained power that was also, effectively, limited.

6.1 Unrestrained but Limited: Policing Vagrancy in Authoritarian Seoul

The South Korean state of the 1960s and 1970s boasted impressive coercive resources. Many of these, at times, were deployed against its own society. The country had one of the largest standing armies. Figures with a military background ran the government. A feared intelligence agency was developed in the early 1960s. The National Security Law provided grounds for detaining people without due process. At times, security forces operated without regard for the law at all. The police agency, founded in the colonial period, was among these security forces.

While police were used for purposes of stifling dissent and haranguing perceived opponents of the authoritarian regime, the police also had more mundane tasks. This chapter examines how the police in Seoul discharged these tasks in the 1960s and 1970s. In this period, encounters between police and ordinary Seoulites were among the most covered topics in newspapers. It was in these encounters that most people saw, or had direct experience with, police.

In a rapidly growing city and with a leadership that had ambitions for social transformation, police roles in Seoul proliferated. Police assumed responsibility for the main areas of administration of the city's large underclass. In fighting crime and working to modernize the city, police took on tasks of providing for the welfare of the city's most desperate residents. To prevent petty crime organizations, police established job centers for youths. To fight prostitution, police corralled young women into facilities where they could learn trades. Rudimentary forms of welfare became tasks for police, a point that has largely gone unnoticed in studies of welfare in South Korea. How do the police cope with expanding responsibilities? Are they effective agents of social transformation in authoritarian settings?

Operating in an authoritarian regime, the police faced few constraints on their power from the government. Respecting the civil liberties of individuals was not a high priority. However, in the context of expanding responsibilities in a developing city, the police faced serious limits on their activities. These limits were not constitutional but imposed by the informal networks they encountered.

6.1.1 Authoritarian Policing and Informal Authority

Authoritarianism is usually depicted as a form of rule involving few rules. A regime follows its whims, disconnected from laws or norms. The South Korean state of the 1960s and 1970s is usually portrayed this way, as a body removed from society. It was an "autonomous" organization,[1] able to make its own decisions and then impose those on society. Discussions of the country's economic transformation begin with such a description. The national police agency has been described the same way. There is some basis to this characterization. The police agency can be treated as a foreign imposition, poorly grounded in Korean society. It is a descendant of the colonial-era police force, and was put back together by the Americans after 1945. Then the agency was wielded by illiberal and eventually downright dictatorial governments. It was also used for political purposes to harass those perceived as opponents of the regime. South Korea's police force in the authoritarian era has been studied alongside other tools of state violence.[2] The police seems to be one of the state institutions most suitably described as separate from society.

However, in discharging their duties, police in a developing society are anything but removed from society. In Seoul in this period, police were the front line of managing social issues. Through their positions on the streets, they confronted all of the problems of a rapidly changing society. In a quickly expanding city, they had to manage growing forms of criminality. Furthermore, working for a regime with ambitious plans to appear "modern," police were often assigned to deal with the cluttering of public

[1] Peter B. Evans, *Embedded Autonomy: States and Industrial Transformation* (Princeton, NJ: Princeton University Press, 1995).

[2] Shenna Greitens, *Dictators and Their Secret Police: Coercive Institutions and State Violence* (New York: Cambridge University Press, 2016).

space by "undesirables." In carrying out such tasks, Seoul's police were charged with a transformative purpose. As deLisle notes in this volume, it has not been uncommon for states in the region to involve the police in transformative projects.[3]

The task of managing these issues involved not only a proliferation of roles, but it also put police into contestation with informal systems of authority. Street gangs saw opportunities in the growing city. They could recruit from among the needy and vulnerable. Private coercive organizations could be more convincing than the police, not only because they could be more threatening. Gangs were involved in more lucrative activities, ranging from extortion of businessmen, entertainers, and residents to intimidation of debtors to petty theft. Destitute people could be useful to them as followers or as sources of income. Coercive organizations took boys out of government shelters, and offered them protection in return for a portion of their earnings from shining shoes or selling gum. They tempted government-run job introduction agents into selling girls to them for resale in the profitable red light districts. Unlike police and state administrators, gangs could use markets to gain from the poorest.

The police faced a situation in which they could battle these informal networks or cooperate with them. In practice, neither of these options worked well on its own; a combination was almost always likeliest. Developing ties to information authority structures could provide the police with information that made keeping order a more regular task. It is useful to think of them as enmeshed in these informal systems of power.[4]

Scholarship on police and criminality in other parts of East Asia has described similar forms of competition, and cooperation, between police and criminal groups. In Republican-era China, for example, chaos and commerce contributed to the ballooning roles of both police and underworld organizations. Political parties sought to gain support from, or intimidate, residents. Secret societies, with their deep reach into communities and labor unions, could play a linking role. Shanghai's Green Gang was the most notorious of such groups, and the Kuomintang saw its value for trying to win control.[5] Although Korea

[3] Jacques deLisle, Chapter 14 in this volume.

[4] On criminality and a relational perspective on state power, see Edward Aspinall and Gerry van Klinken, "Introduction," in Aspinall and van Klinken (eds.), *The State and Illegality in Indonesia* (Leiden: Brill, 2011): 1–30.

[5] For accounts of policing and criminal activity in this period, see Parks Coble, *The Shanghai Capitalists and the Nationalist Government, 1927–1937* (Cambridge, MA: Council on East Asian Studies, Harvard University and Harvard University Press, 1980).

has never had underworld groups with the pedigree of their Chinese counterparts, who could draw on longer histories and connections to the anti-Qing movement, Seoul by the 1960s was a site of confrontation over regular (and especially vulnerable) people between police and criminal groups.

The multiplication of police functions can be found in other contexts. In Taiwan, too, police took on a wide range of administrative and service-related roles. Observing this expansion in tasks, Chen notes that the expansion of police roles – in combination with the division between secret and civil police – helped give the police legitimacy.[6] Because the police officers that most people interacted with most of the time were helpful and uninterested in monitoring for dissidents, ordinary Taiwanese came to respect the police force.

If Chen's argument about legitimacy elucidates an informal source of strength for a police force, then other effects of informal police relations in society might also be identified. Attention to the position of police in informal systems of power points toward the practical limits on authoritarian policing, illustrated here through the context of Seoul in the 1960s and 1970s. There is a possibility of a mode of policing under authoritarianism that is unrestrained but limited. The political context, and the historical origins of the police organization, may give the police license to use unrestrained force in carrying out their work. The stories of individuals can corroborate such a view, as police could be unjustly and extremely violent. If police are understood in relation to informal authority, and a broader perspective is taken, then limits appear. In practice, because they came up against – and sometimes worked through – informal authority networks, their actual power and range of options could be limited.

These points relate to other work on policing, including in this volume. A distinction appears in several chapters in this volume between functions of suppressing organized resistance and managing day-to-day affairs. Martin's chapter on Taiwan and Hong Kong, for example, addresses police management of organized political movement.[7] Police in South Korea have, of course, also performed that role. The focus in this chapter, however, is on other policing tasks. A further distinction can be drawn between policing a city for local purposes as opposed to for wider geopolitical purposes. Ng, in his chapter on Hong Kong,

[6] Chen, "Chapter 8 in this volume."
[7] Martin, Chapter 7.

reveals that media censorship in that city was historically less a local matter than an international one.[8] Policing in Seoul could be studied in a similar way. Police agencies were entangled in Cold War geopolitics. Organized criminals could be deployed to fight for those in power against alleged communists. However, the significance of these wider conflicts for policing Seoul was far from constant over time. In the late 1940s, especially during the period of rule by an American army government, counterintelligence officials and police coordinated with street criminals to defeat leftists.[9] Later, such cooperation declined. By the 1960s, policing the capital was a local, and sometimes national, matter. None of this is to say that the policing discussed here was apolitical or merely administrative. Rather, police were wrapped up in forms of politics other than monitoring or suppression of outright dissent.

6.1.2 Informal Authority on Seoul's Streets in the Early 1960s

The period examined in this chapter was the era of rule by former general Park Chung Hee. After a military coup in 1961, Park eventually assumed control. Civilian rule returned in 1963, but with Park as the elected president. By the end of the 1960s, Park had revised the constitution to extend his stay in office, then a period of hardened dictatorship came in the 1970s, as direct presidential elections were suspended. The 1960s and 1970s saw massive social and economic transformation, as people departed agriculture for other work. Seoul at this time was one of the fastest growing big cities the world has ever seen.

The 1961 coup had major implications for the informal networks of authority in Seoul that police encountered. Since the colonial period, petty gangs and protection rackets had been part of life in central Seoul. They took money from merchants, ran entertainment areas, and gave the police a hard time. After the coup, though, the junta sought to reorganize governmental control over society. This effort involved restructuring merchant associations, rounding up criminals, shuffling administrative personnel, and severing gangsters from their sources of income. The concentrated attempt to deepen state authority over social organization in these months set the stage for efforts to battle private coercion over the following two decades.

8 Ng, Chapter 12.

9 Erik Mobrand, "The Street Leaders of Seoul and the Foundations of the South Korean Political Order," *Modern Asian Studies* 50(2) (March 2016): 636–674.

The coup leaders had particular reasons to crack down on these informal leaders. Underworld figures were implicated in the scandals that had led to the collapse of South Korea's first republic in 1960. A criminal group had cozied up with the then-ruling Liberal Party. Led by a figure with ties to a major market association in Seoul, the group helped the Liberal Party to harass opponents.[10] In response to protests against electoral corruption, this group unleashed violence on student demonstrators. The brazen and barbaric attack – in broad daylight – spelled the end of the Liberal Party government that had Syngman Rhee at its helm. Police inaction in the face of violence against supporters of Rhee's political rivals revealed links between police and gangsters, both working in the service of the Liberal regime. The April 19 attack on students from Korea University involved planning by actors as high as Rhee's personal bodyguard.[11] The protests became remembered as the April Revolution and continue to be remembered as South Korea's first democracy movement. In launching the coup a year later, Park and his colleagues claimed to carry the mantle of the April Revolution. The thugs who had worked for the Liberal Party, known as "political gangsters" (*chŏngch'i kkangp'ae*), were a target for purging bad elements from a prior regime.

Just after the coup, these political gangsters were rounded up. Only five days after the coup, 167 such figures wearing nametags were paraded down the main avenues of Seoul under military escort.[12] The top few leaders, whose involvement in the violence of April 19, 1960 was highlighted, faced quick trials and were executed by the end of the year.

At the same time, police tracked down and detained the staffs of the highest profile gangsters and leaders of lesser organized crime rings. The police caught 39 leaders of organizations running markets and entertainment facilities in Seoul in the first week after the coup.[13] The military leaders had declared that arrest warrants were not necessary for placing criminals in custody. By early June, 10,000 known criminals were gathered from the streets. One-tenth of these were sent to labor for national construction projects in mountainous Kangwon province, after promising to give up crime.[14] This would be the beginning of repeated drives

[10] Mobrand, "The Street Leaders of Seoul."
[11] *Korea Times* (KT), May 10, 1960.
[12] KT, May 23, 1961.
[13] KT, May 25, 1961.
[14] KT, June 6, 1961.

to round-up criminals and send them to work on public projects under supervision in other parts of the country.[15]

The new military leaders also attacked criminal organizations' sources of income. An important base for these organizations was the illicit entertainment sector. At the end of June, 1961, Seoul's prostitutes were declared free of debt and were encouraged to leave their occupation.[16] The city quickly set up a guidance center to take in the women leaving red light districts. This attack on investors in the entertainment industry seemed to have some effect, as groups of prostitutes went to the police asking for protection.[17] Some were given tickets back to their homes in the countryside, and by the end of June, seventy-four prostitutes had been sent home.[18] In November, the enactment of an anti-prostitution law again cleared workers in this sector of debt, and by this time rehabilitation centers with opportunities for learning vocational skills had been set up for the women.[19] In 1962, the city did a survey of prostitutes and ordered 4,326 of them to enter institutions. Of these, nearly 3,500 went home and most of the rest were handed over to relatives and friends. Only 171 entered guidance centers.[20] These methods had holes, as one-third of those sent home in the 15 months after the coup were later arrested in the city again.[21] But the fact that police caught the same people multiple times suggests that their crackdown on prostitution was fairly comprehensive, even if rehabilitation measures were not enduring.

The military regime's fight to restructure relations with the streets in the months following the coup did clearly have some success. The executions of a handful of important informal leaders who linked street organization to political offices were key in eliminating old power structures. But the new regime also lacked the resources to govern entirely without the help of private coercive agencies. Several chief "political gangsters" of the Liberal era were handed death sentences and then quietly released. Others were given short sentences. After the 1961 expansion of governmental

15 The practice of campaigns to gather known toughs from the street was not an innovation of the military regime but was a police technique carried over from earlier times.

16 KT, June 20, 1961.

17 See KT, June 21, 1961.

18 KT, June 30, 1961.

19 KT, November 10, 1961.

20 Mun Sŏn-hwa. "Han'guk yullak yŏsŏng sŏndo saŏp e taehan sogo" (A Look at Guidance Projects for Korea's Prostitutes). Social Work Research Association, Yihwa Women's University, *Sahoe saŏp (Social Work)* 5 (1970): 140–141.

21 KT, August 12, 1962.

power, these underworld leaders rebuilt their networks and reemerged in later years.[22] Midlevel figures in criminal organizations, as well as their followers, probably remained for the most part unscathed in the aftermath of the coup, even though their activities were temporarily halted. The police administration could not keep all of those detained locked up for long periods. Most were simply rounded up and soon released. Those who were sent to national construction projects also returned quickly, apparently unreformed.

What the gathering of hoodlums in 1961 did do was familiarize police with local crooks, and give the former increased leverage over the latter. With police discretion given freer rein, police could make life miserable for uncooperative criminals, even though – or perhaps because – they could not punish them all. The coup gave police more resources to serve state goals, but not enough to eliminate criminal organizations. Techniques such as campaigns made police familiar with criminals and scarcity of resources made police able to dole out leniency to whom they chose. This situation created conditions for police patronage of organized crime, though with more police leverage than under the pre-coup regimes. These relationships were crucial for the way police operated in subsequent years. Their significance can be seen by examining several of the areas of daily work for police.

6.1.3 Vagrant Youths

A major task for police was dealing with people who loitered or appeared idle in central Seoul. As more young people poured into the city, the streets filled with all sorts of figures looking for a way up in life. These were mostly not criminal, but they could easily become entangled in groups that were linked to illegal activities. Besides any criminal connection, city and national officials disliked the disorder on the streets. They wanted a city that was better organized and more "modern" in appearance. These agendas pushed police toward dealing with issues such as vagrant youths.

The presence of orphans on Seoul's streets in the early 1960s signaled that recovery from the Korean War was not entirely complete. As the decade wore on, however, war orphans were increasingly replaced by teenagers who had fled their rural homes for the city. Seoul authorities treated runaways from the countryside as a serious social problem during the 1960s and 1970s. Every day, several young people would show up at the train

[22] See, for example, KT, August 22, 1970.

station in Seoul with no clear idea of where to go. Some claimed to have relatives in the city but were unable to find them. Those without prearranged accommodations in Seoul ended up milling around the train station.

Many street children earned a living by offering marginal services, such as selling gum or collecting cigarette butts. Boys shone shoes or sold newspapers. Girls had fewer options than boys, but hoped to find work as housemaids or bus conductresses. A portion of these children were homeless. Seoul at this time had some 6,000 to 10,000 homeless boys.[23] The remainder belonged to the city's poor households, which were almost half composed by children under the age of fifteen.[24]

6.1.3.1 Policies on Young Vagrants

The city policy toward young vagrants arose not only from welfare concerns but also from the fear that street children would grow up to be participants in organized crime. The city attempted, then, to keep young people out of illegitimate employment. Measures aimed at promoting this goal included rounding up homeless children, setting up institutes for homeless children and giving them vocational training, sending runaway children home, and setting up guidance offices at the train station.

As managers of the city's streets, police were the state representatives with the most contact with young vagrants. Police were charged with gathering young people from the streets and operated many of the facilities for them. Governance of young vagrants started with police rounding up wandering youths. In the early 1960s, police covering the area around the train station would find two or three girls from the countryside daily. Four policemen were assigned to the train station specifically with the duty of picking up girls before they fell into the hands of brokers for the red light districts.[25] Periods of drought in agricultural regions brought more country youths into the city and kept the police busier. Over six months of

[23] Estimated from KT, May 16, 1963, and KT, December 12, 1971.

[24] This 1962 survey found that 45 percent of people in poor households were children. Kwŏn Yi-jŏk, et al. "Yŏngsemin e taehan sahoe ŭihakchŏk chosa yŏn'gu" (A Social Medical Survey of the Poor), Seoul National University *Nonmunjip: ŭiyak kye (Theses: Medical Section)* 12 (December 1962): 1. In 1980, more than half of the residents of Seoul's illegal housing areas were children. See Kim Ki-ho, et al. "Sŏul-si pullyang chutaek chigu ŭi chugŏ silt'ae mit ŏrini munche e kwanhan yŏn'gu" (A Study of Residential Conditions and Children's Problems in Substandard Housing Areas in Seoul), Sŏul Taehakkyo hwan'gyŏng taehagwŏn (Environmental Studies Graduate School, Seoul National University), 1980, research report, 12.

[25] KT, February 26, 1963.

drought in 1968, Seoul police found 2,200 wandering young people from only three of the country's provinces.[26] In busy months, police would find some 500 young people on the streets.[27] By the early 1970s, police were looking beyond the train station for wandering young people from the countryside. Every day, fifteen girls from the countryside would be found looking for work at employment centers and tea houses.[28]

Police were also responsible for what happened to vagrant youths once they had found them. The simplest and probably least effective response was to put them back on trains for their hometowns. This option was usually not one preferred by the youngsters, whose parents may have sent them. Police usually could not force them to leave, but they would provide a train ticket. At times, the police launched a campaign to send street youths home, and in one campaign claimed to have sent back over half.[29] Usually, only a small percentage of those stopped by police were sent home, and many of those seem to have returned. In one report, police recorded a higher number of youths sent home than the total number stopped, suggesting that the same youths were sent home multiple times.[30]

Another step taken to keep rural girls off the streets was to set up guidance offices at the train station and other locations.[31] Counselors took young women off a train into their offices and discussed their options. The first goal of these offices was to prevent women from falling into the hands of procurers, who might lure them away with promises of work as housemaids. The offices would then encourage the girls to return home, and in the peak years of migration to Seoul in the late 1960s City Hall allocated these "guidance centers" with a budget for purchasing train tickets to send girls home.[32] According to a 1967 survey, a quarter of the girls were runaways, with no purpose in the city other than getting away from home.[33]

[26] KT, September 7, 1968.

[27] Calculated from KT, March 11, 1971. In one month in 1974, police counted 1,700 young people who had left "recklessly" for Seoul. KT, February 23, 1974.

[28] KT, May 20, 1972.

[29] KT, March 15, 1963.

[30] KT, December 12, 1971.

[31] In 1969, the city had four counselors at the main train station and two at each of three other stations. *Sijŏng kaeyo* (*Outline of City Affairs*), (Sŏul t'ŭkbyŏl si (Seoul Special City), various years), 193–194.

[32] KT, April 7, 1968. These centers handled 3,800 young women from the countryside in the first six months of 1972. The average age of the women was 17. KT, March 29, 1973.

[33] The survey found half of the girls at guidance centers were in the city looking for work, and so would probably be less inclined to return home. Yi Ch'ung-yu, "Yullak yŏsŏng munche ŭi haegyŏl pang'an: Sŏul t'ŭkbyŏlsi rŭl chungsim ŭro" (Solutions to the Problems of Prostitutes: A Case Study of Seoul). *Sijŏng yŏn'gu (Studies in Municipal Government)* 2 (1968): 116.

But the state had to struggle for the loyalty of guidance center staff, who were tempted to collaborate with the procurers of young women for illicit business or with job introduction offices seeking cheap labor. In one case, a guidance worker was arrested for introducing elementary school-age girls from the countryside to employment as housemaids.[34]

A final method for dealing with vagrant youths was to admit them to welfare institutions and train them for legitimate jobs. In 1961, Seoul had 13 asylums with 1,200 boys, who had been taken in after being found begging. There they would be offered vocational training in occupations that would seem to require few skills, including newspaper delivery, shoe-shining, and cake-selling.[35] Vocational training of this sort continued and was aimed mostly at boys. When taking in boys for training, authorities stated the reason was to deter them from turning to crime or to discourage them from criminal activities they were already undertaking. Seoul's 12,000 homeless teenagers in the early 1960s were reported to account for half of those responsible for juvenile crime, which had taken risen tremendously since the late 1950s.[36] At one point, Seoul police planned to offer technical education to 30,000 young vagrants,[37] but most measures were on a far smaller scale. Most facilities could not handle more than a few hundred at a time. By the mid-1960s, city shelters still had a combined capacity of just 1200 youths.[38] Police stations would also offer night courses to a few hundred vagrant boys.[39]

Police rather than other government agencies, for example those dealing with welfare, took primary responsibility even for the institutions that sheltered and instructed vagrant youths. Given the understood link between vagrancy and crime, police presumably had the greatest stake in reforming young people: if they failed, the police would have more challenges fighting crime. The city also urged private charities to take care of destitute youth. One welfare center for girls, run jointly by a Christian organization and the city, handled some 30,000 cases, mostly girls in their late teens from southern provinces, over seven years.[40] Welfare centers,

[34] KT, September 11, 1977.

[35] KT, November 19, 1961. In the months after the coup, young beggars were taken off the streets of Seoul and put into institutions, some located in the provinces. KT, October 24, 1961.

[36] KT, September 5, 1963. By this time, police claimed to have rehabilitated 10,000 homeless children nationally and 17,000 other needy children.

[37] KT, March 27, 1969.

[38] KT, October 29, 1965.

[39] KT, December 23, 1969.

[40] KT, December 10, 1975.

however, had to compete with other organizations over the city's uprooted youths. One church dormitory reported that gang leaders often came and tried to kidnap or otherwise induce boys to join them.[41] Training given to vagrant youths may have even encouraged gang recruiters to pursue them, because organized toughs could gain from the earnings generated from those skills.

6.1.3.2 Non-State Providers

Street youths often had adults behind them supporting, and gaining from, their activities. Some desperate parents used their children to beg or sell gum.[42] At one point, two places in Seoul reported that they had some 1,000 children selling candy and gum.[43] Some adults coerced children and teenagers into creating income for them. A woman was arrested for forcing teenage girls from the countryside to work without pay.[44] A man drugged twenty youths and made them beg, taking money from them each day.[45]

Young vagrants represented a source of funds for criminal organizations. Many young criminals were wrapped up in underground networks. In 1969, it was reported that fully 40 percent of youth crime was organized. Organized criminal rings used street children to expand their ranks and resources. In some cases, coercion was more like taxation; in others, it involved making youths take on certain activities. Taking a portion of young beggars' earnings was a common method of providing one resource base for gangs.[46] Another means by which gangs generated revenue was encouraging young vagrants to steal. Police revealed groups that had assembled teams of 20–40 teenage boys from the countryside to work as pickpockets. These clientelist relationships could be very stable, persisting over several years.[47] Older boys were also known to organize the younger ones for similar activities.[48]

Gang recruiters' methods could be highly coercive: one migrant boy who failed to locate his Seoul relatives slept on a bench outside the train

[41] KT, December 7, 1960.
[42] See, for example, KT, December 14, 1963, and KT, August 7, 1964.
[43] KT, April 28, 1964.
[44] KT, December 12, 1962.
[45] KT, July 5, 1967.
[46] See, for example, KT, January 27, 1967, and KT, May 16, 1964. One gang took "tips" from a poor youth who survived by donating blood. KT, May 5, 1974.
[47] KT, October 1, 1967, and KT, May 4, 1968.
[48] KT, October 26, 1966. A group of young women were also found earning a living from the gum sales of rural-born children in Seoul. KT, December 21, 1962.

station. He was approached by teenage scavengers and beaten to death after refusing to work for them.[49]

On the other hand, many patrons of young vagrants offered them the security and shelter that they could not get from other sources. Shoe shine boys belonged to particularly tight-knit organizations that provided for them, as well as extracting from them. Shoe shine boys tended to organize in small groups of five to ten, led by an older boss. Bosses appropriated shoe shine boys' earnings and then paid them monthly wages. Bosses earned far more than shoe shiners, but they provided the boys with housing and food. In addition, by the mid-1970s, securing a street corner for shining shoes was very costly, and someone with more funds was necessary to make the high rental payments.[50]

At times, police cracked down on shoe shine bosses, for their extortion of young shoe shiners. One boss successfully pleaded for his release on the grounds that he was important to the boys because he offered them protection. Punishing bosses was said not to help, because boys respected the bosses and aspired to be one in the future.[51] The activity of shoe shining was legal but its organization tended not to be. The police and other agencies struggled to figure out how to deal with the structures that gained from the industry.

6.1.4 Homelessness

Homelessness was not a widespread problem in Seoul in this period. Setting up a shack was inexpensive. One only needed to find a location and gather scraps of wood, tent material, and, if lucky, corrugated iron. Still, Seoul always had a population of drifters who made their beds under the open sky. These did not make a up a big part of the poor, but the homeless were visible.[52] In their efforts to build a modern society,

49 KT, April 22, 1961.

50 KT, November 27, 1975.

51 KT, February 15, 1976. A large-scale survey of shoe shine boys in 1977 (KT, April 20, 1977) revealed that they tended to have elementary school education and to have come from the countryside before the age of fourteen. None of the surveyed boys worked alone, and downtown they were organized in larger groups with divisions of labor – some boys shined while others found customers. It appears that shoe shining became increasingly organized like a corporation over the 1960s and 1970s. Earlier it had been a more individualistic enterprise, with solitary shoe shiners wandering the streets and calling for customers. Later, it became more of a group activity, with shoe shiners rooted in particular locations.

52 In the early 1960s, some 1,200 families lived in caves and under bridges in Seoul. A few hundred people made their homes in cement pipes. See KT, January 17, 1960, and KT, November 15, 1963.

government leaders did not want vagrants lingering in the streets and making the city unpleasant-looking. This cosmetic motive shaped the city's plans for the homeless.

In the first half of the 1960s, the military regime took drastic measures to minimize homelessness. One measure was to round up homeless people and send them out of the city. In the weeks after the coup, vagrants were gathered together with criminals and sent out to mountainous areas to work on government projects.[53] In August 1961, the city announced that 6,000 of the poorest families would be resettled in the countryside.[54] In fact, 1,200 families did depart for new areas under government instruction.[55] By December, however, only 1,040 houses were built under the rural resettlement program.[56] Vagrants were also sent to camps for "rehabilitation." In the two years after the coup, 14,146 vagrants nationally were taken to the camps, 9,763 were still being held in mid-1963, and plans were underway for further campaigns to pick up more vagrants to send to the camps.[57]

Efforts were also made to use Seoul's street dwellers to reclaim tidal land in remote parts of the country, where they would begin new settlements. In 1963, nine former prostitutes were sent to a reclamation project run by 700 ex-vagrants in South Ch'ungch'ŏng province and were to select their husbands from among them.[58] The colony grew, and the following year the city of Seoul funded a mass wedding there of 225 pairs of rehabilitated prostitutes and vagrants.[59] A similar project in South Chŏlla province, organized by the Health Ministry, met with very little success. Men and women from the streets of Seoul were sent to that area and created problems with the locals, who were jealous of the nice homes that their new neighbors were granted with government funds. There were complaints that those resettled were poor workers and within months were already out begging again.[60] By the late 1960s, these experiments in social engineering had petered out.[61]

53 KT, June 11, 1961, and KT, June 21, 1961.
54 KT, August 9, 1961.
55 KT, August 20, 1961.
56 KT, December 5, 1961.
57 KT, June 6, 1963.
58 KT, March 14, 1963.
59 KT, November 25, 1964. The colony continued to expand, at least for another year, to 1,676 inhabitants with 350 married couples in 1965. KT, June 27, 1965.
60 KT, December 26, 1964, and KT, March 10, 1965.
61 That is, public reports of them no longer emerged.

When these ambitious programs failed, responsibilities fell again to the police. In winter, the city would set up accommodations for vagrants so that they would not freeze in Seoul's harsh winters. In 1962–1963, the city expected about 900 vagrants in need of shelter – a very small number for a city of some 3 million inhabitants.[62] In some years, police would round up people sleeping on the streets whenever the temperature dropped below freezing.[63] Hostels for people without homes operated separately for men and women, and by 1965 public relief stations had a capacity of 2,500.[64]

The government's welfare interests were driven more by concerns about public order than the well-being of the homeless. Allowing vagrants to freeze to death in winter did not look good for the regime. The priority in sheltering them was thus getting them off the streets rather than caring for them. Vagrants were forcibly admitted to public institutions, where the treatment was reportedly bad. At one point in 1967, for example, the city's vagrant rehabilitation center housed 891 people, many of whom were sick and were attended by only one doctor. Nearly two people were dying daily in the institution.[65]

6.1.5 Prostitution

An area where police came most directly into contact with informal authority systems was in dealing with prostitution. Many young women from the countryside ended up in the illicit entertainment industry, which was another arena for confrontations between the state and the underworld.[66] Seoul in the 1960s was home to a handful of designated red light districts and tea houses, which grew from the hundreds to the thousands

62 KT, November 30, 1962.
63 KT, December 21, 1965.
64 KT, October 24, 1965.
65 KT, May 16, 1967.
66 According to one survey, over 85 percent of the city's prostitutes were born outside Seoul. The Chŏlla provinces accounted for a third of places of origin. See Yi Myŏng-ch'ŏl, and Ch'oe Yŏng-gyu, "Sŏul si nae yullak yŏsŏng ŭi silt'ae chosa" (A Survey on the Conditions of Seoul's Prostitutes), Chungang Taehakkyo Sahoe Saŏp Hakkwa, *Sahoe bokji yŏn'gu* (*Studies in Social Welfare*) 12 (March 1978): 111. A survey ten years earlier also came up with over 85 percent being non-natives of Seoul. See Chang Tong-ch'il, "Yullak yŏsŏng ŭi silt'ae e kwanhan sogo: Chongno-gu wa Yŏngdŭngp'o-gu ŭi sŏndo chiyŏk ŭl chungsim ŭro" (Reflections on the Condition of Prostitutes: Based on Guidance Areas in Chongno and Yŏngdŭngp'o Districts), *Sahoe pokji yŏn'gu che 2 chip* (*Social Welfare Studies*), Chungang University *Sahoe saŏp hakhoe* (*Social Work Society*) 2 (1967): 125.

and were staffed by young women. As we have seen, procurers for tea houses and red light establishments recruited from institutions that were nominally set up for the purpose of helping the poor find work in the city. According to one survey, 18 percent of prostitutes were lured to the work by job agencies and 26.5 percent by procurers directly.[67] Some were previously employed as house maids but, dissatisfied with that work or losing their job, went in search of other options and ended up in the hands of procurers.[68]

6.1.5.1 Job Centers as Sites of Contestation

Employment introduction agencies, or job centers, became places where police sought to fight prostitution. The establishment of job centers was a measure to deal with employment problems in the city and discourage young people from turning to illegal occupations. The job center was an idea of the early 1960s. In 1963, the city had only one and proposed to create sixty more.[69] By the late 1970s, the country had approximately 400 authorized job agencies, both public and private. The public agencies were run by the labor administration. Private agencies required licenses to operate. In Seoul, some of these offices resembled the guidance centers installed to deter young migrants from the countryside from falling into the wrong hands. Some public job centers encouraged migrants to return home before trying to find work for them.[70]

Job centers handled a fair volume of employment arrangements, but public centers still left many applicants without work. In 1969, for example, some 11,000 jobs were arranged through government-run centers in Seoul. However, this represented 35 percent of applicants.[71] Private job agencies helped lighten the burden on public ones. The vast majority of

[67] KT, November 17, 1968. Another 28 percent were introduced to the job through their friends. Ten years later, a report indicated that over 70 percent entered the industry through their friends or through their own initiative. See Yi Myŏng-ch'ŏl and Ch'oe Yŏng-gyu, "Sŏul si nae yullak yŏsŏng," 117.

[68] Mun Sŏn-hwa. "Han'guk yullak yŏsŏng sŏndo saŏp e taehan sogo" (A Look at Guidance Projects for Korea's Prostitutes), Social Work Research Association, Yihwa Women's University, *Sahoe saŏp* (*Social Work*) 5 (1970): 138. One survey found that one-quarter previously worked in factories, another quarter in restaurants, tea houses, and bars, and 12 percent as house maids. See Yi Myŏng-ch'ŏl and Ch'oe Yŏng-gyu, "Sŏul si nae yullak yŏsŏng," 115.

[69] KT, January 30, 1963.

[70] KT, August 9, 1968.

[71] KT, May 31, 1970.

applicants, 94 percent, according to one statistic,[72] were young women seeking work as housemaids or in restaurants.

The necessity of private job agencies and the overwhelming numbers of young female applicants created the conditions to make such agencies points of human trafficking. Because the centers were magnets for vulnerable young women, procurers for the entertainment industry knew to go to them to find recruits. The situation also created lucrative opportunities for the staff of job agencies. Unlicensed agencies sprung up and were hard for the state to crack down on. Unauthorized agencies were found running advertisements in newspapers along with legitimate agencies, and distinguishing the two was not easy.[73] These job brokers would take fees from job seekers and then introduce them to fictional employers, or would encourage them to switch work frequently in order to collect more fees.[74]

The real money, however, was in inducing young women to enter the entertainment world, and it was this business that made job agencies sites of contestation between public and private coercive organizations. Trafficking in young women was most brisk in the spring, when girls came to Seoul for work. In 1968, Seoul police counted 97 unlicensed job agencies in the city and discovered a broker who had sold around 1,000 women to red light districts in the space of 15 months.[75] Some agencies were run directly by procurers for red light districts; others were in league with them. They used newspapers advertisements to lure young women with promises of work as housemaids, then detained and sold them to tea houses or other entertainment places.[76]

Human trafficking was not limited to unlicensed job agencies. Many licensed agencies purchased their permits, especially after 1973 when the labor administration handed responsibility for licensing to the city. Discoveries of authorized agencies sending young women to brothels gave way to concentrated efforts to clamp down on private job offices, especially in the latter half of the 1970s. By 1976, Seoul had an estimated 200 unlicensed agencies and 95 licensed private agencies.[77] The city and labor authorities tried to weaken job brokers by closing many private

[72] KT, April 10, 1970.
[73] KT, June 6, 1969.
[74] KT, November 25, 1967, and KT, November 1, 1972.
[75] KT, April 5, 1968.
[76] See, for example, KT, November 20, 1971.
[77] KT, October 27, 1976.

offices down and ordering them to collect fees only from employers and not from job seekers.[78]

6.1.5.2 Management of Red Light Districts

The red light district was another site of struggle for police. Rather than force prostitution wholly underground, red light establishments were permitted to operate in certain areas of Seoul. That way their activities could at least be monitored. Administration of red light districts was another duty that fell to Seoul's police. In the early 1960s, the police oversaw ten authorized red light districts. In this role, the police found themselves caught between the demands of organizers of red light businesses, their employees, nearby residents, and governmental superiors.

Handling conflicts between those in the red light sector and their neighbors was one task for police as administrators of the districts. Brothels not only made for poor neighbors but also depressed land prices. Large red light districts were located downtown – near the train station, near Tongdaemun market, and at the heart of the commercial district.[79] Residents took action, such as filing petitions, in order to have red light districts moved.[80] As the city developed, the police started to clear out the districts. In doing so, they encountered resistance. Some prostitutes responded by holding demonstrations.[81] To clear red light areas near the train station, 1,000 riot police were mobilized to evacuate an approximately similar number of workers in the sector. When a similar campaign was launched to remove brothels from the Tongdaemun area, police lost the battle.[82]

From 1968, red light districts were no longer authorized. The remaining legal prostitutes, who numbered over 2,800,[83] were rounded up, their debts cancelled, and they were offered free transportation to their homes.[84] Still, the police remained linked to illicit entertainment activities. Two years after the clearing of red light districts, residents

[78] See KT, December 15, 1976, and KT, February 6, 1979.

[79] When the red light district at Chongno samga – at the center of the business district – was finally cleared in 1968, land prices there immediately doubled. KT, October 3, 1968.

[80] See, for example, KT, December 6, 1963, and KT, October 6, 1967.

[81] KT, September 22, 1963.

[82] KT, October 6, 1967.

[83] This figure is reported in Yi Ch'ung-yu, "Yullak yŏsŏng munche ŭl haegyŏl pang'an: Sŏul t'ŭkbyŏlsi rŭl chungsim ŭro" (Solutions to the Problems of Prostitutes: A Case Study of Seoul), *Sijŏng yŏn'gu* (*Studies in Municipal Government*) 2 (1968): 56–66.

[84] KT, September 24, 1968, and KT, September 28, 1968.

complained that police had allowed another to grow.[85] Because police both monitored and, in effect, made policies on illicit entertainment, they were important patrons for the industry. Outside authorized areas and after those were shut down, police offered to ignore their activities in return for a cut in the earnings.

The clientelist networks of the prostitution industry operated as follows. At the lowest level were young women who were often indentured servants, having been told they had to work off a sum of money that gave them their introduction to the work. Above them were the owners and operators of the establishments where they worked. These owners and operators tended to be middle-aged women. Above the establishments were the underground organizations that specialized in procuring women and guarding them. Finally, the underground organizations and the establishments turned to local police, who brokered the law. The opportunity was a lucrative one for police, who could charge bribes a bit lower than the fines a summary court would assign the establishments. In this way, the vulnerability of young women from the countryside – and demand for their services by a portion of the male urban populace – powered a money-making industry that supported clientelist networks that could compete with some success against the state for the loyalty of administrators of the law.[86]

6.1.5.3 Rehabilitation

Another way of dealing with prostitutes was to send them home or to institutes where they would be rehabilitated. Ordering them home was not a viable long-term solution, because most would not stay. One survey found 30 percent of prostitutes stayed in their occupation simply because they did not want to return home; another 20 percent needed the work to support their family at home.[87] Instead, police tried to get prostitutes into rehabilitation centers. These institutions were run by a number of different organizations, including the city, the Health Ministry, and voluntary organizations. Prostitutes caught in campaigns against illegal prostitution would be taken to the facilities, if not sent to their rural homes, where they could stay temporarily, receive medical treatment, and learn skills

[85] KT, August 4, 1970.

[86] When police were caught collaborating in this industry, operators of establishments had no qualms about detailing their interactions with police. This paragraph is based on their statements, as reported in KT, May 28, 1965, KT, August 19, 1966; KT, August 20, 1966; and KT, January 18, 1968.

[87] Pak Suk-ja, "Yullak yŏsŏng e taehan koch'al" (A Study of Prostitutes), Social Work Research Association, Yihwa Women's University, *Sahoe saŏp* (*Social Work*) 8 (1973): 186.

for other occupations. Vocational programs, such as one at the Happy Garden (*haengbok wŏn*) facility, offered training in knitting, hairdressing, driving taxis, raising chickens, telephone operation, and beauty care.[88]

While appearing to be care institutions, the rehabilitation centers for prostitutes, like those for vagrants and beggars, were repressive. Their main concern was keeping the women out of their former occupation rather than ensuring a healthy transition to another. Most women did not enter the centers on their own accord but were brought in by police.[89] When one red light district was being evacuated, prostitutes who were put on a bus bound for a rehabilitation center attempted to break out of the bus.[90] At one center, 124 women did successfully escape, although most were caught and brought back the next day.[91]

The police role in addressing prostitution points to intriguing linkages between policing and welfare provision. Police became de facto agents of welfare provision. These forms of welfare were rudimentary and often coercive. They aimed as much at controlling the population and maintaining order as providing support. These links between policing and welfare should serve as a reminder that the separation of these functions is a product of a later period.

6.1.6 Strains on Police Resources

While the widespread use of police for governing is often seen as a sign of the brutality of Park Chung Hee's regime, the expansion of police functions also spread resources thin and challenged the state's ability to exercise authority. Police were responsible for the administration of welfare programs, especially taking in vagrant youths and homeless people. When inflation concerns rose, police assembled teams to check stores to make sure prices complied with government regulations. When the government launched austerity drives, police had to raid nightclubs, measure and trim men's hair,[92] and monitor the length of miniskirts.[93] At one point, police gathered hundreds of shopkeepers for being "unkind" to customers.[94]

[88] KT, February 14, 1969, and KT, April 9, 1976.

[89] According to one survey, 55 percent were brought in by police. Mun Sŏn-hwa. "Han'guk yullak yŏsŏng sŏndo saŏp e taehan sogo," 144.

[90] KT, October 6, 1968.

[91] KT, November 9, 1963.

[92] One day, for example, the city police force cut the hair of 1,400 men. KT, October 2, 1971. Over the course of one year, police made 150,000 men get haircuts. KT, July 25, 1975.

[93] KT, March 11, 1973.

[94] KT, May 19, 1973.

6.1.6.1 Resource Limitations

If police were to perform all of these tasks, they needed commensurate increases in resources. But police personnel and funding increased only marginally over the two decades. Police expansion could not keep up with population growth. The ratio of population to police, shown in Table 6.1, hovered between 500 and 600 in the 1960s, then averaged over 600 in the following decade.[95] Looking only at patrolmen reveals a clear decline in police presence on the streets of Seoul. The 1966 ratio of 581 Seoulites per patrolman jumped to 1010 by 1970 and saw little change over that decade, closing out at 1004 in 1979 (Figure 6.1). The wave of in-migration that hit the city in the late 1960s gave police stations more work per personnel, and throughout the 1970s the police administration was unable to compensate for the sharp increase in population per patrolman. Summary courts were also overworked. One court attempted to deal with 2,000 people per day.[96] Personnel was so limited at the courts that 30 percent of court fees went unpaid.[97] Stations were also short of funding, as the operating expenses of Seoul police stations ran at four to five times the amount allocated.[98]

6.1.6.2 Coping with Limited Resources

Short of manpower and funding, police turned away from the state to other power structures for help in performing and financing their work. Night watchmen, paid by residents, patrolled streets and became increasingly similar to police, despite their private origins. Police tried to make night guards share some of their burden, by offering them monetary incentives to catch thieves.[99] Night watchmen later demonstrated publicly against being forced to do police work.[100]

Police also tried to get support from better-off residents of their jurisdictions. Some police substations stations relied on "various voluntary contributions" and appointed cooperative and influential residents as

[95] According to another source, between 1954 and 1964 the population of Seoul tripled, but the absolute number of police decreased from 6,800 to 5,700. Those figures do not match with ones given in official statistics, but they do reflect the broader point that the size of the Seoul police force remained steady as the population started to expand quickly. KT, August 2, 1964.

[96] KT, May 30, 1965.

[97] KT, February 10, 1970.

[98] KT, July 9, 1975.

[99] KT, June 28, 1964.

[100] KT, November 16, 1973.

Table 6.1 *Seoul Police Force, 1960–1979*

	1960	1961	1962	1963	1964	1965	1966
Police	4,851	4,639	4,937	5,914	6,677	6,761	8,377
Population per police	504	556	604	550	513	513	453

	1967	1968	1969	1970	1971	1972	1973
Police	8,187	8,727	8,952	8,807	9,046	9,495	10,369
Population per police	485	497	534	627	647	640	607

	1974	1975	1976	1977	1978	1979
Police	10,890	10,922	11,696	12,149	13,064	13,308
Population per police	601	631	620	619	599	610

Source: Calculated from *Sŏul t'onggye yŏnbo 1966, 1970, 1975, 1982.*
Note: The figures for police include firemen.

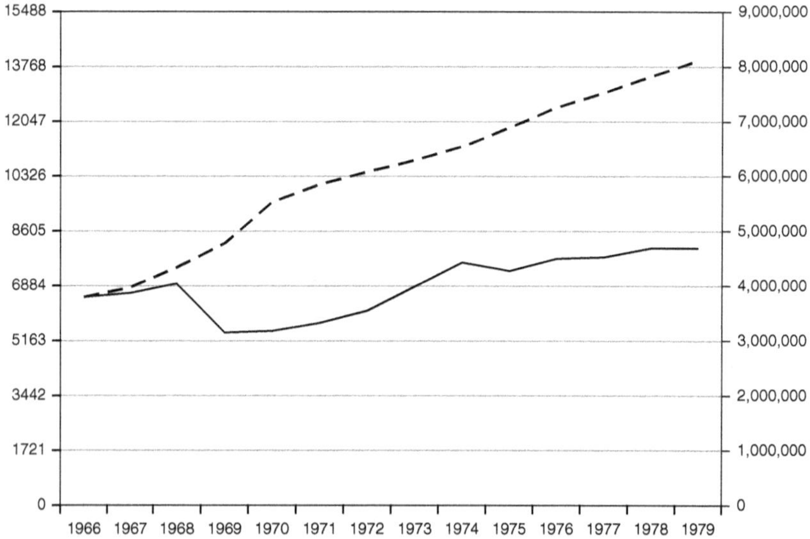

Figure 6.1 Residents and Patrolmen in Seoul, 1966–1979
Source: Calculated from *Sŏul t'onggye yŏnbo* 1970, 1975, 1982.
Note: The dashed line indicates Seoul's population, corresponding to the vertical axis on the right side of the graph. The solid line represents the number of patrolmen in the city, corresponding to figures on the left vertical axis. If the ratio of population to patrolmen had remained constant at the 1966 level of 581:1, then the solid line would follow the dashed one.

"honorary chiefs."[101] In another case, a police station was found to have organized a traditional rotating credit association (called *kye*) and forced wealthy businessmen to join.[102]

With serious limits on their resources, police turned to cheaper methods of doing their work. The most common way of addressing organized crime was to launch campaigns to pick up hoodlums. The police would periodically assemble lists of thousands of criminals and then round up as many of them as they could over a period of days or weeks. In some years, these round ups occurred a few times. The police would then book a few of the detained criminals, send more to summary court, and release the rest. Some would then be sent to work on government projects for a period of time. From soon after the coup, the government started sending hoodlums out of the city to construction projects. They were compensated a small amount. The National Construction Corps they made up had nearly 15,000 members but was disbanded the year after the coup.[103] Still, smaller numbers of criminals continued to be sent to construction projects. Doing so kept them out of the city temporarily, and so was only a short-term solution. They would routinely be allowed back to the city after a few months of work. Police would sometimes claim that the criminals had reformed themselves and so would be released, only to get into fights on the train back to Seoul.[104]

Police could round up criminals but lacked the resources to keep them detained for long. Seoul police might bring in thousands of people, but detainment rooms at the stations had a combined capacity of only 1,400.[105] This meant that police would have to choose who would be punished and who would be let go. At the same time, the habit of rounding up criminals made police and criminals quite close. The situation created personal bonds between police and criminals, and allowed police to become patrons for organized crime. Police could dole out leniency to those who cooperated with their demands, which might include working as an informant or cutting police in on their business. These could be reinforced by the practice of assigning each patrolman to a particular

[101] Oh, Sung-Hwan. "The National Police System of South Korea" (MS thesis, California State University, 1976), 140. This source reports that these "contributions" reached 30 percent of operational expenses (although it is not clear if this was an average across several substations).

[102] KT, November 11, 1969.

[103] KT, November 30, 1962.

[104] KT, October 6, 1968, and KT, August 15, 1969.

[105] KT, May 5, 1968.

beat, so that he kept close relationships with people in the neighborhood.[106] The exchange links between police and criminals were reflected in the discovery at one police station of a "luxury room," where those detained had access to cigarettes, food from restaurants, and bedding – all available for the right price.[107] The country's Attorney General at one point blamed connections between police and gangs for the failure to keep organized crime in check.[108]

Police became involved in bribe-taking, extortion, and collaboration with criminals. They allowed the wealthy to get away with traffic violations in return for cash.[109] Taxi drivers who were detained for not handing all of their earnings over to their employers preferred to pay bribes to police rather than go to court.[110] The most scandalous of irregularities was police involvement in organized theft. One incident emerged in 1966, when forty police were implicated in a pickpocket bribery case. One group of pickpockets admitted to giving large sums in bribes to twenty-five police who were assigned to an anti-pickpocketing team.[111] A larger scandal broke out nine years later, when some officers offered protection to pickpocket gangs during a national crackdown. One gang was found to be turning over one-fifth to one-half of its earnings to police, and further investigation revealed 130 police officers involved in taking bribes from organized thieves.[112] Tight links between police and organized crime sometimes led to the participation of former police in crime rings.[113]

The state could not keep police loyal.[114] Administrative measures were sometimes taken to strengthen control over police. Station chiefs were occasionally changed en masse.[115] The number of ranks was increased in order to generate greater incentives for police to mind their duties.[116] After the 1975 pickpocket scandal, 119 Seoul police were fired, but that was

106 This policy is noted in Oh, "The National Police System of South Korea," 127.
107 KT, July 6, 1975.
108 KT, January 11, 1970.
109 KT, April 20, 1974.
110 KT, January 14, 1968.
111 KT, March 22, 1966.
112 KT, July 22, 1975; KT, June 15, 1975; KT, June 20, 1975; and KT, June 21, 1975.
113 See KT, January 21, 1961, and KT, March 15, 1962.
114 The police officer's dilemma of projecting impersonal authority – and ineffective – or personal authority – and effective – is discussed, in the American context, in James Wilson, *Varieties of Police Behavior: The Management of Law and Order in Eight Communities* (Cambridge, MA: Harvard University Press, 1968): 31–34.
115 KT, October 29, 1967.
116 KT, December 26, 1968.

the exception rather than the rule when dealing with misconduct.[117] In Seoul in 1967, 723 police were found involved in irregularities. Only 56 were dismissed, and most of the remaining were merely reprimanded.[118] According to one report, 70 percent of Seoul police found guilty of corruption received no discipline.[119]

6.2 Conclusion

Soon after the 1975 police bribery scandal died down, pickpocketing on the streets of Seoul soared again. Many of the arrested thieves had been let out and were back at work. Police responded by compiling a list of thieves and tracking them down, as usual. This time, though, the police administration faced a serious obstacle to fighting pickpocketing. The punishments that were dealt out following the scandal had frightened police officers, making them reluctant to employ organized crooks as agents.[120] The informal links that provided a crucial tool to resource-starved police were cut, and administrators found themselves unable to respond effectively as crime rose.

This situation encapsulates the fundamental dilemma facing police in authoritarian-era Seoul. On one hand, measures to encourage police to be more responsive to central demands – by generating turnover in personnel, making arrest procedures fall in line with legal codes, punishing corruption, and so forth – made police less effective in maintaining order. On the other hand, policies to make police more effective – such as decentralization of arrest authorizations, loosening police from the court system, and leniency on irregularities – shifted power away from the state.[121] The state had only limited resources, and the latter option tended to win out. The result was to empower informal ties between police and private

117 KT, July 25, 1975.

118 KT, December 20, 1967. Another 184 were handed salary reductions – a punishment that would seem to encourage continued irregularities.

119 KT, June 9, 1968. Corruption was not limited to police. Another report claimed that 20 percent of officials working in City Hall had been disloyal to their office, with bribery and embezzling of welfare goods the most common charges. KT, October 20, 1968.

120 KT, June 15, 1977, and KT, July 28, 1977.

121 This dilemma is spelled out for a Chinese city at an earlier time in Frederic Wakeman Jr., *Policing Shanghai, 1927–1937* (Berkeley, CA, and Los Angeles: University of California Press, 1995), chapter 10. Wakeman describes how pressure to both enforce laws and maintain social order – in a city with a vast supply of drug money – led police to become involved in organized crime.

coercive agents. These ties made policing cheaper for the state, but meant a sacrifice of state power over the streets.

South Korea's police force in this period cannot be accurately described as a component of a state that was shut off or autonomous from society – even if the authoritarian context provided no guarantee that police would refrain from treating citizens brutally. It was profoundly enmeshed in society, including in networks that were linked to criminality. Police tolerated organized crime groups, because they had no other way to maintain order, despite what their administrative superiors desired. In attempting to govern Seoul's streets, the South Korean state had to fight for the loyalty of its police force, whose resources were stretched as its responsibilities expanded. Lingering links between governmental elites and private coercion further undermined state efforts to command authority over the streets. The lesson learned from Seoul is that authoritarian policing can have systematic limits, despite the absence of democratic protections. Such limits are exposed when the focus is shifted away from suppression of dissent and toward the everyday management of society.

PART III

Democratic Transition and Authoritarian Resilience

7

Public Order, Social Drama, and Legitimate Force

Policing Popular Uprisings in Hong Kong and Taiwan, 2014

JEFFREY T. MARTIN

The year 2014 saw large-scale youth-led civil uprisings on either side of the Taiwan Straits. In March, Taiwan's Sunflower Movement seized and held the national legislative building for three weeks. At the end of August, Hong Kong's Umbrella Movement took over sections of the city and occupied them for about three months. Both places saw normal governing arrangements break down, and politics temporarily take the form of physical struggle between police and dissidents. Given the different constitutional structures of these two places, juxtaposing the two events presents something like a natural experiment in comparative policing.

This chapter compares the different roles played by police within the larger historical processes playing through these two events. I focus on the contrast between the democratic qualities of Taiwanese policing and the authoritarian qualities of Hong Kong's policing system. I address this using a line of analysis suggested by Peter Manning's dramaturgical theory of policing, describing of the events of 2014 as "social dramas."[1] Within this, I concentrate on connections between the dramaturgical aspects of legitimation and physical control of space. I situate these two events in time by supplementing Manning's idea of police dramaturgy with Victor Turner's analysis of the ritual structure of social dramas,[2] and Carl von Clausewitz' theory of violent politics.[3] I apply this theoretical apparatus to a comparative description of the overall trajectory of these two populist movements,

[1] Peter K. Manning, *Police Work: The Social Organization of Policing* (Long Gove, IL: Waveland Press, 1997); Manning, Peter K. *Democratic Policing in a Changing World* (Boulder, CO: Paradigm, 2010); Peter K. Manning, "Drama, Police, and the Sacred," in Tim Newburn and Jill Peay (eds.), *Policing: Politics, Culture & Control* (Oxford: Hart Publishing, 2013).

[2] Victor Turner, *The Forest of Symbols: Aspects of Ndembu Ritual* (Ithaca, NY: Cornell University Press, 1967).

[3] Carl Von Clausewitz and Anatol Rapoport, *On War* (Harmondsworth: Penguin Books, 1968).

from the initial moment in which an insurgent movement overwhelmed the material capacity of the state to control space, through the different ways dissident actors used their temporary hold on territory as a means to communicate meaningful demands for political change, and into the resolution that eventually reaggregated the dramatically different political regimes on either side of the Taiwan Straits. The overall question I wish to explore is how what the police do during a liminal moment of exception affects the *longue durée* patterns linking what comes afterwards to what went before.

Taiwan is a self-governing island inhabited by twenty-three million people with a policing apparatus shaped by a history of Japanese colonial rule.[4] Hong Kong is a city of seven million, a Special Administrative Region of the People's Republic of China (PRC), with police institutions initially established under British colonial rule.[5] Both cases involved social movements driven by political anxieties and economic concerns generated by China's rising geopolitical power. Connections between the two places were explicitly understood by participants themselves (on both sides of the police lines) who studied and communicated with one another before, during, and after the events in question. The explicit, self-conscious comparability of the two events makes the contrast between their institutional differences and their radically different outcomes all the more stark. Taiwan's Sunflower Movement was resolved relatively quickly through back-room politicking, becoming a generational icon in the genealogy of social movements that have driven Taiwan's democratic process since the first stirrings of the Dangwai Movement in the 1970s. In other words, it quickly became a historical event of a recognizable type that folded back into the island's established tradition of democratic self-governance. By contrast, Hong Kong's Umbrella Movement created a historical rupture, a pivotal crisis for the transitional form of governance under which the city returned to Chinese sovereignty in 1997, and ultimately revealed hard limits to the democratic meanings once associated with "One Country Two Systems." The resolution of the 2014 Hong Kong uprising involved not political compromise but a creative application of legal rights that avoided ceding any power to democratic forces, and set the stage for the more acute confrontations in 2019–2020.

[4] Jeffrey T. Martin, *Sentiment, Reason, and Law: Policing in the Republic of China on Taiwan* (Ithaca, NY: Cornell University Press, 2019); Liqun Cao, Lanying Huang and Ivan Y. Sun, *Policing in Taiwan: From Authoritarianism to Democracy* (New York: Routledge, 2014).

[5] Carol A. G. Jones, and Jon Vagg. *Criminal Justice in Hong Kong* (London: Routledge, 2007); Kam C. Wong, *Policing in Hong Kong (International and Comparative Criminal Justice)* (Farnham: Ashgate Publishing Group, 2012).

To reflect on similarities and differences in these two events, I will describe them side by side, organizing my account through the dramaturgical framework of "ritual process" developed by the cultural anthropologist Victor Turner.[6] This framework explains the process by which collective life is renewed or transformed through symbolic means by breaking it into three distinct stages. Section 7.1 examines the initial stage, termed "disaggregation," in which the established structures of political order were loosened or dissolved. In Section 7.2, I examine the intermediate, or "liminal" period that obtained during the weeks or months of occupation, focusing on how police action fitted into the creative or constitutive dynamics playing out under exceptional conditions of "antistructure." And in Section 7.3, I consider how the social order eventually "reaggregated" into a new social order transformed by the political dynamics of the event.

7.1 Disaggregation: Things Fall Apart

Both the Sunflowers and the Umbrellas forced police to center stage in a moment of exception, when politics broke through the procedural channels of the constituted system and spilled out into a physical struggle for control of space. Such situations are an opportunity to study the raw dynamics linking the material and the meaningful dimensions of politics. This is not the conventional framework for analyzing the qualities of a police system. Generally speaking, questions about "democratic" policing are addressed to the institutional arrangements that fit police powers into a state's constitutional form.[7] This follows a conventional understanding of modern governance in terms of a division of powers between executive, legislative, and judicial functions. "Democratic" police are associated with systems of governance that effectively contain violence within the state as a sovereign monopoly, and organize their executive "law enforcement" function in a manner restrained by independent legislative and judicial institutions. This is the familiar normative idea in which law is called upon to supply a counterpower to police.[8] In this framing, policing is understood as democratic to the degree that representative processes are used to make law, and independent judicial

[6] Victor Turner, *The Forest of Symbols: Aspects of Ndembu Ritual* (Ithaca, NY: Cornell University Press, 1967).

[7] Robert Reiner, *The Politics of the Police*, 4th ed. (New York: Oxford University Press, 2010).

[8] Cf. Markus Dubber, *The Police Power: Patriarchy and the Foundations of American Government* (New York: Columbia University Press, 2005).

powers effectively hold police powers within that law. Authoritarian policing, by contrast, is identified with the capacity to act without legal basis or judicial accountability.

That conventional approach is very useful, but here I wish to develop an alternative way of thinking about "democratic" policing. Rather than taking the division of powers as my theoretical point of departure, I begin from an anthropological conception of the human world as an "anthropological fact" constituted in the intersection between its material and its meaningful dimensions.[9] On this conceptual foundation, I develop a Clausewitzian analytic of the interplay between physical and moral forces. That is, policing, like military action, is a mode of politics conducted through the admixture of other means, that is physical violence. Policing differs from warfare in the way its moral (or meaningful) and physical dimensions interact. Understanding this is the purpose of Peter Manning's focus on the communicative or "dramaturgical" aspect of policing. Policing is a sociological enterprise that serves to hold a community together within a common order by providing signs that this common order holds. The drama of policing is "about" the order of social life. Of course, Manning argues, the idea of order that police provide is always, to some degree, an ideological illusion created by hiding the contradictions and antinomies intrinsic to collective life. In ordinary practice, police manage their exposure to pluralism by segmenting different audiences and trying to control appearances in a way that accommodates the divergent expectations of these different audiences. When successful, this strategy allows police to give the impression that a political consensus exists, within which they occupy a neutral position. In moments of acute conflict, however, social antinomy can no longer be managed by such superficial dramaturgical strategies. Police must abandon the pretention to uphold an inclusive consensus, make a choice about whose sensibilities matter most, and take sides in an overt political struggle. Taking this approach suggests a diagnostic principle to distinguish democratic from

[9] Contemporary cultural anthropology uses interpretive methods developed on the basis of Durkheim's idea of the social fact, while also accommodating the post-structuralist challenge to Durkheim's maxim that social meaning should be understood as a sphere of phenomena *sui generis* (i.e. unrelated to external causes). The idea of an "anthropological fact" is part of a broad conversation about how to move beyond the classical opposition between idealist and materialist paradigms. For a programmatic statement of this particular phrase, see Jonathan Marks, "The Nature/Culture of Genetic Facts," Annual Review of Anthropology 42 (2012):247–267. For a monograph-length application of this methodological framework to the study of policing, see Martin, *Sentiment, Reason, and Law*.

autocratic policing, evident in the contrast between Taiwan's Sunflowers and Hong Kong's Umbrellas, lying in the way that police under pressure align themselves with particular audiences. Policing can be called democratic when it chooses to side with "the people" under circumstances of intractable conflict, as (I argue) happened in Taiwan. By contrast, it is autocratic when it aligns itself with some elite fraction within the political field, as it did in Hong Kong.

Clausewitz' idea of "moral force" provides a way of thinking about the way physical violence functions as a medium for the conduct of this kind of semiotic politics. The physical aspect of policing is contentious politics, organized as a Clausewitzian "trial of moral and physical forces" in which both the symbolic and the material dimensions matter. This framing helps situate Manning's police dramaturgy within an anthropological understanding of the "performativity" of signifying practices. Performativity is a way of thinking about the constitution of anthropological facts. Its conceptual core is the analytic distinction between the "illocutionary" force of an actor's action and the "perlocutionary" forces embedded in the sociohistorical context. These somewhat clunky terms were coined by philosopher John Austin to distinguish between the "illocutionary" skill with which a speaker speaks and the "perlocutionary" sensibilities through which the audience hears.[10] It is the calibration between these two dimensions of a speech act that generates its consequences. From this beginning in "ordinary language philosophy," Austin's idea of semiotic performativity has grown into a mode of analyzing the ontological constitution of social reality.[11] Here I propose to use it as a framework for reflecting on how the very different forms of policing historically institutionalized in the perlocutionary patterns of Taiwan and Hong Kong accommodated the unprecedented illocutionary act of populist street occupation.

In Taiwan, national politics crossed decisively into the realm of physical forces at half-past nine on Tuesday March 18, 2014, when a group of activists broke into Taiwan's parliamentary building. The initial entry involved about seventy people working in two coordinated groups. One cohort made a frontal assault on the main entrance while the other broke through a side door, pushed past the forty-odd policemen stationed inside the building, and opened the main door from the inside. Once the front door was open, this vanguard was joined by several hundred more

[10] John L. Austin, *How to Do Things with Words* (Oxford: Clarendon Press, 1962).

[11] Sara Salih, "On Judith Butler and Performativity," in Karen E. Lovaas and Mercilee M. Jenkins (eds.), *Sexualities and Communication in Everyday Life* (New York: Sage, 2006), 55–68.

people drawn from participants in protests ongoing outside. Aided by sympathetic legislators (who enjoyed immunity from arrest inside the halls of parliament), the occupiers barricaded the doors of the legislative chamber with furniture and, to their surprise, successfully held their position against police attempts to enter, all the while broadcasting the course of events through social media such as Facebook and Twitter. Dawn the following day saw a crowd in the thousands growing in the streets outside the occupied building, as people from various walks of life arrived in support of the students inside. Thus began the historic twenty-four-day occupation of Taiwan's legislature that became known as the "Sunflower Movement."[12]

Six months later, on the other side of the Taiwan Straits, a comparable moment of physical politics played out. On the night of Friday, September 26, a group of students climbed a fence and occupied a courtyard in front of the city's Central Government Offices. Police were deployed; they kettled the protesters and arrested their leaders, but failed to clear the space as more people arrived to support those trapped inside the police lines. By Sunday, September 28, the streets around the Government Complex were filled with people, and police at the scene began to feel overwhelmed. The crowd gathering in sympathy with the students was growing rapidly, flooding out of nearby subway stations, spilling off sidewalks into the streets, and bringing traffic in the city center to a halt. At five that afternoon police made a fateful decision to deploy chemical agents. Over the next few hours, riot police fired dozens of volleys of tear gas into the surrounding crowds. Whatever immediate tactical objective this was intended to achieve, it proved a strategic disaster. Broadcast on live television and social media, the lines of police in riot gear advancing through plumes of white smoke detonating from the explosives they fired repeatedly into the milling throng of young people around them created an image of state repression that shocked public sensibilities. The effect of the spectacle on the political tensions underlying the situation was like gasoline poured on a fire. Citizens of every stripe came out into the streets in defense of the young citizens under assault. By the next morning, multiple areas of the city center were completely shut down by a mass occupation of the roadways. The protestors brought

[12] Jeffrey T. Martin, "Policing an Occupied Legislature: Symbolic Struggle over the Police Image in Taiwan's Sunflower Movement." *Hong Kong Law Journal* 45 (1) (2015): 229–248; Ming-sho Ho, *Challenging Beijing's Mandate of Heaven: Taiwan's Sunflower Movement and Hong Kong's Umbrella Movement* (Philadelphia, PA: Temple University Press, 2019).

out tents and turned the streets into a temporary residential space. They maintained the occupation for nearly three months, an event that came to be known as the "Umbrella Movement."[13]

In Taiwan's case, the precipitating cause of the disaggregation had been a point of parliamentary procedure. For eight months prior to the dissidents' raid on parliament, a treaty establishing rules for Chinese investment in Taiwan had been making its way through a tortuous process of legislative review. This treaty – the Cross-Straits Services Trade Agreement (CSSTA) – emerged from collaboration between two nongovernmental organizations that manage the relationship between the governments of China and Taiwan: China's Association for Relations Across the Taiwan Straits (ARATS) and Taiwan's Straits Exchange Foundation (SEF). After these ostensibly private bodies concluded their closed-door discussions, the President of the Republic of China – at that time Ma Ying-jiu – declared that, so far as Taiwan was concerned, the nascent policy was an internal issue rather than an international treaty. As such, it fell within the scope of the Act Governing Relations between the People of the Taiwan Area and the Mainland Area, granting him authority to promulgate it as law without any intervening public or legislative review. This presumptive diktat by the president induced a rare moment of unity in a divided legislature, and Ma was convinced to reconsider his position. He subsequently agreed to expose the contents of his treaty to a process of item-by-item review, organized in sixteen legislative sessions, half of which would be chaired by the president's ruling Chinese Nationalist Party (KMT) and the other half by the main opposition party, the Democratic Progressive party (DPP).

Public hope that the review process would illuminate the substance of the impending policy was frustrated by various forms of bad-faith procedural manipulation. The review was marked by every dirty trick in the Taiwanese political playbook, ranging from party-on-party fistfights for control of the podium, to a (failed) attempt by the president to orchestrate removal of the speaker of the parliament through a special criminal investigation. Elements allied with the president managed to reduce review sessions chaired by the KMT to cursory formalities, concluding them with minimal opportunity for discussion. The DPP took the opposite approach, preventing any progress at all in the sessions they chaired, and threatening to drag the proceedings out indefinitely. In the fog of this war of dirty tricks, little of substance was said about the content of the bill.

[13] Ho, *Challenging Beijing's Mandate of Heaven*, 121–125.

After eight months of this, things came to a head. On Monday, March 17, a KMT legislator, Chang Ching-Chung, was scheduled to convene one of the KMT-led review sessions, even as a DPP-led session initiated the previous week was still frozen in official gridlock. By this time, the struggle over the review process had reduced the rules of legislative procedure to a parody of their intended purpose, using them as the basis for such tactics as hiding all the official microphones so that someone authorized to speak could not, officially, be heard. Chang came prepared for exactly this kind of struggle. He clipped a hidden microphone inside his collar, which broadcast his voice to another KMT legislator who secretly relayed it through an official microphone into the records of parliamentary process. Chang expected to be physically prevented from taking the podium, so he brought with him a fake "official" microphone as a decoy. When a phalanx of opposition party legislators moved to block his ascent to the convenor's position, he allowed the dummy microphone to fall into their hands, giving them a false sense of control over the proceedings. Chang then fell back to a bathroom exit, appearing to give up, while remaining close enough to the podium to claim technical conformity with procedural rules. There, crouching next to the bathroom, Chang began whispering into his collar, secretly assuming his scheduled role as convenor of a legislative hearing. His formal parliamentary voice authorized by the opening of his scheduled session, Chang then invoked a procedural rule in the Legislative Functions Act, which imposed a ninety-day limit on all processes of legislative review. For Chang was not just convenor of that day's review session, he also happened to chair the legislature's Internal Administrative Committee. In this role he was authorized to speak consequentially about broader procedural issues. He announced that the review process had surpassed its ninety-day limit, was therefore concluded, and the bill returned to the executive for ratification. He then closed his clandestine congress and wandered back into the crowd of legislators, most of whom were unaware of the covert formality he had just effected.

The announcement, a few hours later, that the review process had been concluded in this manner caused outrage. Chang's preposterous subterfuge crystallized a diffuse collection of popular anxieties generated by shifts in cross-straits relations, and provided a concrete target onto which they could focus. The base of these popular anxieties was the political significance of Chinese capital as an instrument of policy for the Chinese party-state. Opening Taiwan's service sector to Chinese investment threatened to expose Taiwanese democracy to a sort of financial capture, as it would become possible for businessmen allied with the

Chinese Communist Party to buy the economic foundations of Taiwanese middle-class political autonomy. This was a threat that resonated with the recent purchase of a media conglomerate by a Taiwanese tycoon who had close ties to China. After the purchase, the newspapers and television stations operated by that conglomerate shifted their editorial line dramatically to champion pro-China positions. Taiwan's historical memory of life under Leninism is less than thirty years old. Much of the population has first-hand familiarity with the way an authoritarian party uses media and financial institutions as a mechanism for governmental control. Taiwan's institutions of parliamentary representation are seen as a bulwark against this kind of autocratic behavior. In the course of the democratic transition, political dissidents used access to parliamentary representation as the wedge by which they pried the state free of single-party control. Senator Chang's flamboyantly cynical manipulation of the rules of procedure marked an institutional failure of Taiwan's parliament to uphold its traditional democratic function of protecting the people from executive abuse. It seemed to have become a facilitator for, rather than a bulwark against, the vanguardist ambitions of a president-cum-party-chairman who was quite openly using party discipline to steer Taiwan's future back into the fraught legacies of the Chinese civil war.

Public response to the "30-Second Review" was immediate. A coalition of civic associations gathered in front of the Legislative Assembly that evening, issuing a call to "Defend Democracy" against the president's autocratic implementation of the CSSTA. The capacity of these groups to mobilize at short notice was a legacy of ongoing resistance to Ma's cross-straits agenda. Ma was then in his sixth year as president, and civil opposition to his overtures toward China were a defining feature of his administration. Unrest began shortly after he took office in 2008, when he invited the head of China's ARATS, Chen Yunlin, to Taipei for a meeting with his SEF counterpart. This was the first quasi-diplomatic China–Taiwan meeting held in Taiwan since the founding of the PRC. It provoked widespread demonstrations, culminating in a physical battle between police and a line of protesters that encircled Chen's hotel, to prevent him from reaching the location of his formally scheduled meeting. In the aftermath of that battle, the first named student movement of the Ma era emerged: the so-called "Wild Strawberries." The Wild Strawberries focused on a campaign to reform the Parade and Assembly Law that specified police powers in relation to street demonstrations. The Strawberries eventually prevailed in this reform effort, even as a panoply of other activist groups began to organize around other issues, such as land takings for development projects and the emergence of the previously mentioned media monopoly. These issues could all, more-or-less tendentiously, be associated with the flow of Chinese capital into the Taiwanese economy, endowing the loose coalition of emerging dissent movements with a common ethos that marked a clearly new historical phase in Taiwan's democratic discourse. The old ideological differences separating China's communist and nationalist parties were reconciled within a common pursuit of developmental profit, and the old quasi-ethnic fracture line of Taiwanese versus Mainlander that had structured political discourse during the democratic transition lost relevance. It was replaced by an idealistic fusion of progressive social justice and legal constitutionalism coalescing among a youthful precariat alarmed by the prospect of a cross-straits capitalist oligarchy.

It was this youthful voice, embodied by student leaders Lin Fei-fan and Chen Wei-ting, that addressed the public from the occupied legislature. By the evening of the 19th, twenty-four hours after the students entered the legislative chamber, nearly 10,000 citizens had gathered outside the legislature in support of the occupation. The scale of public support for the students revealed how profoundly the president's camp had miscalculated the strength of purely procedural legitimacy. The formal admissibility of Chang's tactic was nullified by the public outrage it generated. Legality per se had been pushed beyond its breaking point. The legislature's capacity to manipulate formality in pursuit of political goals collapsed into a constitutional crisis that brought the entire system into suspicion. Outrage over Chen's "30-Second Review" called into question Ma's role in engineering the review process under "domestic" rather than "international" rules, which cast a strange light on Ma's presidential status and called into question the balance of powers defining the relationship between parliament and executive branches of government. And so an unelected conglomerate of twenty-year-old activists shouting "Return Parliament to the People!" won, for a time, public support as legitimate occupants of the legislative chambers; or, at least, more legitimate occupants than the people who had been feuding there so unproductively for the previous eight months. These broader dynamics help explain why the most obvious contradiction of the Sunflower Movement – a group advocating rule of law from inside a legislative chamber they held under blatantly illegal auspices – did not weaken the rhetorical force of the students' position.

In contrast to Taiwan's democratic system, electoral institutions in Hong Kong never managed to rise above the role of an instrument for autocratic indirect rule. Hong Kong's procedural arena of democratic empowerment is constrained within a formal carapace of autocratic legality that limits popular voice to a consultative role. This is a legacy of the city's colonial history. Late colonial Hong Kong (1967–1997) figured law as a kind of substitute for democracy. This rationale – a kind of legal fetishim – was the product of a calculated ideological campaign, remarkably successful even as the city's actual system of legislative policy formation remained elitist and exclusionary.[14] Over the decades between 1967 and 2014, Hong Kong's police developed a strategy of legitimation by legal fetishism. They claimed fidelity to law marked a shift to the democratic style of "policing by consent,"[15] associated with the metropolitan UK, rather than the autocratic colonial form associated with the Royal Ulster Constabulary, which the Hong Kong police had practiced before the 1967 riots. The practice of this new version of policing was designed to "quietly [manage] problems generated by unresolved contradictions at higher levels of government, while making sure not to scandalize a public ideologically committed to the rule-of-law ideal."[16] For many years, this mode of policing successfully squared the circle of maintaining a consent-based argument for police legitimacy within a constitutional system designed for autocratic governance. The Umbrella Movement attacked the ambiguity at the heart of this arrangement, overtly rejecting the "administrative absorption of politics."[17] The collapse of the ostensibly "democratic" significance of the law made it impossible for police to continue conflating the legality of their power to control with the democratic consent of those they controlled.

A useful framework for understanding this shift in the meaningful place that law held in the legitimation of police authority can be established on the basis of the normative idea that law should possess a degree of relative autonomy from the extralegal dimensions of politics.[18] Indeed, liberal theories of law take this normative ideal as a constitutive element in the definition of legality per se.[19] Applying this concern with autonomy

14 A. Y. C. King, "Administrative Absorption of Politics in Hong Kong: Emphasis on the Grass Roots Level," in A. Y. C. King and R. P. L. Lee (eds.), *Social Life and Development in Hong Kong* (Hong Kong: Chinese University Press, 1981), 130–146.

15 J. C. Alderson, *Policing Freedom: A Commentary on the Dilemmas of Policing in Western Democracies.Social Topics Series* (Estover: Macdonald and Evans, 1979).

16 Jeffrey T. Martin and Wayne W. L Chan, "Hong-Kong-Style Community Policing: A Study of the Yau Ma Tei Fruit Market," *Crime, Law, and Social Change* 61(4) (2014): 413–427, at 425.

17 King, "Administrative Absorption of Politics in Hong Kong," 130.

18 Christopher Tomlins, "How Autonomous Is Law?" *Annual Review of Law and Social Science* 3(1) (2007): 45–68.

19 Isaac D. Balbus, "Commodity Form and Legal Form: An Essay on the 'Relative Autonomy' of the Law." *Law & Society Review* 11(3) (1977): 571–588.

to the historical dynamics of contemporary Hong Kong focuses analysis onto the "relational other" against which the constitutive autonomy of law is defined.[20] The historical meaning of "One Country Two Systems" positions Hong Kong's government, explicitly and self-consciously, in a transitional state between the British colonial past and the Chinese authoritarian future.

Manning's dramaturgical theory of police is predicated on the idea that different audiences matter differently. In Hong Kong, elite audiences looked to the police to secure the rule of law as assurance that financial interests would be protected. A nonelite mass looked to law for something else, for a promise that their fundamental interests in maintaining a modicum of control over their political circumstances would not collapse completely into the elite capacity for economic domination.

The first significant fracture line in the capacity of law to suture these contradictory expectations came in a 2003 march against the prospective "Article 23" security law on treason and subversion. This marked a new level of overt localist resistance to Chinese state control. Article 23 did not pass. This was followed, in April 2004, by an National People's Congress Standing Committee (NPCSC) interpretation addressing the method of selecting government officials after 2007, which "reserved unlimited discretion for Beijing to set the pace of democratization by reinterpreting the criteria of the 'actual situation' and 'gradual and orderly progress' from time to time as political expediency dictates."[21] In December 2007, the NPCSC issued a further decision rejecting universal suffrage for the 2012 election. It did not, however, preclude such for 2017 or 2020, and thereby created a prospective "focal point" organizing constitutional-scaled political action.[22] In January 2010, five popularly elected LegCo members resigned as a block to stand for reelection on a platform of "universal suffrage in 2012," which they won with an overwhelming majority. Beijing responded with a reform package that partially expanded the space of electoral participation.

As municipal politics go, this was all quite orderly. It had no effect on Hong Kong's all-important place in the global financial markets. Public offerings by Chinese state-owned enterprises made the city one of the world's biggest initial public offering markets by the late 2000s. Elite

[20] Tomlins, "How Autonomous Is Law?"

[21] Eric Ip, "Constitutional Conflict in Hong Kong under Chinese Sovereignty," *Hague Journal of the Rule of Law* 8(1) (2016): 75–99, at 87.

[22] Ibid.

interests were being effectively managed within the terms of the modus vivendi, and the rumblings of localist street politics action stimulated by the global response to Occupy Wall Street (which produced Hong Kong's first "Occupy Central" movement as a tent city in front of the HSBC building during the latter half of 2011) did not threaten to align with any force effective in higher level politics.

The language of occupation, however, remained active, and the gap between youth in the streets and elites in the halls of powers began to close in March 2013, when two professors and a pastor announced a plan to connect a demand for universal suffrage to a threat of civil disobedience. Borrowing language from the global Occupy Movement, they called their plan "Occupy Central with Peace and Love" (OCPL). Beijing's response to this public agitation was the first decisive step toward replacing the ambiguous modus vivendi of "One Country, Two Systems" with a more definite administrative hierarchy subordinating Hong Kong to Beijing. On June 10, 2014, the Information Office of the State Council of the PRC issued a White Paper: "The Practice of the 'One Country, Two Systems' Policy in HKSAR," which asserted that all officials, legislators and judges in Hong Kong must be loyal to the PRC. In response, the Occupy Central organizers held an informal plebiscite on universal suffrage ("choose-your-constitution"); 800,000 people participated, with 90 percent wanting international standard free and fair elections with open nominations and universal suffrage. On August 31, 2014, the NPCSC issued a decision saying all candidates must be approved by the PRC's Nominations Committee and be ideologically aligned with PRC policy. This decision, "probably intended by Beijing to be the focal point that would compel Hong Kong residents to adjust their democratic expectations in light of the Basic Law's revised meaning according to the final authority of the People's Republic of China," became instead a fracture point that brought the street-level mode of contentious politics practiced by an increasingly radical youth movement into alignment with activities by more elite policy entrepreneurs who were involved in prodemocracy politics.[23]

The trajectory of 2014 shifted leadership of the nascent movement away from the elite architects of OCPL to youth activists in the streets. "Scholarism," a student group active in high schools that came to prominence protesting plans for patriotic educational reform, and the Hong Kong Federation of [University] Students called for a boycott of classes and a public demonstration in front of the Legislative Council

[23] Ibid.

on September 26. This led to the first set of physical confrontations with police, which escalated over the next two days into the situation on the evening of September 28, when tear gas was deployed. The spontaneous mass reaction to that confrontation motivated the presumptive leadership of OCPL to announce that what was happening might as well count as delivery of their earlier promises to engage in civil disobedience. They somewhat passively injected their elite-level voice into the scrum of contestation playing out in the streets. And with this, the modus vivendi that had for decades integrated a complex plurality of voices and interests, allowing them to muddle through contradiction by tactful silence and ambiguity, crystallized into an overt and unambiguous binary opposition between two sides, arrayed against one-another in physical confrontation.

7.2 Liminality: Dramaturgy in a Moment of Exception

The political eventfulness at stake in such a physical confrontation can be productively considered through Clausewitz' idea of politics conducted with an "admixture of other means."[24] Clausewitz developed this framework to characterize war as an enterprise directed to pursuit of a "moral" (in contemporary terms, social-psychological) outcome: destroying the enemy's will to resist. Physical harm may serve as a means toward this goal, but (short of the complete physical destruction of the enemy) physical force is not on its own sufficient to achieve this end because the meaningful aspects of human life are as decisive as the physical in constituting collective will. Practical understanding of war is, therefore, an understanding of the intersection and interaction between moral and physical forces.

Conceptualizing war as something involving moral force was Clausewitz' signature contribution to modern political thought. Yet he was explicitly vague in defining "moral force," describing it as an idea that "seeks to escape from all book knowledge." His use of the concept locates it in an intersection between the dynamics of organized large-scaled collective action (i.e. modern warfare) and the semiotic embeddedness of human experience in broader frameworks of symbolic meaning. He used a broad palette of terms – spirit (*geist*), soul (*seele*), understanding (*vestand*), sensibility (*gemut*), and sentiment (*gefuhle*) – to paint a picture of

[24] Clausewitz and Rapoport, *On War*; Raymond Aron, *Clausewitz: Philosopher of War* (New York: Simon & Schuster, 1985).

the "moral virtues" of leadership that mobilize and sustain the industrial-scale destruction required to crush the collective will of a modern army.[25]

When translated into the performative/dramaturgical theoretical paradigm outlined at the beginning of this chapter, Clausewitz' idea of moral force appears as a version of ritual performativity. Clausewitz focused on war, but this theoretical approach can be applied to any form of physically mediated politics. Policing, no less than war, is a practical field defined at the intersection of moral and material forces. There is, however, a very important distinction to be made in applying military theory to policing practices. War and peace are radically different undertakings. Clausewitz characterized the essence of war as a project of destroying an enemy's will to resist. By contrast to this, policing would appear a project of constituting (or reconstituting) a community's will to coexist. This difference in ends has consequences for the analysis of means. Perhaps the most famous of Clausewitz' analytic observations was the logical telos he discerned within war's use of violence as a political instrument. The violence of war is an instrumentality that tends toward unrestrained destruction, making the ideal-typical form of war "absolute war," with no rational basis for restraint. The necropolitical logic of modern absolute war can be counterposed to the biopolitical logic emergent in contemporaneous ideas about (what might be called) "absolute police." Where absolute war is defined by a telos to unrestrained material destruction, absolute policing is defined by a telos of unrestrained moral construction. This quality of police is captured by Foucault's famous characterization of the emergence of modern police as the embodiment of a historical shift from juridical to disciplinary power.[26] Modern policing arose as a novel concept of administrative technology through which sovereign power would penetrate and reconstruct the subjectivity of its population, pursuing the totalitarian dream of a society organized in a perfectly singular order. What state power could destroy by its newly modern capacity to make war, said theorists of high modern totalitarianism, it could create through its newly modern capacity to make peace.

Absolute war and absolute peace are ideal types. Reality exists somewhere in between. In empirical consideration of physical politics, it is difficult to draw a clear theoretical line between acts of coercion that keep a settled peace, and those that aggravate the conflicted or unpeaceful

[25] Aron, *Clausewitz*, 132.

[26] Michel Foucault, *Security, Territory, Population: Lectures at the Collège de France, 1977–78* (New York: Palgrave Macmillan, 2007).

aspects of a situation. Nonetheless, making a theoretical distinction between the telos of total war toward physical annihilation, and the contrasting telos of total peace toward a unified moral order, provides a useful frame of reference for making sense of the historical role of police in moments of constitutional upheaval. Using Peter Manning's dramaturgical framework to consider policing as meaningful performance focuses attention on the ways police agencies use symbolic means to manage the antinomies and contradictions of status quo "order" they are tasked with maintaining. Such policing succeeds when it preserves the affective inertia of ordinary life as a settled situation, that is: the peace. And it fails when the structural violence of social order breaks out from behind the screen of ideological rationalization to become open physical conflict.

Mass street politics is generally an amateur affair. The Sunflower and Umbrella Movements were made up of unarmed civilians who faced in the police a disciplined body of armed professionals capable of physically destroying them. It was not material advantage that allowed the dissidents to hold their ground. Nor was it legal right. It was, rather, their successful application of nonviolent political tactics. The dissidents artfully placed themselves into a position of spectacularly immediate danger from the state's abstract juridical power, so immediate that no individual with authority to deploy that power as material force dared do so. There was no screen of abstract legitimacy available to hide from public view the violence of a decision to crush the dissidents by force. The police violence was constrained by their mandate to prevent escalation toward a collapse of civil order.

Policing is a domain of social action characterized by coercion. Most policing hinges, somehow, on achieving nonconsensual outcomes. This feature led Muir to suggested we theorize policing as a mode of social action defined by "coercive reciprocity," and conducted in the form of "extortionate transactions." Muir described the "extortionate transaction" as a relationship between victim and victimizer mediated by "the hostage." The hostage is anything valued by a victim and controlled by the victimizer. It is by gaining control of a hostage that the roles of victim and victimizer are defined, and it is through this control that the victimizer imposes a nonconsensual outcome.[27] The use of physical violence in routine policing is predicated on using people's bodies as the "hostage," affording police leverage to impose nonconsensual outcomes. The

[27] William K. Muir, *Police: Streetcorner Politicians* (Chicago: University of Chicago Press, 1979).

nonviolent political strategy of the protest reversed this logic. The protesters effectively held themselves "hostage" to the political conscience of the general public. By so doing, they transformed the physical threat police posed to their well-being into an instrument that served their movement's political objectives. This was, to be sure, a calculated risk. The protesters were banking on the broader moral economy of the situation to endow their physically vulnerable position with a defense in the sphere of legitimacy. In this case, their venture paid off. Victory in the abstract struggle for legitimacy – winning the moral high ground, as it were – effectively secured their physical control of space.

This reveals a link between the ideological and the material dimensions of policing: ideological processes can, in some cases, become the determining factor and effectively constrain the scope of material power. In a context of widespread democratic sensibilities activated as the perlocutionary power of an audience gazing at a police standoff, public sentiments can become attuned to issues of political justice in a manner that imposes a moralizing framework onto the state's putative monopoly on physical force. This turns the monopoly on physical force into a liability for those held accountable for its effects. Police power becomes a double-edged political sword, as violation of public sensibilities by police behavior advances discursive counterpowers against the legitimacy of the established regime. These semiotic dynamics, present to some degree in any political system legitimized by consent, shaped the liminal period for both movements. In Taiwan, for more than three weeks the police were physically unable to defend the space of state offices from capture and control by unelected forces. The nonviolent strategy of the student movement successfully imposed a meaningful framing of the situation that rendered police powers politically counterproductive. Any deployment of physical force toward Ma's objectives was transformed, by the principled public exposure of the student's vulnerable bodies, into a political force working against the legitimacy of those same objectives.

The protesters' entry to the legislative chamber precipitated a spatial order that consolidated into two concentric rings: dissidents in the chamber surrounded by a police line, the police line surrounded by a mass public demonstrating support for the dissidents. This configuration persisted as a stable standoff throughout the twenty-four days of the occupation. As the physical standoff persisted, it generated political pressures that mobilized not just the country's whole police force, but the state's entire constitutional structure. Over the long weeks that the mobilization was sustained, its tensions exposed weaknesses in the constituted arrangements of state offices, aggravated contradictions between executive, legislative, and judicial powers, and pushed these contradictions to the forefront of political struggle. One feature of this period of extraordinary politics was the collapse of the conventional rationale for the legitimacy of police repression in a democratic order. It became impossible to present police coercion as "law enforcement" that embodied the will of the people as the constituted law of the land. The occupation unsettled the status quo, and exposed the received conventions of state operations as a system of structural irrationality and injustice. In this unsettled situation, the political landscape lost legal clarity, and the question of (future) accountability for (present) police action became one of the issues staked to the outcome of the political struggle. It was a difficult environment in which to conduct police operations. Yet police stood at the center of the event throughout its entire development and resolution. They defined the physical line at which opposing political forces met, stood guard at the point of their confrontation, and labored to maintain the messy peace defined by the shifting balance of political powers-in-contradiction. That the broader political crisis was eventually resolved without significant violence (this is a contested interpretation, discussed later) is a testament to the quality of police leadership evident on the ground. The police successfully maintained a micro-peace in the streets adequate to allow the macropolitical trajectory of a constitutional crisis to recover from an extraordinary rupture, and recompose itself as a self-evident status quo in which police power could again plausibly cloak itself in the legitimacy of a settled "nonpolitical" order.

The exercise of police power inside a legislative chamber is an institutionally complex issue. In a democratic system, the separation of powers should insulate the legislature from executive interference. In Taiwan the policing system is centralized under the Minister of the Interior in the president's cabinet. What powers, exactly, do these executive agents have to interfere in legislative business? In the trajectory of events leading from Chang's "30-Second Review" to the students' occupation, the constitutional complexity of this question interrupted the operational chain of police command. The first reinforcements of regular police arriving to support the skeleton staff of special legislative policemen came from a municipal police department located only one block away from the legislative building. These reinforcements did not arrive until several hours after the students made their initial entry to the legislative chambers, a delay that was decisive in successfully establishing the student position. According to police I spoke with later, that delay was caused by confusion over procedures authorizing regular police to enter the legislature, combined with political interests working to maximize that confusion to their advantage.

The students themselves were clearly aware of this situation. Among their first public statements was an appeal to Parliamentary Speaker Wang Jin-ping not to exercise the special "police powers" he held in the context of legislative operations. During an emergency conference Wang held with the premier and the head of the National Police Administration on the night of the 18th, Wang insisted that the "dignity" of the legislature be upheld and no students be harmed, a position consistent with supporting the occupation against police eviction. Wang's first public statement, given about twenty-four hours after the students entered the chamber, was a bit more nuanced. By that time, thousands of people had gathered in support of the students and the broader political contours of the event were becoming evident. Wang felt comfortable distancing himself from any formal defense of the occupation. He made a distinction between the special police powers he held in the context of legislative proceedings, and broader issues of social order outside the scope of his special jurisdiction. Because students were not legislators, he said, they were not an "object" (*duixiang*) of his special police powers. It was the National Police Administration's responsibility to deal with any criminal or order-maintenance problems the students caused. However, he went on, the issue of legislative autonomy was at stake in the situation. The overriding principle under which the situation should be managed was, therefore, avoiding precedents that might increase the capacity of the executive to interfere in legislative operations.

Tension between legislative and executive powers were embodied in a history of personal conflict between Speaker Wang and President Ma. They both belonged to the KMT, but as members of different factions. Wang had worked against Ma in the process that compelled the president to submit his CSSTA to legislative review. This provoked a personal struggle between the two, playing out as one dimension of the review process. Ma's attempt at retribution came through a cabinet-level Special Investigation Bureau (SIB), acting under what was presumably Ma's direction, which produced wiretap evidence of Wang's interference in a corruption trial, and brought criminal charges against him. These charges allowed Ma, in his role as KMT party chairman, to strip Wang of his party membership (a move which, by Taiwan's electoral law, would require Wang to resign from the legislature). Wang countered by filing a motion in Taipei District Court claiming the wiretap evidence was illegal, and got an injunction that prevented Ma from implementing party discipline until a ruling was made on the legality of the SIB's evidence. Wang thus remained speaker as investigation into the SIB wiretaps proceeded. That investigation ruled the SIB's conduct was in fact illegal. Ma's chief prosecutor was convicted of criminal misconduct, forced to resign, and sentenced to jail. This decisive legal victory of Wang over Ma, announced the week before the students broke into the legislature, seemed to indicate the clear dominance of the legislative over executive branch, at least in the arena of struggle to influence highly contested judicial outcomes.

This was the context in which the police were mobilized: a constitutional crisis characterized by tensions and ambiguities of immediate practical relevance to the work of policing. Even though Taiwan's police system is formally centralized under the executive branch, its budget and personnel decisions are attached to parliamentary bodies at the local level. These local councils are integrated into the politics of the national legislature through the webs of clientage that define Taiwanese party politics. Wang Jin-ping, as speaker of the national legislature, served as a sort of national godfather involved in managing conflict between the bosses and faction-leaders who run local political machines. Police at the local level served two masters: their commanders in the bureaucratic hierarchy that culminated in President Ma, and their patrons in local councils who operate as nodes in a web of patronage over which Speaker Wang sat as the biggest spider of all. The crisis in the legislature brought the two forms of power to which police were beholden into a relationship of overt hostility. The credibility of Ma's executive command was called into question by public outrage over his handling of the CSSTA. Meanwhile Wang's public statement, that the students were the National Police Administration's (NPA) problem but he expected them to manage their problem without intruding on his sphere of control, was an exemplary assertion of the power of a backstage boss. He expected those less powerful to assume legal responsibility for solving a problem to his satisfaction. Any police hope that the judiciary might supply an independent perspective on proper lines of legal accountability was confronted by Wang's amazing victory in his battle with Ma. Evidence of Wang's ability to interfere in judicial processes had been produced by the country's chief prosecutor, with the result that the chief prosecutor went to jail. Policemen making decisions about what to do were clearly on their own in trying to predict how their performance would be held to account after the political crisis was resolved. For the students, this was a golden opportunity. The constituted power of the state had unraveled in a manner that exposed its moral foundations to nonviolent intervention.

Hong Kong's "One Country Two Systems" was a form of government predicated on ambiguity. Beijing understood it as One Country, temporarily adjusted to accommodate the process of ironing out the local quirks of colonial history. The people of Hong Kong imagined "Two Systems" as the creation of a novel form of Chinese federalism. Prior to 2014, these contradictory interpretations of Hong Kong's political future coexisted in an awkward silence, neither one making any non-negotiable 'final' demands on the other beyond patience. This ambiguity endowed the police with a space of presumptive neutrality in which they could claim to stand for an inclusive general public welfare, regardless of how that welfare was imagined in relation to prickly differences between Hong Kong and China. The Umbrella Movement attacked and destroyed this space of presumptive neutrality. It used tactics of direct action designed to induce an antagonistic situation that would force people to choose sides. It was a strategy of schismogenesis, leveraging polarization to consolidate a localist position as the mirror image of the (now, evidently, equally polarizing) centralist position.[28] The cost of this strategy was destruction of the ambiguous, ineffable middle ground over which Hong Kong's politics had managed to muddle since the 1970s. During the period of the occupation, power over the political affairs of Hong Kong's government was temporarily seized by the people through their control of physical space. When the situation was finally brought back under governmental control, it deployed the form of jurisprudential genius that had successfully maintained the ambiguity for so long. Hong Kong's courts have historically been the locus to which its citizens have addressed hopes for popular sovereignty. "Although lacking allocative or coercive powers, [these courts] have none the less continually used their judicial independence to generate focal points facilitating convergence between SAR authorities and complainants on a common standard of Basic Law and statutory interpretation."[29] This was, in fact, precisely how the occupation was finally dispersed. After three months of political stasis, Hong Kong's courts issued civil injunctions on behalf of plaintiffs who had sued the protestors under a claim that the occupied streets negatively affected their ability to make a living. The police then "assisted" court bailiffs to enforce the injunction, clearing the streets in a putatively "nonpolitical" act of civil law enforcement. The moment of exception

[28] Cf. Brian Fong, "One Country, Two Nationalisms: Center–Periphery Relations between Mainland China and Hong Kong, 1997–2016," *Modern China* 43(5) (2017): 523–556.

[29] Ip, "Constitutional Conflict in Hong Kong under Chinese Sovereignty," 85.

was concluded by a procedurally neutral act of law enforcement, which, coincidentally, secured the political dominance of an undemocratic central authority over the political aspirations of the governed.

7.3 Reaggregation: A New Normal

When people look at police what do they see? What do they *want* to see? A community that imagines itself as self-governing wants to see itself. Democratic ideas of police reform invoke the Peelian ideal of a police/public relationship as one of identity, for example, residence rules or race or gender proportionality. Colonial policing, by contrast, practices the strategy of "policing by strangers."[30] Ruling elites who use police powers to govern a population as an efficient means to the end of imperial glory (and a profitable return on investment) expect the policed to look at their police with fear, not recognition.

What people imagine stands behind the police gaze structures the way they behave in the face of that gaze; perception of police creates the reality of policed behavior. Understanding the larger institutional significance of this is the focus of Peter Manning's dramaturgical theory of policing. It is necessary to account for the semiotic mechanisms by which police action becomes meaningful as one of the foundations for the institution's practical power. And this, as Manning has argued at length, makes democratic policing very difficult.[31] Maintaining the self-image of a peaceful pluralistic society requires police to satisfy divergent audiences, producing representations of police power that supply plausible legitimacy on multiple and potentially contradictory grounds. Achieving this balancing act, disposing of this impossible mandate, is not always possible. There are moments when police cannot make everyone happy. In those moments they must pick their audience and choose whose legitimating gaze to validate and whose to invalidate. This choice is expressed by police engagement with some fraction of the policed population by the terms of a relationship in which legitimacy is not a practical concern, that is an arena of pure material domination.

Those moments of choice are the times when the police must take sides. The moment police shift from the impossible aspiration of maintaining an inclusive-if-contradictory peace to a realist posture at war with some political fraction of the population under their power is the moment they cease

[30] Mike Brogden, "The Emergence of Police: The Colonial Dimension," *British Journal of Criminology* 27(1) (1987): 4–14.

[31] Peter K. Manning, *Democratic Policing in a Changing World* (Boulder, CO: Paradigm, 2010).

to be democratic. The divergent outcomes across the Taiwan Straits in 2014 can be understood by reference to this distinction. Taiwan's police never abandoned their democratic pretensions, even when this rendered them practically incapable of fulfilling any order-keeping function. Hong Kong's police, by contrast, remained committed to the supremacy of order, and never ceased to operate as an efficient means to that end. That they acted under the cover of law gave them ground to claim they had not abandoned democratic ideals, but in fact they had. The sovereign voice that spoke through Hong Kong's courts engineered an end to the occupation through civil judgments. This championed the liberal ideal of contracts all the way down, a consent-based world defined by the rational balance of individual civil and economic rights. But this was a legalistic solution to a political problem. It defined the problem it solved by willfully ignoring the political meaning of the occupation. The occupation itself had already established, as an indelible "focal point," a demand for clarification regarding the democratic representativeness of Hong Kong's constituted government. The occupation was not about traffic in the streets; it was about representation in the political process. The police effectively restored traffic to the streets without addressing the real significance of the conflict.

As jurisprudence, the conclusion of the 2014 occupation was a brilliant demonstration of the skills Hong Kong's courts have relied on to maintain the ambiguity between legalism and democracy at the heart of the One Country Two Systems arrangement. In this case, however, the occupation had destroyed the political utility of such ambiguity. The use of civil injunctions to resolve the physical occupation did not preserve a productive constitutional ambiguity so much as mark the political capitulation of the Hong Kong courts, an acceptance of the new division of jurisprudential labor in which Hong Kong's law was exclusively for the management of economic life and sovereign decisions about political conflict would be left entirely in the hands of the Party. "The public order coordination dilemma between the local authorities and protesters had been resolved, but the greater constitutional conflict between the Party-state and the democratic forces of Hong Kong persisted."[32] It did not persist for long, however, as the decision by the NPCSC on November 7, 2016 revealed. The return to business as usual after December 15, 2014 marked a historical movement forward into an unprecedented disjuncture between the people's concerns with economic traffic in the city streets, and the Party's unchallenged sovereignty over political matters.

[32] Ip, "Constitutional Conflict in Hong Kong under Chinese Sovereignty," 93.

8

Adaptive Authoritarian Policing

A Journey from China and Japan to Taiwan

WEITSENG CHEN*

8.1 Introduction

Taiwan was one of the East Asian developmental states that embraced the rule of law even though their political systems remained authoritarian or dictatorial until democratization in the late 1980s. This model appears to be a viable approach for establishing the rule of law down the road for countries, including Taiwan, South Korea, Singapore, and Hong Kong, during their journey of economic development within a relatively short period of time after World War II. To understand how such instrumental adoption of legal institutions was made possible and later transformed into a functional and trustworthy legal system is theoretically intriguing and may offer insight for countries that are on a seemingly similar path, such as China and Vietnam.

The police system and the exercise of police power play a central role in the operation of legal systems in these jurisdictions. In Taiwan, the police system formerly served as a coercive arm of the authoritarian regime while simultaneously conducting law enforcement vital for the rule of law to take root in society. Despite the repressive role of the police under authoritarian rule, one interesting trait of Taiwan's police system, both before and after democratization in the late 1980s, is its high degree of legitimacy and trustworthiness as perceived by the general public. With its origins from mainland China and Meiji Japan, the adaptation of authoritarian policing in Taiwan might shed light on the operation of the authoritarian legal system – if the authoritarian regime can get the police system correct, it should not be difficult to achieve a functional

* This essay benefited from comments by Hualing Fu and Frank Upham, as well as research assistance from Benjamin Heng. The author is also grateful for the financial support of NUS AcRF (R-241-000-163-115).

legal system. In this regard, studies of authoritarian policing in Taiwan could unveil the idea of the rule of law and legal institutions' evolution and transition in the authoritarian context.

Furthermore, the police system is a good testing ground to see how an authoritarian legacy has affected a young democracy posttransition, considering the police system's organizational hierarchy and the continuity of personnel and institutional culture. Some of the foregoing jurisdictions have gone through a fully-fledged political transition in addition to their economic modernization. Political democratization, however, does not necessarily lead to democratic policing. Rather, authoritarian continuity always poses a challenge for the integration between a young democracy and coercive policing since the police once acted as an extension of the military and intelligence agencies during authoritarian rule. In this regard, Taiwan's police system also presents a case study of the changing role of the police during the country's democratic consolidation. This chapter examines the link between the police and the political system, and the police adaptation to the fundamental change in political climate and institutional environment in Taiwan's postauthoritarian era. This chapter also aims to explore whether and to what extent authoritarian continuity within the police system has affected the performance of the democratic government in contemporary Taiwan.

To clarify, legal reforms under authoritarian Taiwan did not necessarily make the country as one with the rule of law, although the nascent legal system did constrain the government to a certain degree and pave the way for a transition away from authoritarianism. As such, this chapter uses the term "authoritarian legality" to refer to legal reforms promoted by strong authoritarian states, where an instrumental and strategic commitment to law could nonetheless develop and even solidify without radical democratic and/or political reform.[1] This definition of authoritarian legality constitutes a dynamic, conceptual space where legality, genuine rule of law, authoritarianism, and regime legitimacy are intertwined and therefore codevelop during the transition toward rule of law in Taiwan and several of its neighboring countries.[2] The remainder of this chapter is

[1] Weitseng Chen and Hualing Fu, *Authoritarian Legality in Asia: Formation, Development and Transition* (Cambridge: Cambridge University Press, 2020).

[2] Other concepts such as rule by law or authoritarian rule of law exist to conceptualize similar phenomena in authoritarian countries. To avoid long-lasting debates on the definition of rule of law and rule by law, I use authoritarian legality to unveil the dynamic process of evolution from rule by law to rule of law in Taiwan.

divided into five parts. Section 8.2 provides a general account on authoritarian legality and policing. Section 8.3 explores the historical foundation of authoritarian policing in Taiwan after World War II. Section 8.4 discusses the role of the police in authoritarian governance from various perspectives, including their functions in the governance structure and their interaction with the party-state. Section 8.5 discusses the legacy of authoritarian policing and its impact on democratic governance and the rule of law. Section 8.6 concludes the essay.

8.2 Authoritarian Legality and the Police

The Nationalist Party (or Kuomintang, also known as KMT) ruled Taiwan from 1945 to 2000. It took over the governance of Taiwan after World War II from Japan, which had colonized the island for 50 years. Later, after losing the civil war to the Chinese Communist Party in mainland China, the KMT relocated to Taiwan and instituted fully-fledged authoritarian rule that lasted more than four decades. Thereafter, democratization began in 1987 with the lifting of martial law and was achieved in 1996 when the first-ever direct presidential elections were held. Taiwan's democratization can be considered as one of only a few successful Asian cases as it was peaceful and was accompanied by economic prosperity. Furthermore, unlike many other parties that had instituted authoritarian rule, the KMT stayed in power for more than ten years before losing the presidential election in 2000 – only to later regain presidential power between 2008 and 2016. A stable, de facto two-party political system has been in place ever since, and the rotation of ruling parties at both central and regional levels is now the norm.

Interestingly, from the very beginning of the KMT's authoritarian rule, the party-state had embraced the idea of both the rule of law and democracy. The acceptance was instrumental and strategic as it was mainly for the sake of economic development and for establishing the party's legitimacy. However, rather than paying lip service to democracy, the party elites genuinely believed that the rule of law was necessary, and thus created a functional, viable legal system during the party's rule.

This model of authoritarian legality served several crucial functions for the KMT. First of all, it helped create the market economy, facilitate business transactions, and attract foreign direct investment. This model is closely associated with the party's performance-centric way of measuring accountability and maintaining legitimacy, as opposed to a procedural, democratic framework for state accountability. Second, this model improves and institutionalizes coordination between various levels of government and regulatory agencies. Third, this model has a symbolic function so that the KMT can distinguish itself from communist China and thereby earn international support, both politically and economically.

The police system served as a crucial mechanism for pursuing this model of authoritarian legality. In theory, the police as part of the executive branch of government investigates criminal cases, while the courts as the judicial branch of government are responsible for final adjudication. In practice, however, the police can act more swiftly and solve problems in a more efficient manner than the courts, especially since access to justice is often limited and costly for ordinary people. In comparison, the courts under authoritarian regimes are often expected to be a functional extension of the executive branch and to work together with the government, including the police, to identify and solve social problems and any irregularities.[3] The distribution of work between the police and the courts depends on political contexts, and it is not uncommon that prosecutors and the police, instead of the judiciary, are the ones truly at the center of law enforcement.[4]

The police system in Taiwan is a case in point. Taiwan's culture of authoritarian policing was formed during its colonial period (1895–1945) and played a central role under the Japanese colonial government, which was effectively a police state in that the police force penetrated the society and closely monitored the people. After World War II, the KMT inherited and resumed this police system, but also had authoritarian policing play a more sophisticated role, as the legitimacy of the KMT regime did not rely solely on coercive power but also on governmental performance.

After democratization, Taiwan's authoritarian policing has been gradually transformed into democratic policing, which follows procedures required by the law and is subject to judicial review.[5] Nonetheless, as Taiwan's peaceful

[3] For a discussion in the context of the Chinese and Japanese courts, see Frank Upham, "The Illusory Promise of the Rule of Law," in Andras Sajo (ed.), *Human Rights with Modesty: The Problem of Universalism* (New York: Springer, 2004): 279–313; Frank Upham, "Reflection on the Rule of Law in China," *National Taiwan University Law Review* 6(1) (2011): 251.

[4] See, for example, Do Ha Hai and Pip Nicholson, "Vietnamese Deliberative Authoritarianism and Legality," in Weitseng Chen and Hualing Fu (eds.), *Authoritarian Legality in Asia: Formation, Development and Transition* (Cambridge: Cambridge University Press, 2020), 227–254.

[5] For a general review, see Liqun Cao, Lanying Huang, and Ivan Sun, "From Authoritarian Policing to Democratic Policing: A Case Study of Taiwan," *Policing and Society* 26 (6) (2016): 642–658.

democratic transition did not come with radical political changes, its authoritarian legacy persists and continues to affect policing practices.

8.3 Creation of Authoritarian Policing

The police system created by Japanese colonial government in Taiwan was quite efficient and powerful, and responsible for not only maintaining social order but also handling economic matters. The police were in charge of ensuring the monopoly of certain businesses that the government and government-linked enterprises operated, such as tobacco and liquor. The police were a de facto military force by which Japan governed its colonies in a repressive manner.

Compared with Japan's other colonies in Korea and Manchuria, the police system in Taiwan was more organizational, with wide-ranging powers and a more intrusive role.[6] Taiwan did not have a modern police system at the time, and Japan thus had full latitude in creating a system that suited its governance needs in this new territory. Japanese police monitored all aspects of social life and household activities that could disturb their social engineering or cause concerns about stability, market order, hygiene, and public health. Subject matters of police power at the time that deviated from normal policing included, for example, funeral services, sewage treatment, vaccine injection, quarantine orders, tattoo making, toilet cleaning, nursing, haircut and hairstyles, and the forms and layout of houses.[7] The colonial government relied on the police to ensure social stability and deliver governmental services, and therefore delegated more administrative power to the police in Taiwan than their counterparts in Manchuria and Korea.[8] Consequently, Japan was able to exert more direct control over Taiwanese society through the police force than in Manchuria, which Japan governed through a puppet regime.[9] Japan also faced less resistance in Taiwan than in Korea, as the latter was a nation state before Japan's invasion whereas Taiwan was an immigrant society peripheral to the Chinese empire at the time.

[6] Li Lee (李理), *Research on the Police System During the Japanese Occupation in Taiwan* (*日據台灣時期警察制度研究*) (Taiwan: Strait Academic Press, 2007), 309–335.

[7] For a detailed historical account of Japanese police and policing in the context of daily life under the colonial rule, see Dai Bao-Cun (戴寶村), *The Inferiors and the Superiors (小的與大人)* (Taiwan: Jade Mountain Publishing, 2020).

[8] Li, *Research on the Police System*, 333.

[9] Ibid., 325.

One example of this pervasive and intrusive police system in Taiwan is the mandatory, comprehensive household registration system, which the police administered. Every household was registered and assigned into a network that the police closely monitored. This system also existed in Japan and its colonies in Korea and Manchuria, but not as pervasively as in Taiwan.[10] The household registration system was closely linked to the introduction of a new legal system by the Japanese. This transformed the basis on which legal relations are entered – replacing Chinese customary law and social norms with varying legal rights that are provided and protected by a modern legal system. This legal system was exclusive in that legal protection and benefits would not be offered to citizens who failed to register. Unregistered property rights, for example, would not be protected, and married couples' right to inherit each other's property would also not be recognized if their marriage was not registered. People quickly accepted this system as they came to appreciate the institutional benefits of the modern, authoritarian state based on right-centric legality.[11]

This police system was highly oppressive, but it governed efficiently. The KMT inherited this police apparatus when it relocated to Taiwan in 1945. The party initially dispatched 932 newly-recruited and briefly-trained police officers from the mainland to Taiwan as the main force to expel Japanese forces. However, the party leaders realized that it was more efficient to govern the country using the existing police system instead of replacing it with their own from mainland China.[12] In this way, the KMT could also benefit from the police's supreme authority in society at the time. For example, anyone walking by police stations, regardless of whether there were policemen inside or not, had to stop and bow in the direction of the police station before they moved on.[13] As a result, the authoritarian regime began its rule and promoted legality with a relatively efficient police force as part of its powerful state apparatus.

[10] Carter J. Eckert, Ki-Baik Lee, Young Ick Lew, Michael Robinson, and Edward W. Wagner, *Korea Old and New: History* (Cambridge, MA: Harvard University Press, 1990). In Japan, a similar but less oppressive system existed too at the time. Even now, the Japanese police retain their strong presence in the local communities and enjoys a high degree of legitimacy. See, for example, Mark West, "Losers: Recovering Lost Property in Japan and the United States," *The Law & Society Review* 37 (2003): 369–424.

[11] Kuo Yung-Hua, "Personal Identity under a Modern State" (Master's thesis, National Taiwan University College of Law, 2010), 64.

[12] Tsai Hwui-Yu (蔡慧玉), *Taiwan Take-Over and Police Administration Post-WWII* (*光復臺灣與戰後警政*) (Taipei: Academia Sinica Institute of Taiwan History, 2013), 5–6.

[13] Chang Re-De (張瑞德) and Cao Xi (曹忻), *From Junior Officer to Police Chief: Interview with Lu Yu-Chun* (*從一線一星到警政署長：盧毓鈞先生訪談錄*) (Taipei: Academia Historica, 2011), 52.

8.4 Authoritarian Policing and Governance

8.4.1 Governing through the Police

Like several other Asian states, legality in Taiwan was promoted by a strong authoritarian state before genuine rule of law was achieved. A dilemma therefore exists: legal system development is both dependent on and constrained by strong authoritarian states. This greatly complicates the function of legality and the trajectory of the rule-of-law development.

Nonetheless, several characteristics of this trajectory of rule of law development in East Asia can be identified. First of all, rule of law and democracy are not intertwined in that the law serves as a means of authoritarian governance rather than imposes any democratic constraint on the government. Second, law is aimed at promoting economic growth, improving state capacity, and consolidating political power; thus, law empowers rather than constrains the state.[14] Accordingly, any breach of law by the government could be justified if the breach could enhance the performance of the state. For example, it is a norm that industrial policies and political maneuvers can trump law, as law is used later to codify the outcome of mature policy experiments. Moreover, public enforcement is emphasized while private enforcement is de-emphasized. The police system arguably served as a more crucial mechanism than the courts for the purposes of public enforcement.

Furthermore, the police force was integral to survival for the KMT in order to rebuild a political regime that was devastated by the effects of World War II and the subsequent civil war.[15] Constrained by limited resources, the KMT was cost-conscious when designing its governance structure, including the police system. The KMT's attitude toward the household registration system is a case in point. When the KMT came to power in Taiwan, the party elites considered Japan's household registration system overly repressive and thus decided to loosen it.[16] Consequently, throughout the 1950s, the police were authorized to collect household information for the purpose of crime control only, and

[14] Weitseng Chen, "Hybrid Regimes: Constitutionalism and Economic Development" in David Law, Holning Lau, and Alex Schwartz (eds.), *Oxford Handbook of Constitutional Law in Asia* (Oxford: Oxford University Press, 2022). See also Katharina Pistor and Curtis Milhaupt, *Law & Capitalism* (Chicago: University of Chicago Press, 2008): 31–38.

[15] For a review of varying functions, see Chen Tien-Shou (陳添壽), *The History of Social Order in Taiwan: An Interaction between Police and Political Economy* (*台灣治安制度史：警察與政治經濟的對話*) (Taipei: Literary Times, 2010), 352–353.

[16] Kuo Yung-Hua, "Personal Identity under a Modern State," 70.

a separate, specialized agency was placed in charge of administering the household registration system. However, since the late 1960s, the KMT decided to restore the old colonial system, which party leaders considered more efficient and effective for their authoritarian rule. As such, the Household Registration Act was amended, thereby putting the police in charge of the system once more. As a result, the police also served as census-takers, with legitimate authority and enormous power to visit and monitor any changes within individual households on a regular basis.[17]

The relationship between the police and mafia also exemplifies the KMT's cost-consciousness in formulating its governance strategy. To effectively and efficiently rule a society where the KMT was considered as a minority émigré regime, the party delegated some jobs to the mafia, albeit informally. Unlike the police, the mafia could utilize market mechanisms under the shadow of policing and law enforcement, such as collecting service fees in exchange for maintaining order for the illegal prostitution industry and providing security for prostitutes and customers.[18] The mafia was also able to resort to extralegal means for collecting intelligence for the police and disciplining breakers of laws or norms at a time when the legal system and law enforcement were substandard. In fact, before its relocation to Taiwan, the KMT was infamous for collaborating with the mafia in metropolitan cities such as Shanghai, thereby giving rise to close ties between the mafia and the KMT's intelligence agencies. Along with its increase in political influence, the mafia was also involved in provincial politics and local elections throughout the period of the KMT's authoritarian rule in Taiwan.[19]

For the purpose of strengthening its political control and mobilization, the KMT further incorporated the police system into its party apparatus. For instance, the police played a crucial role in elections. They were responsible for collecting intelligence about opposition candidates and mobilizing voters for KMT candidates. Local police leaders were also involved in the party's nomination process as they were usually at the center of the local political networks. Local police chiefs also served in the KMT's party organization.[20] The KMT would also use the police and the

[17] This peculiar system ceased in 1992 after democratization.

[18] Erik Mobrand, in Chapter 6 in this volume, also discusses the role of the mafia in South Korea and its ability to utilize the market mechanism to main social order.

[19] Zhao Yung-Mao (趙永茂), *The Characteristics and Development of Local Politics in Taiwan* (台灣地方政治的變遷與特質) (Taipei: Han-Lu Book Publishing, 2002), 384–403.

[20] Chang and Cao, *From Junior Officer to Police Chief*, 56–57.

prosecutorial system to protect loyal politicians while punishing political dissidents and disciplining those who had disobeyed party rules. This could be done by initiating criminal investigation or merely by frequently visiting the targeted persons or their family members at home.[21] Given the enormous power they possessed, without any substantive mechanism for accountability, some policemen also capitalized on their power, and consequently, structural and collective corruption was not uncommon.[22]

Moreover, the police played a role in the structure of state capitalism that the KMT had designed. The party-state borrowed Japan's idea of an "economic police force" responsible for maintaining market order and ensuring the state's monopoly over certain industries such as tobacco and alcohol.[23] The police were delegated enormous power to investigate market irregularities and behaviors that violated the laws protecting the state monopoly in the market.[24] As a result, the KMT, thanks to state- and party-owned enterprises, was once considered the richest political party in the world. All in all, the police were a vital mechanism that supported the KMT's model of authoritarian governance based on political control, state capitalism, and authoritarian legality.

8.4.2 The Party-State's Controlling Mechanisms over the Police

The KMT tightly controlled the police force through a centralized, military-style personnel system. The most important control mechanism is personnel control and the subordination of the police force to intelligence and secret police agencies. The KMT's military and intelligence personnel controlled and dominated the highest offices of the police apparatus, including its personnel system. Policemen trained in orthodox police educational institutes were deemed inferior to military and intelligence officers.

The operation of this controlling mechanism was rocky sometimes but generally stable and self-enforcing, in that various involved actors abided by this control. Policemen trained under the orthodox police education track often complained about military officers-turned-policemen

[21] Wang Chin-Shou "Judicial Independence Reform and the Breakdown of the Kuomintang Clientelism," *(Taiwan de sifa duli gaige yu guomindang shicong zhuyi de bengkui) Taiwan Political Science Review* 10 (2006): 103, 120.

[22] Chang and Cao, *From Junior Officer to Police Chief.*

[23] Xi Shien-De (習賢德), *Police and 228 Incident* (警察與二、二八事件) (Taipei: Shihying Publishing House, 2012), 24.

[24] *2002 Annual Report of Corrective Measures of the Control Yuan (Taiwan)* (中華民國九十一年監察院糾正案彙編(三)), 1673–74, volume III (2002).

regularly abusing their power, adopting military-style leadership, and lacking professional skills.[25] Nonetheless, being part of the mighty military and intelligence apparatus also made the "orthodox police" more powerful. The KMT's reliance on the military to control the police force resulted in certain institutional changes. For example, in order to resolve a dispute involving a military general's unhappiness about his corresponding rank and salary after being appointed as the police chief, the government enacted an ad hoc law that generally permitted retired military officers to serve as policemen with favorable corresponding ranks and salary packages.[26] This "back door" for military personnel further enhanced military control over the police force and in turn sparked factional politics within the police system. For instance, it was common for different factions within the police system to unite in order to compete collectively with military personnel over key posts and control over certain agencies.[27]

Prior to democratization, all of the police chiefs were military generals who once served in the army and intelligence agencies. Some other key positions in the police force were also dominated by military personnel. For example, the head of the Superintendent's Office of National Police Administration was always held by officials previously from the army's propaganda units.[28] It was only in 1989, two years after the lifting of martial law, that a senior police officer (Chuang Heng-Dai) was appointed for the first time as the police chief. Before this unprecedented appointment, the competition among various police factions for this appointment was initially fierce. However, these factions eventually harmonized in the face of their mutual enemy – a military candidate.[29] The police factions won as a result of their unity as well as the change in the political culture postdemocratization.

The other controlling mechanism is direct party control. The KMT set up numerous party cells that were spread across police agencies to control and monitor this system. These party cells existed in every branch of the police force. These cells and cadres were controlled by a centralized party organization called Liu Zhong-Xin (which literally means a revival of the party-state).[30] Most policemen were also KMT party members, who were

25 Chang and Cao, *From Junior Officer to Police Chief*, 16.

26 Ibid., 15–19. The law referred to here is the Act for Examination and Appointment of Retired Military Personnel for Civil Positions (後備軍人轉任公職考試與比敘條例) (1967).

27 Chang and Cao, *From Junior Officer to Police Chief*.

28 Ibid., 248. The National Police Administration is the top police administration agency in Taiwan.

29 Chang and Cao, *From Junior Officer to Police Chief*, 258–261.

30 Chen Tien-Shou, *The History of Social Order in Taiwan*, 131.

required to join the party upon being admitted to police schools. Those who refused to join the party would receive unfair treatment during the training.[31] Liu Zhong-Xin lasted for decades, and was only abolished in 1987 under the pressure of democratization. However, the links between the party and the police system remained, though not as openly and shamelessly as before. These links remained a crucial mechanism for the KMT to mobilize the police at critical moments, such as elections and political campaigns, although some other functions such as ideology control slowly faded away along with democratic consolidation and the professionalization of the police system. That being said, such party links demonstrated the continuity of authoritarianism after democratization (as will be discussed later), and this continuity later led to a decrease in state capacity and, consequently, the performance of Taiwanese democracy as a whole.

Another softer and more natural mechanism for control was the use of established territorial bonds between party elites and policemen. Along with the party's relocation to Taiwan, the KMT also brought over thousands of military personnel to join the police force. Additionally, thanks to the KMT's language policy, "mainlanders", which refer to people that relocated together with the KMT from mainland China and accounted for approximately 15 percent of the total population in Taiwan, had an advantage in the entrance exam of police schools over their local Taiwanese competitors, who usually spoke only Japanese or Chinese dialect.[32] As a result, in Taiwan's early years, mainlanders accounted for 70–80 percent of policemen.[33] Furthermore, they were natural supporters of the KMT, which was itself led by mainlanders, and was thus considered as a minority émigré regime ruling the majority of local Taiwanese.[34] In fact, the factions within the police system were first formed according to the respective provincial hometowns of these policemen in mainland China. For example, three major factions in the police force were constituted by members from Fujian, Shandong, and Jiangsu provinces banded together by their respective provincial affinities.[35]

31 Chen Pe-Chi, "The Hardship of Junior Policemen" (初入花世界？菜鳥保警苦), May 11, 2014, udn.com, https://theme.udn.com/theme/story/6114/217887 (accessed March 5, 2020).

32 Chang and Cao, *From Junior Officer to Police Chief*, 19.

33 During the colonial era, only a few Taiwanese were hired to serve as low-ranking policemen. The KMT, therefore, did not have to deal with legacy personnel in the police system postcolonial era.

34 Ibid. For a further discussion, see `Weitseng Chen, "Twins of Opposites: Why China Will Not Follow Taiwan's Model of Rule of Law Transition toward Democracy," *American Journal of Comparative Law* 66 (2018): 481–535.

35 Fujian, Shandong, and Jiangsu are three provinces in China.

8.4.3 *The Party's Legitimacy Engineering*

An intriguing question about the party's rule through the police is how the police in Taiwan obtained high levels of legitimacy despite the constabulary's repressive role in the authoritarian regime. Citizens generally respect and trust police officers as public servants and the police force as the nation's law enforcement agency. People call the police to intervene not only when crimes happen, but also when other personal episodes happen.[36] In the countryside, it is common to see policemen having tea with local residents for hours in the shade of a tree or in front of shops or houses. This differs from some other Asian countries such as India where people avoid calling the police unless it is unavoidable. Thanks to such credibility and legitimacy, the police might discredit and discipline political dissidents merely by visiting their homes because the police's presence in itself could serve as a "bad" label on the dissidents, especially in a close-knit society where family members and neighbors might thereafter exert pressure on the targeted persons.

Under its authoritarian rule, the KMT's ultimate strategy to maintain the legitimacy of the police is to create a dual-track police force: the regular police and the secret police. Martial law delegated jurisdiction over certain political acts, such as anticommunist operations and the restriction of freedom of speech and assembly, to the military courts, military police, and the intelligence and secret police agencies. In cases involving overlapping jurisdictions, regular policemen were likely to be subjected to the command of the secret police, even if the secret policemen deployed were of a lower rank. In practice, as of the early 1990s, the National Police Administration, which was the top police administration office, remained part of a national intelligence network, and therefore was subordinate to the National Security Bureau (NSB), the top intelligence agency.[37]

In comparison, regular policemen were put in charge of civil matters that were closer to the daily lives of ordinary citizens. Their authority was limited compared with the secret police. For example, the secret police monopolized surveillance capacity while the regular police force had to rely on the secret

[36] One extreme example, disclosed by a police officer I interviewed, is that a person had called the police for help when he discovered that a public restroom he was at was short of toilet paper.

[37] The NSB effectively led four agencies, which were set under different administrative branches: Investigation Bureau of Ministry of Justice, the Military Police Command, Taiwan Garrison Command, and the National Police Administration under the Ministry of Internal Affairs. Chang and Cao, *From Junior Officer to Police Chief*, 284–285.

police's cooperation when surveillance footage was necessary for a criminal investigation.[38] It was common for regular policemen to complain that the secret police refused to share or even stole the former's intelligence.[39] In the face of increasing social unrest, coupled with an increase in economic prosperity and in turn legal consciousness, the KMT created a special security police that operated in a military fashion and were trained and based in military-style barracks. The special security police were not responsible for duties that were handled by the regular police. Rather, they specialized in dealing with social protests and functioned as riot police.[40] As a result, this 'good cop/bad cop' style of work allocation preserved and enhanced the legitimacy of the police system as a whole under the authoritarian regime, whose continued ability to rule depended highly on the police.

This dual-track allocation of duties was reflected in the KMT's approach to personnel control over the police. Prior to democratization, all police chiefs were military generals from the top intelligence and secret police agencies. Interestingly, all of these generals served as a deputy chief in their respective agencies prior to their appointment as police chief. This indicates the subordination of regular police to the intelligence and secret police agencies. Among the generals-turned police chiefs, the only one who had never served in a secret police agency is General Kong Ling-Cheng, but he was extremely close to both President Chiang Kai-Shek and his son and successor Chiang Ching-Kuo. Before leading the police force, he served as the chief of the Presidential Security Agency, which is in fact a specialized quasi-intelligence agency.

8.5 Authoritarian Continuity in a Liberal Democracy

The dual structure of the authoritarian police apparatus that the KMT designed enabled the police to smoothly go through Taiwan's democratic transition. Democratic reforms quickly eliminated the "bad cop" part of the apparatus that was once put at the center of authoritarian rule. Meanwhile, the "good cop" part continued its functions for everyday policing and became the face of the police apparatus. While this largely explains the adaptability of the police in the posttransition era, it also accounts for the authoritarian continuity within the police apparatus owing to the merger between the two.

38 Chang and Cao, *From Junior Officer to Police Chief*, 316–317.

39 Ibid.

40 Chen, "Twins of Opposites."

8.5.1 Legacies of Authoritarian Policing

Authoritarian continuity persists through various channels, such as legacy personnel and their perception of legality and democracy (e.g. crime control justifies the infringement of human rights; factual finding trumps due process requirement), and therefore affects policies, institutional design, and law enforcement. To analyze such continuity and its impact, two general approaches exist. The institutionalist approach assumes that institutions shape individuals' incentives, strategy selection, and preference formation. Even though a new institutional equilibrium has been reached and has become self-enforcing after the democratic transition, it is not formed in a vacuum but rather is influenced by preexisting norms and institutions, thereby reflecting/revealing authoritarian continuity. In comparison, the culture-centric approach focuses on actors of a field at issue and suggests that policing practices in Asia are affected by a composition of communitarian ideas (such as *guanxi*, trust, harmony, or face) embedded in political life.[41] In this regard, authoritarian continuity is a natural product of cultural continuity.

In Taiwan, this continuity comes with an intriguing phenomenon with respect to the legitimacy of the police. Throughout the authoritarian years and the following democratic period, the police force has generally a strong legitimacy and has been perceived as one of the most trustworthy government agencies, regardless of its changing nature. For example, surveys over the past two decades show that people trust the police more than congressmen, journalists, and judges. In a 2019 survey about social trust, 76.5 percent of the interviewees expressed their trust in the local police officers, compared with 39.6 percent for judges and 53.9 percent for lawyers.[42] This public attitude shows that the police system has been very adaptive in Taiwan to earn public trust, whereas judges and lawyers, despite the improving quality of personnel and decisions coupled with institutional reforms over the years, remain distant from the public. That being said, considering that legacies persist and continue, this part of the chapter examines the legacies' impact on democratic governance and legal reforms in the posttransition era.

[41] See, for example, Jeffrey Martin, "A Reasonable Balance of Law and Sentiment: Social Order in Democratic Taiwan from the Policeman's Point of View," *Law & Society Review* 41 (2007): 665–698; Jeffrey Martin, "The Hukou and Traditional Virtue: An Ethnographic Note on Taiwanese Policing," *Theoretical Criminology* 17 (2013): 261–269

[42] Global Views Monthly, "2019 Survey on Social Trust in Taiwan" (2019台灣社會信任調查), May 23, 2019, gvm.com, www.gvm.com.tw/article/61091 (accessed March 10, 2020).

The most observable continuity exists in the organizational structure and personnel culture. For example, the Taiwan Garrison Command, a notorious secret police organization during the martial law era, was restructured in 1992 and transformed into the Coast Guard Command and Military Reserve District Command. Infamous for suppressing speech, publications, and activities promoting democracy, socialism, and Taiwanese independence, the Taiwan Garrison Command was also involved in illegal arrests and torture, as well as military trials that had broad jurisdiction over such activities. After democratization, the same personnel stayed and operated the reorganized system, albeit in a very different political climate with reassigned work.

In addition, the training of police officers has retained its authoritarian approach.[43] Teaching materials have generally incorporated discourse on the rule of law and emphasized the importance of human rights protection. However, one can still find some materials that focus on how to identify the "enemies" of society, and treat the freedom of assembly not as an expression of opinion but a disruption of social order.[44] Enforcement styles developed in the early years also continue in this system that emphasizes experience, seniority, and hierarchy.

Continuity also exists in law. During the martial law era, the normal constitutional order was suspended and overruled by martial law, giving rise to a number of laws being passed that suppressed political, social, and economic rights. Politically, for example, elections at central level were suspended and restrictions on the establishment of new political parties were imposed. Economically, state-owned enterprises benefited from financial repression under which private, small-, and middle-sized firms had difficulty in obtaining credit from state-controlled banks. Socially, the KMT set up party cells in universities, social organizations, and governmental agencies to monitor members of society. After democratization, martial law and relevant special legislation were quickly lifted. However, many restrictive laws that existed in the normal legal system survived democratization, although with less severe penalties.

For example, laws concerning police powers, which were usually transplanted from Germany and Japan in the early 20th century, are typically

[43] Hsu Jen-Show, "Rethinking the Legal System of Policing Protest in Taiwan: Focusing on Protest Policing and Anti-Repression Strategy after Party Alteration" (LLM thesis, National Taiwan University College of Law, 2015), 217.

[44] Ibid., 134, 217.

loosely constructed with broad language to allow the executive branch of the government, including local governments, to further supplement. Furthermore, police power is highly centralized and usually provided in various types of laws at the central level.[45] For instance, laws that authorize the police to intervene in the freedom of speech are not just the Police Law but also the Criminal Law, Assembly and Parade Act, and a few others. Unless a thorough review of all legislation that concerns important aspects of social life can be conducted, the legacy of authoritarian policing will linger for a long period of time.

8.5.2 Democratic Progress and Political Decay

After democratization, the police and the exercising of policing power have been quickly democratized and professionalized. The authoritarian legacy and persisting culture of law enforcement emphasizes not only law but also sentiment, reason, *guanxi*, and harmony. For example, policemen usually play the role of moderator in their jurisdiction to defuse disputes between complainants and wrongdoers, rather than rigidly enforcing the law that is being violated.[46] That said, there is no doubt that the police system has gone through an institutional overhaul based on democratic values and rule of law principles.[47] Both the judiciary and the police authority have introduced stringent evidence rules into the investigation procedure to prevent duress and undue influence and to examine the reliability of a confession.[48]

Nonetheless, authoritarian continuity, the byproduct of an incremental and peaceful democratic transition, triggered a backlash against the authoritarian legacy after democratization. Such tensions between authoritarian legacy and democratic values gave rise to long-lasting political struggles and, consequently, weakened state capacity and harmed the performance of the democratic government. This "democratic civil war," as some commentators coined it, led to decay in both authoritarianism as well as liberal democracy.

45 Hsu, "Rethinking the Legal System of Policing Protest in Taiwan."

46 For more examples, see Martin, "A Reasonable Balance of Law and Sentiment."

47 In fact, soon after Taiwan's democratization, the problems of the police system were studied and published by the KMT's own think tank. See Lin May-Ling (林美玲), *The Issues about Social Order and Policing* (治安問題與警力運用) (Taipei: Institute of National Policy, 1994).

48 Chen Yin-Tsong (陳英淙) and Huang Hui-Ting(黃惠婷), *Policing and Its Authority under the Rule of Law* (法治國之警察理念與權限) (Taipei: Angle Publishing, 2007), 266–278.

This decaying process reflects an inherent defect of nonrevolutionary democratic transition, which usually results in a disconnect between democratization and political reforms.[49] Like South Korea, Taiwan's democratization process was generally peaceful and less revolutionary than many other democratic transitions in Eastern Europe and Latin America. Praised as a successful model of democratic transition, this nondisruptive process was not accompanied by drastic political reforms at the time. The disconnect between democratization and actual political and institutional reforms also explains why the authoritarian party still enjoys a certain level of popularity owing to its legitimacy during the authoritarian era. In theory, it implies that the parties might return to power if they could adapt to the new democratic polity. Indeed, this was the case for the KMT, which regained the presidency only eight years after losing the presidential election to a rival party in 2000. As a result, in the face of fragmented reform results, activists continued to call for reforms posttransition, while KMT party elites persistently resisted.

During this prolonged process, reformists resorted to liberal values and, when possible, implemented them in judicial policies, including the restructuring of governmental organizations such as the police (e.g. to decentralize police power), provide new interpretations of law (e.g. to limit police discretionary powers by applying the rule of proportionality), engage in judicial reforms (e.g. to enhance judicial review, to restrict martial court jurisdiction), and other political agendas relevant to the judicial system (e.g. to call for transitional justice). In comparison, those who benefited under the authoritarian regime continued to do what they had been doing in gray areas, and did so very well, even after they had formally stepped down.[50] Overall, Taiwan's authoritarian legacies were transformed and incorporated into a political force guarded by conservative values, although "conservative" is probably the wrong label for

[49] Shen Yu-Chun (沈有忠), "Dominant Party and Democracy: Case of Taiwan" (優勢政黨與民主：台灣經驗), in Sun Tsai-Wei and Wu Yu-Shan (eds.), *Dominant Party and Democracy: Asian Experiences* (優勢政黨與民主：亞洲經驗) (Taipei: Chuliu Publising, 2017), 93.

[50] For example, retired party cadres or military and police officers could easily find a new position in state-owned and party-owned enterprises. A related phenomenon is that democratization somehow serves as a process of legalizing illegality under the authoritarian regime. For example, certain personnel, who usually lacked educational qualification and/or did not pass the recruitment examinations, could become public servants protected by law. See also Michael Albertus and Victor Menaldo, *Authoritarianism and the Elite Origins of Democracy* (Cambridge: Cambridge University Press, 2018), 3 (who suggest that many young democracies are often confronted with the problem of authoritarian continuity).

these legacy authoritarians as they do not necessarily believe in limited government, deregulation, free market and other conservative values in the conventional sense.

Protracted political conflicts between liberals and legacy authoritarians have continued for more than two decades and led to severely divided politics. This division has spread widely to many aspects of public policy, including election campaigns, political discourse, economic policies, foreign relations, and education reform. Partisan fighting leaves little room for policy deliberation. While insecure authoritarians resisted liberal reforms and compromised on the implementation of any kind of reform, frustrated liberals in turn resorted to more drastic reform measures. Consequently, divided politics became a chronic political disease, and the treatment process unwittingly led to a decay in state capacity, compromising the state's ability to provide public goods, deliberate over public policies, and engage in civil society.

The police system also reflects the decay in state capacity. Decentralization of executive power as part of the overall postdemocratization reforms caused the police to become subject to local politics. With the main opposition party, the Democratic Progressive Party (DPP), gaining control of local governments through elections, the KMT and DPP competed with each other for administrative control over the police force. There were several occasions when local governments forbade local police from following the orders of the central police leadership. When the DPP governed the country's capital Taipei while the KMT controlled the presidential office, some extreme scenarios happened. In one instance, the DPP mayor directed the local policemen to confront their fellow policemen who were dispatched by the central police bureau to dismiss pro-DPP social protestors. This was possible because of unclear and overlapping jurisdiction between local and central governments over certain matters. Similar tensions were fueled by an increase in calls for greater autonomy for local governments, to further decentralize executive power that was once centralized by the KMT and thus considered as a symbol of authoritarianism. Hence, police power was gradually decentralized in the new political climate.

Furthermore, although the decentralization agenda seemed politically correct in the postdemocratization political climate, it embroiled the police force in factional and nasty local politics unleashed by democratization. During authoritarian rule, local police budgets mainly came from the central government. From 1991 onwards, this centralized system gradually changed. After the first presidential election in 1996, local police relied on budgetary support from local governments.[51] Budget constraints made coordination and mutual support between different police forces less efficient than before.[52] As a result, cost consciousness interestingly changed the police attitude toward social protests, making them more conflict-averse so as to incur lower administrative costs.[53] Moreover, under the decentralized budgetary system, local congressmen and politicians extended their influence over law enforcement and police personnel affairs. Politicians lobbied over law enforcement measures that would affect their political supporters, including matters ranging from traffic tickets, to the ways to respond to social protests, and to criminal investigations including corruption investigation.[54]

Electoral politics also caused the increased influence of local politics over the police. After democratization, the KMT transformed its own party governance structure, from an elite/technocrat-centric structure to one controlled by politicians from all sectors of society with varying backgrounds (including gangsters). This was as long as the KMT-nominated candidates had a high chance of being elected. Such change in power structure further intensified undue influence over local police forces.[55] For example, local congresspersons would retaliate against the local police officers who initiated corruption investigations against the congresspersons during their campaign by, for example, cutting budgets or intervening in the promotion decisions with respect to particular police officers.[56] To be fair, this was not just a practice of congresspersons from the KMT, but also of those from the DPP and other parties. Thus, this was a structural issue.

Increasing judicial scrutiny over the police's acts further constrained the police. In cases involving political assemblies; for example, courts in the early years would respect the police's exercise of discretion to decide whether to dismiss an assembly on grounds of security concerns, as long as the procedural requirements set by law were satisfied.[57] But such practices

[51] For example, budget for purchasing police cars, operating training centers, and constructing offices and dormitories. Po-Jen Chen, "The Political Economy of Local Police Budgeting System in Taiwan" (Master's thesis, National Taiwan University, 2012), 59–60, 75.

[52] Hsu, "Rethinking the Legal System of Policing Protest in Taiwan," 136.

[53] Ibid., 146.

[54] Chen, "The Political Economy of Local Police Budgeting System in Taiwan," 52–53.

[55] Some scholars have begun to call for the recentralization of administrative power over police personnel and the budget of the police force.

[56] Chen, "The Political Economy of Local Police Budgeting System in Taiwan," 54.

[57] Article 26 of Act of Assembly and Parade.

changed in 2002, and the courts are now more willing to conduct substantive reviews to discover whether such decisions were made according to the rule of proportionality, in addition to procedural requirements.[58] Furthermore, the Constitutional Court began to intervene in and impose constitutional constraints on police power.[59] This differs from the court's activities during the authoritarian era: it was once embarrassed by the KMT's ignorance over its decision to announce a police law unconstitutional. At the same time, liberal reforms after democratization empowered nongovernmental organizations and activists to pursue reforms through social movements. In the face of various social movements, the police have become more tolerant of, and even cooperative with, social protests – partly because they try to avoid legal disputes in which the police feel that they would lack support from the judiciary in a liberal political climate.[60]

A related phenomenon is the overall change in gauging government performance, from growth-oriented to service-oriented performance. In the face of divided politics and a challenging economic climate, the new democratic government failed to deliver rapid economic growth as the authoritarian, developmental state had done until 2000. In response, under reelection pressures, various levels of governments turned to the provision of good service as an alternative. As a result, this change in the orientation of governance has been reflected in police operations as well. For example, local police administration offices enhanced the police's involvement in community services, including, for instance, regular visits to seniors living by themselves. Similarly, a secret police officer once in charge of speech and publication censorship could be made accountable to the people by providing public services for the people he used to secretly monitor for speech and assembly control.[61] Accordingly, people expect such services from the police as well. In some extreme cases, people have

[58] Hsu, "Rethinking the Legal System of Policing Protest in Taiwan," 133–135, 166.

[59] For example, Interpretation No. 718 (2014) confirms that it is unconstitutional for police to impose an approval requirement on incidental or urgent assemblies and demonstrations. See also, Jiunn-Rong Yeh, "Marching towards Civic Constitutionalism with Sunflowers," *Hong Kong Law Journal* 45 (2015) 315–330.

[60] Hsu, "Rethinking the Legal System of Policing Protest in Taiwan," 129, 137–138.

[61] This is similar to the second republic regime of South Korea in the early 1960s, which reformed and laid off 17,000 policemen under democratic pressure. This in turn decreased the state's governance capacity as the government relied on the police system to penetrate the local society in order to govern, as the Liberal Party itself did not have sufficient support to control the local people. See David Kang, *Crony Capitalism: Corruption and Development in South Korea and the Philippines* (Cambridge: Cambridge University Press, 2002).

even called the police when they were unable to withdraw cash from faulty ATM machines, failed to successfully catch mice in their own homes, or needed help with fixing pipe leakages.

In short, this mix of continuity and democratic changes has led to role confusion, thus affecting the allocation of human and financial resources. Consequently, despite the democratic achievements and the reforms made to the policy system, it diminishes police capacity, which is in fact a partial manifestation of the overall decay of state capacity.

8.6 Conclusion

Authoritarian legality is functional and stable only if it is self-enforcing. People are willing to comply with the law if they feel they are better off within rather than outside the legal system. In Taiwan, the police system as the center of the KMT's authoritarian legality was initially established by the Japanese colonial government with absolute power in the face of local rebellions. The colonial government was a police state but was also quite legalistic. The oppressive police system was introduced by the Japanese together with a modern legal system that streamlined social and economic relations under Chinese customary law and hence facilitated market transactions. People soon felt the benefits of compliance and accepted this police system. The post-World War II socioeconomic conditions allowed the KMT to inherit this police apparatus and assume authoritarian legality. A strong, capable and legitimate police system made the KMT secure to pursue other reforms, which in turn enhanced the legitimacy of the authoritarian regime.[62]

Specifically, the police as a law enforcement agency played a key role in ensuring authoritarian legality. The police functioned not only as a conventional law enforcement agency but also as census-takers, public service providers, intelligence units, election campaign organizers, and party cadres. The KMT maintained the legitimacy of its police state by splitting jurisdictions into "good cops" in charge of civil matters and public services, and "bad cops" in charge of political control. It also devised a number of controlling mechanisms to ensure the subordination of normal police to the party, military, intelligence agencies, and the secret police.

[62] This colonial legacy means that Taiwan's experience is not necessarily replicable. In China, for example, compared with the KMT, the CCP appears to be insecure, and such insecurities have incentivized the CCP to tighten social and political control.

The legacy of Taiwan's authoritarian policing lingered after democratization, which eliminated the "bad cop" part quickly and merged it into the overall police apparatus. Personnel, institutions, and culture persisted owing to the peaceful, nonrevolutionary nature of Taiwan's political transition. From a broader perspective, similar continuity and issues are also manifested in Taiwan's posttransition politics and struggles. The mix of authoritarian continuity and prolonged political conflicts between liberals and authoritarians led to divided politics and a decay in state capacity. Liberals resorted to drastic approaches to push for reforms and continue to develop and engage in social movements. As a result, the "strong state – weak society" political structure that characterized the authoritarian era gradually transitioned into one of "weak state – strong society" after democratization. Despite its democratic achievement, this structure seems to be paradoxically detrimental to the performance of this young democracy, resulting in disappointment among both liberals and authoritarians as it could be a source of populist sentiment and the revival of illiberalism – a phenomenon we have witnessed around the world over the past decade.

9

Organizational Legacies of Authoritarian Police in Postwar Japan

KOICHI NAKANO

This chapter provides a political-sociological study of the authoritarian police tradition in postwar Japan through an analysis of the organizational change, career paths, and retirement patterns of elite police bureaucracy.

The data set that serves as the basis of this study was collected by the author for all of the 199 elite bureaucrats who occupied and/or retired from the posts of bureau chief (director-general) or above in the state police administration between 1945 and 2013 and covers both their career paths and post-retirement posts. These posts comprise the following: the Police Affairs Bureau Chief of the Ministry of the Interior; the Commissioner-General, Deputy Commissioner-General, Police Affairs Bureau Chief, Chief Secretary, Criminal Affairs Bureau Chief, Security Bureau Chief, Traffic Bureau Chief, Community Safety Bureau Chief, Info-Communications Bureau Chief of the National Police Agency (NPA), or their equivalent positions in its predecessor organizations; the Head of the Imperial Guard Headquarters; and the Superintendent-General of the Tokyo Metropolitan Police Department (TMPD). Several more senior bureaucrats from the recent years have also been surveyed to update and complement the database as necessary.

Commonly, the police are subdivided into the following three categories. First, there are the "political police" (*seiji keisatsu*), whose role consists of the maintenance of public security and regime order led by the Security Bureau (Keibi Kyoku) of the NPA; they include the Public Security Department (Kōan Bu) of the TMPD, the public security divisions of other local police forces, and also the Imperial Guard Headquarters. Secondly, there are the "criminal police" (*keiji keisatsu*), who are overseen by the Criminal Affairs Bureau of the NPA and the criminal departments and divisions of the local police forces. Finally, there are the "administrative police" (*gyōsei keisatsu*), referring to police work conducted by the Community Safety Bureau and the Traffic Bureau. In addition, there are organs within the NPA that deal with the organizational and personnel management of the police administration and forces nationwide: the Commissioner-General's Secretariat (headed by the Chief Secretary) and the Police Affairs Bureau (until 1994). The Info-Communications Bureau is in charge of information and communications technology and is staffed by technical experts (called *gikan* (technicians)), while the rest of the NPA is dominated by law-trained, cadre-track bureaucrats, many of whom are graduates of the Law Faculty of the University of Tokyo.

Through an analysis of this data set, this chapter assesses the organizational impact of the democratization reforms of the police bureaucracy implemented during the US Occupation. It also pays attention to the persistence and revival of some important institutional and cultural legacies of the prewar police in spite of the regime change. These are the legacies of the prewar "political police," most notoriously known and remembered as the Special Higher Police (SHP, Tokubetsu Kōtō Keisatsu or Tokkō Keisatsu, for short) in the postwar period, and the persistent, and recently reinforced, dominance of the "political police" (security police) in the police administration. The evolving institutional ties of the police bureaucracy with other state institutions, political parties, and socioeconomic actors shall be analyzed throughout the era of the political contestation that followed in the 1960s and 1970s, as well as the neoliberal turn of politics and economy in the 1980s and 1990s and, finally, the renewed polarization of politics and society from the 2000s to date.

9.1 Postwar Democratization of the Police Administration and Its Limits

Police administration was a central part of the very mighty Ministry of the Interior (Naimushō) throughout the process of modernization in Japan until the US Occupation reforms. Comprising not only police administration, but also local affairs, public works, health and welfare, and even State Shintoism, the Ministry of the Interior was among the most powerful ministries in the prewar regime in part because of its extensive jurisdiction. There was a general tendency for the elite bureaucrats of the ministry to follow a specialized track in either one of the policy areas, but there was also a certain degree of intraministry mobility that nurtured a sense of unity. Such were the prestige and influence of the Interior Ministry that they extended to some other organs of the imperial bureaucracy as well. One notable instance was the Ministry of Education.

For instance, a bureaucrat originally from the Interior Ministry, Nagai Hiroshi, was the Student Mobilization Bureau Chief of the Ministry of Education at the time of the Japanese war defeat and surrender. Even more prominent was the case of Ōmura Seiichi, who had an illustrious career in the Ministry of the Interior, successively occupying the posts of Local Affairs Bureau Chief, Police Affairs Bureau Chief, and Social Affairs Bureau Chief, and then serving on two different occasions in the wartime and immediate postwar as the vice-minister of the Ministry of Education, after having served as the governor of two prefectures. Ōmura went on to serve as the vice-minister of the Ministry of the Interior and was subsequently made the Minister of the Interior in the first Yoshida government. At that time, he turned to politics, and later served as the Director-General of the Defense Agency (cabinet-rank ministerial position). In Ōmura's case, it was as if the end of the war and the Occupation had no negative impact on his career.

The Ministry of the Interior, and with it the police administration, however, went through fundamental reorganization during the US Occupation. The Supreme Commander of Allied Powers (SCAP) understood that the Ministry of the Interior, and its police bureaucrats in particular, played key roles in the suppression of freedom and rights in the militarist regime, and took the radical step of abolishing the Ministry of the Interior at the end of 1947 in an attempt to democratize the defeated country and decentralize the powers that were previously held in the hands of state elites. The transitory Bureau of Internal Affairs was disbanded just two months later, and the police were decentralized. Japan was to have a US-style local police system, each with its own commissioner and board. At the national level, all that remained was the National Headquarters of Local Police (Kokka Chihō Keisatsu Honbu).

This was a mortifying humiliation and intolerable injustice for the statists who were the police bureaucrats. The orphaned bureaucrats of the Ministry of the Interior continued to explore the possibility of reestablishing their defunct ministry up until the 1960s to no avail, and it was not until July 1954 that the municipal police forces were more or less fully renationalized with the setting up of the National Police Agency. The loss of prestige was so enormous for the National Headquarters of Local Police that they hired only four new cadre-track bureaucrats between 1950 and 1952, and none of them was from the prestigious Law Faculty of the University of Tokyo. The police bureaucrats had to rely on their former colleagues from the Ministry of the Interior to offer recruitment assistance during these wilderness years.

The local affairs bureaucrats (the crème de la crème in the prewar Ministry of the Interior alongside the police bureaucrats), who similarly became "homeless" after the ministry was disbanded through the SCAP's ambitious democratization and decentralization reforms, were a step ahead in finding a new organizational home in the form of Local Autonomy Agency in June 1949, and they recruited several elite bureaucrats on behalf of the police administration. For instance, Fukuda Katsuichi, who rose to become the Superintendent-General of the Tokyo Metropolitan Police Department (TMPD) in the mid-1980s, was initially recruited by the Local Affairs Agency in 1950 to be transferred to the newly established National Police Agency in 1954. (The Superintendent-General of the TMPD is a top post for police bureaucrats, second only to the Commissioner-General of the NPA.)

The Impact of the US Occupation was not simply on the organization of the police administration. Having abolished the SHP in October 1945, the SCAP purged nearly 5,000 SHP bureaucrats and officials nationwide, though the policy was implemented rather unevenly in reality.[1] The police bureaucracy more broadly was also subject to the purge during the Occupation. Established in 1928, following the enactment of the notorious Public Security Preservation Law in 1925, the SHP was a special, but integral, part of the prewar police bureaucracy.

Table 9.1 shows how the purge affected the Police Affairs Bureau Chiefs of the Ministry of the Interior in the immediate postwar years. Mizuike Ryō, who had a long background in the SHP, including as the SHP department chief of the TMPD, and was the Police Affairs Bureau Chief at the time of the Japanese surrender, was purged and spent his postwar career in the private sector. Hashimoto Masami, who succeeded to Mizuike at the top of the Police Affairs Bureau, became the deputy mayor of Osaka City once depurged. Izumi Gorō retired from the police to the private sector as he was purged. We do not know whether Hashimoto and Izumi had a spell in the SHP. Tanigawa Noboru is the only Police Affairs Bureau Chief on the list who was not an elite bureaucrat of the Ministry of the Interior, and thus without any background in SHP – he was an official from Tokyo City.

Tanaka Naramichi, in contrast, was an elite police bureaucrat who built his career in the SHP. Tanaka's first post was in the Public Security Department of the Police Affairs Bureau, the very nerve center of the SHP

[1] Ogino Fujio, *Tokkō Keisatsu* (Tokyo: Iwanami Shinsho, 2012), 215–218.

Table 9.1 *Police Affairs Bureau Chiefs, Ministry of the Interior (1945–1947)*

Name [Term]	Purge	Postwar Career
Mizuike Ryō [1945]	Yes	CEO, Pulp/paper company
Hashimoto Masami [1945]	Yes	Deputy Mayor, Osaka city
Izumi Gorō [1945–1946]	Yes	CEO, Traffic sign manufacturer
Tanigawa Noboru [1946–1947]	Yes	Member, Lower House
Tanaka Naraichi [1947]	Yes	Deputy Governor, Osaka Prefecture
Hisayama Hideo [1947]	No	Executive, People's Association

in the Ministry of the Interior. He was subsequently posted to Harbin, Ōita, Kagoshima, and Beijing to conduct SHP work, and also had spells in the censorship department in SHP, before he was promoted to more general and elevated managerial positions in national and local police administration. He was only purged for a year and a month, and after an aborted appointment to the newly established Police Reserve (the predecessor organization of today's Self-Defense Forces), became the Superintendent-General of the Osaka Prefecture Police Department. After retirement as a police bureaucrat, he spent over ten years as the Deputy Governor of Osaka Prefecture.[2]

The last occupier of the post of Police Affairs Bureau Chief as the Ministry of the Interior was abolished was Hisayama Hideo. As a junior official, Hisayama was in charge of SHP in Fukui and Aomori, but that did not disrupt his postwar career. Exempt from the purge, and after having served in the police administration in different capacities even after the abolition of the Ministry of the Interior, he retired to serve as an executive board member of the People's Association (Kokumin Kyōkai) foundation, today's People's Political Association (Kokumin Seiji Kyōkai), which is essentially the fund-collecting arm of the conservative, ruling Liberal Democratic Party (LDP).

Table 9.2 shows the careers of the Superintendent-Generals of the Tokyo Metropolitan Police Department in the immediate postwar period. Machimura Kingo led a long and successful political career after he was depurged once Japan regained sovereignty, having served as a Lower House member, Governor of Hokkaido, Upper House member,

[2] Yanagase Tadashi, *Kokuhatsu Sengo no Tokkō Kanryō* (Osaka: Nihon Kikanshi Shuppan Sentā, 2005), 18–22.

Table 9.2 *Superintendents-General, TMPD (1945–1948)*

Name [Term]	Purge	Postwar Career
Machimura Kingo [1945]	Yes	Member, Lower House; Minister
Saka Nobuyoshi [1945]	Yes	CEO, Chemical company
Takano Genshin [1945–1946]	Yes	Executive, Printing company
Fujinuma Shōhei [1946]	Yes	Advisor, Radio Station
Suzuki Mikio [1946–1947]	No	Member, Lower House
Hirooka Kenji [1947]	Yes	Chair, Emigration Agency
Toga Muneo [1947]	Yes	Vice-Minister, Defense Agency
Saitō Noboru [1947–1948]	No	Member, Upper House; Minister

and also Minister of Home Affairs. Saka Nobuyoshi, in turn, had a long postwar career in various companies in the private sector. Takano Genshin, too, served on the executive boards in companies as a lawyer, while Fujinuma Shōhei took a position as the advisor of a radio station. Even though Suzuki Mikio had a background in SHP as its foreign affairs department chief, he was not purged, and became the last Vice-Minister of the Ministry of the Interior before he entered national politics. Hirooka Kenji, who had a strong background in SHP, took up several private sector managerial positions while purged, but eventually returned to state bureaucracy in 1956 as the Secretary-General of the Defense Council of the Prime Minister's Office, and subsequently retired into a cushy position at the Emigration Agency, a government organization. Toga Muneo, who was in charge of SHP in Saga as a young police bureaucrat, followed the footsteps of Hirooka in having a second bureaucratic postwar career in the field of defense. He rose to be the Administrative Vice-Minister of the Defense Agency between 1960 and 1963. Saitō Noboru, while a bureaucrat of the Ministry of the Interior, seemed not to have had much police experience, and played an important role in the transition period as the SCAP was reforming the police administration. He became the Superintendent-General of TMPD after having served as the Vice-Minister of the Ministry of the Interior, and then also became the Commissioner-General of the National Headquarters of Local Police before he was appointed the first Commissioner-General of the National Police Agency. Saitō became an Upper House member of the LDP upon retirement from the NPA and served the Transport Minister and Health and Welfare Minister in the later postwar period.

9.2 The Legacies of the Special Higher Police in the Postwar Period

Table 9.3 lists the successive Commissioner-Generals of the national police bureaucracy since the abolition of the Ministry of the Interior, starting with Saitō, in the first two decades of the postwar era. Saitō served as the General Affairs Bureau Chief of the Air-Raid Headquarters, which was in charge of the coordination of anti-air-raid measures for the country, and in that sense was apparently mostly involved in the defensive aspects of civilian life in wartime. But his two immediate successors as Commissioner-Generals, at the time Japan regained independence and established the National Police Agency, were far more implicated in the aggressive side of imperialist expansion, attesting to the onset of what is commonly referred to as the reactionary "Reverse Course" – a backlash against the earlier democratization and demilitarization efforts of the Occupation. Ishii Eizō headed the SHP in Fukui and Shizuoka prefectures and served as the Police Affairs Division Chief of the Government-General of Korea before assuming the equivalent post in the Police Affairs Bureau of the Ministry of the Interior back in Japan. He also served as the Police Affairs Bureau Chief and the Personnel Bureau Chief of the newly established Police Reserve (today's SDF) prior to his return to the top echelon of the national police bureaucracy proper.

Kashiwamura Nobuo, who succeeded Ishii, was also a top bureaucrat who worked for the reestablishment of the police administration in the postwar era with a SHP background – he headed the SHP in Iwate Prefecture, and also served in the Censorship Division of the main Ministry of the Interior. Kashiwamura also worked at the General Affairs Agency of Manchukuo. After the war, he had a stint as the Security Department Chief of the National Headquarters of Local Police before he was transferred to help establish the new Public Security Intelligence Agency: both organizations, the Security Department/Bureau (Keibi) of the NPA and the Public Security Intelligence Agency (Kōan Chōsa Chō), are informally called *kōan* in Japanese and are seen as the postwar reincarnation of the SHP, if in a milder form. Eguchi Toshio, who followed Kashiwamura, was a civil administrator in the territories occupied by the Imperial Navy in wartime. He was the head of *kōan* as the Security Bureau Chief of the NPA during the turmoil leading up to the revision of the US-Japan Security Treaty in 1960. He left the position as Prime Minister Kishi Nobusuke resigned, but was rewarded amply for his work when he became Commissioner-General of the NPA three years later.

Table 9.3 *Commissioners-General, NPA (1948–1965)*

Name [Term]	Notable Prewar Posts
Saitō Noboru [1948–1955]	General Affairs Bureau Chief, Air-Raid HQ
Ishii Eizō [1955–1958]	SHP; Police Affairs Division Chief, GG of Korea
Kashiwamura Nobuo [1958–1963]	SHP; General Affairs, Manchukuo
Eguchi Toshio [1963–1965]	Civil Administrator, Imperial Navy

Table 9.4 *Superintendents-General, TMPD (1948–1965)*

Name [Term]	Notable Prewar Posts
Tanaka Eiichi [1948–1954]	Economic Police
Eguchi Mitoru [1954–1957]	N/A
Kawai Hisato [1957–1958]	SHP
Ogura Ken [1958–1961]	SHP
Hara Bunbei [1961–1965]	SHP

As we have seen, it was never as if the Tokyo Metropolitan Police Department, by far the nation's largest police force on top of being in charge of the nation's capital, was fully democratized, or rid of control and influence from the prewar authoritarian police traditions, but the impact of the "Reverse Course" was similarly obvious in the same turbulent period leading up to the first half of the 1960s.

Tanaka Eiichi, as Table 9.4 indicates, had a background in economic policing, that is to say, the policing of economic crimes, and he served as Economic Bureau Chief of the Tokyo Metropolitan Government in the immediate postwar period. He was followed by Eguchi Mitoru, whose prewar posts remain unclear, but is noted for an unusually varied career after the Ministry of the Interior was disbanded after the war. This, in turn, strongly suggests that he was likely a "generalist" rather than a highly specialized police bureaucrat. (We shall review Eguchi's postwar career developments in detail later.) The restoration of SHP bureaucrats to the top post of the nation's capital was resumed as Kishi's influence in the government grew and his revisionist agenda was reinforced. Kawai Hisato, the head of SHP in Ishikawa prefecture before the war, reclaimed the post of Superintendent-General of TMPD as an ex-SHP after about ten years, in January 1957. He was succeeded by Ogura Ken, former SHP head in Ōita and Tottori prefectures, who oversaw the police force in Tokyo during the turbulent times when the nation was severely divided over Kishi's attempt to revise the US–Japan Security Treaty (Anpo). Hara Bunbei then took over in 1961. He had previously served as the chief of SHP in Kagoshima during the war. None of these three former SHP officials was purged from public office in the postwar era, although two were made to take a temporary leave. Hara led a highly successful career as an Upper House member after he retired from the police force, including a spell as the Director-General of the Environment Agency (cabinet rank), ultimately rising to be the Speaker of the Upper House.

The priorities of the SHP, even after it was formally disbanded in the postwar period, are clearly indicated by Table 9.5, which lists the Head of the Imperial Guard Headquarters between 1948 and 1958. All of the six top police officials in charge of the security of the emperor and the imperial household in this decade had SHP experience.

Kimura Kōzō oversaw SHP operations in Kagoshima and Hiroshima prefectures in the prewar years, and after he headed the Imperial Guard Headquarters, he also served as the President of the National Police Academy, Affairs Bureau Chief of the Prime Minister's Office, and Safety Bureau Chief of the National Police Agency. Fujita Jirō was SHP head in Toyama prefecture, Kabayama Toshio in Miyazaki prefecture, Takesue Tatsuo in Chiba and Hyōgo prefectures, Kawai in Ishikawa prefecture, and Harada in Yamagata prefecture.

While there was a particularly high concentration of ex-SHP police bureaucrats among the Heads of the Imperial Guard Headquarters, and even among the most successful officials who made it to become Commissioner-General of the NPA or Superintendent of the TMPD, there were other high-ranking NPA bureaucrats with SHP background as well (Table 9.6). Nakagawa Atsushi, for instance, was the SHP head in Iwate prefecture, who served as the Police Affairs Department Chief of the National Headquarters of Local Police. He was subsequently posted to a series of top police posts in the Osaka area. Having retired as the Chief of Osaka Prefectural Police Headquarters, he led the life of an Osaka local notable. Similarly, Sakai Tokitada, an ex-SHP head in Saitama prefecture, established his post-police career in Osaka's neighboring Hyōgo prefecture. After he retired from the police force as the head of the Kinki District of the NPA,[3] he was given a post-retirement job as a board member of the

[3] Kinki region includes Osaka, Kyoto, and Hyōgo (including Kobe city).

Table 9.5 *Heads, Imperial Guard Headquarters (1948–1958)*

Name [Term]	Notable Prewar Posts
Kimura Kōzō [1948–1949]	SHP
Fujita Jirō [1949–1950]	SHP
Kabayama Toshio [1950–1952]	SHP
Takesue Tatsuo [1952–1954]	SHP
Kawai Hisato [1954–1956]	SHP
Harada Akira [1956–1958]	SHP

Table 9.6 *Other High-Ranking Police Bureaucrats with SHP background*

Name	Police Posts [Term]	Notable Subsequent Post
Nakagawa Atsushi	Police Affairs DC [1948–1952]	Chief, Osaka Police
Nakagawa Tōji	Criminal Affairs BC [1952–1960]	CEO, Metal company
Sakai Tokitada	Chief Secretary [1955–1958] Police Affairs BC [1958–1960]	Governor, Hyōgo Prefecture
Noda Akira	Safety BC, NPA [1962–1963]	Auditor, OTCA
Yamaguchi Hiroshi	Security BC [1970–1971]	Deputy Governor, Hyōgo Prefecture

Hanshin Expressway Public Corporation and was then nominated as a deputy governor of Hyōgo prefecture.[4] In 1970, he managed to get elected as the Governor of Hyōgo. He served for a total of sixteen years. During his tenure, Sakai recruited his junior police bureaucrat, Yamaguchi Hiroshi, who also had an SHP background in Shimane prefecture, to be his deputy governor, though the latter passed away prematurely in office in his fourth year. Nakagawa Tōji was a Criminal Affairs Bureau Chief with a prewar background in SHP in Niigata and Aichi prefectures. Noda Akira was an SHP head in Shiga prefecture, who rose up the police hierarchy to be the

[4] Hanshin means Osaka and Kobe, which is the prefectural capital of Hyōgo.

Safety Bureau Chief of the NPA, and subsequently served as the Statistics Bureau Chief of the Prime Minister's Office. He retired as a bureaucrat to become an auditor of the Overseas Technical Cooperation Agency. Incidentally, his son, Noda Takeshi also became a police bureaucrat, and served as the Superintendent-General of TMPD and Deputy Chief Cabinet Secretary for Crisis Management.

Even more surprising than the persistent presence of SHP bureaucrats in the top echelon of the postwar police administration is their influence over education policy in supposedly democratized Japan. When Ōdachi Shigeo, a former Interior Ministry bureaucrat by background, was appointed as the Minister of Education in the fifth Yoshida Shigeru cabinet in 1953, he placed two former SHP bureaucrats in the top administrative positions of his ministry. Ōdachi himself was a one-time suspected class-A war criminal incarcerated in Sugamo prison, who was later released but purged from public office. In the prewar period, Ōdachi was the top bureaucrat in Manchukuo, vice-minister of the Ministry of the Interior, Mayor of the occupied Shōnan (Singapore) City, Mayor of Tokyo, and Minister of the Interior. The two SHP officials Ōdachi elevated to the highest-ranking posts in the Ministry of Education were Tanaka Yoshio, Administrative Vice-Minister, and Ogata Shinichi, Elementary and Secondary Education Bureau Chief.[5]

Tanaka served as the head of SHP in Gunma and Nagasaki prefectures, and he was later transferred to education in the prewar era, serving notably in the Thought Bureau and also in the education department in Manchukuo. Once he was depurged, he was appointed Elementary and Secondary Education Bureau Chief before being promoted to the top post in the Ministry of Education. A former SHP official in charge of Aomori and Mie prefectures, when Ōdachi became the Mayor of Singapore, Ogata was appointed as the city's police department chief. Upon depurge, Ōdachi made Ogata the Elementary and Secondary Education Bureau Chief. Ogata later reached the apex of the Ministry of Education as the administrative vice-minister, right after he served as the Higher Education Bureau Chief, at the time the student revolts against the remilitarization agenda and the ratification of the US-Japan Security Treaty were at their peak. Ōdachi, Tanaka, and Ogata joined forces to pass measures and legislation that sought to constrain the unionized teachers' "political activities." Even after Ōdachi resigned as Minister, Tanaka and Ogata stayed on as top bureaucrats, and oversaw the reversal

[5] Tadashi, *Kokuhatsu Sengo no Tokkō Kanryō*, 58–71.

of the Occupation democratization reform by making the elective education boards appointive again.

9.3 Spheres of Influence of Police Bureaucrats in the Postwar Period

Such collaboration among the bureaucrats of the defunct Ministry of the Interior was not uncommon even in the postwar period. The abolition of the Ministry did not mean that its officials were permanently removed or forcefully retired. In reality, the police bureaucrats retained their influence across formal ministerial divisions, at least as long as the cohorts that were originally recruited and trained by the Ministry of the Interior continued to occupy high positions in the national bureaucracy. The last of them retired as recently as the late 1970s and 1980s.

We have already mentioned some of the police bureaucrats who played key roles in the establishment of the Self-Defense Forces and security policy in the postwar era. In reality, ever since the Defense Agency/SDF was initially set up as the Police Reserve in 1950 until 1978, all but one of the thirteen bureaucrats who occupied the top administrative post (Administrative Vice-Minister) were police bureaucrats by background. The position was then taken over by the bureaucrats who were originally from the Ministry of Finance and, eventually, those who were recruited by the Defense Agency proper, but as recently as 1990–1991 a police bureaucrat made it to the bureaucratic apex of the Defense Agency.

Similarly, police bureaucrats were occasionally placed in top posts in some other ministries and agencies that had roots in the prewar Ministry of the Interior (Table 9.7).

There were two police bureaucrats who rose up to occupy the top administrative position of the Ministry of Construction, formerly the Civil Engineering Bureau of the Ministry of the Interior, Shibata Tatsuo and Yamamoto Sachio. Shibata was an "all-round player" from the prewar years, and in that sense, he was more of an Interior Ministry official than a more focused police official to begin with. In that postwar period, he served as the Chief of the Osaka Prefectural Police Force, the General Affairs Department Chief of the National Headquarters of Local Police, and the first Chief Secretary of the newly reorganized National Police Agency. It was at that time that he was transferred to the Ministry of Construction to serve as its Chief Secretary before he was further promoted to be its Administrative Vice-Minister. Yamamoto's career overlaps considerably with that of Shibata's, though Yamamoto was more of a

Table 9.7 *Top Police Bureaucrats in Ex-Interior Ministries*

Name	Notable non-Police Post [Term]	Notable Police Post [Term]
Eguchi Mitoru	AVM, Labor [1948–1950]	SG, TMPD
Shibata Tatsuo	AVM, Construction [1958–1961]	Chief Secretary, NPA
Gotōda Masaharu	Tax Chief, Local Autonomy [1959–1962]	CG, NPA
Yamamoto Sachio	AVM, Construction [1963]	Chief Secretary, NPA

police bureaucrat in the Interior Ministry years. Yamamoto was appointed as the Personnel Bureau Chief of the Defense Agency, then brought back to NPA as its Chief Secretary, and after a spell in Osaka as the Chief of its Police Force, he was headhunted to be the Chief Secretary of the Ministry of Construction, and then promoted to be the Administrative Vice-Minister in his adoptive home.

These personnel moves had to do with the fact that the Construction Ministry (and indeed the Civil Engineering Bureau in the Interior Ministry) was dominated by bureaucrats with civil engineering backgrounds (called *gikan*, technicians) and thus also lower in prestige and power in the officialdom as a whole that was dominated by law-trained bureaucrats (called *bunkan* or *jimukan*, administrators). Even the post of the administrative vice-minister was contested between the technicians and the administrators, and the latter was generally on the defensive. It was in this context that some police bureaucrats, who enjoy higher prestige and standing, were brought in to counter the domination of the technicians.

The career paths of Eguchi Mitoru and Gotōda Masaharu, In turn, serve as illustrations of the bigger role and influence of the Interior/police bureaucrats in the postwar political and administrative context. Eguchi was the Chief Secretary of the TMPD in the immediate postwar period and was soon promoted to be the Labor Standards Bureau Chief of the Ministry of Health and Welfare. When the Ministry of Labor was newly established in September 1947 as part of the Occupation democratization reform, Eguchi was moved sideways as the Labor Standards Bureau Chief of the Ministry of Labor (and briefly also the Labor Statistics Research Bureau Chief), and then its Administrative Vice-Minister. As the Police Reserve was established in 1950, he was transferred to serve as the administrative head of the Police Reserve Headquarters. Eguchi was then made a Deputy Chief Cabinet Secretary before he retired as a bureaucrat as the Superintendent-General of the TMPD. The fact that a police bureaucrat such as Eguchi, who also contributed to the rearmament of postwar Japan, was centrally involved in the founding of the Ministry of Labor clearly indicates that the conservative ruling elites of Japan had every intention to resist the strengthening of the labor movement and the democratization of the economy that were pursued by an important segment of the SCAP.

Upon retirement from the bureaucracy in 1957, Eguchi was parachuted into the board of Ōmikenshi, a major textile company in Osaka that was going through a serious boardroom battle, pitting the banks against the founder-owner, in the aftermath of a historical labor dispute several years previously. Eguchi then worked at two public entities that were placed at the heart of Japan's fledgling nuclear power industry, the Power Reactor and Nuclear Fuel Development Corporation and the Japan Atomic Energy Research Institute. Eguchi also served as the Executive Director, Secretary General, and then Chairman of the People's Political Association, the fund-gathering arm of the ruling LDP.

If Eguchi, like Hisayama whom we mentioned earlier, worked for the LDP backstage, as it were, Gotōda became the most successful of the LDP politicians with a police background. Gotōda was Chief Secretary and Tax Bureau Chief of the Local Affairs Agency (later Ministry) to help out his former colleagues in the Local Affairs Bureau of the Ministry of the Interior but was swiftly brought back to the NPA to climb up the ladder, as Chief Secretary, Security Bureau Chief, Police Affairs Bureau Chief, Deputy Commissioner-General, and finally, Commissioner-General. He was then handpicked by Prime Minister Tanaka Kakuei to serve as his Deputy Chief Cabinet Secretary. Upon retirement from officialdom, Gotōda sought entry to politics as a member of the Tanaka faction of the LDP, and led a spectacular second career as a Lower House member, with half a dozen key ministerial appointments that included two spells as the Chief Cabinet Secretary in the government of Nakasone Yasuhiro, his junior in the Ministry of the Interior in the 1980s, culminating as Deputy Prime Minister in the Miyazawa Kiichi cabinet in 1993.

The post-retirement careers of Eguchi and Gotōda raise interesting questions about police bureaucrats' relations with socioeconomic actors and political power, respectively, but before we examine them, let us first take a closer look at the position and influence of security police (*kōan keisatsu*) inside the postwar police administration.

9.4 The Organization of the *Kōan* (Security) Police and Its Dominance

The broader concept of *kōan* (security, or public security) encompasses the purviews and activities of the Public Security Intelligence Agency under the jurisdiction of the Ministry of Justice that is controlled by the prosecutors as well, and indeed, the Public Security Intelligence Agency, too, had started with an influx of ex-SHP officials in the postwar period. What is referred to as *kōan keisatsu* (security police) more narrowly, on the other hand, consists of the Security Bureau of the NPA and the Security (*keibi*) or Public Security (*kōan*) departments and divisions of the prefectural police forces and stations, the biggest and the most important being the Public Security Department of the TMPD – they are the direct descendants of the prewar SHP (see Figures 9.1 and 9.2).

As early as October 1945, Tsugita Daisaburō, Chief Cabinet Secretary of the then Shidehara Kijūrō government, remarked, "We have no choice but to abolish the organization of the SHP entirely. However, while we have to abolish the SHP completely once, I think we will have to create an alternative organization fast."[6] Two months later, the public security (*kōan*) division was established in the Police Affairs Bureau of the Ministry of the Interior, and the setting up of security (*keibi*) divisions at the prefecture level soon followed, as alternatives to the SHP, with the permission of the SCAP.[7]

According to the Police Law (*keisatsu hō*), Article 24, the Security Bureau of the NPA is in charge of the following: (1) matters concerning security police (*keibi keisatsu*), (2) protection of the members of the imperial household (*keiei*), (3) protection of foreign and domestic VIPs (*keigo*), (4) implementation of security (*keibi*), and (5) planning and implementation of measures in emergency situations as stipulated in Article 71 of the Police Law.[8] In addition, the Foreign Affairs and Intelligence Department in the Security Bureau is in charge of the security police, who are concerned with foreigners and foreign-based Japanese. The riot police (*kidōtai*) are special units that are at the disposition of the security police. At the heart of the security police are the *kōan keisatsu* (public security police), who are focused on what they regard as subversive anti-state activities and protests not only by the violent extreme right and left, hostile foreign states, and

[6] Fujio, *Tokkō Keisatsu*, 221.

[7] Ibid., 222.

[8] Article 71 stipulates that in case of such emergency situations as major disasters and riots, the prime minister may declare the state of emergency upon recommendation of the National Public Safety Commission, if he deems it necessary to do so to preserve order.

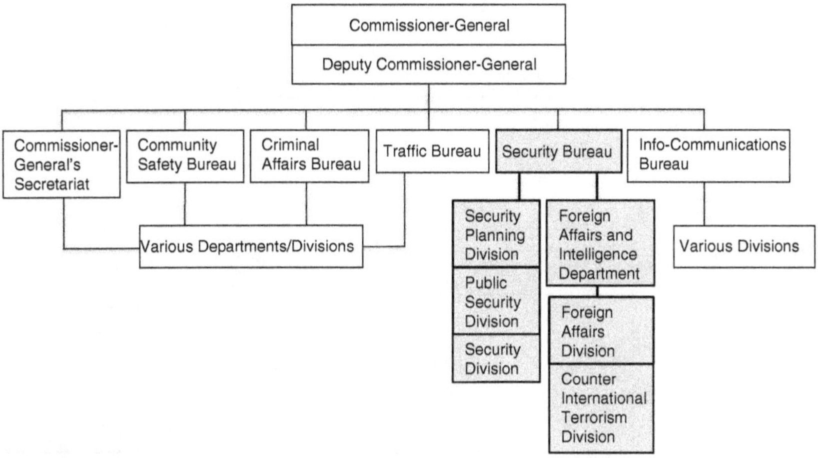

Figure 9.1 Organization of NPA (as of 2018)

terrorist groups, but also by student protesters, labor movements, anti-US bases and anti-war civic movements, and anti-nuclear power protesters, among others.[9] Even today, the police fail to clearly differentiate between violent terrorist groups and peaceful civic movements, or between anti-state (anti-regime) riots and anti-government protests.

Broadly in charge of the maintenance of public security and order, the security police are directly funded and directed by the NPA even at prefectural and local levels. Article 37 of the Police Law lists the expenses that are incurred by the prefectural police forces but are nevertheless to be covered by the state budget, and the eighth item is about the business of *kōan keisatsu*: "expenses that are necessary for the investigation of crimes that concerns the public security (*kōan*) of the state and other special crimes." There is a phrase, *kōan trumpet*, which means that security police can exaggerate the threats and danger to the state all it wants and never have to justify or explain what they really are because of the secrecy that is required in such investigations. The exact amount of the security police budget and the use to which it is put are only known to members of the security police, and because of central control through the budget, the command structure in the security police is extremely centralized, even by the standards of the Japanese police. The Security Bureau of the NPA

[9] The Japan Communist Party, too, continued to be monitored by the security police, even though it has long since renounced violent means to establish a communist regime.

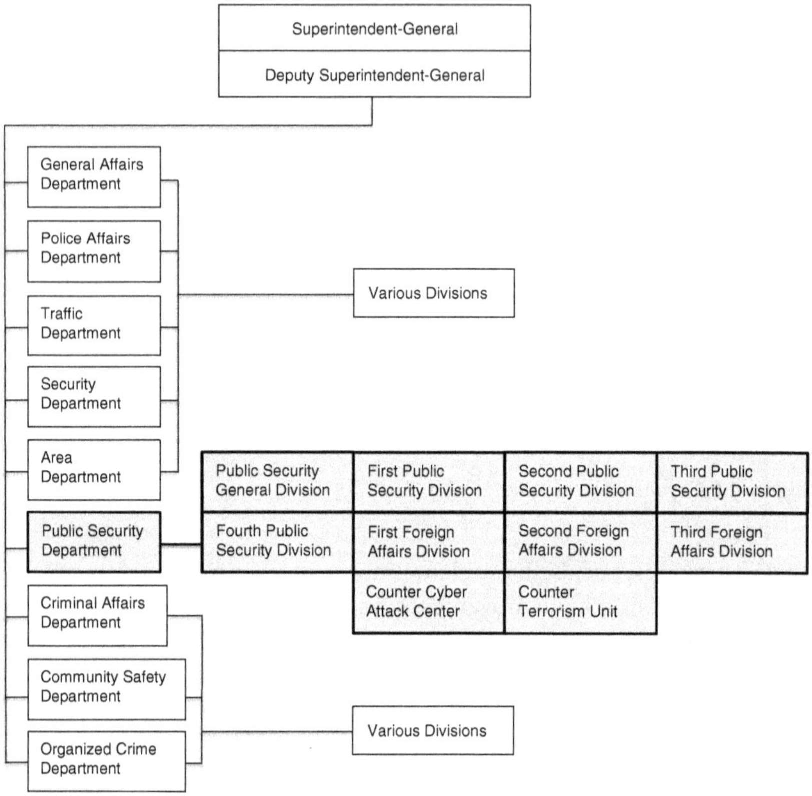

Figure 9.2 Organization of TMPD (as of 2018)

has direct control over the prefectural and local security police officers on the ground, and the nominal heads of the prefectural police forces are completely sidelined. Furthermore, because security police officers are considered to be the best and the brightest, the extremely hierarchical and secretive nature of the security police ends up as a model for the rest of the police administration. In fact, investigative journalists have pointed out that the *kōan* budget has been used to reward police officers outside the public security sections who helped obtain useful *kōan* intelligence.[10] This has, in effect, the consequence of turning all police officers into de facto public security police informants, and reinforces the domination of the security police bureaucrats in the police administration.

[10] See, for instance, Aoki Osamu, *Nihon no Kōan Keisatsu* (Tokyo: Kōdansha Gendai Shinsho, 2000), 26–27.

Like the SHP, the security police have been an integral part of the police administration overall, and while some police bureaucrats can be identified as being primarily security police bureaucrats, others follow a more diverse and mixed career path that includes spells in security-related posts (police officers on the ground are much more clearly separated between those who are in the security police and those who are not, e.g. criminal investigation). There is no doubt, however, that the security police are at the very heart of postwar Japanese police administration, and that those who build their careers primarily in security police are far more likely to go up the government hierarchy than those whose careers center around community police, traffic, or even criminal investigation. Among the twenty Commissioner-Generals of the NPA between 1955 and 2009, ten served as Security Bureau Chief before assuming the top post, while six had experience as the Criminal Affairs Bureau Chief, four had bureau-chief level experience in organizational management (e.g. Chief Secretary and/or Police Affairs Bureau Chief), and just one was a former Traffic Bureau Chief.[11] This is in addition to the growing presence of police bureaucrats in the prime minister's office, who are really in the security and intelligence field.

Further evidence of the authority and prestige of *kōan* police within the police administration as a whole can be found in the high proportion of those who served as a Security Bureau Chief of the NPA and/or the Public Security Department Chief of the TMPD who subsequently attained Administrative Vice-Minister (*jimu jikan*) ranking, including the Commissioner-General of the NPA, Superintendent-General of the TMPD, Director of Cabinet Intelligence (formerly the Cabinet Intelligence Office Chief), and Deputy Chief Cabinet Secretary for Crisis Management. As can be seen in Table 9.8, out of the thirty-three Security Bureau Chiefs of the NPA between 1948 and 2016, exactly two-thirds (66.7 percent) of them (twenty-two) went on to climb up to an Administrative Vice-Minister rank post. Out of twenty-eight Public Security Department Chiefs of the TMPD between 1952 and 2011, sixteen (57 percent) retired at an Administrative Vice-Minister rank position (Table 9.9). In comparison, the rival Criminal Affairs Bureau Chiefs, while also competitive, did not do as well with sixteen out of thirty-four (47 percent) between 1948 and 2018 subsequently reaching Administrative Vice-Minister rank (Table 9.10). It bears underlining that the Public Security Department

11 Suzuki Sadatoshi served as both Criminal Affairs Bureau Chief and Security Bureau Chief, but tellingly in that order – indicating clearly in the parlance of Japanese bureaucratic hierarchy that the latter position was superior to the former.

Table 9.8 *Security Bureau Chiefs, NPA (1948–2016)*

Name [Term]	Final Administrative Posts
Kabayama Toshio [1948–1950]	Head, Imperial Guard Headquarters Kinki District Chief, NPA
Kashiwamura Nobuo [1950–1952]	Commissioner-General, NPA
Yamaguchi Hisao [1952–1958]	Kinki District Chief, NPA
Eguchi Toshio [1958–1960]	Commissioner-General, NPA
Miwa Yoshio [1960–1963]	Administrative Vice-Minister, Defense Agency
Gotōda Masaharu [1963–1965]	Commissioner-General, NPA Deputy Chief Cabinet Secretary
Hatano Akira [1965–1966]	Superintendent-General, TMPD
Takahashi Mikio [1966–1967]	Commissioner-General, NPA
Kawashima Hiromori [1967–1970]	Cabinet Intelligence Office Chief Deputy Chief Cabinet Secretary
Yamaguchi Hiroshi [1970–1971]	
Tomita Tomohiko [1971–1972]	Cabinet Intelligence Office Chief Director-General, Imperial Household Agency
Yamamoto Shizuhiko [1972–1975]	Commissioner-General, NPA
Mitsui Osamu [1975–1978]	Commissioner-General, NPA
Suzuki Sadatoshi [1978–1981]	Commissioner-General, NPA
Yamada Hideo [1981–1984]	Commissioner-General, NPA
Shibata Yoshinori [1984–1985]	Kinki District Chief, NPA
Mishima Kenjirō [1985–1987]	
Nitta Osamu [1987–1988]	Chief, Osaka Prefectural Police Force
Kiuchi Yasumitsu [1988–1990]	Commissioner-General, NPA
Yoshino Jun [1990–1992]	Superintendent-General, TMPD
Suganuma Kiyotaka [1992–1994]	Chief Secretary, NPA
Sugita Kazuhiro [1994–1997]	Director of Cabinet Intelligence Deputy Chief Cabinet Secretary for Crisis Management Deputy Chief Cabinet Secretary
Date Okiharu [1997–1999]	
Kanashige Yoshiyuki [1999–2001]	
Uruma Iwao [2001–2002]	Commissioner-General, NPA Deputy Chief Cabinet Secretary
Okumura Masuo [2002–2004]	Superintendent-General, TMPD
Segawa Katsuhisa [2004–2005]	
Kobayashi Takehito [2005–2006]	

Table 9.8 (*cont.*)

Name [Term]	Final Administrative Posts
Yonemura Toshirō [2006–2007]	Superintendent-General, TMPD
Ikeda Katsuhiko [2007–2010]	Superintendent-General, TMPD
Nishimura Yasuhiko [2010–2013]	Superintendent-General, TMPD
Takahashi Kiyotaka [2013–2015]	Superintendent-General, TMPD
Okita Yoshiki [2015–2016]	Superintendent-General, TMPD

Chiefs of the TMPD, which is formally inferior in rank and seniority to the Criminal Affairs Bureau Chiefs of the NPA, have a substantially higher chance of making to it to the very top of the bureaucratic hierarchies than the latter – and this clearly indicates the domination of "political police" in the police administration overall.

9.5 "Descent from Heaven" (*Amakudari*)

Let us now turn our attention to the police bureaucrats' relations with socioeconomic actors through an examination of the industries and companies that accepted high-raking police bureaucrats as they retired as public servants, in a phenomenon that is widely known in Japan as "descent from heaven" (*amakudari*) – a terminology that is distinctly different from similar phenomena in the US ("revolving door") or even in France ("pantouflage," or changing of slippers). Arguably, the Japanese phenomenon is sharply different from its equivalents in the US and France in two important ways. First, there is a strongly implied hierarchy in the relationship between the state bureaucracy (in this case, the police administration) and the private sector businesses. The state–society relations are not conceptualized and understood as horizontal on an equal footing, but strictly vertical (even in comparison with the statist France). Needless to say, this paradigm may be traced back to the Meiji slogan "Revere Officialdom and Despise the People" (*kanson minpi*). Second, the change of career is typically one-way without a return ticket back to officialdom, or a complementary "ascent to heaven" in the other direction (though there are some limited exceptions). The only time when a retired official makes a comeback to officialdom is in the case of political appointment, ordinarily in the prime minister's office (*kantei*) (or as an advisor to a minister). Private-sector employees are sometimes sent on secondment to the state

Table 9.9 *Public Security Department Chief, TMPD (1952–2011)*

Name [Term]	Final Administrative Posts
Hara Bunbei [1952–1954]	Superintendent-General, TMPD
Kosugi Heiichi [1954–1955]	Head, Imperial Guard Headquarters Kantō District Chief, NPA
Noda Akira [1955–1959]	Safety Bureau Chief, NPA Statistics Bureau Chief, Prime Minister's Office
Ishioka Makoto [1959–1961]	Cabinet Intelligence Office Chief Deputy Chief Cabinet Secretary
Hatano Akira [1961–1963]	Superintendent-General, TMPD
Kawashima Hiromori [1963–1967]	Cabinet Intelligence Office Chief Deputy Chief Cabinet Secretary
Yamamoto Shizuhiko [1967–1971]	Commissioner-General, NPA
Mitsui Osamu [1971–1973]	Commissioner-General, NPA
Nakajima Jirō [1973–1975]	Deputy Superintendent-General, TMPD
Fukuda Katsuichi [1975–1978]	Cabinet Intelligence Office Chief Superintendent-General, TMPD
Kamakura Sadame [1978–1980]	Superintendent-General, TMPD Director-General, Imperial Household Agency
Shibata Yoshinori [1980–1982]	Kinki District Chief, NPA
Fukui Tomoaki [1982–1985]	Kinki District Chief, NPA
Kiuchi Yasumitsu [1985–1988]	Commissioner-General, NPA
Kunimatsu Takaji [1988–1989]	Commissioner-General, NPA
Ōmori Yoshio [1989–1991]	Cabinet Intelligence Office Chief
Maeda Kenji [1991–1992]	Superintendent-General, TMPD
Watanabe Motoo [1992–1994]	President, National Police Academy
Sakurai Masaru [1994–1996]	Kinki District Chief, NPA
Hayashi Norikiyo [1996–1998]	Criminal Affairs Bureau Chief, NPA
Okumura Masuo [1998–1999]	Superintendent-General, TMPD
Andō Takaharu [1999–2001]	Commissioner-General, NPA
Yonemura Toshirō [2001–2003]	Superintendent-General, TMPD
Itō Shigeo [2003–2004]	Kinki District Chief, NPA
Suei Seishi [2004–2006]	Traffic Bureau Chief, NPA
Takaishi Kazuo [2006–2007]	Deputy Superintendent-General, TMPD
Uematsu Shinichi [2007–2008]	Director of Cabinet Intelligence
Aoki Gorō [2008–2011]	Chūbu District Chief, NPA

Table 9.10 *Criminal Affairs Bureau Chiefs (1948–2018)*

Name [Term]	Final Administrative Posts
Mutō Fumio [1948–1952]	Kinki District Chief, NPA
Nakagawa Tōji [1952–1960]	Kantō District Chief, NPA
Arai Hiroshi [1960–1962]	Commissioner-General, NPA
Miyaji Naokuni [1962–1963]	
Hihara Masao [1963–1966]	
Utsumi Hitoshi [1966–1969]	AVM, Defense Agency President, Personnel Authority
Takamatsu Keiji [1969–1972]	DG, Defense Facilities Administration Agency
Sekine Hirofumi [1972–1973]	Kantō District Chief, NPA
Tamura Noriaki [1973–1975]	President, National Police Academy
Tsuchikane Kenzō [1975–1977]	
Suzuki Sadatoshi [1977–1978]	Commissioner-General, NPA
Kobayashi Sunao [1978–1979]	
Nakahira Kazumi [1979–1982]	
Kanazawa Akio [1982–1985]	Commissioner-General, NPA
Nihira Kunio [1985–1988]	Superintendent-General, TMPD
Chūmon Hiroshi [1988–1991]	Chief, Osaka Prefectural Police Force
Kunimatsu Takaji [1991–1993]	Commissioner-General, NPA
Kakimi Takashi [1993–1995]	President, National Police Academy
Noda Takeshi [1995–1996]	Superintendent-General, TMPD Deputy Chief Cabinet Secretary for Crisis Management
Satō Hidehiko [1996–1999]	Commissioner-General, NPA
Hayashi Norikiyo [1999–2000]	
Igarashi Tadayuki [2000–2001]	
Yoshimura Hiroto [2001–2002]	Commissioner-General, NPA
Kurimoto Hideo [2002–2004]	
Okada Kaoru [2004–2005]	
Nawata Osamu [2005–2007]	Chief, Osaka Prefectural Police Force
Yoneda Tsuyoshi [2007–2009]	Commissioner-General, NPA
Kanetaka Masahito [2009–2011]	Commissioner-General, NPA
Funamoto Kaoru [2011–2013]	
Takatsuna Naoyoshi [2013–2014]	Superintendent-General, TMPD
Kuryū Shunichi [2014–2015]	Commissioner-General, NPA
Miura Masamitsu [2015–2016]	Superintendent-General, TMPD
Yoshida Naomasa [2016–2017]	Superintendent-General, TMPD
Kinoshita Takashi [2017–2018]	

bureaucracy, but these instances are still limited in number, time period, and significance in most cases, and are relatively recent phenomena.

In other words, the *amakudari* phenomenon in Japan, while generally seen as symptoms and products of collusive relations between the ministries and the industries (as in the "revolving door" syndrome and "pantouflage"), the seemingly mutual beneficial and desired exchange between the state and business elites is predicated on the authoritarian position of the state bureaucracy. While there is no denying the fact that the recipient companies and industries of the retired bureaucrats request and benefit from *amakudari*, it is because they obtain access to the authority of the state and its decisions in that way.[12] In other words, through *amakudari*, we get to find where the police administration is extending its tentacles beyond the official state machinery proper, and in what fields and industries its authority is being utilized for the state to control.

As the case of Eguchi suggested, energy, and nuclear power in particular, has been an important priority for the conservative state. In addition to Eguchi, two police bureaucrats, including a retired superintendent of the TMPD, Nakahara Tadashi, have been sent to the Power Reactor and Nuclear Fuel Development Corporation as auditors in consecutive years. High-ranking police bureaucrats have also retired to join the board of Japan Nuclear Security System, a private security company that was jointly founded by SECOM (Japan's largest private security firm) and the three electricity giants, TEPCO, KEPCO, Chubu Electric Power Co. (regional monopolies in Tokyo, Osaka, and Nagoya regions respectively), and founded in the late 1970s. Indeed, all of these four companies have had a track record of accepting top police bureaucrats. TEPCO, which is responsible for the nuclear power accident in Fukushima in 2011, has kept such top police officials as Andō Tadao and Sugita Kazuhiro on its payroll. Andō became an advisor to TEPCO as he stepped down as the Superintendent-General of TMPD until he was brought back to *kantei* as the first Deputy Chief Cabinet Secretary for Crisis Management in 1998. Sugita is a *kōan* (security) expert, who followed in the footsteps of Andō as both Deputy Chief Cabinet Secretary for Crisis Management and TEPCO advisor, after having served as the Security Bureau Chief of NPA and the Director of Cabinet Intelligence. Sugita was brought back to *kantei* again as Deputy Chief Cabinet Secretary of the Abe government since December 2012, embodying Abe's commitment to

[12] See Koichi Nakano, "Becoming a 'Policy' Ministry: The Organization and Amakudari of the Ministry of Posts and Telecommunications," *The Journal of Japanese Studies* 24(1) (1998): 95–117, for a full discussion of the *amakudari* phenomenon.

nuclear power in so many words. TEPCO is a considerable employer of retired police bureaucrats, and some are even found working in TEPCO subsidiaries. The builders of nuclear power plants, including Toshiba and Hitachi, have also employed high-ranking police bureaucrats. As the Nuclear Regulation Authority was established in September 2012 as the nuclear power accident in the previous year exposed the failure of oversight in the existing regulatory framework, Ikeda Katsuhiko, a prominent police bureaucrat with a background in security police and then Superintendent-General of TMPD, was made its first Secretary-General.

SECOM is not the only private security firm that has hired police officials upon their retirement. For instance, Kawai Hisato, who retired as the Superintendent-General of the TMPD, helped establish the private security firm that offers services to the Reprocessing Plant in Rokkasho village in Aomori prefecture and served as its founding chief executive officer. Needless to say, private security firms do not just provide security to the nuclear industry, and its ties (as well as conflict of interests) with the police are obvious. Tsubakihara Masahiro, a former Police Affairs Bureau Chief of NPA who retired as the Chief of Osaka Prefecture Police Force, was the deputy president and deputy chairman of SECOM for over a decade from 1991. ALSOK, the second largest company in the business, obtained the services of Miwa Yoshio, former Security Bureau Chief of NPA and former Administrative Vice-Minister of the Defense Agency, during the company's pioneering years in the 1960s.

Retired police bureaucrats are to be found in smaller, specialized security firms as well, providing services to airports, for instance. Indeed, through police jurisdiction over security of important hubs and means of transport, a number of police bureaucrats have retired to the major international airports (e.g. Narita and Kansai), Japan Airlines as well as All Nippon Airways, JR Central and JR East, in addition to highway corporations and some auto-makers (e.g. Toyota) as well.

The cozy ties between the Japanese government and the media conglomerates, most notably the conservative Fuji-Sankei group and Yomiuri group have often been noted.[13] In fact, Japan's (indeed the world's) largest newspaper company, Yomiuri, was acquired by a police bureaucrat, Shōriki Matsutarō, who was responsible for spreading rumors that aggravated the massacres of ethnic Koreans in the aftermaths of the Great Kantō

[13] See, for instance, Koichi Nakano, "The Right-Wing Media and the Rise of Illiberal Politics in Japan," in Jeff Kingston (ed.), *Press Freedom in Contemporary Japan* (New York: Routledge, 2017), 30–39.

Earthquake in 1923, in the interwar years. Shōriki maintained a firm control over his media empire through the war and postwar years, using it to launch a political career after he was depurged. He even served as the Director-General of the Science and Technology Agency (cabinet rank) on two occasions during the "Reverse Course" years, and came to be known as the "Father of Nuclear Power" in Japan. Shōriki eventually passed the control of the Yomiuri media empire to his son-in-law, Kobayashi Yosoji, who was also a former bureaucrat from the Ministry of the Interior (though in the field of local affairs, rather than the police). Our data set also showed that a Cabinet Public Relations Secretary and a Security Bureau Chief of NPA retired to be Advisors of Dentsu, while a former Cabinet Public Relations Secretary and Director of Cabinet Intelligence found a post-retirement job in Hakuhodo – Japan's top two PR firms.

The actual scope of *amakudari* for the police bureaucrats is wider, and of course, subject to change over time.[14] As we have seen, energy, transport, and mass communications have been areas of priority for the police administration of the conservative state since early on in the postwar era, but in general, unlike such economic ministries as the Ministry of Finance and the Ministry of Economy, Trade, and Industry, given that the NPA has no direct regulatory control over specific sectors and industries, it was not a central government organ that was known to have an abundance of *amakudari* posts on offer for retiring officials. Indeed, it initially had to rely on its "brother" Ministries of Construction and Welfare for post-retirement jobs in parastate, public corporations under their respective jurisdictions. These charitable gifts, as it were, from the other offshoots of the Ministry of the Interior included the Presidency of Hanshin Expressway Public Corporation, an auditor post in Teito Rapid Transit Corporation (today privatized as Tokyo Metro Co.), and board memberships in Japan Housing Corporation, Pollution Prevention Agency, Japan Railway Construction Public Corporation, and Japan Highway Public Corporation among others.

Some of the police's own parastate entities have provided *amakudari* positions as well. The Japan Police Support Association (established in Meiji era), Japan Police Scholarship Association, and Police Mutual Aid Association are all associations that were established to offer support to rank-and-file police officers and their families that are also providing cushy

[14] See Koichi Nakano, *Sengo Nihon no Kokka Hoshu Shugi* (Tokyo: Iwanami Shoten, 2013), 116–119.

retirement positions to the top police bureaucrats. The others are all in the field of "administrative police," particularly traffic safety-related, which is ironic since it is at the bottom of the police pecking order, and yet it offers *amakudari* posts to the elite police bureaucrats, most of whom come out with little background in that particular policy area. Japan Traffic Safety Association, Japan Federation of Authorized Drivers School Associations, Japan Automobile Federation, Japan Road Traffic Information Center, Japan Safe Driving Center, and Japan Traffic Management Technology Association were all established in the 1960s and 1970s and offered consistent *amakudari* posts for the NPA.

The neoliberal turn In the 1980s opened a new frontier in the police bureaucrats' search for post-retirement jobs. The NPA reinforced its control over Japan's thriving *pachinko* (pinball) gambling business through the revision of the Entertainment and Amusement Establishments Control Law, and that led to the Security Telecommunication Technology Association (Security Communication Association today) in 1982, which provides positions for the retiring technicians in the NPA in particular. This venue of *amakudari* has expanded to the amusement/video game industry since, with jobs for even the non-technicians among the police bureaucrats in CAPCOM, ARUZE (Universal Entertainment today), and KONAMI. The legalization of casinos in 2018 offers exciting new opportunities for the industry, and, no doubt, for the police bureaucrats who are supposed to regulate it.

Elite police bureaucrats who go high up enough to attain Administrative Vice-Minister rank retire later, and there are enough parastate organs that offer *amakudari* posts, but there used to be a general shortage for those who retired somewhat earlier at Bureau Chief rank or lower for the NPA. In the early 1980s, these former bureau chiefs started to obtain post-retirement jobs as advisors, auditors, and board members in banking, insurance, manufacturing, and construction. In the second half the 1980s, Tsuchida Kuniyasu and Kamakura Sadame, both former Superintendent-Generals of the TMPD, became advisors to Daiichi Kangyō Bank and Mitsubishi Bank respectively. From the 1990s, former Commissioner-Generals of the NPA started to find occupations in all sorts of blue-chip companies. This was also to do with the revision of commercial law in 1993 that made it mandatory for big companies to appoint auditors from outside the companies (*shagai kansayaku*), supposedly in order to enhance accountability to prevent corporate crimes. It has been pointed out, however, that this change had the effect of boosting *amakudari* opportunities for police bureaucrats and prosecutors –raising the suspicion that the measure may have merely reinforced the "rule of man" rather than the "rule of law." The police bureaucrats are in demand, not because they are expected to monitor corporate malpractice severely, but rather as they are "bouncers" who can fend off external organized crimes, or worse, guard corporations from unwanted scrutiny by law enforcement.

In its original sense, the tradition of *kanson minpi* ("Revere Officialdom and Despise the People") meant that no self-respecting police bureaucrat would willingly retire into the private sector (unless forced by the purge), but today, the persistence of the spirit provides ample opportunities for police bureaucrats to cash in on their own administrative prestige and connections at the time of their retirement from officialdom.

9.6 The Changing Relations between Politics and Police

Gotōda Masaharu, while the most successful, was by no means the only police bureaucrat who had a second career in politics. In fact, he was among the more "dovish" of them. Yanagase Tadashi, who studied the postwar career of SHP bureaucrats, lists as many as forty police bureaucrats from the Interior Ministry era with some SHP background in the prewar period who subsequently entered national politics in the postwar period.[15] Perhaps the most eye-catching among the former SHP was Okazaki Eijō, who developed his career almost uniquely inside SHP, having risen to be the SHP Department Chief of the TMPD by 1945 and then Public Security Division Chief in the Police Affairs Bureau of the Ministry of the Interior before he was purged. Okazaki was reelected to the Lower House for a total of six times, was made the Deputy Chief Cabinet Secretary of Kishi Nobusuke's government and served as Political Vice-Ministers on a couple of other occasions, until the late 1960s. More prominent as a right-wing politician was Okuno Seisuke, who was the head of SHP in Kagoshima prefecture, but moved to the Local Affairs administration in the postwar period and rose to the very top of the Ministry of Local Affairs. Okuno was reelected a total of 13 times and lived to be 103. During his long forty-year career as a Lower House Member, he was made Minister of Education, Minister of Justice, and Director-General of the

[15] Yanagase Tadashi, *Kokuhatsu Sengo no Tokkō Kanryō*, 52–55. One needs to take note, however, that Yanagase's definition of SHP does not simply include those who were posted to SHP posts narrowly understood, but also those who served in such positions that supervised SHP such as Police Affairs Bureau Chief of the Ministry of the Interior, Minister of the Interior, Vice-Minister of the Interior, and the Superintendent-General of the Tokyo Metropolitan Police Department.

National Land Agency (cabinet rank). Okuno was notorious for his right-wing, revisionist views.

It was not uncommon for police bureaucrats from the Ministry of the Interior to enter national politics upon retirement, particularly among the former Commissioner-Generals of the NPA and the former Superintendent-Generals of the TMPD, up until the 1980s. Since then, those police bureaucrats who seek national elective offices do so when they are still mid-career.

There have also been changes in the way police bureaucrats, and *kōan* (security) bureaucrats in particular, get senior positions that are at the intersections of politics and administration. I have pointed out elsewhere that police bureaucrats (including those with SHP background) commonly occupied the post of Deputy Chief Cabinet Secretary, the top position for bureaucrats in the prime minister's office (and later of the entire bureaucracy) until the mid-1970s (Table 9.11).[16] Hosoya Kiichi and Ishioka Makoto, who together occupied the post throughout the 1960s, a decade known for political strife, had SHP backgrounds in the prewar era. As the conservatives in the LDP sought to calm the political opposition and consolidate their hold on power, the police bureaucrats were then shunned as being too overly political and controversial to be the virtual head of the civil service – since the police bureaucrats have access to intelligence that include sensitive information about politicians, of the opposition parties in particular.

After an interval of over thirty years, the rightward shift of the ruling LDP, and the intensification of political opposition to it, seems to have brought police bureaucrats back to the virtual head of the Japanese civil service in recent years. Uruma Iwao was a close associate of Abe Shinzō, who worked closely with him on the North Korea abduction issue and was rumored as a possible Deputy Chief Cabinet Secretary when Abe ascended to the premiership in 2006. Though that did not materialize, Uruma was picked by Abe's successor, Asō Tarō, two years later when the latter became prime minister. This was a controversial appointment, not just because a police bureaucrat was nominated to this sensitive intersection between party politics and state bureaucracy, breaking an over three-decade-long taboo, but all the more so because it was absolutely clear from

[16] Koichi Nakano, "Neoliberal Turn of State Conservatism in Japan: From Bureaucratic to Corporatist Authoritarian Legality," in Hualing Fu and Chen Weitseng (eds.), *Authoritarian Legality in Asia: Formation, Development and Transition* (Cambridge: Cambridge University Press, 2020), 343–349.

Table 9.11 *Deputy Chief Cabinet Secretaries with Police Background (1946–2018)*

Name [Term]	Previous Administrative Posts
Eguchi Mitoru [1952–1954]	VM, Labor Ministry Deputy Chief, Police Reserve
Taniguchi Yutaka [1954]	Deputy DG, National Police Agency
Tanaka Eiichi [1955–1957]	Superintendent-General, TMPD
Okazaki Eijō [1957–1958]	Public Security Division, Police Bureau
Hosoya Kiichi [1960–1964]	Kagawa Prefectural Police Chief
Ishioka Makoto [1964–1970]	Cabinet Intelligence Office Chief
Gotōda Masaharu [1972–1973]	Commissioner-General, NPA
Kawashima Hiromori [1973–1976]	Cabinet Intelligence Office Chief
Uruma Iwao [2008–2009]	Commissioner-General, NPA
Sugita Kazuhiro [2012–]	Director of Cabinet Intelligence Deputy Chief Cabinet Secretary for Crisis Management

the moment Asō assumed office that his mission was to face down the ascendant opposition, the Democratic Party of Japan, as a Lower House election was due within a year. Uruma's loyalty to right-wing ideology, commonly shared by Abe and Asō, and his access to police intelligence were obviously the reason behind his promotion. As a matter of fact, Uruma invited strong criticism as Deputy Chief Cabinet Secretary, when he made an off-the-record comment that LDP politicians are unlikely to be investigated in the Nishimatsu scandal (which was directly implicating Ozawa Ichirō, the then leader of the DPJ) even though some key figures in the LDP were also known to have received funds from the company in the months before the Lower House election was called. Uruma was forced to emerge from anonymity and apologize for his comment. As the DPJ won the election and came to power, Uruma stepped down from his post, but when Abe brought the LDP back to power three years later, and as he went on to establish the National Security Council through a controversial legislation, Uruma was nominated as a member.

As Abe took power back from the DPJ in December 2012, he appointed Sugita Kazuhiro, as we noted earlier. Sugita is a thoroughbred *kōan* (security) bureaucrat, who has served as the Security Bureau Chief of the NPA, the Director of Cabinet Intelligence, and the Deputy Chief Cabinet Secretary for Crisis Management, and was in conservative circles as advisor to both TEPCO and JR Central (headed by Kasai Yoshiyuki, known as a close ideological companion of Abe's) before he was brought back to government. It matters that a police bureaucrat occupies the top bureaucratic post in the country because police presence in the prime minister's office (*kantei*) is already strong as it is. The Director of Cabinet Intelligence (formerly the Cabinet Office Intelligence Chief) has always been a police bureaucrat, and since 1998, the Deputy Chief Cabinet Secretary for Crisis Management was established as a position for a senior police bureaucrat. In addition, NPA has always been a supplier of the Executive Secretary for the Prime Minister, alongside the Ministry of Finance, the Ministry of Foreign Affairs, and the Ministry of Economy, Trade, and Industry.

The enhanced police presence in the prime minister's inner circle is clearly a background to Abe's more assertive, PM-led (as opposed to Ministry of Foreign Affairs-led) foreign and security policy as well as his more authoritarian approach to law-and-order legislations on the domestic front, including the state secrets law in 2013 and the conspiracy law in 2017.

10

Authoritarian Policing and Democratization

The Case of Thailand

EUGÉNIE MÉRIEAU

10.1 Introduction

As David Bayley remarked in his seminal study of policing, "Police activities determine the limits of freedom in organized society, an essential feature in determining the character of government [...] A government is recognized as being authoritarian if its police are repressive, democratic if its police are restrained."[1] In other words, the type of policing practiced in a society is indicative of regime type, broadly conceived as either authoritarian or democratic. Hence, during democratization processes we should observe corresponding changes in modes of policing, from "authoritarian" to "democratic policing."[2]

A key distinction between authoritarian and democratic policing lies in the difference between law enforcement, service-oriented policing and the policing of political activities. As societies democratize, the police undergo a process of "professionalization" whereby they progressively relinquish their political activities to focus on law enforcement. Derived from the nine principles of "the founder of modern police" Sir Robert Peel,[3] professionalization entails specialization on crime reduction (referred to as "low policing") as opposed to political policing ("high policing").[4]

Against this background, the literature on policing identifies three historical stages: prior to the eighteenth century, policing was essentially

[1] David H Bayley, *Patterns of Policing, Crime, Law and Deviance* (New Brunswick: Rutgers University Press, 1985), 5, 189.

[2] Liqun Cao, Lanying Huang, and Ivan Sun, "From Authoritarian Policing to Democratic Policing: A Case Study of Taiwan," *Policing and Society* 26(6) (August 17, 2016): 642–658.

[3] Keith L. Williams, "Peel's Principles and Their Acceptance by American Police: Ending 175 Years of Reinvention," *The Police Journal: Theory, Practice and Principles* 76(2) (April 2003): 97–120.

[4] Jean-Paul Brodeur, "High Policing and Low Policing: Remarks about the Policing of Political Activities," *Social Problems* 30(5) (1983): 507–520.

political in that its function was to consolidate a specific regime and protect its power-holders; from the eighteenth to the twentiethcentury, as the police professionalized, they increasingly focused on suppressing crime; and, from the late twentieth century onwards, "communitarian policing," with its emphasis on delivery of public goods and trust-building, became the new standard in democratic states.[5] In line with the tenets of modernization theory, political policing is considered to recede along with democratization, thereby acting as one of the key markers of the authoritarian/democratic dichotomy, which also maps onto a nonmodern/modern divide.[6]

The Thai case is particularly relevant in any testing of the hypothesis that sees policing as a function of regime type in the broader frame of modernization theory. Since the overthrow of absolute monarchy in 1932, Thai political history has been dominated by long periods of military dictatorship punctuated by shorter periods of democracy. For the first forty years of its history (1933–1973), Thailand was ruled by military juntas, although elections were sometimes held. The so-called Third Wave of democracy hit the kingdom in 1973, one year before the Portuguese Carnation Revolution[7], but it was short-lived. The "democratic parenthesis" lasted only three years, before a coup plunged the country back into military dictatorship in 1976. Following the ouster of the junta a few years later, Thailand was labeled a "semi-democracy": notwithstanding election results, prime ministers would inevitably come from the ranks of the military.[8] In 1991, yet another military coup gave rise to a popular movement for democracy that called for an end to military rule and a new constitution. The outcome of this process, the 1997 Constitution, was a watershed moment in the history of the country. The fragile young Thai democracy appeared to be morphing into a consolidated, participatory democracy. Yet in 2006, a twelfth military coup ushered in a return to military rule, followed by a short period of democracy (2008–2014), military rule again (2015–2019), and the return to a "semi-democracy" headed by a soldier legitimized by elections.

To test the hypothesis of policing as a function of regime type, this chapter focuses on the evolutions of political policing in light of recent

[5] George L Kelling, "The Evolving Strategy of Policing," *Perspectives on Policing* 4 (1988): 1–16.

[6] Peter K. Manning, "Jean-Paul Brodeur on High and Low Policing" (2012) Champ penal, http://journals.openedition.org/champpenal/8285.

[7] Samuel P Huntington, "Democracy's Third Wave," *Journal of Democracy* 2(2) (1991): 12–34.

[8] Chai-Anan Samudavanija, "Democracy in Thailand: A Case of a Stable Semi-Democratic Regime," *World Affairs* 150(1) (1987): 31–41.

Thai political developments – as only political policing is expected to be affected by democratization/modernization. As Bayley puts it, "[r]egime character does not affect the nature of tasks performed by police, apart from those related to politics."[9] Indeed, whether in times of fully-fledged military dictatorship or in times of electoral democracy, routine service-oriented, law-enforcement policing remains relatively constant. For instance, in the 1970s, as the Thai police were involved in violent counterinsurgency practices including extrajudicial killings, enforced disappearances, and torture on a massive scale, they still performed highly service-oriented "low policing" tasks on a daily basis. Asked about his everyday routine, a Thai policeman tells of his role in the following terms:

> The police are charged with serving the public. This police service includes the rendering of facilities and assistance to the public, such as giving information on location of places, streets, or, when requested, seeing that vehicles or other things left with the police will not be tempered with, taking a sick person to hospitals, giving advice and opinion in civil cases, helping in the settling of compoundable offences, helping children and the aged across the street, removing such obstructions as vehicles and other things from roadways, helping others with personal service when possible such as lifting loads onto vehicles, giving first aids in emergency, finding the home of children who have lost their way, returning lost property to the rightful owners and others. In other words a policeman is a friend of all and is always helpful to the public.[10]

In contrast to "helping children and the aged across the street," the quintessential marker of "high" policing signaling authoritarianism is the policing of political dissent. Dissent manifests itself in variegated ways, including in the staging of street protests. Protest policing might be one of the domains where the dichotomy between authoritarian and democratic policing appears most sharply: "brutal versus soft," "illegal versus legal," "confrontational versus consensual," "repressive versus accommodative."[11] In a democratic society, political dissent manifesting itself in street protests will be channeled and protected, whereas in an authoritarian polity it will be violently repressed. Democratic policing is defined as a minimal use of state violence against the citizen, and whenever it is used, there

[9] Bayley, *Patterns of Policing*, 210.

[10] Quoted in Albert C. Weed, *Police and the Modernization Process: Thailand* (Princeton, NJ: Woodrow Wilson School of Public and International Affairs, 1970), 25.

[11] Janjira Sombatpoonsiri, "The Policing of Anti-Government Protests: Thailand's 2013–2014 Demonstrations and a Crisis of Police Legitimacy," *Journal of Asian Security and International Affairs* 4(1) (April 2017): 95–122.

will be a concomitant interest in restraining its use.[12] In a democracy, "police view their job to be managing, rather than repressing, protest, protecting the right to demonstrate, and guaranteeing (even to those whose views they may find intolerable) due process of law."[13] Besides restraint in the use of force and due process of law, police accountability and transparency are key characteristics of democratic policing.

By contrast, authoritarian policing involves a reliance on secret police, arbitrary arrests and unlawful detention, extrajudicial killings, torture, and enforced disappearances. Moreover, police violence is understood, in the authoritarian context, as structural as opposed to deviant and impunity as the norm rather than the exception. Democratic policing must be neutral and accountable,[14] whereas authoritarian policing is both politicized and unaccountable.[15] Several studies also associate democratic policing with decentralization of police structures, and authoritarian policing with hypercentralization.[16]

In this chapter, I argue that post-1970s democratization in Thailand had minimal effects on the entrenched practices of authoritarian policing. Democratization, in fact, did not put an end to these practices; instead, correlated with their legalization has been the enactment of a set of empowering legislations. This empirical finding invites a reconsideration of the hypothesis that there exists a covariation between regime type and policing practices. Section 10.2 provides a brief overview of the genealogy of the Thai police.

10.2 The Birth of the Modern Thai Police: Colonial Origins and Foreign Models

Thailand is the only country in Southeast Asia to have never been directly colonized. A stone inscription from the Sukhothai era (thirteenth–fifteenth

[12] Gary T Marx, "Some Reflections on the Democratic Policing of Demonstrations," in Donatella Della Porta and Herbert Reiter (eds.), *Policing Protest: The Control of Mass Demonstrations in Western Democracies*, 253–269, at 253.

[13] Marx, *Some Reflections*, 254.

[14] Puangthong R. Pawakapan, *Central Role of Thailand's Internal Security Operations Command in the Post-Counter-Insurgency Period*, Trends in Southeast Asia, no. 17 (Singapore: ISEAS Publishing, 2017), 3. Peter K. Manning, "The Study of Policing," *Police Quarterly* 8(1) (March 2005): 23–43.

[15] "Democratic policing refers to the police practice where political neutrality holds in domestic conflicts and a civilian supremacy prevails. Police officers are accountable to the law and ultimately to a democratically elected parliament." Cao, Huang, and Sun, *From Authoritarian Policing*, 645.

[16] Kevin Carty, *Guidebook on Democratic Policing*, 2nd ed., SPMU Publication Series 1 (Vienna: OSCE, 2008).

centuries) refers to the role of inspectors or *phu truat* mandated by the king for various missions of public ordering.[17] During the Ayuthaya era (fourteenth–eighteenth centuries), bureaucracy was divided into military and civilian domains.[18] A form of "metropolitan police" tasked with patrolling around the palace appeared during that time.[19] The word for police, *tamruat*, can be found in sixteenth-century court chronicles.[20] The police function was then exclusively to provide security to the royal family.[21] Policing was influenced by the Hindu models of kingship that had spread in the Siamese kingdoms of Sukhothai and Ayuthaya as part of a long process of "Indianization."[22] In the eighteenth century, the newly founded kingdom of Rattanakosin attracted a large influx of Chinese, and a "police constabulary division" was formed to police Bangkok's Chinese residents activities involving opium trafficking and gang warfare in Chinatown (Sampeng area).

From the second half of the nineteenth century onwards, Siam was cryptocolonized;[23] that is to say, the government was involved in the hiring of numerous foreign advisors to build and reform the state on a Western model. In 1860, King Mongkut created a "police constabulary" under the command of a British former official, Samuel Joseph Bird Ames. The unit comprised Malayan and Indian constables,[24] as well as many British officers.[25] In 1871, King Chulalongkorn undertook a study trip to Singapore and in 1875, he asked Samuel Joseph Bird Ames to reform the police, based on the Singaporean-British model. More than fifty regulations were issued to that end, assigning specific duties to constables based on their locations.[26] In 1897, Rama V established a provincial gendarmerie on the French model,[27] while simultaneously recruiting British colonial

[17] Eric Haanstad, "A Brief History of the Thai Police," in Paul Chambers (ed.) *Knights of the Realm: Thailand's Military and Police, Then and Now* (Bangkok: White Lotus Press, 2013), 447–498, at 452.

[18] Reign of King Trailokanat (fifteenth century); Haanstad, *A Brief History*, 453.

[19] Eric James Haanstad, "Constructing Order through Chaos : A State Ethnography of the Thai Police" (Doctor of Philosophy (Anthropology) thesis, Wisconsin-Madison, 2008), 50.

[20] Weed, *Police and the Modernization Process*, 14.

[21] Haanstad, *Constructing Order*, 42.

[22] George Coédès, *The Indianized States of Southeast Asia* (Honolulu, HI: East-West Center Press, 1968).

[23] M. Herzfeld, "The Absent Presence: Discourses of Crypto-Colonialism," *South Atlantic Quarterly* 101(4) (October 1, 2002): 899–926.

[24] Haanstad, *A Brief History*, 455.

[25] Weed, *Police and Modernization*, 15.

[26] Haanstad, *Constructing Order*, 52.

[27] Weed, *Police and Modernization*, 15.

officers in India to build a "Patrol Police Unit."[28] Under the supervision of key European advisors, the police force professionalized its training and practices: the first training academy was established in 1901, and a set of binding regulations based on the British model were codified in 1903.[29]

The reign of Chulalongkorn was one of state-building, centralization, and consolidation of royal power. The highly educated Prince Damrong, brother of Chulalongkorn, headed the Ministry of the Interior. In 1906, he established the first secret police composed of officers in plainclothes, whose role was to gather information on criminals involved in possible conspiracies against the regime. Meanwhile, criminal law was modernized with the help of foreign advisors: numerous laws criminalizing offences to the state, including laws against *lèse-majesté* that emulated those from Prussia, were introduced in Thailand, and later included in the first modern Penal Code (1908).[30] In that context, Chulalongkorn hired French advisors to draft a martial law in 1907,[31] modeled on the French *état de siège*. Revised in 1914, martial law allowed the military to take over civilian administration and rule by decree, make arbitrary arrests, and order detention without charge. It granted immunity for acts by the military, while military officers as well as targeted civilians were put under the exclusive jurisdiction of martial courts.[32] Martial law was put to use for the first time in 1912 to quell a revolutionary attempt to overthrow the monarchy and replace it with a republic. In 1913, a Criminal Investigation Department was created to centralize intelligence on criminals and conspirators.[33] At that point, the Thai police still included many foreigners, including Westerners filling the top ranks. In 1915, the French-influenced Provincial Gendarmerie merged with the British-influenced Patrol Department. During the 1920s and early 1930s, Siam increasingly emulated Japan and reformed its police forces accordingly.[34]

In June 1932, a faction of foreign-educated civil and military bureaucrats seized power from King Prajadhipok, replacing absolute monarchy

28 A. J. Jardine was the first Patrol Police Unit director. Eric St. J. Lawson succeeded him in 1904; Haanstad, *Constructing Order*, 54.

29 Ibid., 56.

30 Eugénie Mérieau, "Thailand's Lèse-Majesté Law : On Blasphemy in a Buddhist Kingdom," *Buddhism, Law and Society* 4 (2019): 54–92.

31 The Criminal Code was promulgated in 1908, the Civil and Commercial Codes in 1935, and the first constitution in 1932.

32 Article 7 of the 1914 Martial Law.

33 Haanstad, *Constructing Order*, 56.

34 Weed, *Police and Modernization*, 16.

with constitutional monarchy. The People's Committee centralized the Royal Thai Police and put it under the direction of a powerful director-general. In November 1932, a few months after the revolution/coup, King Prajadhipok issued the Santiban Act, creating a Special Branch of the police tasked specifically with the protection of the monarchy and threats to national security. The Royal Thai Police Department developed into the main intelligence unit conducting data collection on dissident activities. Plainclothes officers were assigned to monitor anti-royalist communists.

In 1941, Siam declared war on the Allies and expelled all European advisors including those in the police. Prime Minister Field Marshal Phibun Songkhram, a fervent admirer of Mussolini, declared martial law while Japan occupied Siamese territory. He reorganized the police on the very centralized "Asian Police Organization" model. As Eric Haanstad puts it, "the martial law period under Phibun during WWII was a watershed moment for the centralization and expansion of the Thai police."[35] The Santiban Police was to spy on political opponents. Phibun intended for the project to merge the police and the army, but it failed. Nevertheless, both branches of the security forces were not strictly separated: they shared a common system of ranks and titles and officers could easily move from one body to another. This is how General Luang Adul Detcharat, chief of the national police during World War II and key figure of the anti-Japanese resistance movement, became, at the end of the war, army chief. In 1944, as the Allies were winning the war, Phibun was forced to resign and the Police Department was reformed toward gaining more autonomy: instead of being placed under the Ministry of the Interior, its director became solely responsible for its management.

10.3 Policing under Military Dictatorship: Extrajudicial Killings and Enforced Disappearances

After the war, the United States (US) inaugurated, as part of its policy of anticommunist containment, a "special relationship" with the Thai security forces in the domains of intelligence gathering and covert operations.[36] In 1950, American officials including Office of Strategic Services veteran Willis Bird and Central Intelligence Agency (CIA) official William

[35] Haanstad, *Constructing Order*, 60.

[36] Daniel M. Fineman, *A Special Relationship: The United States and Military Government in Thailand, 1947–1958* (Honolulu, HI: University of Hawai'i Press, 1997).

Lair met with leading Thai generals and the police chief to launch intensive cooperation. An initial anticommunist act was passed in 1952, called the Anti-Communist Activities Act (ACAA). It empowered the police to define "Communist-infiltrated" zones and to subsequently limit civil liberties, especially freedom of movement, in these areas. At first, the US directed its efforts at the Thai police, at the time under the leadership of Police Chief Phao Sriyanond, rather than at the military. The CIA armed and trained the Thai police, supporting the Santiban Police as well as helping in the establishment of the Border Patrol Police (BPP) in 1955, which would become "the paramilitary force of the Royal Thai Police."[37] The BPP's mission was extremely broad: it included border security, counterinsurgency and intelligence, as well as more traditional antismuggling and counterbanditry activities.[38] It also engaged massively in the building of schools and hospitals in impoverished areas.[39]

By the end of the 1950s, the Thai police was fully formed, trained, and equipped to carry out counterinsurgency missions as part of the US anticommunist insurgency policy. Already in 1951 the *New York Times* had noted that the Thai police was bigger than the military, and was very well equipped and trained, including in counterguerrilla warfare.[40] The massive American aid delivered to the Thai police installed Phao Sriyanond, the head of the police, as the strongman of Thailand and locus of power. As police chief, he engaged in extrajudicial killings and the enforced disappearances of his opponents. He was notoriously known for having his own police bodyguards, the Knights of the Diamonds Ring, or *Asawin*, assassinate whomever he pleased, before disappearing the body, either in the Chao Phraya River or elsewhere.[41] He notably had four Members of Parliament killed by the police.[42]

[37] Pawakapan, "Central Role of Thailand's Internal Security Operations Command," 3.

[38] Paul Chambers, "Securing an Alternative Army," in Pavin Chachavalpongpun (ed.), *Routledge Handbook of Contemporary Thailand*, 1st ed. (Abingdon; Routledge, 2019), 102–117, at 103, https://doi.org/10.4324/9781315151328-8.

[39] Sinae Hyun, "Mae Fah Luang : Thailand's Princess Mother and the Border Patrol Police during the Cold War," *Journal of Southeast Asian Studies* 48(2) (June 2017): 262–282, https://doi.org/10.1017/S0022463417000078; Sinae Hyun, "Integrating a Nation from the Margins: The Remote Area Security Development of the Border Patrol Police in Northern Thailand 1," *Rian Thai: International Journal of Thai Studies* 3 (2010): 233–258.

[40] "Thai Police Force Bigger than Army, Equipment Includes Bren Guns and Mortars – Some of Men Get Guerilla Training," *New York Times*, July 23, 1951.

[41] Thak Chaloemtiarana, *Thailand: The Politics of Despotic Paternalism* (Ithaca, NY: Cornell University Press, 2019), 60.

[42] Ibid., 48.

In order to reestablish military dominance over security issues and Thai politics at large, Army chief Sarit Thanarat staged a military coup in 1957 and another in 1958. To consolidate his rule, he staffed the entire police apparatus with military men.[43] He enacted an interim constitution granting him full powers, including broad police and judicial powers, which he used to execute his opponents.[44] Around this time, the CIA switched allegiances, favoring the Thai military and Sarit. In 1962, with the help of the CIA, he established the Central Security Command to centralize counterinsurgency actions. Following the failure of Sarit's Central Security Command, his successor General Praphat Jarusathien established the Communist Suppression Operations Command in 1965.[45] This was a hybrid command center, coordinating the actions of the police and the army with support from the CIA. In 1969, a second ACAA was passed, allowing the military to detain suspected communists for up to 480 days without charge.[46] Several other anticommunist acts succeeded one another: Revolutionary Announcement 78 followed by Revolutionary Announcement 199, the latter allowing indefinite detention of suspected communists.[47] In 1973, the Communist Suppression Operations Command became the Internal Security Operations Command (ISOC). Its mission was to conduct surveillance of political opposition, activist populations, and coordinate the suppression of threats to national security. ISOC included members of the army as well as the police chief.[48]

As can be expected, policing during the first decades of the Cold War period involved the perpetration of extrajudicial killings and enforced disappearances against alleged communists and political opponents, to the extent that "state killings" became a defining feature of post-World War II politics. As Ben Anderson puts it, "Political murders by

[43] Haanstad, *A Brief History*, 68.

[44] Article 17, 1959 Interim Charter.

[45] Pawakapan, "Central Role of Thailand's Internal Security Operations Command," 7.

[46] Tyrell Haberkorn, *In Plain Sight: Impunity and Human Rights in Thailand* (Madison, WI; University of Wisconsin Press, 2018), 78.

[47] Ibid., 78.

[48] "The original command structure gave the directorship of ISOC to the Army commander; the deputy director was the deputy commander of the Army; four assistant director posts belonged to two assistant Army commanders, to the permanent secretary of the Ministry of the Interior and the national police chief; and the position of ISOC chief of staff went to the Army chief of staff" (Pawakapan, "Central Role of Thailand's Internal Security Operations Command," 8). In 1987, by order of then Prime Minister Prem Tinsulanond, the prime minister became the director of ISOC instead of the army chief.

the ruling cliques have been a regular feature of modern Thai politics – whether under Marshal Phibunsongkhram's dictatorship in the late 1930s; under the Phibunsongkhram – Phao Sriyanond – Sarit Thanarat triumvirate of the late 1940s and 1950s, or the Sarit Thanarat – Thanom Kittikachon – Praphat Charusathien regime of the 1960s and early 1970s."[49] There was little distinction between an extrajudicial killing and a judicial execution, as the military had, under Sarit's rule, the power to order executions. Execution and the threat of execution were also used to crack down on ordinary crime including even breaches of social regulations. In one legendary example, Sarit, confronted with the proliferation of deadly fires in factories, promised the death penalty to factory owners whose buildings ever caught fire – and, so the story goes, the fires instantly stopped.[50]

The period also saw the creation of paramilitary police organizations. Most notably, the Village Scouts, established by the BPP in 1971, had massive outreach: in 1975, their membership peaked at roughly 10 percent of the Thai adult population[51]. Paradoxically, the intense militarization of the Thai police and society at large coincided with a period of democratization.

10.4 Policing in Times of Democratization: More Extrajudicial Killings and Enforced Disappearances

In 1973, students took to the streets to call for an end to military rule and a new constitution, as well as the dissolution of ISOC. The military resigned – the so-called three tyrants even left the country. A three-year period of democracy ensued. Yet occurrences of extrajudicial killings surged in the "democratic parenthesis" of the 1970s. Reminiscent of techniques used in the Argentinian dirty war, suspected communists and labor activists were killed and their bodies disappeared, thrown out of helicopters or burnt in boiling drums. In the province of Patthalung (South), police and military officers conducted a campaign of massive extrajudicial killings. Villagers were arrested, knocked unconscious, and their bodies dropped in boiling drums, while their screams were covered by sounds of truck engines – the

49 Ben Anderson, "Withdrawal Symptoms: Social and Cultural Aspects of the October 6 Coup," *Bulletin of Concerned Asian Scholars* 9(3) (September 1977): 13, https://doi.org/10.1080/14672715.1977.10406423.

50 As recalled by Tarend J. Terwiel, informal discussion, May 2018, Göttingen.

51 Pawakapan, "Central Role of Thailand's Internal Security Operations Command," 3.

thang daeng killings[52]. In 1975, halfway through the "democratic parenthesis," extrajudicial killings peaked tremendously[53].

The next year, on September 25, 1976, two labor activists were found hanged in Nakhon Pathom Province, allegedly by the police. This prompted students to stage protests against the methods used by security forces to silence labor activists within the broader context of anticommunist operations. They gathered at Thammasat University in Bangkok on October 6, 1976, only to be raped, shot, hanged, and drowned by security officials including police, military, and paramilitary organizations. The BPP had a leading role in the massacre, prompting scholars and intellectuals to question the American responsibility in the bloodbath.[54] This episode, epitomizing authoritarian policing, ended the democratic experiment: by the evening of that day, the military seized power in a coup, ousting the government of Seni Pramot. The 1976 coupmakers issued many "revolutionary decrees" affecting policing. They increased the jail penalty for *lèse-majesté* to fifteen years and issued a number of other security laws.[55] In any case, the democratic experiment did not lead to either a halt in state violence or even some first steps toward accountability of the security forces. As Tyrell puts it: "Even if only the three years between 14 October 1973 and 6 October 1976 are examined, let alone the periods before or since, impunity was the established norm for state violence."[56]

In the 1980s, the "semidemocracy" under the premiership of Prem Tinsulanonda, a nonelected yet parliamentarily-accountable ex-general, seemed to have called violent crackdowns on protesters to a close. ISOC

[52] Tyrell Haberkorn, "Getting Away with Murder in Thailand, State, Violence and Impunity in Phattalung," in N. Ganesan and Chull Kim Sung (eds.), *State Violence in East Asia* (Lexington, KY; The University Press of Kentucky, 2013), 185–208, https://muse-jhu-edu.ezp-prod1.hul.harvard.edu/book/21100.

[53] Ibid., 202.

[54] Scholars also questioned the role of the monarchy, given the close relationship between the king, the queen, and the BPP. As Vasit Dejkunjorn and others put it, "The close relationship between HM King Bhumipol and the BPP, especially the PARU, was well-known in uniformed circles" (Vasit Dejkunjorn, Busakorn Suriyasarn, and Christopher Moore, *In His Majesty's Footsteps: A Personal Memoir* (Bangkok: Heaven Lake Press, distributed in Thailand by Asia Document Bureau, 2006), 2).

[55] David Streckfuss, *Truth on Trial in Thailand* (New York : Routledge, 2011); Tyrell Haberkorn, "The Hidden Transcript of Amnesty: The 6 October 1976 Massacre and Coup in Thailand," *Critical Asian Studies* 47(1) (January 2, 2015): 2. In its revised version, Article 112 of the Thai Penal Code reads: "Whoever defames, insults or threatens the King, the Queen, the Heir-apparent or the Regent, shall be punished with imprisonment of three to fifteen years."

[56] Haberkorn, "The Hidden Transcript of Amnesty," 3.

was downsized and its power reduced. It refocused its activities on the monitoring of the Malay Muslim insurgency in the south of the country. In the three southernmost provinces of Thailand, the majority population of Malay Muslims had voiced demands for autonomy from the Thai Buddhist state and a possible reunion with Malaysia as part of a federation of Malaya (a sultanate of Patani). Prem instructed several military-dominated agencies, notably the Southern Border Provinces Administrative Center (SBPAC), to adopt a conciliatory approach with the insurgents – to be coordinated by ISOC.[57] In spite of this relative democratization, enforced disappearances did not stop. Between 1976 and 1982 alone, some sixty cases of enforced disappearances were recorded, mostly involving environmental and human rights activists.[58]

Yet following the 1991 coup, which inaugurated another period of semi-dictatorship under the prime ministership of civilian liberal Anand Panyarachun, protests against the army's resilient role in politics were met with the same violence: protesters were shot by the security forces during the "Black May Incident."[59] Deaths and disappearances remained part of the possible means of political policing. The violence of policing sparked renewed calls for democratization and "political reform." In 1996, the Thai government ratified the International Covenant on Civil and Political Rights, signaling a new era for Thai politics and a possible embracement of the values of "democratic policing." Meanwhile, Thailand drafted its new, liberal, constitution. The next year, then-prime minister Chuan Leekpai launched a reform of the police, transferring it from the supervision of the Ministry of the Interior to the direct supervision of the prime minister.[60] The hypercentralization of the Royal Thai Police, with a powerful commissioner-general at the top reporting directly to the prime minister was a direct outcome of democratization. The 1997 constitution – the most democratic Thai constitution to date – was promulgated that same year. Under the new charter, a former policeman, Thaksin Shinawatra, was elected prime minister with a near-absolute majority. Thaksin was a former policeman who had also

57 Both agencies were created by decrees of Prem Tinsulanond in 1981. Human Rights Watch, *No One Is Safe: Insurgent Attacks on Civilians in Thailand's Southern Border Provinces* (Bangkok: Human Rights Watch, 2007), 16.

58 Haberkorn, *In Plain Sight*, 166.

59 William A. Callahan, *Imagining Democracy: Reading "The Events of May" in Thailand* (Singapore and London:Institute of Southeast Asian Studies, 1998).

60 Tony Glendinning, "Police Reform in Thailand Post-2006," *International Journal of Criminology and Sociology* (2013): 372.

completed a degree in criminology from the US.[61] Yet under his rule, brutal policing including extrajudicial killings and enforced disappearances peaked, probably at levels not experienced since the rule of military dictator Sarit Thanarat in the late 1950s.

Upon his election in 2001, one of Thaksin's first measures was to launch a massive "War on Drugs." Drawing inspiration from the policing techniques of ex-police chief Phao Sriyanond, whom he liked to quote, he once declared to "his" policemen: "Police General Phao Sriyanond said 'There is nothing under the sun that the Thai police cannot do.' So I'm confident that drugs are something that the Thai police can deal with. Do it to the full."[62] Launched in February 2003, Thaksin's War on Drugs lasted three months and caused more than 2,500 deaths, most of which were presumably extrajudicial killings, with no investigation into the deaths whatsoever.[63] Another key measure of Thaksin was to adopt a more "law and order" approach to the conflict in the South. He dissolved the military-dominated, dialogue-oriented SBPAC to make room for the police in the Deep South. When, in January 2004, southern insurgents raided an army compound and seized weaponry including assault rifles, grenades, and ammunition, Thaksin responded by declaring martial law, which allowed searches, raids, and arrests without warrant, as well as administrative detention for up to seven days. Although he did empower the army, Thaksin made sure that the police took the lead in the operations.[64] He dispatched teams from the Crime Suppression Division to the southern areas – and let them engage in acts of torture and extrajudicial killings.[65] In April 2004, security forces raided a mosque where suspected insurgents were hiding, killing thirty-two men.[66] In July 2005, Thaksin enacted an Emergency Decree, which empowered the police to conduct searches without warrant and to put alleged offenders under pretrial detention

61 Pasuk Phongpaichit and Chris Baker, *Thaksin: The Business of Politics in Thailand* (NIAS Press, 2004).

62 January 14, 2003, quoted in Pasuk Phongpaichit and Chris Baker, *Thaksin: The Business of Politics in Thailand* (Copenhagen : NIAS Press, 2004), 153.

63 Human Rights Watch, *Not Enough Graves: The War on Drugs, HIV/AIDS, and Violations of Human Rights* (Bangkok: Human Rights Watch, 2004).

64 Human Rights Watch, *No One Is Safe : Insurgent Attacks on Civilians in Thailand's Southern Border Provinces* (Bangkok : Human Rights Watch, 2007), 33.

65 Ibid., 34.

66 Krue Se mosque raid. General Chavalit's orders focused on negotiation, when General Panlop Pinmanee, deputy director of ISOC, ordered the killing of the suspected insurgents.

for up to thirty days – more than the seven days allowed under martial law.[67] Meanwhile, Thaksin Shinawatra issued the 2004 Police Act allegedly to improve and deepen "community policing," but in fact to reinforce the prime minister's control over the police.[68] In October of the same year, a protest in front of a police station in the southern province in Narathiwat was met with firing of live shots, killing seven protesters, as well as the arrest and humiliation of all remaining protesters. Stripped, laid on the ground in the burning sun before being taken to an army camp in the back of a truck, almost a hundred of those arrested died of dehydration and suffocation before reaching the detention center.[69] This episode tragically exemplifies the violence of authoritarian policing in times of democratization.

Another technique considered characteristic of authoritarian policing is the recourse to enforced disappearances. In this domain as well, the coming to power of Thaksin had tragic effects. The most prominent case of enforced disappearances under the government of Thaksin is that of Somchai Neelapaichit, a human rights lawyer specialized in defending Muslims from the Deep South in cases of terrorism. One day, in March 2004, he was kidnapped by police officers in a busy street in Bangkok, and never reappeared.[70] Five police officers were initially charged for kidnapping but later acquitted for lack of evidence and released.[71] Other less prominent cases of enforced disappearances were recorded during Thaksin's rule. The Thai nongovernmental organization Justice for Peace Foundation documented fifty-nine disappearances between 2002 and 2012,[72] a period of democratic flourishing.

In 2005–2006, mass anti-Thaksin protests erupted in the capital city. Unlike in the Deep South, mass protests in Bangkok were not met with deaths or grave injuries. Thaksin refrained from declaring a state of

[67] International Commission of Jurists, *More Power, Less Accountability: Thailand's New Emergency Decree* (Bangkok: International Commission of Jurists, 2005), 3. The new law was passed on July 15, 2005 and enforced four days later in the southernmost provinces of Thailand.

[68] Glendinning, "Police Reform in Thailand Post-2006," 373.

[69] Eighty-five of them lost their lives. This is referred to as the "Tak Bai Incident."

[70] See the book written by his widow Angkhana. Angkhana Neelapaichit, *Reading between the Lines* (Bangkok: Working Group on Justice for Peace, 2009).

[71] For a detailed account of the court cases, see International Commission of Jurists, *Ten Years Without Truth: Somchai Neelapaijit and Enforced Disappearances in Thailand* (Bangkok: International Commission of Jurists, 2014).

[72] Haberkorn, *In Plain Sight*, 167.

emergency under the 2005 Executive Decree on Public Administration in Emergency Situations. It seemed that Thaksin was intent on embracing the policy of deescalation of street protests, a key pillar of democratic policing. He did not deploy the army to quell the protests, which self-dispersed when Thaksin dissolved the House of Representatives. Thaksin was later that year removed in a military coup. Under martial law, declared as part of the coup, gatherings of more than five people were banned and street politics wound down. The military government established two new police divisions: the Protection and Crowd Control Division attached to the Metropolitan Bureau and the Technology Crime Suppression Division attached to the Central Investigation Bureau.[73] Head of the junta General Surayud Chulanont attempted to reform the police organization, aiming to withdraw it from the Prime Minister's control, but it failed owing to police resistance.[74] Surayud reenacted martial law in the South[75]. The military drafted a new security legislation, the Internal Security Act, reintroducing a military-dominated and powerful ISOC empowering the military to indulge in renewed "political policing" activities.[76]

The 2007 Constitution reestablished civil liberties, prompting another wave of political protests. In 2008, "yellow-shirts" protested against the elected government – up to the point of closing down the airport entirely for several weeks. Notwithstanding the scale of the protests, the army was not deployed nor was a state of emergency declared. Democratic policing seemed to be entrenched and the police to be bound to the rule of law. Yet the 2008 Internal Security Act reinstating ISOC was passed, although after intense debate, it was placed under the supervision of the prime minister rather than the Army commander in chief.[77] From 2009 to early 2010, "red-shirt" protests against the resilient role of the military in Thai politics were met with "deescalation" techniques by the police. But in May 2010, the military-backed civilian government of Abhisit Vejjajiva, using the new Internal Security Act, sent the army to crack

[73] Arisa Ratanapinsiri, "A History of Police Reform in Thailand," in Paul Chambers (ed.), *Knights of the Realm: Thailand's Military and Police, Then and Now* (Bangkok : White Lotus Press, 2013), 523.

[74] Ibid., 500.

[75] International Commission of Jurists, *Implementation of Thailand's Emergency Decree, July 2007* (Bangkok: International Commission of Jurists, 2010), 3.

[76] International Commission of Jurists, *Thailand's Internal Security Act: Risking the Rule of Law?* (Bangkok: International Commission of Jurists, 2010), part v.

[77] Ibid., part vi.

down on the protests. Scenes of urban guerrilla action unfolded, leaving 90 people dead and more than 2,000 injured.[78] Under the following civilian government of Yingluck Shinawatra, elected in 2011, mass protests were not handled by the army but by the police. The 2013 mass protests were also "de-escalated" by the police,[79] until the military seized power in yet another coup in 2014, promulgating martial law and putting a durable end to the street politics that is so familiar in Thailand.

During this time, the practice of enforced disappearances continued unabated. In April 2014, environmental activist Porlajee "Billy" Rakchongcharoen reported to the police – and never reappeared. Continually harassed by the police, he was well known for his struggle for justice for Karen families living in national parks.[80] As in the case of Somchai, some police officers were charged for the murder but released on lack of evidence. In 2012, Thailand had signed the Convention on the Protection of All Persons from Enforced Disappearances, five years after its ratification of the Convention on Torture, then under the military dictatorship of Surayud Chulanont. Under the military dictatorship of Prayuth Chan-Ocha, a draft Act on the Prevention and Suppression of Torture and Enforced Disappearances was submitted to the National Legislative Assembly in 2015 – but, as of 2022, no progress has been made since.

10.5 Explaining the Resilience of Authoritarian Policing in Times of Democratization: Thailand's Dual State Structure

Why are security forces not responsive to democratization? Why are practices of torture, enforced disappearances, and extrajudicial killings so robust during times of democracy? The answer lies in the nature of the Thai state: Thailand's security apparatus remains autonomous from elected politicians, and is therefore irresponsive to democratization. The Weberian ideal-type, according to which the bureaucracy comes under government control, does not hold for Thailand where the bureaucracy is the principal

[78] Tyrell Haberkorn, "Truth and Justice When Fear and Repression Remain," in Michael J. Montesano, Pavin Chachavalpongpun, and Aekapol Chongvilaivan (ed.), *Bangkok, May 2010: Perspectives on a Divided Thailand* (Singapore: ISEAS–Yusof Ishak Institute, 2012), 42–54.

[79] Sombatpoonsiri, "The Policing of Anti-Government Protests."

[80] International Commission of Jurists, "Thailand: at fourth anniversary of enforced disappearance of 'Billy', still no resolution," 2018 www.icj.org/wp-content/uploads/2018/04/Thailand-Billy-disappearance-4th-year-News-web-story-2018-ENG.pdf.

and the government the agent.[81] Thailand has been analyzed as a "bureaucratic polity" characterized by a bureaucracy autonomous from politics and endowed with veto powers over the sphere of the political.[82]

Thai bureaucracy can be described as a compound of several competing power centers tied together in complex nonhierarchical relations or networks.[83] As Craig J. Reynolds puts it, "what prevails most of the time is a multi-centred autocracy with many centres of power that sometimes do what they want autonomously, without instruction and with impunity. Even with elections, autocratic rule is the norm, not the exception."[84] Among these entities, the military and the Santiban police are two power centers, both highly autonomous from the government. The Thai bureaucracy is also fragmented along the lines of what Ernst Fraenkel calls a dual state.[85] In a dual state, two autonomous systems coexist, one system governed by the "rule of law" and another by arbitrary power, the former being subservient to the latter. Fraenkel built on John Locke's analysis of the royal prerogative – characterized by discretion – to call the realm of arbitrary rule the "prerogative state," while referring to the legalistic one as the "normative state." In his account, the normative and the prerogative state are competitive. In the case of Thailand, the normative state can be identified as taking its orders from the elected government of the day, and the prerogative state from the military. The prerogative state is a type of "deep state" composed of specific state agents who oppose the rise of electoral politics and eventually the very idea of electoral democracy, from low-ranking civil servants to the highest-ranking officials, including security forces.[86]

[81] Max Weber, "Bureaucracy," in Tony Waters and Dagmar Waters (eds.), *Weber's Rationalism and Modern Society: New Translations on Politics, Bureaucracy, and Social Stratification* (Palgrave, 2015); Jacob I. Ricks, "Agents, Principals, or Something in between? Bureaucrats and Policy Control in Thailand," *Journal of East Asian Studies* 18(3) (November 2018): 321–344.

[82] Fred Riggs, *Thailand: The Modernization of a Bureaucratic Polity* (Honolulu, HI: East-West Center, 1966).

[83] Duncan McCargo, "Network Monarchy and Legitimacy Crises in Thailand," *The Pacific Review* 18(4) (December 2005): 499–519.

[84] Craig Reynolds calls the Thai State an "un-State"; Craig Reynolds, "Time's Arrow and the Burden of the Past," 4.

[85] The book, initially published in 1941, analyzed the case of Nazi Germany. Ernst Fraenkel, *The Dual State: A Contribution to the Theory of Dictatorship* (Oxford: Oxford University Press, 2018).

[86] Eugénie Mérieau, "Thailand's Deep State, Royal Power and the Constitutional Court (1997–2015)," *Journal of Contemporary Asia* 46(3) (July 2, 2016): 445–466. See also Eugénie Mérieau, "The Legal–Military Alliance for Illiberal Constitutionalism in Thailand," in ed. Björn Dressel and Marco Bünte (eds.), *Politics and Constitutions in Southeast Asia* (New York: Routledge, 2017), 140–160.

They refuse to take their orders from elected governments as they see them unfit to administer the country. Civilian governments have limited or no control over such a "state within the state." Neither a mafia nor a shadowy set of connections, Thailand's deep state is grounded in law, especially in a set of emergency legislations. Fraenkel traces the origin of the prerogative state to martial law. Martial law indeed creates a parallel state, with its own rules, its own executive, and its own judiciary. While democratization affects the normative state, it does not affect the deep or prerogative state, which continues to function according to fully-fledged authoritarianism and to its own set of norms and hierarchies.

The history of the Thai police is one of shifting trajectories between the prerogative and the normative state, between the realm of the highly militarized deep state and that of the traditional civilian sphere under government control. Since the 1950 Naresuan meeting of army strongman Sarit Thanarat and police chief Phao Sriyanond with US officials,[87] a meeting that can, in many ways, be understood as the birth moment of Thailand's deep state, the police and the army have been in a relationship of competition for the control of the state's security apparatus. In this political competition, authoritarian policing of political activities is a key instrument of control. As Paul Chambers puts it, "Civil – military relations in terms of Thailand's internal security turn on the question of who – civilians or soldiers – exerts more authority over the maintenance of order in emergency situations, counter-insurgency and counter-terror programs, domestic intelligence gathering, daily policing and border control."[88]

Phao and Sarit had together established a strong dictatorship founded on police-military cooperation, until Phao was ultimately defeated by Sarit in 1957. By eliminating Phao, Sarit did in fact expel the police from the deep state. As Ben Anderson puts it, "By the coups of 1957 and 1958, Sarit destroyed the power of the police, and made the army, which he controlled, the undisputed master of Thai political life."[89] Since then, whenever the police threaten to become more powerful than the army, the latter stages a military coup.[90] By gaining and maintaining control

[87] Hyun, "Integrating a Nation from the Margins."

[88] Paul Chambers, "In the Shadow of the Soldier's Boot: Assessing Civil–Military Relations in Thailand," in Marc Askew (ed.), *Legitimacy Crisis in Thailand* (Chiang Mai: Silkworm, 2010), 204.

[89] Anderson, "Withdrawal Symptoms: Social and Cultural Aspects of the October 6 Coup," 26.

[90] This rationale explains in part the Sarit Thanarat coup against Phao Sriyanond in 1957 and 1958, the 1971 coup against Police Chief Prasert Ruchirawong, the 2006 coup against elected politician Thaksin Shinawatra, and the 2014 coup against his sister Yingluck Shinawatra.

over the deep state, the military has displaced the police to the periphery of the bureaucratic polity, potentially putting it under the orders of the elected government – a move the police resists by continuing to practice, in a rather autonomous fashion, authoritarian policing of political activities. This rivalry best accounts for the evolution of practices and norms of policing in contemporary Thailand, as exemplified in the proliferation of competing emergency legislations (martial law versus emergency decrees), empowering security forces to derogate from the normative state.

Therefore, current efforts at exporting "democratic policing" by introducing more decentralization in the Thai police structure might be, in their current form, misguided. As Bayley puts it, "Police structures should not be read as a symptom of governmental character, because identical command structures can accommodate regimes of vastly different types."[91] Moreover, if the Thai police is at present highly centralized, with a police chief reporting directly to the prime minister, it is de facto highly autonomous: decentralizing it might make it even more autonomous.

10.6 Conclusion: On Modernization, Regime Type, and Policing

Thailand's history of policing is one of continuity rather than discontinuity. From the early 1950s onwards, methods of authoritarian policing have flourished on the backdrop of anticommunist/proroyalist acts.[92] They have empowered security forces to conduct extrajudicial killings, arbitrary arrests, torture, and enforced disappearances of key enemies of the state while shielding them from prosecution by granting them full judicial immunity. Tyrell Haberkorn considers the number of unresolved cases of enforced disappearances since 1952 to amount to

Paul Chambers identifies the following coups as being at least partly motivated by the need to constrain police powers: 1957, 1958, 1971, 1991, 2006, and 2014. Chambers, "Securing an Alternative Army," 110.

91 Bayley, *Patterns of Policing*, 73.

92 Tyrell, quoting Jaran Kosanan, provides a full list: "Act on Communism of 2476 [1933], Amended Act on Communism of 2478 [1935], Anti-Communist Activities Act of 2495 [1952], Junta Announcement No. 12 (issued on 22 October 2501 [1958]), Junta Announcement No. 15 (issued on 27 October 2501 [1958]), Act on the Control of Anti-Communist Activities Defendants of 2505 [1962], Act Amending Junta Announcement No. 12 of 2506 [1963], Act (version 2) on the Control of Anti-Communist Activities Defendants of 2506 [1963], Act (version 3) on the Control of Anti-Communist Activities Defendants of 2511 [1968], Anti-Communist Activities Act of 2512 [1969], Junta Announcement No. 12 (issued on 22 November

roughly 5,000:[93] even if some police officers were prosecuted, no one has ever been convicted, let alone punished. Meanwhile, as of 2022, Martial law remains in permanent force in about half of all provinces of Thailand.[94] Authoritarian methods of policing experimented with and developed during periods of dictatorship are remarkably resilient. One of the key variables pertains to the military versus civilian control of policing at large – even though the line between military and civilian security forces appears at best rather blurred. In the words of the Royal Thai Police Reform Commission in the early 2010s, the RTP is regarded as "the fourth branch of the armed forces,"[95] along with the Army, the Navy, and the Air Force.[96] The Thai police was and remains an "alternative military,"[97] a political actor engaged in power struggles with the military to which "political policing" is instrumental to survival.

In the context of Thailand, regime type, either civilian or military, democratic or authoritarian, and any combination thereof, does not significantly impact the level of violence being used to quell dissent (protesters, activists) nor crime (drug users). This is explained by the fact that the authoritarian nature of the state is largely autonomous from electoral politics – therefore, so far, democratization of electoral politics has not led

2514 [1971]), Junta Announcement No. 78 (issued on 16 February 2515 [1972]), Junta Announcement No. 199 (issued on 10 August 2515 [1972]), NARC Order No. 5 (issued on 6 October 2519 [1976]), NARC Order No. 8 (issued on 6 October 2519 [1976]), NARC Order No. 14 (issued on 6 October 2519 [1976]), NARC Order No. 25 (issued on 17 October 2519 [1976]), NARC Order No. 43 (issued on 21 October 2519 [1976]), Ministry of Interior Announcement on the Restriction of Printed Material (issued on 6 October 2520 [1977]), Anti-Communist Activities Act of 2522 [1979]), Ministry of Interior Announcement on the Restriction of Printed Material (issued on 6 June 2523 [1980]), and Ministry of Interior Announcement on the Restriction of Printed Materials (6 November 2523 [1980])." Haberkorn, *In Plain Sight*, 250; see Jaran Kosanan, *Law, Rights, and Liberties in Thai Society: Parallel Lines from 1932 to the Present* (Bangkok: Coordinating Group for Religion in Society, 2528 [1985]), 71–75.

93 "By conservative, partial estimates of the scattered cases of disappearance from 1952 to the present that I mentioned at the beginning of this chapter, there are at least 179 unresolved cases of disappearance, and this number grows to over 5,000 if one adds the suspected deaths that occurred during the thang daeng killings in 1972 and the 'War on Drugs' in 2002." Haberkorn, *In Plain Sight*, 186.

94 Martial law is in force in 31 provinces and 185 districts of Thailand's 77 provinces, including most of the provinces along Thailand's border with Myanmar, Laos, Cambodia, and Malaysia. Martial law is in force in almost all border areas as well as the Deep South.

95 Quoted in Glendinning, "Police Reform in Thailand Post-2006," 372.

96 Chambers, "Securing an Alternative Army." This is exemplified by the Democracy Monument erected in the heart of the old Bangkok: the monument features a statue of the Constitution on its golden tray surrounded by four obelisks representing the three branches of the Thai Armed Forces and the Police.

97 Ibid.

to a democratization of the state apparatus nor to "democratic policing." Brodeur argued in the 1980s that policing, whether democratic or authoritarian, is always a political means of maintaining a preferred sociopolitical order.[98] Authoritarian as opposed to democratic policing might rather be a function of perceived threats to the sociopolitical order than to regime type. Then, authoritarian practices of policing can in some circumstances inversely correlate with levels of democracy.

This claim finds some support in the pattern of *lèse-majesté* cases filed from the 1950s until now. One of the first cases of *lèse-majesté* occurred in 1946, at a time of great democratization and parliamentarization of Thai political life – but also of fading monarchism.[99] The number of cases soared from the 2000s onwards, a time of democratization – but also of rising anti-monarchism.[100] Benedict Anderson took notice of this paradox in the late 1970s: "not long after liberal democratic government was installed and censorship abolished, prosecutions for lese majeste began to be inaugurated."[101] By contrast, at present, as the military is firmly in power, *lèse-majesté* prosecutions have ceased entirely.[102] Besides *lèse-majesté*, cases of enforced disappearances have also dramatically increased during the "democratic parenthesis" of the 1970s, while continuing to pile up under the elected governments of Thaksin and Yingluck Shinawatra. There lies a prima facie puzzle, which can be solved by thinking not in terms of regime type but of regime stability – whether in authoritarian or democratic settings.

98 Brodeur, "High Policing and Low Policing."

99 Prominent jurist Yut Saeng U-Thai was prosecuted for explaining on radio the meaning and scope of the king's powers. The case was later dismissed.

100 Serhat Ünaldi, "Working towards the Monarchy and Its Discontents: Anti-Royal Graffiti in Downtown Bangkok," *Journal of Contemporary Asia* 44(3) (July 3, 2014): 377–403, https://doi.org/10.1080/00472336.2013.842260.

101 Anderson, "Withdrawal Symptoms," 23.

102 Eugénie Mérieau, "Thailand in 2018: Military Dictatorship under Royal Command," in Daljit Singh and Malcolm Cook (ed.), *Southeast Asian Affairs 2019* (Singapore: ISEAS–Yusof Ishak Institute Singapore, 2019), 333.

PART IV

The Singapore and Hong Kong Exceptions

11

Democratic Policing in an Authoritarian State?

A Historical Look at Singapore

KEVIN Y. L. TAN

11.1 Introduction

There is no authoritative definition of what is meant by authoritarian policing. This should not be surprising, given how difficult it is for us to even agree on what "authoritarianism" means. I have highlighted this difficulty previously in the context of so-called "authoritarian constitutionalism", and argued that while it is interesting to create models or ideal types of political systems, such exercises are ultimately of limited utility.[1] So what do we mean when we talk about authoritarian policing? Does it refer to the form of policing that takes place in an authoritarian state (assuming we can confidently define what that means)? Or does it refer to some form of non-democratic policing? Can democratic states practise authoritarian policing,[2] or conversely, is it conceivable that democratic policing takes place in authoritarian states?

The literature on forms of policing is as disparate as it is voluminous, but few efforts have been made to define what is meant by authoritarian policing. Many scholars proceed on the assumption that the term is self-explanatory or that forms of policing in authoritarian regimes are necessarily authoritarian as well.[3] Others prefer to deal with the issue by discussing what democratic policing entails or requires.[4] For the purposes

[1] Kevin Y. L. Tan, "Is Singapore an Authoritarian Constitutional Regime? So What If It Is?" in Chen Weitseng and Hualing Fu (eds.), *Authoritarian Legality in Asia: Formation, Development and Transition* (Cambridge: Cambridge University Press, 2020), 189–191.

[2] See Yanilda Maria Gonzalex, *Authoritarian Police in Democracy: Contested Security in Latin America* (Cambridge: Cambridge University Press, 2021).

[3] See, for example, Cathy Schneider and Paul E. Amar, "The Rise of Crime, Disorder and Authoritarian Policing," *NACLA Report on the Americas* 37(2) (2003): 12–16; and Liqun Cao, Lanying Huang, and Ivan Sun, "From Authoritarian Policing to Democratic Policing: A Case Study of Taiwan," *Policing & Society* 26(6) (2016): 642–658.

[4] See, for example, David H. Bayley, *Democratizing the Police Abroad: What to Do and How to Do It* (Washington, DC: US Department of Justice, 2001); Peter K. Manning, *Democratic*

		Policing in	
		Authoritarian States	**Democratic States**
1	Primary mission	• Protect regime • Control subjects or citizens	• Uphold rule of law • Protect citizens against crime and disorder • Prevent and combat crime • Provide assistance and services to the public
2	Loyalty to …	Regime	Constitution & Rule of Law
3	Levels of coercion and force	High	Low
4	Accountability and transparency	Low	High
5	Relations with Public	Surveillance and Reporting on behalf of regime	Positive relationships between community and police
6	Trust by Public	Low	High

Figure 11.1 Nature of policing in democratic and authoritarian societies

of this chapter, I adopt the matrix found in Figure 11.1, which aggregates factors identified by various scholars to distinguish between policing in authoritarian and democratic regimes.[5]

Most legal and political commenters classify Singapore as an authoritarian state.[6] Does this mean that it necessarily practises an authoritarian

Policing in a Changing World (Boulder, CO: Paradigm, 2010); Otwin Marenin, "Police Training for Democracy," *Police Practice & Research* 5(2) (2004): 107–123; Barry Friedman and Maria Pnomarenko, "Democratic Policing," *New York University Law Review* 90(6) (2015): 1827–1907; and Michelle D. Bonner, "What Democratic Policing Is … And Is Not," *Policing & Society* (2020) 30(9): 1044–1060.

5 See Michael D. Wiatrowski and Jack A. Goldstone, "The Ballot and the Badge: Democratic Policing," *Journal of Democracy* 21(2) (2010): 79–92; Liqun Cao, Lanying Huang, and Ivan Sun, "From Authoritarian Policing to Democratic Policing: A Case Study of Taiwan," *Policing & Society* 26(6) (2016): 642–658; Michelle D. Bonner, "What Democratic Policing Is … And Is Not," *Policing & Society* 30(9) (2020): 1044–1060; David H. Bayley, *Democratizing the Police Broad: What to Do and How to Do It* (Washington, DC: US Department of Justice, 2001); and Senior Police Adviser to the OSCE Secretary-General, *Guidebook on Democratic Policing*, 2nd ed. (Vienna: OSCE, 2008).

6 See, for example, Rebecca Grace Tan, "Defanging Public Discontent in an Authoritarian Regime: Grassroots Volunteering and Immigration in Singapore," *Commonwealth & Comparative Politics* 58(4) (2020): 452–475; Elvin Ong, "Complementary Institutions in Authoritarian Regimes: The Everyday Politics of Constituency Service in Singapore," *Journal of East Asian Studies* 15(3) (2015): 290–361; Jothi Rajah, *Authoritarian Rule of Law:*

form of policing? In this chapter, I will argue that while there exist authoritarian elements in Singapore's modern police system – especially in laws providing for executive or preventive detention – it is far more democratic than may otherwise be assumed. This argument is based on a historical study of Singapore's policing system and the supporting laws and institutions that have been enacted and established over the years to deal with both internal and external threats.

For almost 140 years, the British ruled Singapore, first as part of the Straits Settlements (1824–1946), and then as a separate crown colony (1946–1963). In the earliest years, Singapore's policing system was rudimentary and much of law and order was left to a combination of private ordering with minimal state intervention.[7] However, as Singapore's importance as a colony grew, and as the British poured more and more investments into the island, threats to public order, and more importantly to the colonial state, led to increasingly draconian legislative interventions by the British. However, this did not necessarily make policing of the state any more authoritarian because the colonial state lacked the wherewithal to subjugate the population and could not control the criminal elements of the secret societies right up till the time of Singapore's self-governance in 1959. It was only after the People's Action Party (PAP) came to power that things began to take a turn. Concerned first to establish order, the PAP government was prepared to go against the grain of British legal tradition to break the backs of the secret societies, stamp out corruption in the civil service and then rebuild a society founded on the rule of law.

It was in the field of political policing that we see authoritarian elements being introduced. Starting from the time of the Sepoy Mutiny in 1915, the colonial authorities in Singapore stepped up surveillance on political organisations and individuals who threatened the security and existence

Legislation, Discourse and Legitimacy in Singapore (Cambridge: Cambridge University Press, 2012); Lynette J. Chua, *Mobilizing Gay Singapore: Rights and Resistance in an Authoritarian State* (Singapore: NUS Press, 2014); Lily Zubaidah Rahim and Michael D. Barr (eds.), *The Limits of Authoritarian Governance in Singapore's Developmental State* (Singapore: Palgrave Macmillan, 2019); Garry Rodan, *Transparency and Authoritarian Rule in Southeast Asia: Singapore and Malaysia* (New York: Routledge, 2004); Stephan Ortmann and Mark R. Thompson, "China's Obsession with Singapore: Learning Authoritarian Modernity," *The Pacific Review* 27(3) (2014): 433–455; Stephan Ortmann, "Singapore: Authoritarian but Newly Competitive," *Journal of Democracy* 22(4) (2011): 153–164; and Denny Roy, "Singapore, China and the 'Soft Authoritarian' Challenge," *Asian Survey* 34(3) (1994): 231–242.

7 See Tan Cheng Han, "Private Ordering and the Chinese in Nineteenth Century Straits Settlements," *Asian Journal of Comparative Law* 11(1) (2016): 27–53.

of the colonial state. This was done through a slew of tough laws, including the Sedition Act and the Preservation of Public Security Ordinance, that were introduced, allowing the state to, among other things, preventively detain suspects without trial. Many of these laws were kept in place after Singapore attained self-government, thus making certain aspects of Singapore policing authoritarian. However, these tough measures went hand in hand with reforms in the police force, public education and the fostering of better relations between the police and the populace. These post-independence developments, especially in the professionalism of the police force and extensive efforts in community-oriented policing have contributed greatly to Singapore now operating one of the most democratic policing regimes in Asia.

11.2 Policing in Colonial Singapore[8]

In 1819, Stamford Raffles, Lieutenant-Governor of Bencoolen, arrived in Singapore and signed a Treaty of Friendship and Alliance with Sultan Hussein Shah and Temenggong Abdul Rahman allowing the British East India Company (EIC) to establish a "factory" or trading post on the island. Much was in flux in the first five years of British presence on the island owing to competing Dutch claims on the island, and it was not till 1824 – when the British and the Dutch concluded the Treaty of London (also known as the Anglo-Dutch Treaty) – that the Dutch gave up Malacca and all claims on Singapore in exchange for British territories in Sumatra, including Bencoolen. That year, the EIC purchased the island outright from the Sultan and Temenggong, and two years later merged it with Prince of Wales Island (Penang) and Malacca, to form the Straits Settlements.

There was no real local policing to speak of and security in the port area proved to be a major headache for its administrators since the EIC provided no budget for a proper police force. The first Resident, Major William Farquhar – who took charge of administering Singapore from 1819 to 1823, and who reported to Raffles in Bencoolen – formed the first police squad in January 1820 with his son-in-law, Francis Bernard, as officer-in-charge.

[8] In the following account, I have relied on Peer M. Akbur, *Policing Singapore in the 19th and 20th Centuries* (Singapore: Singapore Police Force, 2002); C. M. Turnbull, "Internal Security in the Straits Settlements 1826–1867," *Journal of Southeast Asian Studies* 1(1) (1970): 37–53; Roland St J. Braddell, "Crime: Its Punishment and Prevention," in William Makepeace, Gilbert E. Brooke, and Rolkand St John Braddell (eds.), *One Hundred Years of Singapore* (London: John Murray, 1921), 244–300; and Tay Seow Huah, *The History of the Singapore Police Force, 1819–1889*, BA Honours Academic Exercise (Singapore: University of Malaya, 1956).

By this time, Singapore had grown from a small fishing village of less than 1,000 inhabitants, into a settlement of some 5,000 persons. To finance the fledgling police force, and much to Raffles' chagrin, Farquhar issued gambling licences to gain revenue. As the EIC had a very limited budget to spend on policing, it was agreed that local residents would contribute to the cost. A committee consisting of three European and three native merchants was established to take charge of all matters relating to the police and a Night Watch Fund was established; merchants contributed to the fund by way of subscriptions. With the subscription moneys, the committee hired one *jamadar,*[9] as well as eight native policemen.[10]

In 1823, when Raffles returned to Singapore for the last time, he abolished the Night Watch Fund and allocated a budget for the police force. However, the growth of this force ran in tandem with the rapid growth of the settlement's population. By 1827, there were only three European constables, five *jamadars* and twenty-four peons in the force even though the population was by then close to 14,000.[11] The period from 1828 to 1843 has been described as a "period of stagnation and increasing inefficiency" owing to the lack of proper supervision and a breakdown in the discipline of the men in the force.[12] This was made worse by the fact that many more immigrants flocked to Singapore from China and the region. Between 1830 and 1840, the population of Singapore more than doubled, from 16,634 to 35,389.[13] Despite a constantly increasing budget for the policing, the police force was poorly trained, incompetent, corrupt and inept. As a consequence, crime was rampant, and much of it was perpetrated by members of the various Chinese secret societies on the island.[14]

With the passage of Act III of 1847, the Straits Settlements governor was given direct control over the police and this led to the appointment of Thomas Dunman as the first Superintendent of Police and an expansion of the force.

9 A 'jamadar' or 'jemadar' was originally an armed official of the Zamindar (feudal lord) in India. Later it was used as a rank in the British Indian Army – the lowest rank for a commissioned officer.

10 Akbur, *Policing Singapore in the 19th and 20th Centuries*, 13–15.

11 Ibid., 16–20.

12 Tay, *The History of the Singapore Police Force*, 6.

13 Saw Swee Hock, *The Population of Singapore*, 3rd ed. (Singapore: Institute of Southeast Asia Studies, 2012), 9.

14 On secret societies in Singapore, see Wilfred Blythe, *The Impact of Chinese Secret Societies in Malaya: A Historical Study* (London: Royal Institute of International Affairs, 1969); and Mak Lau Fong, *The Sociology of Secret Societies: A Study of Chinese Secret Societies in Singapore and Peninsular Malaysia* (Kuala Lumpur: Oxford University Press, 1981).

However, this remained insufficient, and in 1856, Act XIII was passed to vest the administration of the police in the hands of the Commissioner of Police – a post created in 1851 – who was to be appointed by the Governor of the Straits Settlements. The commissioner was also empowered to fix the size of the police force. It was thanks to Dunman that the police force became professionalised. He increased the salaries of policemen, instituted long-term contracts for job stability and compensation schemes for injuries or death sustained in the course of public duty, and forged strong ties with leaders of the community, including known gang leaders. By the time of his retirement in 1871, policemen – once despised for their corrupt and inept ways – had come to be respected by the population at large.[15]

During this period, the function of the police was primarily crime control and the apprehension and prosecution of criminals. While the police could certainly be considered the colonial state's key instruments of coercion, it was generally too weak to be a major oppressive force on the population. Indeed, despite Dunman's reforms and the exertions of his successor Samuel Dunlop, it was a constant struggle to maintain the morale and efficacy of the police force. The poor salaries and working conditions resulted in the force failing to attract the best candidates for the job. This in turn led to internal unhappiness and corruption throughout the ranks. The situation grew so bad that two commissions of inquiry were established to examine the situation in the police force, the first in 1879,[16] and the second in 1890.[17]

11.3 The First (and Stubbornly Persistent) Threat: Secret Societies

Despite Dunman's reforms and improvements, the police force was still inadequate to deal with the secret societies. Riots between rival societies and protest riots against government policy were a common feature of nineteenth-century Singapore. For a start, many Chinese were members of the secret societies. It was estimated that in 1881, almost 18 per cent of the Chinese population were members of secret societies.[18] The worst riots occurred in May 1854 when fighting broke out between the Hokkien and Teochew branches of the Ghee Hin secret society. The riots lasted for 10 days, and over 500 persons were killed and 300 homes destroyed. Dunman

15 Akbur, *Policing Singapore in the 19th and 20th Centuries*, 18.
16 Straits Settlements Legislative Council, *Report of the Police Commission*, 1879.
17 Straits Settlements Legislative Council, *Report of the Police Commission*, 1890.
18 Andrew Phang Boon Leong, *The Development of Singapore Law: Historical and Socio-Legal Perspectives* (Singapore: Butterworths, 1990), 187.

called for military reinforcements to quell the riots, but his request was initially rejected by Governor William Butterworth, who underestimated the gravity of the situation. Later, the military was brought in and the Temenggong of Johore sent 200 Malay soldiers to assist. This was by no means the only major riot to occur.

The use of ordinary criminal law to prosecute the rioters and other society-linked criminals proved futile as these secret societies struck so much fear in the local population that no one dared to testify as witnesses against them. Indeed, Jonas Vaughan, Superintendent of Police for Penang from 1851 to 1856 wrote:

> ... at every Sessions cases are thrown out from want of evidence. It is quite apparent that the fraternity is the root of all evil here. Were they suppressed, the Chinese would be brought under the influence of our laws and made to respect them, but at present the Hoey is looked up to as the only legitimate Court of Justice, and Magistrates, Judge, Courts of Judicature, etc are viewed as merely engines of tyranny.[19]

To deal with the secret societies, residents and merchants agitated for new legislation. In 1857, a Draft Act for the Better Controlling of Chinese Secret Societies in the Straits of Malacca was proposed. The draft gave the governor power to deport and to criminally punish deportees who returned to the Straits. At the same time, the governor's decision would not be reviewable in any court of law and no writ of habeas corpus would be available to deportees.[20] This proposed draft was rejected by the Indian authorities – who governed the Straits Settlements as a subordinate presidency – as being contrary to principles of British justice. A subsequent draft, which was less draconian and recommended a system of licensing and registration of societies, was submitted to the Indian authorities, but nothing came of it.[21]

The authorities were pushed into action again in 1867, following the massive Penang Riots that lasted nine days, when the Red Flag Society clashed with the White Flag Society. The Preservation of Peace Act was passed.[22] Among other things, this Act provided for the appointment of "special constables", the power of deportation of persons who were not natural-born subjects of the queen, the issuance of a proclamation under

19 Daniel Vaughan, "Notes on the Chinese of Pinang," *Journal of the Indian Archipelago and Eastern Asia* 8 (1) (1854): 23–24.

20 Governor to Bengal, January 10, 1857, *Straits Settlements Records* SSR R30: Governor: Letters to Bengal, 1856–1857, 232.

21 Phang, *The Development of Singapore Law*, 190–191.

22 Ordinance 20, 1867.

which persons might be detained so long as the proclamation was in force, and the suspension of the writ of habeas corpus. The Act was to last a year but was extended by the Preservation of Peace Extension Ordinance 1868.[23] The enactment of this legislation and its extension drew protests from the Chief Justice, Sir Peter Benson Maxwell, and prominent business leader William Henry Read. Maxwell and Read considered the deportation provisions and the lack of habeas corpus to be "at variance" with the most important "constitutional principles", which could be justified "by nothing short of the greatest emergency".[24]

A period of hand-wringing and dithering followed. Members of the Legislative Council were divided between those who wanted tough criminal laws to suppress the secret societies and those who wanted to control the societies through a system of registration. The result was the enactment of the Dangerous Societies Suppression Ordinance in 1869.[25] This sounds a lot more oppressive and draconian that it really was because the mode of control prescribed therein was for the registration of societies, rather than their suppression. It took another twenty years for the Legislative Council to act decisively. In 1889, it finally passed the Societies Ordinance,[26] which required all societies of ten or more persons to be registered. It also empowered the authorities to declare any society illegal and de-register them. Although colonial policy had steadfastly shifted from tolerance to suppression, the Societies Act did little to stem the activities of the secret societies, and they remained a major force to be reckoned with right up till the Japanese Occupation (1942–1945).

We will return to the threat of secret societies in Section 11.5.4 as the various moves taken to tackle this problem head-on needs to be understood within the context of other post-war developments.

11.4 The Second Threat: Anti-Empire Movements and Political Policing

11.4.1 The Start of Political Policing: The Sedition Act

While secret societies posed a serious internal threat to law and order, the greater threat was the rising tide of nationalism within the British Empire, especially in India. Concerned for the safety of the empire, the British

[23] Phang, *The Development of Singapore Law*, 191–192.
[24] Report of the Straits Settlements Legislative Council Proceedings, May 17, 1869, 20.
[25] Ordinance 19, 1869.
[26] Ordinance 1, 1889.

passed increasingly draconian criminal legislation that included, among other things, the power to detain suspects without trial. Indian nationalist activity against the British arrived in Singapore in the form of the Indian Sepoy Mutiny of February 1915.[27] From the early 1900s, the Indian Ghadar Party began agitating Indian troops stationed abroad against the British.[28] One of these was the Muslim 5th Light Infantry, which was stationed in Singapore. The mutiny began when Kassim Mansoor, a Gujarati Muslim coffee-shop owner, influenced the troops by sowing ill-will against the British. When rumours circulated that the Light Infantry would be sent to fight against their "Muslim brothers" in Turkey, they revolted. The mutiny lasted ten days and forty-four British soldiers and civilians and fifty-six sepoys were killed. The mutiny triggered two things: first, the establishment of a political intelligence bureau (Special Branch) in Singapore;[29] and second, the enactment of the Sedition Act.

The offence of sedition originated in the common law,[30] but was ultimately placed on a legislative footing in Britain in 1819 with the enactment of "An Act for the more effectual Prevention and Punishment of Blasphemous and Seditious Libels".[31] The offence of sedition appeared in the first draft of Lord Macaulay's Indian Penal Code (1837–1839) as section 113. However, when the Penal Code was finally passed into law in 1860, it was omitted. It was subsequently added in 1870 by way of a verbal amendment by Sir James Stephen, as section 124A of the Penal Code. The Indian Penal Code was re-enacted as the Penal Code of the Straits Settlements in 1871, which came into force in September 1872. Section 124A of the 1872 Straits Penal Code provides:

> **124.** – Whoever by words, either spoken or written, or by signs, or by visible representation, or otherwise, brings or attempts to bring into hatred or contempt, or excites or attempts to excite feelings of disaffection towards

[27] On the Sepoy Mutiny, see Umej Bhatia, *Our Name Is Mutiny: The Global Revolt Against the Raj and the Hidden History of the Singapore Mutiny 1907–1915* (Singapore: Landmark Books, 2019); and R. W. E. Harper and Harry Miller, *Singapore Mutiny* (Singapore: Oxford University Press, 1984).

[28] See, generally, Maia Ramnath, *Haj to Utopia: How the Ghadar Movement Charted Global Radicalism and Attempted to Overthrow the British Empire* (Berkeley, CA: University of California Press, 2011).

[29] Leon Comber, "The Singapore Mutiny (1915) and the Genesis of Political Intelligence in Singapore," *Intelligence and National Security* 24(4) (2009): 529–541; and Ban Kah Choon, *Absent History: The Untold History of Special Branch Operations 1915–1948* (Singapore: Raffles, 2001).

[30] See James Fitzjames Stephen, *Digest of Criminal Law*, 4th ed. (London: Macmillan, 1887).

[31] 60 Geo. III and 1 Geo. IV c 8.

> His Majesty or the Government established by law in the Colony, shall be punished with penal servitude for life, to which fine may be added, or with imprisonment for a term which may extent to three years, to which fine may be added, or with both.

The expression of "dissatisfaction" included disloyalty and "all feelings of enmity",[32] but comments "expressing disapprobation of the measures of Government with a view to obtain their alteration by lawful means, without exciting or attempting to excite hatred, contempt or dissatisfaction", do not constitute sedition.[33] At the same time, any comments "expressing disapprobation of the administrative or other action of the Government without exciting or attempting to excite hatred, contempt or dissatisfaction" also do not constitute sedition.[34]

In 1915, following the Sepoy Mutiny, the colonial government decided that more needed to be done to stem the rising tide of anti-British material flooding the colony and agents fomenting rebellion. To this end, the Straits Settlements government passed the 1915 Seditious Publications (Prohibition) Ordinance,[35] to "suppress the circulation in the Colony of seditious publications".[36] As Europe edged toward war, in 1938, the Straits government proposed amending the Penal Code to include a provision that would complement Section 124A of the Penal Code to make it a "punishable offence to promote hatred between different classes of the community".[37] As Attorney-General Howell informed the Legislative Council, this new provision was drawn "from the corresponding provision in the Indian Penal Code".[38] However, this Bill never made it to its second reading, largely because it provoked controversy both locally and as well as in London. Instead, a separate Sedition Ordinance,[39] with a complementary Undesirable Publications Ordinance,[40] was enacted

[32] Explanation 1.
[33] Explanation 2.
[34] Explanation 3.
[35] Ordinance 11, 1915 (Straits Settlements).
[36] "Speech of Attorney-General GA Goodman, First Reading of the Seditious Publications (Prohibition) Bill, 25 June 1915," in *Proceedings of the Legislative Council of the Straits Settlements for the Year 1915* (Singapore: Government Printing Office, 1916), B40.
[37] "Speech of Attorney-General CG Howell, First Reading of the Penal Code (Amendment) Bill, 25 April 1938," in *Proceedings of the Legislative Council of the Straits Settlements for the Year 1938* (Singapore, Government Printing Office, 1939), B25.
[38] Ibid.
[39] Ordinance 18, 1938 (Straits Settlements).
[40] Ordinance 19, 1938 (Straits Settlements).

in 1938. Speaking at the first reading of the Sedition Bill on June 13, 1938, Attorney-General C.G. Howell explained:

> The present law of the Colony with regard to sedition is briefly dealt with in section 124A of the Penal Code, but it is desirable that this subject should be dealt with in rather more detail than it is possible to do in that way, and the present Bill reproduces substantially the provisions of the common law of England with regard to sedition.[41]

The Sedition Act absorbed the crime of sedition under Section 124A of the Penal Code (offence against the state) and enlarged it to include the incitement of feelings of enmity and hatred to other groups or classes of individuals in the community. With the broadening of the offence of sedition, Section 124A of the Penal Code was accordingly repealed. Likewise, the new 1938 Sedition and Undesirable Publications Ordinances rendered the 1915 Seditious Publications (Prohibition) Ordinance obsolete,[42] and the latter was accordingly repealed.[43] The offence of sedition under the Sedition Ordinance was punishable by imprisonment of up to two years or a fine of up to $1,000 in the case of a first-time offender, whereas a subsequent offender was subject to an imprisonment of up to three years.[44] Just three years after the passage of the Sedition Ordinance and Sedition Enactment, British Malaya and Singapore were overrun by the Japanese, who occupied the territories from 1942 to 1945.

11.4.2 The Special Branch

The Sepoy Mutiny of 1915 laid bare the weakness of British political policing in the Straits Settlements. The events that led to the mutiny were not the result of ordinary local criminal activity, but the confluence of international, regional and local forces that culminated in the breakout. The British realised that given the unique geography and economy of the Straits Settlements and of Malaya generally, internal security required the involvement of "all the dimensions of intelligence gathering, including detection or the forward collection of information, its collation and interpretation in a regional if not

41 "Speech of Attorney-General CG Howell on the Sedition Bill, 13 June 1938," in *Proceedings of the Legislative Council of the Straits Settlements for the Year 1938* (Singapore, Government Printing Office, 1939), B46.

42 Ordinance 19.

43 Sedition Ordinance 1938 (Straits Settlements), s 10.

44 Ibid., s 4(1).

international context".[45] And Singapore, being a major trade hub, "would always be exposed to the winds of wars and conflicts even if these were far away in India or even Europe"; the trouble that erupted might be local, but "its origin was in nearly every instance elsewhere".[46]

To deal with this growing challenge of intelligence gathering, the Straits Settlements authorities proposed the setting up of a Criminal Intelligence Department (CID) within the Police Force. In 1918, the CID was established under as the local counter-espionage and political intelligence department under the directorship of Assistant Superintendent V.G. Savi.[47] The term "criminal" in its official name was a misnomer since the CID did not investigate ordinary crime but was instead "responsible for political and security intelligence".[48] It was effectively the Special Branch of the Straits Settlements Police Force and was organised closely along the lines of the Metropolitan Police Special Branch in the United Kingdom.[49] In 1933, it was renamed the Special Branch.[50] This was later deployed as a key policing tool by both the colonial and local authorities, especially in conjunction with preventive detention, a matter to which we will return in Section 11.5.4.

11.4.3 Communism

The Sepoy Mutiny of 1915 proved to be the most serious of the troubles the British were to face in the period leading up to the Second World War. If anything, it was a precursor of things to come as the forces of "Bolshevism, anti-colonialism, nationalism and religion … compete[d] for the hearts and minds of the colonized people".[51] Communist activity is believed to have begun as early as 1919 with the arrival of three anarchists from China, all members of the anarchist Truth Society.[52] But it was only in 1925 that seven agents of the Kuomintang were dispatched to Singapore to organise the Malayan Chinese, and this led to the establishment of the Nanyang

45 Ban, *Absent History*, 63–64.
46 Ibid., 64.
47 Comber, "The Singapore Mutiny," 539–540.
48 Ibid., 539.
49 On the British Special Branch, see Rupert Allason, *The Branch: A History of the Metropolitan Police Special Branch* (London: Seeker & Warburg, 1983).
50 Ibid., 540.
51 Ban, *Absent History*, 44.
52 C. F. Yong, "Origins and Development of the Malayan Communist Movement, 1919–1930," *Modern Asian Studies* 25(4) (1991): 625–648, at 626.

Public Bodies Union in 1926, which the British considered the first communist organisation in Malaya.[53] In 1928, the Provisional Committee of the Nanyang Communist Party was established under the auspices of the Chinese Communist Party,[54] but this was dissolved following the third Representatives' Conference on April 30, 1930, when the Soviet-led Communist International (Comintern) ordered the establishment of the Communist Party of Malaya (CPM).[55]

Communist agents in Singapore were seen as major threats since the Comintern's avowed aim was to create national-revolutionary movements in each colony to overthrow the colonial powers and replace them with communist governments. Comintern agents fomented revolution by organising acts of violence and sabotage (e.g. attempting to assassinate Governor Franklin Gimson),[56] infiltrating schools and labour unions and turning them into front organisations and recruitment bases, and circulating seditious propaganda and literature. By this time, the Special Branch was already fully operational, and was fairly successful in identifying and arresting several key Comintern agents and leaders and banishing them under the Banishment Ordinance.[57]

11.5 Toward an Authoritarian Tightening of Political Policing

While the British certainly took steps to strengthen and bolster the police force and pass increasingly tougher laws to deal with the twin menace of local crime and foreign subversion, the kind of policing practised in Singapore up to this point could hardly be described as authoritarian. For a start, the police force was too small and weak to deal with the secret societies and other criminal elements. And while the governor had the power to banish subversive elements, this was a blunt instrument that did not effectively eradicate these threats. So while the colonial state might well be described as authoritarian – there being no representative government – the policing it administered was not authoritarian. It was only after the end of the Second World War that far greater resources were poured into the building of a far more effective police force, and laws providing for detention without trial were enacted to cripple the

[53] Ibid., 634.
[54] Ibid., 639–640.
[55] Ibid., 647.
[56] See "Midnight Bomb Attack on Gimson," *Straits Times*, April 29, 1950, 1.
[57] See Geoffrey C. Gunn, *Singapore and the Asian Revolutions* (Macau: Geoffrey C Gunn, 2008), 68–83.

secret societies and subversives. It was with these moves that Singapore's policing became more authoritarian.

11.5.1 *The Japanese Occupation and Its Aftermath*

The Japanese armed forces invaded Malaya in December 1941, and by February 1942 had overrun Singapore. Active members of the CPM took to the jungles in the guise of the Malayan People's Anti-Japanese Army in armed resistance against the Japanese. The secret societies went underground as the Japanese military authorities clamped down on all forms of illegal activity with draconian vigour. When the British returned at the end of the Second World War to reclaim their territories, they had determined to constitutionally reorganise these territories. The Straits Settlements – comprising Penang, Malacca and Singapore – was disbanded in 1946, and Penang and Malacca joined the rest of the Federated Malay States and Unfederated Malay States to form a new entity, the Malayan Union. Singapore would be administered as a separate Crown Colony. Owing to Malay opposition, the Malayan Union was disbanded in 1948 and replaced by the Federation of Malaya.

In the meantime, the CPM became a legally registered society in 1946 but almost immediately began agitating and stirring up unrest through the labour unions. In 1948, it was proscribed under the Societies Act, and its more militant members took to the jungles of Malaya to start an armed insurrection in 1948 to displace the British. This led to the proclamation of a state of emergency – a euphemism for what was effectively an undeclared civil war.[58] The CPM conducted their assault on the British and their institutions on two fronts – directly in the jungle through armed struggle and indirectly by infiltrating open front organisations such as trade unions and school associations and conducting a constitutional struggle. The Malayan Emergency and its attendant regulations were extended to Singapore in July 1948.

[58] On the Malayan Emergency, see Edgar O'Balance, *Malaya: The Communist Insurgent War, 1948–1960* (London: Faber, 1966); Anthony Short, *The Communist Insurrection in Malaya, 1948–1960* (London: Muller, 1976); Richard Stubbs, *Hearts and Minds in Guerrilla Warfare: The Malayan Emergency, 1948–1960* (Singapore: Oxford University Press, 1989); Leon Comber, *Malaya's Secret Police 1945–60: The Role of the Special Branch in the Malayan Emergency* (Clayton: Monash Asia Institute, 2008); and Yao Souchou, *The Malayan Emergency: A Small, Distant War* (Copenhagen: NIAS Press, 2016).

11.5.2 Sedition ... Again

To combat the spread of anti-British propaganda, the government proposed a number of legislative measures, including strengthening legislation on restricted residence, seditious publications, printing presses and emergencies.[59] It was in these circumstances that the British government decided to reinvigorate and strengthen the 1938 Sedition Ordinance by passing a new Sedition Act. Speaking at the second reading of the Sedition Bill on July 6, 1948, E.P.S. Bell, the Acting Attorney-General for the Federation of Malaya, stated that previous enactments on sedition within the Federation were identical as they followed "very much the same pattern ... based on a model Ordinance ... sent to this country some years ago by the Colonial Office".[60] Bell explained that the new Bill was "very substantially – indeed, a re-enactment – the same as the existing Sedition Enactments in force throughout the Federation".[61] At the same time, the government was taking the opportunity to "increase the maximum penalties in respect of seditious offences ... and incorporate two new sections which did not exist" previously – giving the court the power to suspend the publication of a newspaper convicted of publishing matters having a seditious tendency as well as a procedure to govern this process.[62]

This was disingenuous because Bell did not tell the Legislative Council that the new Sedition Act completely altered the structure and elements of the offence of sedition. The new Section 4(1)(a) made it an offence for any person to do, attempt to do, or make preparations or conspires with another to do "any act which has or which would, if done, have a *seditious tendency*". This was quite different from the 1938 Ordinance, which was worded similarly, except that the act must be one that was done with a "seditious intention". The new Section 3 defines "seditious tendency" as follows:

> 3. – (1) A "seditious tendency" is a tendency:
>
> (a) to bring into hatred or contempt or to excite disaffection against any Ruler or against any Government;
> (b) to excite the subjects or inhabitants any Ruler or the inhabitants of any territory governed by any Government to attempt to procure

59 See "Decisive Action Being Prepared," *Straits Times*, June 17, 1948, 1.

60 "Speech of the Acting Attorney-General EPS Bell, Second Reading of the Sedition Bill, 1948, 6 July 1948," in *Proceedings of the Legislative Council of the Federation of Malaya for the Period (First Session) February 1948 to February 1949* (Kuala Lumpur: Government Press, 1951), B351.

61 Ibid., B352.

62 Ibid.

in the territory of the Ruler or governed by the Government the alteration, otherwise than by lawful means, of any other matter as by law established;

(c) to bring into hatred or contempt or to excite disaffection against the administration of justice in the Colony;

(d) to raise discontent or disaffection amongst the subjects of the Yang di-Pertuan Agong or of the Ruler of any State or amongst the inhabitants of Malaya or of any State; or

(e) to promote feelings of ill-will and hostility between different races or classes of the population of Malaya.

The new provision makes it much easier to charge someone for sedition since the *mens rea* for the new offence makes "intention" to "incite" or "excite disaffection" irrelevant. All that the prosecution needed to do was to show that the accused intended to either speak the words spoken or execute the deed in question. It did not matter why the accused was motivated to act. Intention to act was sufficient to satisfy the *mens rea* element of the crime.

Malaya's 1948 Sedition Act was extended to Singapore in May 1964 after Singapore became part of the new Federation of Malaysia, along with the Borneo states of Sabah and Sarawak.[63] This legislation was retained in Singapore even after it seceded from the Federation of Malaysia in 1965 and is currently found in Chapter 290 of the Singapore Statutes. The sedition legislation has not, however, been widely used in Singapore. From the time of the Sedition Ordinance's enactment in 1938, right up till 1964 – when the Malayan Act applied to Singapore – there were only about a dozen successful prosecutions, with about half of them occurring before the Japanese Occupation.[64] Immediately after the occupation, it was used in connection with the trials of alleged collaborators such as S.C. Goho and Samad Ismail,[65] or for communists or left-wing agitators.[66] Perhaps the most famous sedition prosecution in the post-war period was the trial of eight university undergraduates in the Fajar case. This highly politicised case saw the emergence of Lee Kuan Yew as

[63] "Sedition Act Extended," *Straits Times*, May 30, 1964, 1.

[64] See, for example, "Four Officials of 'Red' Society Convicted," *Straits Times*, May 17, 1940, 11; "Sedition Charge," *Morning Tribune*, May 28, 1940, 12; "Story Teller Jailed for Sedition," *Malaya Tribune*, July 31, 1940, 2; "Schoolboy as Leader of Sedition," *Morning Tribune*, August 14, 1940, 6; and "Japanese Sentenced for 'Attempt' to Create Trouble," *Straits Times*, September 21, 1941, 9.

[65] "Indian Lawyer and Malay Editor on Collaboration Charges," *Straits Times*, October 26, 1945, 4.

[66] "Communist Party Representative Convicted on Sedition Charge," *Indian Daily Mail*, March 23, 1946, 4; and "Four Face Sedition Charges," *Straits Times*, April 20, 1948, 7.

a major lawyer and political figure, as he engaged the well-known British left-wing barrister Denis Pritt to defend the students, who were acquitted of the charges.[67]

11.5.3 Preventive Detention

Under the Emergency Regulations Ordinance 1948,[68] provisions were made for detention without trial. Initially, all Emergency Regulations had to be reviewed and where necessary, reissued every two months. In 1955, this requirement was removed with the enactment of the Preservation of Public Security Ordinance (PPSO),[69] which was passed following the Hock Lee Bus Riots which was allegedly masterminded by the CPM and its operatives. Under section 55 of the PPSO, the colonial secretary had the power to order the detention (without trial) of any person for a period not exceeding two years provided the Governor in Council was satisfied that the detention was necessary to prevent that person from acting in "any manner prejudicial to the security of Malaya, the maintenance of public order, or the maintenance of essential services".

In 1960, three years after the Federation of Malaya became independent from Britain, the Emergency was declared over. To replace the Emergency Regulations Ordinance, the Malayan Parliament enacted the Internal Security Act (ISA).[70] The provisions were similar to the old PPSO, although the detaining authority was now the Minister of Home Affairs (with the agreement of the Yang di-Pertuan Agong, or king). And when Singapore became part of the Federation of Malaysia in 1963, the ISA was made applicable to that territory as well. It remains in force as Chapter 143 of the Singapore Statutes.

11.5.4 The Criminal Law (Temporary Provisions) Act

While the secret societies all but disappeared during the Japanese Occupation – on account of the brutal and arbitrary treatment meted out by the Japanese military – they quickly made their appearance again when peace was restored. By the 1950s, the secret societies were bigger

67 See Poh Soo Kai, Tan Jing Quee, and Koh Kay Yew (eds.), *The Fajar Generation: The University Socialist Club and the Politics of Postwar Malaya and Singapore* (Petaling Jaya: SIRD, 2010).

68 Ordinance 17, 1948.

69 Ordinance 25, 1955.

70 Act 18, 1960.

and better-organised than they had ever been and were terrorising the local population once more. This led to the passage of the Criminal Law (Temporary Provisions) Ordinance in 1955. Interestingly, this statute was aimed at controlling the movement of persons and vessels in the Straits of Johor to deny supplies to communist terrorists in the jungles. At the same time, it required workers of essential services to give at least fourteen days' notice for any strike or lock-out. The Act, which was, as its name suggests, a temporary measure, had a "sunset clause" and had to be renewed every three years. In 1958, it was amended to give the government authority to order the preventive detention of persons suspected of criminal activities for up to six months.

Speaking at the Second Reading of the Amendment Bill, Chief Secretary Edgeworth Beresford David told the Legislative Assembly that these draconian powers were needed to combat gang fights and other crimes committed by secret society members who could never be brought to justice because victims and witnesses were too afraid to testify against them:

> It is in these circumstances that the Government has decided that more drastic steps must be taken to protect the public from the activities of these gangs, and that since, for the reasons I have given, it is not possible to achieve that protection through the normal judicial processes of the Courts, these safeguards, which are adequate in ordinary times, must, in the present abnormal crime-wave, be supplemented by executive action. It is not only the duty of the Government to do this in discharge of its primary responsibility for the maintenance of peace and good order, but I believe that there is a wide public demand that such action should be taken and that it will meet with wholehearted support from all law-abiding members of the community.[71]

The Amendment was supported by the People's Action Party (then in opposition). Its leader, Lee Kuan Yew stated:

> Let us face the facts: either we bring these gangsters to trial, or we do nothing, or we lock them up without trial. Well, we prefer to bring them to trial if we could. As I know, and I think every practising lawyer in town knows, the point is now reached when police officers frankly admit that gangsters are not scared of the police any more.... Now quite frankly either you surrender and say, well, the judicial process is inadequate and therefore we have been beaten by gangsters, or we say, well what do we do about it? I say, well, if there is no other way, then we had better deal with them firmly.[72]

[71] Singapore Legislative Assembly Debates, August 13, 1958, Volume 7, 605–606.
[72] Ibid., 618.

Although a temporary measure, the Act has been renewed every five years since 1958 and remains in force as Chapter 67 of the Singapore Statutes. This legislation was particularly effective in the fight against the secret societies. In the first year of its implementation, the number of secret societies was cut down from 334 to 168, while 276 suspects were placed under executive detention and another 187 under police supervision. These arrests resulted in a 40 percent drop in incidents involving secret societies between 1959 and 1960.[73]

11.6 Post-War Developments in Policing

The Japanese Occupation left Singapore's policing system in disarray. The British Military Administration – which governed Singapore under martial law from September 1945 to April 1946 – made it its highest priority to re-establish law and order on the island. Remnants of the old police force were slowly reassembled with the help of senior British police officers in the liberating force. The Police Training School was reopened and a major recruitment exercise was undertaken. In addition to recruiting aggressively for the full-time police force, the colonial government also established a Volunteer Special Constabulary in 1946 to supplement the force. Women were also recruited to the force for the first time in 1949, and to improve patrolling activities, a Radio Division was established in May 1946 with four "patrol cars".[74]

To better coordinate police and military resources on the island, a Combined Operations Room was established in 1951. A pan-Malayan Security Service was established in 1946, but this was divided and absorbed into the Malayan and Singapore forces as Special Branches in 1948. Policing and law enforcement activities were reinforced with the establishment of the Security Squad in 1951 (to protect important public figures), a Riot Squad in 1952 and the Airport Police in 1954 (to protect the airport). A Gurkha regiment was also formed in 1949 to protect important public and security installations.

The reorganisation and strengthening of the police force was accompanied by serious efforts on the part of the police to educate the public about their roles and to build better relations with the community, which had hitherto considered the police to be an instrument of state oppression. Police actively assisted in flood rescue operations and distributed food

[73] Akbur, *Policing Singapore in the 19th and 20th Centuries*, 79–81.
[74] Ibid., 53–59.

and supplies to those rendered homeless by floods or fires, thus positioning itself as an ally, rather than an opponent of the community. In July 1958, the first "Police Week" was held, with the police opening up twelve of its key buildings in the evening for a week, "and treating the public to talks, exhibitions and band performances".[75] It was a resounding success, and an estimated 350,000 members of the public attended the various events and activities.

11.7 Policing in Post-Independence Singapore

Up to the time of independence, the historical development of Singapore's policing system mirrors the general pattern of development in other parts of the British Empire.[76] Sir Charles Jeffries, Deputy Under-Secretary of State for the Colonies, writing in 1952, divided the development of the colonial policing tradition into three overlapping phases. The first phase was "one of more or less improvised arrangements for securing the basic essentials of law and order"; the second involved the establishment of "semi-military constabulary forces modelled upon the Royal Irish Constabulary and organised mainly with the view to the suppression of crimes of violence and mass outbreaks against the peace"; and the third involved the "conversion of ... semi-military constabularies into civilian police forces".[77] The third phase was patterned after the British pattern of police organisation, which focused more on crime prevention than on the apprehension and punishment of offenders after the crime is committed,[78] while retaining certain continuing supplementary functions of a military character.[79] This modification of British policing practice was necessary "for the preservation of internal security" especially where "no regular military forces are readily available, and reliance must be placed upon the police to deal with any emergency calling for armed action".[80]

The PAP government inherited and strengthened both the tough legislation the British had passed, as well as the capabilities of the Special Branch, which it renamed the Internal Security Department in 1966. It took a very realistic and practical approach to issues of public order

[75] Ibid., 74.
[76] See, generally, Georgina Sinclair, *At the End of the Line: Colonial Policing and the Imperial Endgame 1945–80* (Manchester: Manchester University Press, 2006), 13–30.
[77] Charles Jeffries, *The Colonial Police* (London: Max Parrish, 1952), 32–33.
[78] Ibid., 24.
[79] Ibid., 32–33.
[80] Ibid., 33.

and security. Lee Kuan Yew, who was prime minister from 1959 to 1990, explained his philosophy in a 1962 speech as follows:

> In a settled and established society, law appears to be a precursor of order. Good laws lead to good order, that is the form that you will learn. But the hard realities of keeping the peace between man and man and between authority and the individual can be more accurately described if the phrase were inverted to "order and law", for without order the operation of law is impossible. Order having been established and the rules having become enforceable in a settled society, only then, is it possible to work out human relationships between subject and subject, and subject and the State in accordance with predetermined rules of law. And when a state of increasing disorder and defiance of authority cannot be checked by the rules then existing, new and sometimes drastic rules have to be forged to maintain order so that the law can continue to govern human relations.
>
> The alternative is to surrender order for chaos and anarchy. So it is that we have to allow the use of extraordinary powers of detention first in the case of political offenders under the PPSO, and next in the case of secret society gangsters under the Criminal Law (Temporary Provisions) Ordinance. It must be realised that if you abolish the powers of arrest and detention and insist on trial in open court in accordance with the strict laws of evidence of a criminal trial, then law and order becomes, without the slightest exaggeration, utterly impossible because whilst you may still nominally have law, order and the wherewithal to enforce it would have disappeared.[81]

With the implementation of the Criminal Law (Temporary Provisions) Act, the police managed to break the back of the secret societies. Although secret society activity was common right into the 1970s, the societies were no longer a law unto themselves and had to operate underground. The use of the Internal Security Act in Operation Coldstore in 1963 – which resulted in over 100 leading communist and pro-communist leaders and organisers being arrested – crippled the CPM and its front organisations. With these two big threats negated, the police then focused on building better relations with the community, and worked toward a more democratic, community-oriented form of policing. It began by enlisting the assistance of members of the public in crime detection and prevention by establishing the Neighbourhood Watch Scheme in June 1981. And in 1983, the Japanese *Koban* style of policing was instituted through the establishment of numerous Neighbourhood Police Posts (NPP) throughout the island.

[81] Lee Kuan Yew, Speech at the Annual Dinner of the University of Singapore Law Society, January 18, 1962, www.nas.gov.sg/archivesonline/data/pdfdoc/lky19620118.pdf.

Each NPP was headed by an inspector who was assisted by a team of some twenty officers who would patrol the neighbourhood on foot or on bicycles to aid in their building better rapport with members of the public.[82] The system of community policing that developed from the early 1980s proved so successful that David Bayley, the leading authority on policing noted:

> Singapore represents the most ambitious and successful attempt in the English-speaking world to change in a short time the fundamental strategy of policing. Since 1981, the Singapore police force has carefully shifted from a reactive, incident-centred mode of operation to full-scale community policing.
>
> … What they have done fits almost anyone's notion of community policing. It certainly fits the rigorous test Jerome Skolnick and I have suggested: (1) community-based crime prevention; (2) reorientation of patrol to emphasize proactive servicing; (3) decentralization of command; and (4) development of accountability to local communities.[83]

To augment and supplement the regular police force, the government decided that it was necessary to build up a reserve of trained officers. This was done in 1975 by introducing full-time national service for the police. All male Singaporeans are conscripted for national service at the age of eighteen. Hitherto, they had been conscripted only for the armed forces, but with the change in the law, national servicemen were now staffing the police ranks. It has been suggested that the large presence of full-time national servicemen in the police is a key factor in Singapore's police force has prevented a "us against them" mentality in relations between the police and the public, thus resulting in much less police brutality and mishandling of situations.[84] Because "a sizeable proportion of the police force consists of citizen-officers whose main identity is as citizens and not as professional policemen" and whose "loyalty lies with home and community", a schism between two distinct groups – the police and the people – is averted.[85]

[82] On the NPP system, see Narayanan Ganapathy, "Conceptualising Community Policing, Crime Prevention and Criminology: A Singapore Perspective," *The Australian & New Zealand Journal of Criminology* 33(3) (2000): 266–286; and David H. Bayley, *A Model of Community Policing; The Singapore Story* (Washington, DC: US Department of Justice, National Institute of Justice, 1989).

[83] Bayley, *A Model of Community Policing*, 1.

[84] "How did Singapore Avoid the Police Brutality Trap? A Story of NSFs and NPCs," *Kopi.*, June 12, 2020, https://thekopi.co/2020/06/12/how-did-singapore-avoid-the-police-brutality-trap-a-story-of-nsfs-and-npcs/.

[85] Ibid.

Today, the Singapore public places great trust in the police and does not see them as instruments of state oppression. Indeed, in a 2017 by the Ministry of Home Affairs, 87 percent of Singaporeans considered the police force to be a "world class crime-fighting organization", while 88 percent of them felt that the police provided "a high quality of service".[86] A remarkable 92 percent of respondents rated Singapore's general safety and security as "good" or "very good".[87]

11.8 Conclusion

While Singapore may be seen as an authoritarian state, its system of policing – save for the existence of preventive detention laws – is largely democratic. In most colonial societies, it is assumed that authoritarian policing takes place because of the need for the colonial state to maintain its rule over unwilling masses. This was not the case in Singapore because the colonial authorities simply had no wherewithal to do so. They were always understaffed and underpaid and the police force was not only inadequate, it was also inept and corrupt. Indeed, notwithstanding the various reforms, the colonial police force still could not deal with the secret societies – the biggest threat to public order – and relied on a mix of welfare, cooperation and selective coercion. This continued right up till the Japanese Occupation when authoritarian policing reached its zenith. Brutal and harsh military law was enforced and even the fiercest secret societies went underground.

The fact that much of the legislation was passed in response to the threats to law and order, subversion, communalism and communism did not allow the police to gain an upper hand against these threats. Laws such as the Societies Act and the Sedition Ordinance were simply too weak and mild to deter would-be secret society thugs or treasonous subversives. Things changed after the war when rebuilding was taking place. The colonial authorities remained under-resourced, but concerted efforts were made to boost their numbers and strength as they had to deal with the kinds of mass protests, sit-ins, hartals and boycotts organised by communist and pro-communist front organisations who largely operated through open front organisations such as trade unions, reading societies and alumni associations.

[86] Seow Bei Yi, "Parliament: 87% of Public View Police as World-Class Crime-Fighting Organisation, Says Survey," *Straits Times*, March 3, 2017, www.straitstimes.com/politics/87-per-cent-of-public-view-police-as-world-class-crime-fighting-organisation-survey.

[87] Ibid.

The turning point came just before Singapore became independent. When the local politicians began grappling with the problem of lawlessness and the secret societies, the British had to enact draconian preventive detention laws – first in the guise of the Malayan Emergency Ordinances and then through the Criminal Law (Temporary Provisions) Act, and then in 1960 in Malaya the Internal Security Act. These laws helped the strengthened the police force to break the backs of the secret societies and the communists. These two pieces of legislation, with their wide scope, made policing authoritarian, especially from the time of their enactment right up to 1989, when the Court of Appeal ruled that the executive discretion to order preventive detention was subject to judicial review.

Even so, the state has not been content to rely solely on draconian legislation to police the population. Starting in the 1950s, the police have been working on becoming more of a community organisation that worked with rather than against the people. This move was further strengthened in the 1970s with the recruitment of regular citizens as national service policemen and reserves, and a conscious move toward a more community-oriented form of policing through the NPP, and later the Neighbourhood Police Centre system of decentralised, active policing.

Returning to the criteria listed for policing at the start of this chapter, Singapore appears to check far more boxes in the democratic than the authoritarian column. Today, Singapore practises a form of policing that is more democratic than authoritarian. But these two forms of policing co-exist and reinforce each other. The view of the state is that if order is to come before law, then order needs to be maintained, even with draconian authoritarian-style policing. But once order is established, democratic policing can flourish. What of the danger that the authoritarian might supplant the democratic? This is a perennial problem of democratic governance political thinkers such as Madison have pondered for centuries: we need first to enable a government to control the governed, but how do we oblige it to control itself?[88]

[88] James Madison, *Federalist No. 51*, February 8, 1788.

12

Empires Collaborate

Geopolitics of Colonial Policing in Hong Kong (1880s–1970s)[1]

MICHAEL NG

Around noon on June 3, 1919, nine schoolboys aged eight to seventeen from Ying To School in the Central District of Hong Kong Island walked westwards along Queen's Road Central clad in their school uniforms and holding open oil-paper umbrellas made in mainland China. The umbrellas featured Chinese characters in white paint that read "Chinese people should buy native goods" or simply "Native goods". The group of young boys carrying umbrellas attracted the attention of passers-by who began to stop and watch or even follow the boys as they walked down the street. More than 100 people joined the impromptu parade. Within less than an hour, a police inspector with the surname Brazil who was patrolling the area intervened and stopped the crowd near the Central Fire Station. He asked one of the students whether he had obtained a permit to organise such an activity. The student said no, but that one of their teachers had instructed them to march. Inspector Brazil arrested the nine students on the spot and then went to the teacher's residence to arrest him as well. All of those arrested were charged with the offence of organising a procession without having obtained a permit under the Regulation of Chinese Ordinance and remanded for trial. The teacher was charged with aiding and abetting the organisation of an illegal procession. After a four-day trial, Magistrate Lindsell

[1] This chapter adopts in part content from the author's monograph, *Political Censorship in British Hong Kong: Freedom of Expression and the Law (1842–1997)* (Cambridge: Cambridge University Press, 2022) and his co-authored article: Michael Ng Zhang Shengyue, and Max Wong, "'Who but the Governor in Executive Council Is the Judge?': Historical Use of the Emergency Regulations Ordinance," *Hong Kong Law Journal* 50(2) (2020): 425–461. The author thanks the publishers for consenting to the use of this content. The work in this chapter was also substantially supported by a grant from Research Grant Council of Hong Kong Special Administrative Region, China (Project No. HKU 17605917).

entered a judgment against one of the defendants, student Wu, who had headed up the procession. Wu was sentenced to pay a heavy fine of HK$10.[2]

In his concluding submission, the prosecutor who was also the Chief Superintendent of Police, with the surname Wolfe, chose not to shy away from the political motive behind the lawsuit. A wave of similar anti-Japanese protests, Wolfe said, had got out of control in many mainland Chinese cities, including Beijing and Tianjin, with the Chinese government there practically overrun by students. As a British colony, Hong Kong had to adopt preventive measures.

The way in which the "umbrella procession" had been dealt with in the Magistrate's Court of Hong Kong was credited as a friendly (to Japan) precedent of suppression shown to an ally. The following report that appeared in one of the leading English-language newspapers in Japan, the *Japan Chronicle*, which adopts a highly racist and strident tone if viewed from today's perspective, reflects how policing in colonial Hong Kong was seen as effectively serving geopolitical interests:

> Nine Chinese students have been arrested by the Hongkong police for the offence of walking around the streets with umbrellas bearing the words "Don't Buy Japanese Goods," or something of the sort. The legality of such a proceeding is very doubtful, though of course it may be wrapped up in phrases about the impossibility of allowing the commerce of the port to be at the mercy of agitators, and all that sort of thing … all British authorities must do everything they can to protect Japan from even its most remote consequences. This action on the part of Hongkong authorities enormously strengthens the hands of the Japanese diplomatic officials all over China. … [The British authorities] compel the Chinese to suppress newspapers which denounce the Shandong settlement in too heated terms and to forbid indignation processions and every manifestation of popular feeling. So far they do not appear to have gone to such lengths as the Hongkong Police, but armed with this precedent, Japanese Consuls will be able to demand practically anything they desire. The boycott is obviously an ineffective weapon, but like a strike, it may be carried out in a legal way. However, as Marquis Okuma said, racial equality is not for uncivilized people like [the] Chinese.[3]

[2] To put the amount of fine in context, in 1919 a low-level coolie employed by Hong Kong government earned approximately HK$9 to 12 per month, see Hong Kong Government, *Hong Kong Blue Book for the Year 1919* (Hong Kong: Hong Kong Government Printer, 1919), 103, 117.

[3] A report of *South China Morning Post* (hereinafter *SCMP*) under the title of "A View from Japan," *Japan Chronicle*, June 20, 1919.

To date, most scholarly work on historical Hong Kong policing has focused on the relationship between the governing and governed within a local setting.[4] This approach explains policing solely within the confines of the juxtaposition of the authoritarian power of the colonial government on the one hand with the individual rights and liberties of the colonised on the other. It thus fails to consider the bigger picture of Hong Kong policing within the geopolitics of East Asia, and the world as a whole, during the long twentieth century and the influence of global politics on policing in colonial Hong Kong. This chapter, which draws upon archival documents from the nineteenth and twentieth centuries showing how public media in Hong Kong were systematically censored, placed under pervasive surveillance and prosecuted for political reasons, argues that collaboration among the imperial empires to safeguard their interests in East Asia contributed significantly to Hong Kong policing during that period. The interests of the British empire's strategic partners at various times, including the Qing empire, Nationalist China, the United States (US) and Japan, had a substantial effect on how the freedom of the Hong Kong people was defined, confined and policed. During the period under study, Hong Kong was one of Asia's most important centres of geopolitical intelligence, a hotbed of subversive activities among agents of various powers and, in the latter part of the period, a site of Cold War politics. Hence, this chapter argues that Hong Kong policing was historically not solely a matter of domestic authoritarian governance but also an issue of global geopolitical relevance. Analysing authoritarian policing in colonial Hong Kong based on the conventional framework of human rights or colonial inequality and racism without considering the bigger picture of global and regional politics is, this chapter argues, seriously inadequate. The bigger picture

[4] There is a handful of academic works on the history of Hong Kong police including Lawrence Ho, *Policing Hong Kong, 1842–1969: Insiders' Stories* (Hong Kong: City University Press, 2012); Kam Wong, *Policing in Hong Kong* (Farnham and Burlington, VT: Ashgate, 2012); Allan Jiao, *The Police in Hong Kong: A Contemporary View* (Lanham, MD: University Press of America, 2007); Colin Crisswell and Mike Watson, *The Royal Hong Kong Police, 1841–1945* (Hong Kong: Macmillan, 1982); Patricia O'Sullivan, *Policing Hong Kong: An Irish History* (Hong Kong: Blacksmith, 2017); Carol A. G. Jones and Jon Vagg, *Criminal Justice in Hong Kong* (London and New York: Routledge-Cavendish, 2007). Crisswell, Watson, and O'Sulliven described very briefly the political tasks handled by colonial Hong Kong police. Carol Jones is among the few who in her work on crimes and criminal justice system in Hong Kong alerts us that geopolitics, rather than crime rates, could drive the practice of criminal justice system in colonial Hong Kong.

is the political-economic situation of China, China's relations with the major world powers and those powers' China strategies over time, as this chapter's archival discovery will discuss.

The chapter begins by discussing the hitherto unknown fact that the monitoring and political censorship of the mass media was the norm rather than the exception under the colonial version of British common law that prevailed in Hong Kong after it became a British colony in 1842. The interests of friendly powers, including France, Japan and sometimes the Chinese government, were protected through censorship measures that evolved from the punitive use of libel lawsuits to punish news editors to the pre-emptive daily vetting of Chinese newspaper proofs – the latter a measure that was introduced in the 1920s and continued throughout the inter-war period. The chapter then turns to the post-war period when Britain collaborated with other world powers, including the US, to monitor and combat the cultural infiltration of Hong Kong by the communist powers. Such international collaboration through policing media turned Hong Kong into an important surveillance centre in East Asia, where intelligence was collected and disseminated among the world powers.

12.1 Policing the Hong Kong Press during the Nineteenth and Early Twentieth Centuries

For the first fifty years of British rule in Hong Kong, criminal prosecutions under libel law were the major tools used by the colonial government against newspaper editors for criticisms not only of government policies, but also reports that upset the geopolitical interests of Britain and its allies in China.[5]

For example, in 1884, criminal actions were directed against four Chinese newspapers, two of which were the major papers in Hong Kong (*Wa Tsz Yat Po* and *Tsun Wan Yat Po*), for their publication of an imperial edict issued by the governors of Guangdong and Guangxi provinces calling for resistance against French military aggression after the outbreak of the Sino-French War. A report from the Acting Hong Kong Governor Marsh to London in 1884 indicated the geopolitical reasons behind the prosecution against the press:

[5] Newspapers in Britain also underwent struggle with libel lawsuits during the nineteenth century. For details, see Martin Hewitt, "The Law and the Press," in Joanne Shattock (ed.), *Journalism and the Periodical Press in Nineteenth Century Britain* (Cambridge: Cambridge University Press, 2017), 147–164; see also Mark Hampton, *Vision of the Press in Britain, 1850–1950* (Champaign, IL: University of Illinois Press, 2004), 30–39.

> My Lord, I have the honour to report that, on the recommendation of the Attorney General, and with the full concurrence of the Executive Council, I have directed criminal proceedings to be taken again the Editors of four local Chinese Newspapers namely: 1.Wa Tsz Yat Po [華字日報]..., 2. Tsun Wan Yat Po [循環日報], 3. Chung Ngoi San Po [中外新報], 4. Wai San Yat Po [維新日報] for publishing what purported to be an Edict issued by the Viceroy of the Two Kwang and the Governor of Kwang Tung. In [the edict], Chinese subjects residing in Hongkong are exhorted to "secretly kill some French Commander, or destroy by fire their munitions of war, or cooperate with the Chinese officers and soldiers in attacking them from within and without, with a view to their being entirely swept away".[6]

In addition to judicial proceedings, the colony also made laws that forbade the import of revolutionary publications against the Qing-dynasty government into Hong Kong. The Post Office Ordinance was amended in 1900 to give the governor power to prohibit dispatching and delivering of any letter, newspaper, book or pamphlet into Hong Kong. Anyone importing a publication into Hong Kong without going through the Hong Kong Post was liable to be charged with an offence. However, such legislative measures soon proved inadequate to relieve the growing anxiety of the Hong Kong government arising from worsening instability on the mainland.[7] After the failure of the Hundred Days' Reform in 1898, many revolutionaries escaped to Hong Kong and published revolutionary newspapers in the colony. Many of them even organised and promoted revolutionary activities against the Qing Empire in Hong Kong.[8]

The rising number of anti-Qing publications and activists in Hong Kong became a headache for the Hong Kong government. Given the then British stance of supporting the Qing government, Chinese Publications (Prevention) Ordinance was passed in 1907. The new law – "[o]wing to the proximity of the Colony of Hongkong to the mainland of China and to the tendency to create internal dissension in that country" – punished any person who published or distributed materials calculated to excite disorder in China, regardless of whether they were printed on the mainland or in Hong Kong. Those convicted of these charges would be liable to imprisonment for any term not exceeding two years and to a fine not exceeding HK$500.[9]

6 Letter from Acting Governor Marsh to the Earl of Derby, September 25, 1884, CO 129/217.

7 The Post Office Ordinance, 1900.

8 Lee Siu-nam, "Chinese and English Press in Hong Kong" (香港的中西報業), in Wang Gungwu (ed.), *Hong Kong History: New Perspectives* (香港史新編) (Hong Kong: Joint Publishing, 2017), vol.2, 563–604.

9 Chinese Publications (Prevention) Ordinance, 1907.

During the Legislative Council meeting considering the legislation, then Colonial Secretary Francis Henry May and Attorney General Rees Davies made the objective of stricter press control clear. The law aimed "to prevent Hongkong becoming a place where seditious pamphlets may be printed and circulated with a view of distribution in China" and "to prevent this Colony being made a centre for seditious publications".[10] The Colonial Secretary justified the passing of the law by saying that the stance of "the native press in this Colony towards the reigning dynasty in China has been a serious source of embarrassment". While addressing the Legislative Council, he held up a publication sold in Hong Kong "in which were represented some of China's leading statesmen sitting with their heads in their hands" (Figure 12.1). "That is," the Colonial Secretary said, "nothing more or less than inciting persons to deliberate rebellion against the great and friendly empire which lies so close to our border".[11]

A letter from the Straits Settlements Sir John Anderson to the Hong Kong governor revealed that the Qing government played a role in enacting this Ordinance:

> Sir, I have the honour to transmit to you for your information a copy of Hongkong Ordinance no. 15 of 1907 [Chinese Publications (Prevention) Ordinance] together with copies of correspondence with the Foreign Office with regard to the request of the China Government that similar enactments should be passed in the Straits Settlements and other British territories in the Far East in order to prevent the publication there of books or newspapers containing matter calculated to excite dissension in China.[12]

Shortly after enactment of the Chinese Publications (Prevention) Ordinance, the British Empire itself also faced anti-imperialist and nationalist movements in its colonies, particularly in India. A new ordinance was thus passed to suppress the spread of anti-British sentiments to Hong Kong. The Seditious Publications Ordinance was passed in 1914 to prohibit anti-government publications against British rule. The new legislation empowered the government not only to punish the publisher of anti-government materials, but also to search for, seize and confiscate such materials. During the Legislative Council meeting held to consider the new ordinance, the Colonial Secretary spoke of the empire's growing unease over its colonies. He noted that "newspapers and documents of

[10] *Hong Kong Hansard*, Hong Kong Government Reports Online (1842–1941), October 3, 1907.
[11] Ibid.
[12] Confidential note addressed to Governor John Anderson, June 19, 1908, CO 129/351.

Figure 12.1 China's leading statesman losing his head, as depicted in *Min Bao* (民報), 1907

a highly objectionable character" had been recently imported into Hong Kong. Although Section 12 of the Post Office Ordinance, 1900 empowered the postmaster to stop such import, many publications "of a highly seditious and disloyal character" entered Hong Kong by means other than through the Post Office. Hence, the government needed legal powers to "detain any articles suspected of containing seditious publications" and to declare them "to be forfeited". Further, it needed the power "to issue search warrants for such publications and for seizure". What worried colonial officials even more was that anti-imperialistic feelings among the Indian population of Hong Kong might be incited by some of the publications emanating from Indian sources. Their publication and appearance in India had already been prohibited.[13]

The Seditious Publications Ordinance provided that any person who published or knowingly had in his or her possession any newspaper, book or other document containing any seditious material (which included any words likely to incite violence or excite hatred or disaffection toward the British government) would be liable to a fine not exceeding

[13] *Hong Kong Hansard*, April 23, 1914.

HK$500 and imprisonment of no more than two years. Extensive powers of search and seizure of seditious materials were given to the police. More importantly, the law was subsequently strengthened to provide that defendants charged with possessing such materials bore the burden of proving their absence of knowledge that the materials were seditious.[14] Although these laws were supposedly applicable to both the English- and Chinese-language press, their actual application shows that Chinese and European papers were not in fact treated equally before the common law system practised in Hong Kong, as the following prosecution against the Chinese newspaper *Chung Kwok Yat Po* (中國日報) shows.[15]

In 1911, the editor of *Chung Kwok Yat Po*, a newspaper founded by the revolutionary Chen Shao-bai (陳少白) in 1900, was prosecuted for publishing an article calculated to excite tumult, disorder or crime in mainland China in breach of the Chinese Publications (Prevention) Ordinance. The offending article condemned the oppressive behaviour of Qing government officials as "If there were no Tsing officials there would be no famine-stricken people … the officials were contemplating selling the country…".[16] The article also called for actions against Qing officials. In defending the editor, barrister Eldon Potter highlighted the unequal treatment in law of English and Chinese newspapers in his cross-examination of A.W. Brewin, the Registrar General of the Hong Kong government, who was responsible for monitoring Chinese newspapers. Brewin testified how the article was calculated to excite tumult in China under the law. Potter read to Brewin a quote from an article in an English-language newspaper: "They [the Qing government] stand out to day in the eyes of all the world, as the most incapable, corrupt, decadent and hopeless race, into whose hands have fallen, the destinies of any conquered people." He then asked Brewin: "Does that not mean the Manchu conquered China and are the worst rulers that the people have even seen? Is it not as strong as anything in here [the *Chung Kwok Yat Po* article]?" Brewin replied: "Yes I suppose it is."

Potter then submitted that "it was a vindictive prosecution. … [The government] boasted that the law was the same for an Englishman as for

[14] Seditious Publications Ordinance, 1914, ss. 2, 3, 3A, 3B and 4.

[15] The Attorney General explained to the legislative councillors that the Chinese Publication (Prevention) Ordinance applied also to materials printed in English language if such materials were founded by the court to have excite tumult or disorder in China; see *Hong Kong Hansard*, October 3, 1907.

[16] *SCMP*, May 23, 1911.

a foreigner. But, unfortunately, in the administration of that particular ordinance, the Chinese were picked out and were prosecuted while others, who were publishing literature much stronger were passed by."[17]

The judge hearing the case, Chief Justice Sir Francis Piggott, in directing the jury, did not consider the foregoing point relevant to the case: "A great deal had been said of the other papers in the colony. They [the jurors] had to remember, however, that two wrongs did not make a right, and that question, so far as they were concerned, was totally irrelevant."[18] Chief Justice Piggott's remarks also reveal the deeper political anxiety of the empire, which in his view should be afforded a higher priority than free speech and equality before the law: "They all know that China subjected herself to criticism, but the basis of the law was that the King's Government had undertaken certain obligations, of friendship and of commerce with the Emperor of China, and it was bound to recognise the existence of the Government as much as the French or German Governments.... It was no new principle."[19]

12.2 Pre-Emptive Political Censorship from the 1920s

Local laws continued to be employed by the colonial government to police potential troubles that might upset Britain's international relations or geopolitical interests in East Asia. In response to the most serious challenge to its legitimacy to date during the large-scale strikes that occurred from 1922 to 1926, particularly in the face of the united front of the Kuomintang (KMT) and the Chinese Communist Party (CCP) in the anti-imperialist movement of 1924, the colonial government made a law to approve Chinese newspaper proofs on a daily basis before they were printed.[20] During the Canton-Hong Kong Strike and Boycott of 1925, the governor made newspaper censorship regulations (hereafter Newspaper Regulations) under the power vested in him by the Emergency Regulations

[17] Ibid.

[18] Ibid.

[19] Ibid.

[20] The strikes were seamen's strikes in 1922 and Canton-Hong Kong Strike and Boycott from 1925 to 1926. For an account of these strikes, see Jung-Fang Tsai, *The Hong Kong People's History of Hong Kong 1841–1945* (香港人之香港史 1841–1945) (Hong Kong: Oxford University Press, 2001), 109–167; Ming K. Chan, "Hong Kong in Sino-British Conflict: Mass Mobilization and the Crisis of Legitimacy," in Ming K. Chan and John D. Young (eds.), *Precarious Balance: Hong Kong between China and Britain, 1842–1992* (Hong Kong: Hong Kong University Press, 1994), 27.

Ordinance. Under these regulations, the extensive power of pre-censorship of the proofs of newspapers and other types of publication was vested in the Secretary for Chinese Affairs, and the governor was even afforded the power to suspend a newspaper from publication.

> 1. No person shall print, publish, or distribute any newspaper, placard or pamphlet containing any matter ***in the Chinese language*** (other than a bona fide trade advertisement) which has not been ***previously submitted to and passed by*** the Secretary for Chinese Affairs. [Emphasis added]
> 2. No person shall import, print, publish, reproduce, have in his possession or under his control, post up or distribute any newspaper, placard, pamphlet, writing or pictorial representation calculated or tending to persuade or induce any person or persons, whether individually or as members of the general public, (1) to refrain from dealing with, trading with, working for or hiring any person or persons in the course of trade, business, occupation, or employment; (2) to do any act calculated or tending to cause a breach of the peace; (3) to interfere with the administration of the law or with the maintenance of law and order.
> 3. No person shall, without the permission of the Secretary for Chinese Affairs, import any newspaper, placard or pamphlet containing any matter in the Chinese language other than a bona fide trade advertisement. No person shall have in his possession any newspaper, placard or pamphlet imported without permission.
> 4. The Governor in Council shall have power to suppress for such period as he may think fit or until further order the printing and publication of any newspaper.[21]

In 1931, the censorship regulations were tightened to empower policemen to seize and detain the printing machinery and writing materials of suppressed newspapers.[22] Not surprisingly, English-language newspapers were not subject to the mandatory daily pre-censorship requirement.

12.3 The Secretive Press Censorship Office

No one has written in detail about how the Hong Kong government pre-censored Chinese newspaper proofs during the 1920s and 1930s, probably because of the lack of official archives pertaining to such shameful operation. Yet the testimonies of government censors reported in newspaper coverage of trial hearing of censorship prosecutions reveal the detailed operation of the government's secretive pre-censorship works. The diary and personal collection of Ng Bar-ling (吳灞陵), a long-time editor of one

[21] G.N. No. 369 of 1925, Hong Kong Government Gazette, June 25, 1925.
[22] G.N. No. 621 of 1931, Hong Kong Government Gazette, October 2, 1931.

of the major Chinese-language newspapers in colonial Hong Kong, *Wah Kiu Yat Po* (華僑日報), also contain valuable information and documents on how the hitherto little known Press Censorship Office operated.

During the Canton-Hong Kong Strike and Boycott, the pre-censorship of newspaper proofs was carried out on a part-time basis by three Chinese justices of the peace, one Chinese staff member of the Secretariat for Chinese Affairs and two Chinese staff members of the Education Department. After the strike, this pre-censorship work was institutionalised under the newly established Press Censorship Office under the leadership of an ethnically Chinese Deputy Secretary for Chinese Affairs by the name of Liu Zhi-ping (劉志平). Liu was a highly educated man who had served as the county governor of Bao An (寶安) County in Guangdong Province, which neighbours Hong Kong.[23] The Press Censorship Office began operating on 17 May 1928.[24] Liu supervised two full-time censors who were charged with "the task of reading every line" that appeared in the proofs of all Chinese newspapers every day. One of the censors was on duty from 4 pm to 6 pm, and the other from 6 pm to 8 pm. Censorship hours were later extended to 11 pm, and subsequently to as late as 1.30 am, to cater for late news coming in from mainland China.[25] Figure 12.2 shows a notice kept by the Chinese press about the opening hours of the Press Censorship Office during the 1930s. The censors sometimes had to ring up the papers at 12.45 am to tell them that if they had any articles to be censored, they were to send them along as quickly as they could. Any later telegrams arriving from China after 1 am had to be sent to the residence of a designated censor for approval.[26] The method of censorship entailed the censors "delet[ing] any objectionable matter by striking it through with a red or blue pencil or an ink cross or line, which indicated that the matter was not passed for publication, or to place his initials in the corner of any objectionable paragraph, which indicated that the particular paragraph was passed for publication".[27]

If the censors struck out objectionable words or sentences from the newspaper proofs, editors had to delete those words or sentences from the

[23] See a newspaper report of April 7, 1970 on Liu's death and his background contained in Ng Bar Ling Collection (1904–1976), Special Collections of The University of Hong Kong Libraries.

[24] Ng Bar-ling, Manuscript of "Materials of Hong Kong Press History," and diary entries of Ng Bar-ling, Ng Bar Ling Collection (1904–1976).

[25] *SCMP*, June 21, 1928, and *SCMP*, June 15, 1928. Two additional censors were subsequently added to the operation; see *Hong Kong Hansard*, August 26, 1936.

[26] *SCMP*, February 5, 1931.

[27] *SCMP*, June 21, 1928.

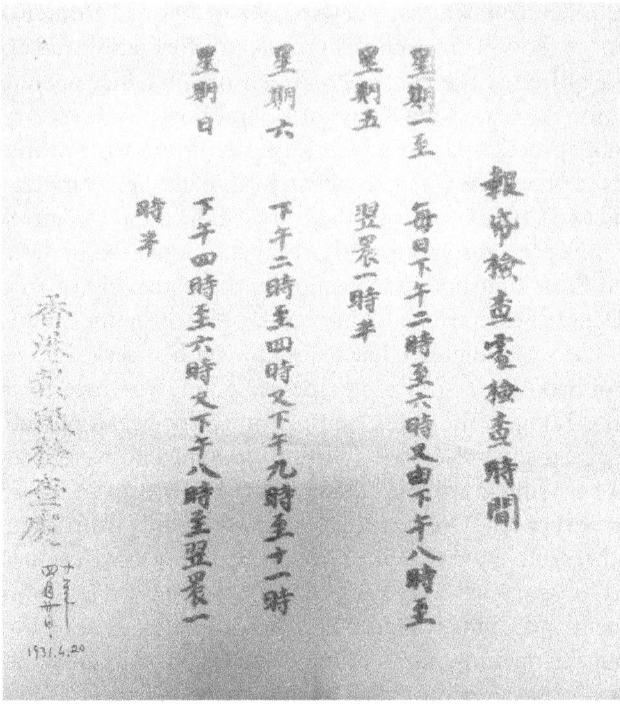

Figure 12.2 Notice kept by the Chinese press about the opening hours of the Press Censorship Office in 1931. It informs the press that the office operates from 2 pm to 6 pm and 8 pm to 1.30 am from Mondays to Fridays; from 2 pm to 4 pm and 9 pm to 11 pm on Saturdays; and from 4 pm to 6 pm and 8 pm to 1.30 am on Sundays.
Source: Ng Bar Ling Collection (1904–1976), Special Collections of The University of Hong Kong Libraries.

proofs. In an age without computer software, editors were left with insufficient time to manually rearrange newspaper layouts to accommodate such deletions. Instead, they had to either replace the deleted words or sentences with a blank space marked "censored" in Chinese or replace them with dots, crosses and/or squares (Figure 12.3) before sending the revised proofs to the printers in a hurry. Veteran journalists later recalled that the government had not liked the idea of revealing to readers that a news story had been censored but could do nothing about it.[28] It was therefore not

[28] A Chinese newspaper report (newspaper title missing), August 22, 1974, kept at Ng Bar Ling Collection (1904–1976).

重慶昨被狂炸大火
激烈空戰×喪七機
公私損失在積極發掘清查中

（某某電）××于昨九六式轟炸機四十五架•組爲五隊•佈成方形之陣•于午後一時四十分左右•由西向東侵入重慶上空投彈•我神鷹空軍於×機未襲之先•即升空準備迎擊•當×機投彈之際•我機迎面擊上•我先頭隊向×猛攻•後續各隊均向當面之×隊攻擊•一時機槍四射•我機以奮銳之勢•均奮勇冒×火突進×機隊形中•緊迫攻擊•連續發射•×機隊形遂形紛散•我機或以數機擊×之一機•或一機對×一機•直至擊落爲止•我各機在追擊中•均至油量最大範圍或彈盡爲止•漏網之×機均倉惶散東逃•至石柱附近•經衝集合東竄•此戰結果•×機三架被我擊中•在空中着火墜於廣陽壩東方山谷中•又×隊長於追攻之際•見×下落墜於重慶南東一帶•另據某隊員目睹•見×機三十八架東飛•×共損失七架•後據石柱情報•在石柱以東×機因油箱擊中•續有墜落•正詳查中•我機兩架跳傘•一架迫降警官學校附近•此役頗爲激烈•爲近來空戰所罕有•×投彈大部落長江及嘉陵江中•一小部落於市區•均係市民住區•×在強弩之末•死命掙扎之際•不惜慘無人道•對我非武裝市民濫施狂炸•吾人不能僅依世界輿論制裁•吾人皆必以吾人之力•遏制××××之××•復已死同胞之仇•（三日）

（中央社重慶電）三日下午十一時廿分•此間防空司令部據玩旋報告•×機多架•由東向西飛行•十二時卅分左右•復接酉陽報告•×機兩批各十八•向西北飛•當于十二時四十五分發出空襲警報•我機亦即升空迎擊•十二時五十五分•發緊急警報•×機于下午一時十七分•侵入市空•其投彈目標似係某某軍事機關•但我軍事機關早已疏散鄉間•而×機師技術又極惡劣•除致附近商店民居•慘遭狂炸•投重量炸彈外•并有多枚燃燒彈•西四街左營街兩處•立即起火•延燒甚久•此時我防護團警察及各救護團體•均于爆發聲中出動搶救•于極端實慨中•精神奮發•工作緊張•其悲憤情緒•與責任觀念•充分表現無依•一般市民亦極鎮定•謹守秩序毫無紊亂•尤見人民已具有最大決心•現死傷人數及公私損失•正在積極發掘清查•同時防空部•并與空襲緊急救濟聯合辦事處•會同辦理善後•至×機•經我機猛烈攻擊•即于下午一時三十分倉惶逃去•聞曾被我擊落一架•現正在鄰近各地搜查中•又本日×機并投下紙包之（大成新牌）香烟數百包•其中是否含有毒氣•現正檢查中•（三日）

（路透社重慶電）今午日機作本年內首次大舉轟炸重慶市內稠密人口區域•轟炸後•繼以大火•預料死傷甚重•（三日）

（路透社重慶電）據華人消息•福州商業區于去月廿一日•廿五•及本月一•二兩日•迭遭日機轟炸•死傷居民千餘•全市成廢墟•日機現繼續轟炸寧波•（三日）

Figure 12.3 A censored Chinese newspaper *Wah Kiu Yat Po* dated 4 May 1939 that reports the military attack of Chongqing city in mainland China by the Japanese air force. Source: Courtesy of *SCMP*.

uncommon to see newspapers filled with dots, crosses and squares for sale in the streets. In addition to striking out individual words and sentences in a newspaper proof, the press censors could also prohibit an entire news story from being published. As shown in Figure 12.4, a censor would sometimes cross out an entire news report and stamp it with an official chop to signify his disapproval. The characters on the outer circle of the chop shown in the figures reads "Hong Kong Press Censorship Office", and the inner one reads "This script is not allowed to be published."[29]

[29] Ng Bar-ling, Manuscript of "Materials of Hong Kong Press History," Ng Bar Ling Collection (1904–1976).

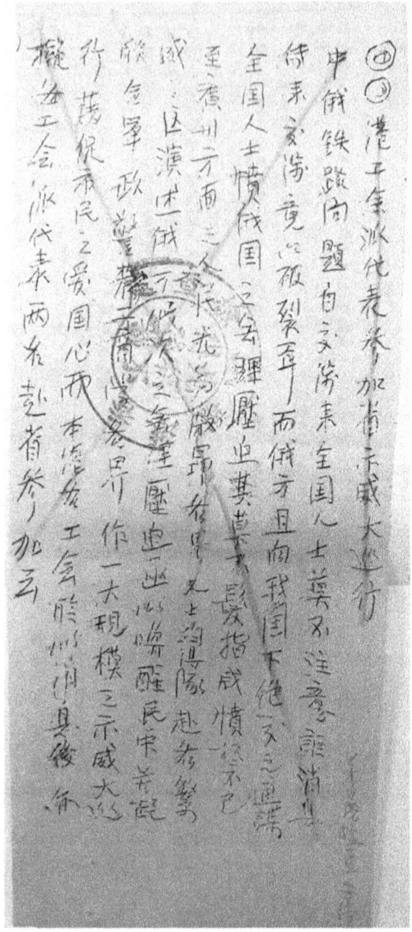
(四)(三)港工会派代表参加省示威大巡行
中俄铁路问题自交涉来全国人士莫不注意讵消息
传来交涉竟以破裂[illegible]而俄方且向我国下绝交之通牒
全国人士愤俄国之无理压迫其暴[illegible]莫不发指咸愤[illegible]不已
至广州方面之人民代表尤为激昂各界人士组织宣传队赴各乡
镇区演述俄方[illegible]之无理压迫以唤醒民众并发起
联合全军政警各界作一大规模之示威大巡
行藉促市民之爱国心而本港各工会[illegible]以[illegible]其后[illegible]
机务工会派代表两名赴省参加云

Figure 12.4 Original manuscript of a news story that was banned by the Press Censorship Office. The story reported that representatives of trade unions in Hong Kong had joined the demonstration held in Guangzhou to protest against the USSR and in support of China during a railway dispute in 1929.
Source: Ng Bar Ling Collection (1904–1976), Special Collections of The University of Hong Kong Libraries.

Furthermore, censors sometimes had face-to-face meetings with editors in which they would tell them what not to report. When one editor was cross-examined in court about what he had been told by a censor, he said, "What he [the censor] told us was not to publish anything violent against Japan".[30] The Secretary for Chinese Affairs also sent notices to the press via the Newspapers Association setting out topics that the press should not report on. For example, a notice kept by Ng Bar-ling shows that the government asked the press not to write stories that would "jeopardize loyalty to the British Empire", "affect British relations with China" or "promote communism".[31] Newspapers could be prosecuted under the Newspaper Regulations if they published any articles that had not been approved.[32] Despite the ending of Canton-Hong Kong Strike and Boycott in 1926, the Newspaper Regulations and the pre-censorship regime continued to operate until Hong Kong was occupied by Japan in December 1941.[33]

12.4 Policing for Allies

What kinds of news stories were banned from publication? What kinds of words warranted deletion by the censors? The colonial government was particularly sensitive not only to reports that criticised its governance of the colony, but also those jeopardising the British Empire's and its allies' geopolitical interests in East Asia, upsetting the power equation in the region or instigating political activism in the Chinese populace. For example, when Britain was collaborating with the nationalist government in China in suppressing the rise of communism in Asia, a left-wing newspaper known as *Siu Yat Po* (小日報) was suppressed in 1929 under the aforementioned regulations not long after it commenced publication. *Siu Yat Po*'s office was searched by the police and its scripts and documents seized.[34] The Press Censorship Office banned news story that might affect the interests of other European powers in China. Figure 12.4 shows the original manuscript of a news story written in 1931 that was banned by the Press Censorship Office. The story reported that representatives of trade unions in Hong Kong had joined the demonstration held in Guangzhou to protest against the USSR and in support of China during a railway dispute in 1929. The British Empire's anxieties

30 *SCMP*, June 15, 1928.

31 A translated letter (undated but likely that it was written in 1936 as it refers to the Legislative Council debate in 1936) from the Secretary for Chinese Affairs to the representatives of Newspaper Association, contained in Ng Bar Ling Collection (1904–1976).

32 *SCMP*, February 5, 1931.

33 Notes of recollection by Ng Bar-ling, Ng Bar Ling Collection (1904–1976).

34 For pro-communist background of *Siu Yat Po*, see Yang Guo-xiong, *Hong Kong Pre-war Newspaper Industry* (香港戰前報業) (Hong Kong: Joint Publishing, 2013), 210–225.

and priorities are clearly reflected in the following important censorship prosecution under the Newspaper Regulations.

In May 1928, a month in which military conflict between China and Japan killed thousands of Chinese civilians and soldiers in the city of Jinan in Shandong Province,[35] the publisher and printer of a local Chinese newspaper, *Shun Po* 晨報, were prosecuted for contravening one of the aforementioned Newspaper Regulations of 1925 by printing certain articles that had not first been sent to the Secretary for Chinese Affairs for approval and publishing an article that advocated the boycott of Japanese goods.[36]

The offending sentences were as follows:

> Warning to our Chinese … all of us who wish to maintain our nationality must refrain from using Japanese goods. If your enthusiasm is going to last for only five minutes, you might as well prepare to become slaves in a lost country…
>
> All our countrymen arise in a body and be active. The Japanese have challenged us and cruelly murdered our Chinese Officials and people. Be unanimous in severing economic relations with Japan.[37]

When sentencing *Shun Po* and its editors, the magistrate Lieutenant Colonel Eaves expressed explicitly what in his view what was more important than freedom of the press in colonial legality: "If the defendants had had the slightest idea of civic responsibility, they must have realised that in the then state of Chinese feeling, the publication of such matter might excite further feeling between the Chinese and Japanese in this Colony…"[38]

As a result, the partners and publisher of *Shun Po* were heavily fined and sentenced to imprisonment for one month. The sentence could be mitigated only if they publicly expressed regret and apologised to the colony's Japanese community in the newspaper, according to the following order of Magistrate Eaves to address his concern over the feelings of the Japanese community in Hong Kong:

> When a person wrongs others through the medium of the press, the least he can do to right the wrong is publicly to apologise through the same medium. I therefore add that if at the expiration of seven days, the

[35] For more information about Jinan incident, see Li Jia-zhen (李家振), *Jinan Tragedy* (濟南慘案) (Beijing: China University of Political Science and Law Press, 1987).

[36] For a detailed analysis of this and other censorship trials, see Michael Ng, *Political Censorship in British Hong Kong: Freedom of Expression and the Law (1842–1997)* (Cambridge: Cambridge University Press), Chapter 2.

[37] *SCMP*, June 21, 1928.

[38] *SCMP*, June 21, 1928.

> defendants have printed and published in the Hongkong Morning Post [*Shun Po*] for two consecutive daily issues an expression of regret and apology to the Japanese community in Hong Kong in the following terms, I shall be prepared to recommend to the proper authority remission of the remainder of the defendants' sentences of imprisonment.
>
> The terms of the apology are: "We . . . trading as the Chung Fat Company, Printers, and Leung Chan, Publisher, all of Hongkong, the Printers and Publisher respectively of the *Hongkong Morning Post*, having on the 9th and 10th May last unlawfully printed and published in the Chinese language in the said newspaper certain matter advocating a boycott of Japanese goods, calculated in this result to injure the Japanese community in Hongkong, and, having been sentenced therefor to fines and imprisonment, hereby express our regret and apologies to the Japanese Community in Hongkong and further counsel and advise the Chinese inhabitants of Hongkong loyally to live in peace and amity and to continue to trade as heretofore with all persons irrespective of their nationality."[39]

It was well known that the Western powers, Britain included, backed Japan's claim to Qingdao in Shandong Province under the terms of the Treaty of Versailles. Japan was also exerting increased pressure on the Western powers to acquiesce to its other territorial ambitions. Both Britain's alliance with Japan in the 1920s and its subsequent "neutrality" in the Sino-Japanese conflict in the late 1930s aggravated the Hong Kong government's use of emergency regulations to police and suppress the press in Hong Kong, where there was mass resentment of Japanese aggression in China. For example, in line with the British Empire's desire to maintain "neutrality" in the Sino-Japanese War prior to the Japanese invasion of Hong Kong,[40] words relating to Japan or the Japanese were very often struck out of news reports, as shown in Figure 12.3, which depicts a censored news report from 1939.

12.5 Cold War Policing of the Hong Kong Media (1950s–1970s)

After the end of the Second World War, the civil war in mainland China led to the coming to power of the CCP. The subsequent loss of China to communism, mass influx of Chinese refugees into Hong Kong, outbreak of the Korean War, global Cold War geopolitics and ongoing

[39] Ibid.

[40] For Britain's accommodative policies towards Japan's aggression in China, see Yoichi Kibata, "British Imperialism in Asia and Anglo-Japanese Relations, 1930s–1950s," in Shigeru Akita and Nicholas J. White (eds.), *The International Order of Asia in the 1930s and 1950s* (Farnham and Burlington, VT: Ashgate, 2010), 49–60.

ideological warfare between the KMT and CCP in Hong Kong through their respective newspapers and magazines, as well as the rise of new mass media forms such as live radio broadcasts, hugely increased the complexity of operating effective media censorship while maintaining a free flow of information for trading and business purposes. The colonial government could no longer rely on pre-emptive daily vetting of newspapers to contain undesirable content and comments. Accordingly, during the second half of the twentieth century, political censorship of the media was facilitated and supplemented by new legal powers and large-scale surveillance operations carried out through a collaborative network of local and international agencies, including the Special Branch of the Hong Kong Police, the London-led Regional Information Office, and the US Information Agency, to name just a few. In 1951, the power to suppress or suspend a newspaper originally exercisable by the governor under subsidiary regulations for emergency situations was elevated to the status of a power under primary legislation under the newly passed Control of Publications Consolidation Ordinance. According to the new law, which consolidated the power of press control granted under such old laws as the Emergency Regulations Ordinance, a perceived state of danger was no longer necessary for the government to suppress or suspend a newspaper. All that was necessary was that a news report be, among other things, considered to have published seditious content.[41] Intelligence collected by this global surveillance network allowed the colonial government to use the new law to nip trouble in the bud, and a number of "troublemakers" (including editors and publishers) were arrested, detained and even deported without trial without any due regard to whether such actions were lawful.[42]

The period from the 1950s to the 1960s also saw CCP cultural infiltration into various sectors of Hong Kong in an attempt to propagate radical anti-colonial ideas and communist ideologies. The CCP not only published, directly or indirectly, newspapers, books and magazines in Hong Kong, but also sponsored schools and film studios and staged theatrical performances. The colonial government responded by extending

[41] Control of Publications Consolidation Ordinance 1951, ss. 3 and 4.

[42] For the use of deportations in eliminating political dissents in colonial Hong Kong during the 1950s and 1960s, see Ng, *Political Censorship of British Hong Kong*, chapters 3 and 4; see also Christopher Munn, "Our Best Trump Card – a Brief History of Deportation in Hong Kong, 1857–1955," in Michael Ng and John D. Wong (eds.), *Civil Unrest and Governance in Hong Kong: Law and Order from Historical and Cultural Perspectives* (London: Routledge, 2017), 26–45.

its monitoring and censoring of such mass media as newspapers and radio to such private and semi-private media as novels, textbooks, films and cultural performances. Cinemas and theatres, for example, could be closed down if the government saw a need to do so. The following sections discuss this encroachment of the imperial collaborative silencing machine on the private lives of Hong Kong citizens.

12.6 Policing without Provoking: Political Censorship of Films and Live Performances

In addition to print media, visual entertainment such as films and live performances was also a target of political censorship by the colonial government. Cold War geopolitics and international relations drove the Hong Kong government's strategies, particularly its anti-communist propaganda policies, and criteria in censoring and banning sensitive films from screening in Hong Kong cinemas. Policing and political censorship of films in Hong Kong had been operating since the early twentieth century, and was formalised by the Film Censorship Regulations of 1953.[43]

Under the broad yet ambiguous power of the political censorship of films under the Film Censorship Regulations, a film could be banned (or have scenes excised) if, in the opinion of the censor appointed by the governor, it would provoke racial hatred, hatred or contempt of the Hong Kong government, damage the colony's good relations with other territories or encourage public disorder, in addition to such usual grounds for censorship as sex, violence and moral decency.[44] The public was unaware of how these principles were applied and interpreted until 1973, when censorship guidelines were published.[45] Yet declassified documents reveal how the government applied the principles in practice. It censored films to as far as possible prevent Hong Kong from becoming a site of cultural and ideological Cold War tensions in Asia. It banned or cut films

[43] For recently published works on the Cold War and film censorship in Hong Kong, see Poshek Fu, "More than Just Entertaining: Cinematic Containment and Asia's Cold War in Hong Kong, 1949–1959," *Modern Chinese Literature and Culture* 30(2) (2018): 1–55; Lee Shuk-man, *Screens of the Cold War: History of Film Censorship in Hong Kong under Geopolitics* (冷戰光影: 地緣政治下的香港電影審查史) (Taipei: Monsoon Zone Publishing, 2018); and Du Ying, "Censorship, Regulations, and the Cinematic Cold War in Hong Kong (1947–1971)," *China Review* 17(1) (2017): 117–151.

[44] *Film Censorship Standards: A Note of Guidance*, issued by Television and Films Division, Secretariat for Home Affairs of Hong Kong Government, May 1973, HKRS 313-7-3

[45] Lee, *Screens of the Cold* War, 197–198.

from the mainland that were "of anti-Nationalist significance" or "anti-foreign significance" or that "eulogised" Mao Ze-dong. The government also censored films from Taiwan that called Chinese communists bandits or made any reference to the "recovery of [the] Mainland".[46] Not only were films from mainland China and Taiwan censored, but so too were anti-communist films produced in the US.[47] This practice reflected Hong Kong's Cold War policy of combating the spread of communist propaganda in Asia according to the UK–US consensus while not provoking Beijing in order to safeguard Hong Kong's security. The following examples of censorship demonstrate the Cold War geopolitical considerations that underpinned film censors' decisions in the 1950s and 1960s.

In 1965, the censors banned the screening of a film called *Waves on the Southern Shores*, which revolves around a family of boat people living in Nan Wan, a fishing village in South China. In a flashback, a female character relates the bitter experience of an old man who was victimised by a villainous owner of farms and fishing boats named Kao, a protégé of KMT army officers, and tells the ill-fated story of a boat girl who was forced to serve as the chambermaid of Kao's daughter-in-law, who was from Hong Kong, as a means of liquidating her father's debt. While being pursued by armed officers of the local KMT government sent at Kao's request, the girl jumps into the sea. The film further portrays the cruelties of Japanese military officers and features the mistreatment and murder of women and children. It was banned in Hong Kong because the film censor considered it to be "ridiculing the KMT administration, glorifying the underground Communist elements … and showing Japanese atrocities during their military occupation". Censorship was also warranted because "Communists [were] referred to throughout the film as invulnerables [and] good shooters" who kept everyone "in awe".[48]

Censorship policies in Hong Kong during the post-war era reflect not only the British Empire's anxiety about the growing popularity of the CCP among the Chinese population in Hong Kong, but also geopolitical collaboration with powers friendly to Britain, including the US. In a letter

[46] Notes and Comments on "A Statement of the General Principles as Adopted on 20 November 1965 by the Film Censorship Board of Review," by William Hung, Chief Film Censor, December 1, 1970, HKRS 508-3-3.

[47] See censorship of US films in Du, "Censorship, Regulations, and the Cinematic Cold War in Hong Kong."

[48] 'Films: Waves on the Southern Shores', memo from R. S. Barry, Secretary to the Panel of Film Censors, to the Board of Review (Hon. S.C.A., Hon. D. of E, Commissioner of Police, S. of S.W.), March 6, 1965, in HKRS 394-26-14.

from an official of the Hong Kong government's Information Services Department sent to the South Film Corporation, a major Hong Kong-based film studio, concerning the panel of censors' decision about a documentary called *Peking Scientific Symposium*, he asked the film studio to "agree to the excision from the speeches and the commentaries of words and sentences about colonialism, imperialism and American imperialism as well as the excision of pictures, speeches and commentaries referring to the war in Vietnam". Otherwise, he warned, the film would be banned from exhibition.[49]

Archival evidence also shows that the US government exerted diplomatic pressure on London to tighten its censorship measures against any Hong Kong media thought to be sponsored or used by Chinese communists. A telegram from the British Foreign Office to the Colonial Office in 1958 reveals such pressure: "In [a] recent discussion in Washington on Anglo-American cooperation in information work abroad the Americans asked whether it would not be possible for the Hong Kong Government to take some action to impede the production in the Colony of Chinese Communist films, books [and] periodicals."[50]

In 1959, the Colonial Office in London conducted a study on the measures that could be taken in response to, among other things, the US request for enhanced media censorship in Hong Kong. As shown here, one suggestion in that study led to increased American involvement in the diplomatic and media battle with leftists in Hong Kong. A telegram from the Colonial Office to the Hong Kong government in the same year advised the government to consider "stimulating" the US government to subsidise counter-communist publishers in Hong Kong in a strategically delicate and skilful way:

> Our study of the memorandum suggests that it might be worthwhile to consider subsidizing, or providing long-term credits to, some of the struggling right-wing publishers in Hong Kong, who would thus be enabled to offer better terms to booksellers and compete more effectively with Communist publishers. As you probably know, however, Her Majesty's Government has little or no money to spend for such worthy purposes. It occurs to us that a possible solution might be to stimulate the United States Government into subsidizing publishers or arranging long-term

49 'Peking Scientific Symposium', letter from R. S. Barry of Information Services Department (ISD) and as the Secretary to the Panel of Film Censors to Southern Film Corporation, May 18, 1965, HKRS 394-26-14.

50 Telegram from P. G. F. Dalton, Foreign Office, to W. I. J. Wallace, Colonial Office, February 5, 1958, CO 1030/582;

> credits for them. I hasten to add that we do not forget what a delicate subject American activities in Hong Kong is, but we think it possible that such subsidizing could be done discreetly and be made such an unobtrusive form of aid that it would add little or nothing to the offensiveness in the Communist eyes of existing American activities in the Colony....[51]

Collaboration in policing films that were considered undesirable portrayals of British allies continued into the 1970s, as Table 12.1 shows a list of films that were banned for political reasons from the 1970s.

It was not only motion pictures that were policed and politically censored; the long arm of government censorship in colonial Hong Kong also extended to theatrical performances. Both the Hong Kong government and the Colonial Office in London closely monitored the frequency of visits by theatrical and musical performance troupes from communist China and subjected the content of their performances to censorship before they were permitted to enter Hong Kong. Moreover, under the Places of Public Entertainment Ordinance, the scripts of all plays and lyrics of all songs had to be sent to government authorities, including but not limited to the Secretariat for Chinese Affairs and Police Special Branch, for censorship before a public performance permit could be granted. As a result, politically undesirable titles were filtered out from the stage.[52] In a telegram sent to the Colonial Office in 1962, Hong Kong government officials summarised their monitoring of performance troupes from China since 1956. The various troupes mentioned, which performed in a variety of genres, came from provinces across China. They included the Chinese Folk Artists Group, Swatow Opera Group, Shanghai Shaoshing Opera Group, Shanghai Youth Opera Group, Shanghai Vocalist Troupe and Kwantung (North-Eastern China) Acrobatic Group. The Hong Kong government was of the view that it was not desirable to prevent "these Communist ventures in the entertainment field altogether". Yet "it is not in [the government's] interests that they should be too frequent and successful or that the Communists should secure a monopoly of popular culture". It also worried that "if such performances became too regular a feature in

[51] Telegram from K. G. Ashton to E. B. Teesdale, January 9, 1959, CO 1030/583.

[52] For the law under Places of Public Entertainment Ordinance (cap. 172) on theatrical censorship, see Johannes Chan, "Freedom of Expression: Censorship and Obscenity," in Raymond Wacks (ed.), *Civil Liberties in Hong Kong* (Hong Kong: Oxford University Press, 1988): 208–242, at 208–209; for archival evidence of censorship of theatrical performances in practice during the 1950s and 1960s, see Cheung Chui-yu, "Hong Kong Government's Strategies in Governing Theatres, 1945–1997" (香港政府治理戲劇的策略, 1945–1997) (MPhil dissertation, Chinese University of Hong Kong, 2013), chapter 2.

Table 12.1 *Films banned for political reasons from the 1970s and the reasons cited for the ban*

Title of films (origin of production and year of censorship)	Reasons for banning for "political overtone"
Battle of Algiers (Italy, 1970, 75)	The film depicts how the Algerian National Liberal Front struggled against the French for independence and "the ruthless French reprisals".
Savage Action and Strict Punishment (North Vietnam, 1975)	"It portrays [the] US and President Nixon in the worst possible light."
The Sand Pebbles (USA, 1967, 74, 75)	The film describes how students in China demanded the treaty powers to leave China and killed an American sailor who had tried to rescue American missionaries.
The Boxer Rebellion (Taiwan, 1975)	The film depicted how Chinese patriotic youths went to stop "ruthless treatment given by the allied troops, but were killed."
Great Victory of Highway 9 (North Vietnam, 1975)	The file shows "an American defeat" and "laid the blame of the Vietnamese war squarely onto the Americans".
The Fisher Boy (China, 1977)	This cartoon made in 1959 carried messages "that the Communist Party has successfully got rid of the foreign powers".

Source: Letter from J. Michie for Secretary for Administrative Services and Information of the Hong Kong Government to C. E. Leeks of FCO, 28 April, 1987, FCO 40/2338; letter from Governor Wilson to FCO, 30 January, 1989, 26 May, 1989, FCO 40/2823.

Hong Kong they might become a target for right-wing [KMT-backed] demonstrations". Therefore, the Hong Kong government set internal limits on the number of visits per year by such groups and requested that they follow "the various conditions laid down by the Commissioner of Police regarding the approval of scripts [and] avoidance of propaganda".[53]

Such a fine balancing act of controlling and censoring the cultural activities of leftist group without banning them entirely did not always satisfy Britain's Cold War partners, most notably the US, as shown by a telegram

[53] Telegram from E. G. Willan, Colonial Secretariat to J. D. Higham of Colonial Office, October 17, 1962, CO 1030/1108.

from the British Embassy in Washington to the Foreign Office in London in 1958. In the telegram, P.L. Carter of the British Embassy requested that the Foreign Office "consider the feelings of the Americans in putting their efforts against Communist opposition on the truly formidable scale". He suggested that the media activities of communists be further curtailed by manipulating such municipal regulations as those pertaining to sanitation and fire precautions if overt political suppression was undesirable from Hong Kong's point of view.[54] The balancing act also did not prevent Hong Kong from becoming a useful hub of political propaganda by the CCP, KMT and the US, as well as an important market for the trading of political intelligence among the Cold War powers.[55] Behaving largely within the confines of political censorship, left-wing trade and labour unions, media groups and schools continued to grow in scale and membership in the 1960s despite the authoritarian policing regime, and their potential influence on the masses was painfully felt by the colonial government in a violent showdown in the 1967 riots.[56]

12.7 Empires Collaborate in Policing Hong Kong

The archival study in this chapter makes it clear that colonial Hong Kong was policed not only for the purpose of maintaining authoritarian law and order within its borders. Colonial policing in Hong Kong also played an important function for Britain and its allies in global politics at the Eastern frontier. The way in which the mass media in colonial Hong Kong were censored and closely monitored reveals an unappreciated fact about the strategic collaboration among world powers to assert and safeguard their regional authority: such collaboration defined, confined and policed the freedoms of the Hong Kong people.

The legal history of colonial Hong Kong told in this chapter points to at least two directions for future research in the history of authoritarian

[54] Top Secret telegram from P. L. Carter of British Embassy in Washington to Donald Hopson of Foreign Office, May 27, 1958, CO 1030/583.

[55] Colonial government did monitor the "activities of intelligence peddlers in Hong Kong" who, for example, sold intelligence regarding CCP to the US; see CO 968/226 for details of these activities. See also Lu Xun, "The American Cold War in Hong Kong, 1949–1960," in Priscilla Roberts and John Carroll (eds.), *Hong Kong in the Cold War* (Hong Kong: HKU Press, 2017), 117–140.

[56] For the 1967 riots and involvement of CCP's dominated organizations in Hong Kong in them, see Gary Cheung, *Hong Kong's Watershed: The 1967 Riots* (Hong Kong: Hong Kong University Press, 2009).

policing that may have been overlooked in previous scholarship. First, authoritarian policing should not be seen as a tool of controlling the society *only* of non-democratic or dictatorial regimes. Leading democracies such as Britain and the US did participate in authoritarian policing of Hong Kong to protect their political and economic interests in East Asia and China, as this chapter reveals. The history of authoritarian policing in colonial Hong Kong also casts doubts on explaining authoritarian policing in East Asia by culturally essentialising Asian values of order and harmony. Echoing Kroncke,[57] this chapter shows that much archival work still needs to be done in understanding exactly what kind of factors drove and constrained authoritarian policing in global history, without adhering to "a reflexive assumption that democratic regimes would have more accountable and less violent policing practices than those in authoritarian regimes". Secondly, while many accounts of authoritarian policing in East Asia are told in the contexts of domestic politics, how such policing responded to the bigger picture of global politics remain largely under-studied. Hong Kong's story continues the long history of the global power struggle among various sovereign powers to protect their geopolitical interests in China and East Asia as a whole from the mid-nineteenth century onwards against the contexts of changing relations between China and the world, as well as the world powers' changing China strategies. That history still has bearing on the global politics of today, as China rises to take its place among those competing world powers and recycles some of the colonial policing measures for Hong Kong to meet China's perceived challenges in geopolitical and geo-economic rivalries.

[57] Kroncke, Chapter 2 in this volume.

13

The End of Soft-Style Protest Policing in a Hybrid Regime

Evidence from Hong Kong[1]

PENG WANG, PAUL JOOSSE, AND LOK LEE CHO

13.1 Introduction

Social movements that conduct highly visible protest actions can pose significant challenges to holders of state power, enabling otherwise powerless people to register complaints about state legitimacy.[2] In such contexts, police often find themselves in the unenviable position of having to weigh one set of societal goods (relating to the importance of political expression) against another (relating to the maintenance of public order).[3] As such, police actions in protest situations are seldom inert: law enforcement responses to protest events can either reduce political tensions or, as it may be, exacerbate societal conflicts.[4] Furthermore, because they are emblematic of law, policy, and the political establishment, police themselves can become targets of social movement actions and, in a spiral of action and reaction, contribute to political processes that either bolster or erode governmental legitimacy.[5]

[1] This chapter is an updated version of P. Wang, P. Joosse, and L. L. Cho (2020), "The Evolution of Protest Policing in a Hybrid Regime," *The British Journal of Criminology* 60(6): 1523–1546. Permission has been granted by Oxford University Press.

[2] Charles Tilly, *From Mobilization to Revolution* (Reading, MA: Addison-Wesley, 1978); Donatella Della Porta and Olivier Fillieule, "Policing Social Protest," in David A. Snow, Sarah A. Soule, and Hanspeter Kriesi (eds.), *The Blackwell Companion to Social Movements* (Malden, MA: Blackwell Publishing, 2004), 217–241.

[3] Benjamin Bowling, Robert Reiner, and James Sheptycki, *The Politics of the Police* (New York: Oxford University Press, 2019); Robert Reiner, *The Politics of the Police* (Oxford: Oxford University Press, 2010).

[4] Robin Lipp, "Protest Policing in New York City: Balancing Safety and Expression," *Harvard Law and Policy Review* 9 (2015): 275–306.

[5] Dennis Lai Hang Hui and Ryan Chi Yan Au, "Police Legitimacy and Protest Policing: A Case Study of Hong Kong," *Asian Education and Development Studies* 3 (2014): 223–234; Tom R. Tyler, "Trust and Legitimacy: Policing in the USA and Europe," *European Journal of Criminology* 8 (2011): 254–266.

In extreme cases, the sway of police allegiance – from the establishment to the anti-establishment side – can determine the survival of political regimes.

The policing of social protest has garnered a great deal of academic attention in democratic contexts. For example, using case studies of protest policing in the United Kingdom (UK) and on the European continent, della Porta and colleagues have produced a number of classifications relating to protest policing styles, from "tough" styles that rely on an escalated force model, to "soft" styles that involve the negotiated management of protests.[6] Smith[7] has discussed the strategy of "negotiated accommodation" as a model for policing civil disobedience campaigns in liberal democracies. Gillham et al.[8] analyzed the practice of "strategic incapacitation" in public order events in the United States during the post-9/11 era. In all of this work, the metric of differentiation among tactics – from negotiation to coercion – relates to the degree to which citizens, as political subjects, are to be engaged as rightful or legitimate participants in the sociopolitical process. The give-and-take nature of protest policing is thus a moment when the social contract – so foundational to Western political theory – reveals itself to be living; subject to adjustment and reformulation in accordance with expressions of public will.

While these previous studies have contributed valuable insights about the role of police in protest situations, little work has been done to examine policing dynamics in political contexts where social contact theory is less foundational to the political culture. We suggest that "hybrid regimes" – with Hong Kong serving as our exemplary case – offer a particularly interesting opportunity for examining the sociopolitical agency of police, precisely because they operate outside the usual political framework. Hybrid regimes are neither fully democratic nor fully authoritarian, with people living under them enjoying only limited political rights and civil liberties.[9] There is some reason to think that hybrid regimes are inherently unstable, and one scholar has noted that Hong Kong's erstwhile stability

6 Donatella Della Porta and Herbert Reiter, *Policing Protest* (Minneapolis, MN: University of Minnesota Press, 1998); Donatella Della Porta, *Social Movements, Political Violence, and the State* (Cambridge: Cambridge University Press, 1995); Della Porta and Fillieule, "Policing Social Protest."

7 William Smith, "Policing Civil Disobedience," *Political Studies* 60 (2012): 826–842, at 826.

8 Patrick F. Gillham, Bob Edwards, and John A. Noakes, "Strategic Incapacitation and the Policing of Occupy Wall Street Protests in New York City, 2011," *Policing and Society* 23 (2013): 81–102.

9 Mikael Wigell, "Mapping 'Hybrid Regimes': Regime Types and Concepts in Comparative Politics," *Democratization* 15 (2008): 230–250; Leah Gilbert and Payam Mohseni, "Beyond Authoritarianism: The Conceptualization of Hybrid Regimes," *Studies in Comparative International Development* 46 (2011): 270–297.

has been somewhat of a curiosity, since "[t]he coexistence of democratic and authoritarian elements within a single political regime would usually be an inherent source of political conflict."[10]

Recently, Hong Kong has indeed been beset by episodes of turbulence that are increasing in severity and frequency. The Occupy movement (2014), the Mong Kok riot (2016), and the Anti-ELAB (Extradition Law Amendment Bill) protests (ongoing from 2019) all evidence a situation where political actors, lacking regular channels of influence, are moving toward innovated, non-sanctioned, and increasingly illegal political tactics. In order to increase our understanding of protest policing in hybrid regimes, this chapter examines the evolving structure of protest policing in Hong Kong, specifically tracking the change of police strategies in handling social protest since the UK's return of Hong Kong to Chinese sovereignty in 1997.

As a Chinese territory that is meant to retain considerable political and cultural autonomy under the principle of "One Country, Two Systems," Hong Kong bears features that will be at least superficially recognizable to observers of modern liberal democracies. It has a representative legislative body called the Legislative Council ("LegCo"), but only limited suffrage: 50 percent of the seats are elected by popular vote from geographical ridings, and 50 percent are filled by "functional constituencies" – professional or industrial sectors that are generally pro-establishment in their orientation. The chief executive of Hong Kong is elected by a 1,200-member panel (also heavily pro-establishment) from a Beijing-approved list of candidates. Since the handover from the UK, Hong Kong has witnessed a growing number of protests concerning economic inequality, cultural autonomy, and political enfranchisement[11]. Recent high-profile protest events have been motivated by the desire to increase democratic participation, including large-scale protests held on July 1 (the anniversary of the handover) every year since 2003, the Occupy Central movement of 2014, and most recently the ongoing antiextradition bill protests.

Over this period, the Hong Kong Police Force (HKPF) has undergone a change in its style of protest policing, moving from rather tolerant, soft, or flexible approaches to more repressive, hard, and proactive methods. This chapter accounts for the change by arguing that several factors, from

10 Brian C. H. Fong, "State–Society Conflicts under Hong Kong's Hybrid Regime: Governing Coalition Building and Civil Society Challenges," *Asian Survey* 53 (2013): 854–882, at 856.

11 Stephan Ortmann, "The Lack of Sovereignty, the Umbrella Movement, and Democratisation in Hong Kong," *Asia Pacific Law Review* 24 (2016): 108–122.

macrostructural to microinteractional levels, have combined to place the HKPF in a particularly fraught position vis-à-vis the protests in Hong Kong. Thus, while the "negotiation spectrum" in the aforementioned literature offers an array of options for police departments and policymakers who operate in modern liberal democracies, the political reality of hybridity in Hong Kong inverts the spectrum from one of various *possibilities* (involving hard and soft approaches that are available for selection) to one of various *impossibilities*, where any action – hard or soft – can be credibly judged to be either overpolicing or underpolicing, depending on one's political stance. In such situations, police are beset by a vocational paradox: while they are increasingly being called upon to shoulder responsibility for dealing with political unrest, they are at the same time increasingly unable to be effective actors in social-protest environments. The macrostructural setting for such dynamics is easy to discern and describe. What is needed – and what we provide presently – is data on the microinteractional realities of policing in hybrid contexts. Using interview and observational data, this chapter delivers a granular depiction of the fraught state of protest policing in hybrid regimes.

13.2 Theorizing Protest Policing Beyond "Policecentric" Approaches

Past research on protest policing develops a "policecentric" perspective that emphasizes the importance of police knowledge – that is, police perceptions and understandings of their own role in a context shaped by various political opportunities and movement characteristics. Such a perspective characterizes police as knowledgeable agents who act strategically, deciding which model of protest policing to apply.[12] For example, when styling themselves as the "King's police" – agents tasked with upholding the political establishment – police will tend to regard demonstrators as trouble makers and as such employ an escalated-force style that features dramatic shows of force, exhibits a disregard for constitutional rights, involves minimal communication with demonstrators, and employs mass arrests as a strategy.[13] When viewing themselves as "citizen police," or as service providers whose legitimation comes from below, police will act in ways that are more accountable to communities and less accountable to political authorities, regarding demonstrators as rational claims-makers and preferring to deploy

[12] Della Porta and Reiter, *Policing Protest.*
[13] Della Porta and Fillieule, "Policing Social Protest."

a negotiated-management model of protest policing characterized by a reliance on dialogue. As such, police will see themselves as *facilitators* of peaceful protest.[14] Thus, changes in self-understandings among police can lead to changes in policing styles.

The policing philosophy approach, as developed by Winter[15] and Smith[16], offers a different yet complementary explanation for differences in policing styles. According to Smith[17], underlying principles of police operations and the normative self-conceptions of police who inhabit their role serve as "important variables in shaping the attitudes and actions of police officers" during protest events. In most existing research contexts then, policing philosophies will tend to be reflective of a wider democratic legitimating structure, such that police will view themselves as being facilitative of the peaceful dimensions of protest, adopting a strategy of negotiated accommodation that at times even cooperates with civilly disobedient activities, assisting in the "commission of a protest that is effective as an expression of their grievance against law or policy."[18]

While these policecentric explanations of policing styles have enjoyed considerable uptake as a framework for analyzing the policing of protest all over the world, there are limitations to their value when studying protest policing in authoritarian and hybrid regimes. One reason for this is practical: because understanding police knowledge and its professional culture usually requires in-depth interviews with senior and frontline officers, these data are often inaccessible in nondemocratic contexts. The perspective also assumes a modicum of independence on the part of police departments from political influence – something that frequently does not obtain in nondemocratic contexts. Across all polities, however, we argue that the policecentric perspective tends to overemphasize the importance of police perceptions while minimizing the social-interactional context in ways that produce one-sided explanatory frameworks.

Viewing policing-styles as a form of culture that is constituted by historical, political, and interactional factors, this chapter develops an alternative, "mixed embeddedness," perspective as a means of accounting for the evolution of protest policing in Hong Kong. The idea of

[14] Donatella Della Porta, A. Peterson, and Herbert Reiter, *The Policing of Transnational Protest* (Aldershot: Ashgate, 2006).

[15] Martin Winter, "Police Philosophy and Protest Policing in the Federal Republic of Germany, 1960–1990," in Porta and Reiter (eds.), *Policing Protest*, 188–212.

[16] William Smith, "Policing Civil Disobedience," *Political Studies* 60 (2012): 826–842.

[17] Smith, "Policing Civil Disobedience," 827.

[18] Smith, "Policing Civil Disobedience," 828.

embeddedness stems from Mark Granovetter's[19] seminal work, originally within economic sociology, which has gone on to find relevance across the social sciences. In contrast to atomized-actor explanations for economic activity (among which we can count the aforementioned policecentric approaches), Granovetter argues that individuals' choices for action are embedded in matrices of social relations that create expectational frameworks that condition the possibility for choice itself, constraining and allowing particular ranges of actions.[20] Rather than conceiving of police as atomized actors who use their powers of observation and analysis to develop optimal strategies vis-à-vis protests, then, the mixed embeddedness approach conceives of policing styles as being refracted through history, politics, community relations, and microlevel interactions with demonstrators in the protest context. To reflect this conception of mixed embeddedness, we differentiate our analysis across macro- meso-, and microscales.

13.3 Methods and Data

Collectively, this research consists of 52 in-depth semistructured interviews, observations of police-protester interactions, and an analysis of news reports and relevant literature in both English and Chinese. All interviews and observations occurred between 2016–2019. The authors' interests in the evolution of social movements and police's changing strategies in handling social protest began in the wake of the 2014 pro-democracy Occupy Central movement. The first and the second authors are university professors based in Hong Kong; they teach both undergraduate students (many of whom are themselves activists) and postgraduate students in a criminology program – many of whom are officials from local disciplinary forces. The third author is a current postgraduate research student who was born and raised in Hong Kong. The social contacts possessed by the authors have thus provided many opportunities to conduct interviews with both protestors and enforcement officers, and enabled them to gain a deep understanding of protest policing in Hong Kong.

The first author conducted six interviews immediately after the occurrence of what came to be known as the Mong Kok Riot or Fishball Revolution in 2016. Occurring during Chinese New Year celebrations,

[19] Mark Granovetter, "Economic Action and Social Structure: The Problem of Embeddedness," *The American Journal of Sociology* 91 (1985): 481–510.

[20] Granovetter, "Economic Action and Social Structure," 481.

police attempts to clear unlicensed street vendors (who are regarded as symbols of localist/nationalist identity in Hong Kong) led to violent clashes between police and protestors, resulting in injuries to roughly 200 police officers.[21] Interviews were conducted with a retired chief superintendent, a senior inspector, a frontline police officer, a researcher, and a university student. These data provided key insights related to social unrest in the new, "Post-Umbrella" phase of Hong Kong politics, and were also illuminating with respect to why the police were seemingly unprepared for handling these new developments. During the 2019 antiextradition movement, the first and third authors conducted seven interviews with police officers and officials from other disciplinary forces in Hong Kong and one interview with a protestor. The data gained in this round were especially useful for understanding recent causes for the police's change in strategy – from a 'soft' style to a 'harder' one – and the major challenges associated with such a change. The second author started his project on Hong Kong's social movement in 2017, collecting 38 interviews among people aged 16–30, all of whom have participated in social movements in Hong Kong. These varied from protesters who advocated civil disobedience and illegal tactics to those who have participated only in peaceful marches and organizing. The interviewees were questioned about their personal history of political involvement, their views on movement leadership, and on their views about the future of Hong Kong as it moves toward 2047 (when Hong Kong's formal autonomy from mainland China ends). The combination of these two sources of data – one policecentric and the other demonstratorcentric – enabled the authors to develop a comprehensive view of protest policing in Hong Kong.

13.4 Historical Backdrop: From Colonial Repression to "Soft" Protest Policing

The HKPF's styles and strategies for protest policing have transformed along with different phases of governance over the course of Hong Kong's history. From the formation of the HKPF in 1841 and until the early 1970s, the HKPF served the colonial government as a classic paramilitary police force modeled on "the recognition of a hostile (usually indigenous) population ruled (usually by an alien colonial power) primarily by coercion with the threat

[21] Kam-Cheung Wong, *Public Order Policing in Hong Kong: The Mongkok Riot* (Cham: Palgrave Macmillan, 2019).

of armed force."[22] Maintaining public order – especially by policing riots and protests – was accorded a higher priority over other functions (such as fighting crime and providing community services).[23] In order to effectively suppress political activity that would threaten colonial rule, the police developed an escalated force model that featured a reactive implementation of law and the use of force to disperse protest activity (whether violent or nonviolent), while exhibiting a low reliance on communication and bargaining. As Tsang[24] argued, the Hong Kong police were able to maintain stability "either by pre-empting major disturbances, politically inspired or not, or by containing and suppressing them efficiently once they started."

The police force was able to meet new demands and deal with emerging challenges through frequent reorganization initiatives and with improvements in equipment and general training. For example, after the Guangdong-Hong Kong strike of 1925–1926, organized by the Communist Party of China to challenge colonial rule, the HKPF established an Emergency Unit that enhanced its ability to tackle civil disturbances. They also formed the Anti-Communist Squad (renamed the Special Branch in 1938), tasking it with gathering political intelligence and monitoring left-wing political agitators.[25] As a response to the Double Tenth Riots of October 1956 (politically motivated riots involving fights between procommunist and pro-Chinese Nationalist factions that caused 60 deaths and 500 injuries), the HKPF established the Police Training Contingent to offer training on internal security and antiriot measures, ensuring the police force's readiness to respond to emerging threats to internal security and public order.[26] The Police Training Contingent became the Police Tactical Unit in the late 1960s.

In 1967, the HKPF earned significant trust from the British government after it quelled a procommunist uprising that began as a labor dispute and developed into a massive general strike and violent demonstrations.[27] The force's firm suppression of local communists and its efforts to restore

[22] Wayne W. L. Chan and Raymond W. K. Lau, "The Police Force," in Eric Wing Hong Chui and T. Wing Lo (eds.), Understanding Criminal Justice in Hong Kong (London: Routledge, 2016), 155–174, at 138.

[23] Charles Jeffries, *The Colonial Police* (London: Max Parrish, 1952).

[24] Steve Tsang, *Government and Politics* (Hong Kong: Hong Kong University Press, 1995), 174.

[25] Hua Ling Fu and Richard Cullen, "Political Policing in Hong Kong," *Hong Kong Law Journal* 33 (2003): 199–230.

[26] Chan and Lau, "The Police Force."

[27] Gary Ka-wai Cheung, *Hong Kong's Watershed: The 1967 Riots* (Hong Kong: Hong Kong University Press, 2010); Ray Yep, "The 1967 Riots in Hong Kong: The Diplomatic and Domestic Fronts of the Colonial Governor," *The China Quarterly* 193 (2008): 122–139.

social order also led to increased recognition and support from the public, especially as a bombing campaign emerged to spread terror in the colony.

The 1967 riots ultimately proved to be a turning point for the HKPF and for Hong Kong as a whole. Prompted by the unrest, the force established the Police Public Information Bureau (later renamed the Police Public Relations Bureau), to improve police–public relations.[28] The colonial authority also decided to modify its governance style, concentrating on social welfare issues and poverty reduction as a means of addressing grievances that posed a threat to social stability. As a means of improving the colonial regime's legitimacy, they also sought to reform the HKPF, which was, according to recent historical work, marked by deep corruption and abuses of power up until the early 1970s.[29] With the establishment of the Independent Commission Against Corruption in 1974, the colonial government sought to curb corruption among officials, especially in the police force, and end police collusion with local organized crime groups – measures that ultimately significantly increased the force's performance in crime fighting and law enforcement.[30] By the mid-1980s, the HKPF had completed its reorientation and transformation, from a colonial paramilitary force that was primarily focused on maintaining public order and internal security, to a modernized police service that was professional and largely free of corruption.[31]

Public service reforms initiated by Chris Patten, the last colonial governor, aimed to promote a "customer service" model for government providers – viewing users of public services as customers whose satisfaction is a key legitimating value.[32] Following Patten's lead, the HKPF established its Service Quality Wing in 1994 and launched the Force Strategy on Quality of Service in order to develop a "customer-focused culture" within the Force.[33] Consequently, the force developed a softer strategy of protest policing (i.e. the negotiated management model), employing negotiation strategies and stressing communication efforts as a means

[28] Hong Kong Police College, *Policing in Hong Kong at the Turn of the Century* (Policy Report, 2007).

[29] Tit Wing Lo, *Corruption and Politics in Hong Kong and China* (Buckingham and Philadelphia, PA: Open University Press, 1993); Sharon Ingrid Kwok and T. Wing Lo, "Anti-Triad Legislations in Hong Kong: Issues, Problems and Development," *Trends in Organized Crime* 16(1) (2012): 74–94.

[30] Lo, *Corruption and Politics in Hong Kong and China*; Ian Scott, "Institutional Design and Corruption Prevention in Hong Kong," *Journal of Contemporary China* 22 (2013): 77–92.

[31] Charles Jeffries, *The Colonial Police*; Chan and Lau, "The Police Force."

[32] Gary Ka-wai Cheung, *Hong Kong's Watershed: The 1967 Riots*.

[33] K. O. Hui, *A Service of Quality* (Hong Kong: Government Printer, 1995).

of cooperatively facilitating demonstrations in ways that minimized the potential for disruption to public order. Amid this strategy, the importance of constitutional rights and freedoms was stressed, and the use of coercive methods was restricted to a last resort.

Since the return of Hong Kong to Chinese sovereignty in 1997, the HKPF has had to handle more frequent, large-scale, and increasingly decentralized social protests that have shown an ability to develop innovative confrontation strategies, blocking roads and occupying public spaces.[34] The number of public order events increased from 247 in 1986, to 1,190 in 1997, and to 11,880 in 2018.[35]

Prior to the 2010s, the HKPF was for the most part able to maintain the noncoercive customer service model established during Patten's governorship. The HKPF policed political assemblies peacefully with "only pepper spray [being] occasionally used in local issue-related protest."[36] Public order events had generally taken place peacefully, amid mutual understanding, communication, and negotiations between police and protestors. As Lo[37] observed, frontline police officers were required to "exercise the use of force cautiously and to adopt the principle of 'not using force but trying to use your mind.'" This was especially the case prior to the Occupy Central Movement in 2014, when a large-scale civil disobedience/sit-in campaign shut down large commercial and administrative sections of Hong Kong for 79 days.

The negotiated management model (soft strategies) for protest policing has proven increasingly ineffective in the latter half of the 2010s, however. It was significantly challenged by protesters during the 2010 movement against the construction of a high-speed rail line that would link Hong Kong with mainland China while displacing residents of the Hong Kong village of Choi Yuen Tsuen.[38] During the Occupy Central Movement in 2014, demonstrators' growing distrust with the government had significantly changed their perception of the police who were seen as "a political tool" employed by the unpopular government to repress prodemocracy

[34] Lawrence K. K. Ho, "Policing Public Order Events in Hong Kong SAR," (2013), www.the-aaps.org/wp-content/uploads/2015/05/14.Ho-Wong_Public-Order-Policing-HK.pdf.

[35] Social Indicators of Hong Kong, "No. of Public Order Events: Social Indicators of Hong Kong," *No. of public order events | Social Indicators of Hong Kong* (2019), www.socialindicators.org.hk/en/indicators/political_participation/2.5.

[36] Ho, "Policing public order events in Hong Kong SAR," 12.

[37] Sonny Shiu-Hing Lo, *The Politics of Policing in Greater China* (New York: Palgrave Macmillan, 2016), 124.

[38] Ho, "Policing public order events in Hong Kong SAR".

activists.[39] As a result, protestors adopted aggressive actions (e.g. poking officers with umbrellas), and in response, police used arrests (over 900) and tear gas to disperse the protestors. Given that the large and lengthy occupation ultimately ended without any deaths, one could argue that police actions, which combined soft- and hardline tactics, were successful.[40] But as an exercise within civil society it was a failure: the movement ultimately ended in political frustration, without any resolution of grievances or concessions from the government.[41]

The 2016 Mong Kok riot, which led to the injury of roughly 200 police officers, was another transformative moment in police–protester relations. At issue was the government's crackdown on unlicensed foodstall hawkers who were selling traditional street food such as fish balls – a strong symbol of local identity. Deep distrust among young protestors toward the police meant that police officers were unable to strike a deal with protesters of the crackdown, and some localists decided to resort to violence against law enforcers.[42] Police commanders ordered frontline officers to confine their repressive measure to the use of pepper spray, which was far from sufficient to protect police officers from the attacks with bricks and other improvised weapons. According to interviews, tear gas was not employed to disperse the crowd because the use of tear gas on demonstrators during the 2014 Occupy Movement caused a public outcry.[43] While the prodemocracy sector of the public criticized an officer for firing his gun in the air to ward off attacks, these events also generated demands within the force and within proestablishment sectors of society for the adoption of "harder" policing styles.

Since these events, a comparatively harder strategy, relying on more coercive means or a combination of coercion and negotiation, has been implemented.[44] For example, during the 2019 antiextradition protests tear gas, pepper spray, rubber bullets, bean-bag rounds, and water cannons – all seldom used previously – have become commonplace on the

39 Interview 39 (senior police inspector), February 2016.

40 Lo, *The Politics of Policing in Greater China.*

41 Ching Kwan Lee and Ming Sing, *Take Back Our Future: An Eventful Sociology of the Hong Kong Umbrella Movement* (Ithaca, NY, and London: Cornell University Press, 2019); Laikwan Pang, *The Appearing Demos: Hong Kong during and after the Umbrella Movement* (Ann Arbor, MI: University of Michigan Press, 2020).

42 Wong, *Public Order Policing in Hong Kong.*

43 Interview 40 (retired senior police officer), February 2016; interview 41 (frontline police officer), March 2016.

44 Interview 46 (senior police constable), December 2019; interview 47 (senior police inspector), December 2019.

streets of Hong Kong. On December 24, 2019, the *Washington Post* published a report showing that 16,000 rounds of tear gas had been used by police since June 12, 2019.[45] By contrast, only 87 rounds were used during the entirety of the 79-day Occupy Movement in 2014.[46]

13.5 Macrolevel: A Legitimacy Crisis in Postcolonial Hong Kong

A century ago, Weber[47] outlined processes through which legitimacy can be won or lost, and showed how authority can be underwritten according to different logics of domination (*Herrschaft*). Sources of state legitimacy can be classified by "the ways in which state power can be justified: by a commonly accepted leader selection procedure; by services that a state provides; and by a promise to bring a better future."[48] Among these methods, democratic regimes are legitimized most often by way of "inputs" from the body politic into political processes. These can involve durable procedures of public election, multiparty competition, and a general state of political liberty. Authoritarian regimes, by contrast, can be said to gain legitimacy ultimately by way of governmental "outputs" involving credibly delivered measures of economic development, the provision of public services, and contributions to projects that increase national pride and impart a sense of grandeur on the international stage.[49] Hybrid regimes such as Hong Kong can thus face significant challenges reconciling these output and input principles amid the conflictual coexistence of democratic and authoritarian modes of legitimation[50].

45 Shibani Mahtani, Timothy McLaughlin, Tiffany Liang and Ryan Ho Kilpatrick, "In Hong Kong Crackdown, Police Repeatedly Broke Their Own Rules – and Faced No Consequences," *The Washington Post* (December 24, 2019), www.washingtonpost.com/graphics/2019/world/hong-kong-protests-excessive-force/.

46 Rikkie Yeung, "Democracy for Hong Kong: The Modest Demands of the Umbrella Protesters," *Brookings* (November 10, 2014), www.brookings.edu/opinions/democracy-for-hong-kong-the-modest-demands-of-the-umbrella-protesters/.

47 Max Weber, "The Nature of Social Action," in W. G. Runciman and E. Mathews (eds.), *Max Weber* (Cambridge: Cambridge University Press, 1978), 7–32.

48 Hongxing Yang and Dingxin Zhao, "Performance Legitimacy, State Autonomy and China's Economic Miracle," *Journal of Contemporary China* 24 (2014): 64–82, at 70.

49 Martin Minogue, "Power to the People?" in Uma Kothari and Martin Minogue (eds.), *Development Theory and Practice: Critical Perspectives* (Basingstoke: Palgrave Macmillan, 2002), 117–135; Yuchao Zhu, "'Performance Legitimacy' and China's Political Adaptation Strategy," *Journal of Chinese Political Science* 16 (2011): 123–140.

50 Steven Levitsky and Lucan A. Way, *Competitive Authoritarianism: Hybrid Regimes after the Cold War* (Cambridge: Cambridge University Press, 2013); Honorata Mazepus, Wouter Veenendaal, Anthea McCarthy-Jones, and Juan Manuel Trak Vásquez, "A Comparative Study of Legitimation Strategies in Hybrid Regimes," *Policy Studies* 37(4) (2016): 350–369.

Legitimacy crises have been a significant challenge for the postcolonial Hong Kong government. On the performance legitimacy/output side, worsening income inequality and a shortage of affordable housing have meant that an increasing share of Hong Kong's population is finding it extremely difficult to maintain financial security. Hong Kong's latest Gini coefficient rating (2016) was 0.539, the highest rating recorded in over four decades, making it the ninth most unequal country in the world:[51] 20.4 percent of the city's population is living below the poverty line.[52] Moreover, Hong Kong has become far and away the world's least affordable housing market, a position it has held for nine years straight. On average, it would take 21 years of salary (spending on nothing else) to buy a home in the city, compared with 12.6 years in Vancouver, the city that ranks second globally.[53] Despite the fact that the government provides heavily subsidized public housing to lower-income families, access is very limited, with the average waiting time for public rental housing being more than five years in 2018.[54]

A widely held view among the general public is that the lower and middle classes are increasingly being cut out of Hong Kong's economic opportunities amid collusion between government and business, especially between real estate developers and senior public officials.[55] This governing coalition with the capitalist class, while beneficial for some in the short run, has over the longer term had a decentering effect within Hong Kong's political economy.[56] As such, the Hong Kong Special Administrative Region's evident decreasing capacity for governance points to an emergent

[51] Michelle Wong, "Why the Wealth Gap?" *South China Morning Post* (September 27, 2018), www.scmp.com/news/hong-kong/society/article/2165872/why-wealth-gap-hong-kongs-disparity-between-rich-and-poor.

[52] 'Poverty Situation,' Census and Statistics Department, The Government of the Hong Kong Special Administrative Region, 2019.

[53] Pearl Liu, "Want to Buy a Home in Hong Kong? This Is How Long You'll Have to Save," *South China Morning Post* (January 21, 2019), www.scmp.com/business/article/2182980/nothing-be-proud-hong-kong-tops-table-worlds-most-expensive-housing-market.

[54] Naomi Ng and Su Xinqi, "Wait Time for a Hong Kong Public Housing Flat Longest in 18 Years," *South China Morning Post* (August 10, 2018) www.scmp.com/news/hong-kong/community/article/2159237/waiting-time-hong-kong-public-housing-flat-longest-18-years.

[55] Stan Hok-Wui Wong, "Political Connections and Firm Performance," *Journal of East Asian Studies* 10 (2010): 275–314; Stan Hok-Wui Wong, "Real Estate Elite, Economic Development, and Political Conflicts in Postcolonial Hong Kong," *The China Review 15* (2015): 1–38.

[56] Tai-lok Liu and Stephen W. K. Chiu, "Governance Crisis in Post-1997 Hong Kong," *China Review* 7 (2007): 1–34.

structural weakness that cannot simply be explained as a function either of civil society's increased political demands or as a result of specific leadership failures[57], but rather as a result of 'the growing disconnection of the business sector from the local community'[58].

On the input side, the Hong Kong government's legitimacy has been weakened owing to its unwillingness to implement universal suffrage in the election of the chief executive – something that was enshrined in the Sino-British Joint Declaration,[59] and Article 45 of the Basic Law,[60] as an ultimate goal for Hong Kong's political reform. In 2003,[61] a social movement developed with the aim of speeding up the introduction of universal suffrage, and in 2007 the central government in Beijing finally promised to introduce it by 2017. But this promise was not realized owing to several details of the electoral model proposed by the Chinese government in 2014, which were regarded by pandemocratic politicians as subverting the spirit of democratic reform.[62] After the rejection of this initial proposal by the LegCo in 2015, there have been no new developments, and the suffrage movement seems to have been permanently stymied. The result has been a growing social divide and increasing public anger.

A loss of political legitimacy, along both its input and output modalities, has thus largely deprived Hong Kong authorities of their ability to govern in ways that rely on generalized, consensual support for law. The Hong Kong people – especially prodemocracy protestors – have become increasingly uncompliant with the government and its police force, something that indicates that, against the backdrop aforementioned macro-structural factors, legitimacy is often both realized and contested at the

[57] Liu and Chiu, "Governance Crisis in Post-1997 Hong Kong."

[58] Fong, "State–Society Conflicts under Hong Kong's Hybrid Regime," 867.

[59] The Sino-British Joint Declaration (the 1984 treaty) is an international treaty signed between Britain and China. The treaty states that under the "one country, two systems" framework, the city would retain a high degree of autonomy and its legal and judicial system will remain unchanged for 50 years. The basic policies are detailed in an annex and stipulated in the Basic Law.

[60] The Basic Law is Hong Kong's "mini-constitution," which came into effect at the handover, in July 1997.

[61] From 2003, Hong Kong started its wide and deep discussions about constitutional reform concerning the election of the chief executive and all LegCo members through universal suffrage, and Hong Kong people believed that universal suffrage could be realized in the year 2007 or 2012.

[62] Albert H. Y. Chen, "The Law and Politics of the Struggle for Universal Suffrage in Hong Kong, 2013–15," *Asian Journal of Law and Society* 3 (2016): 189–207; Benny Tai, "30 Years after Tiananmen: Hong Kong Remembers," *Journal of Democracy* 30 (2019): 64–69.

level of criminal justice institutions and interactions with its agents.[63] In order to provide an explanation of changes in protest policing from a mixed embeddedness perspective, we therefore need to consider meso-level features of trust relationships as they exist between police and the public – a task to which we turn next.

13.6 Mesolevel: The Erosion of Police Authority

Two factors are particularly salient for understanding recent erosions of police authority in Hong Kong. First, the public increasingly views the police as having lost political neutrality. Second, the prevalent use of video and internet technologies has increased the visibility of police violence, leading to a reevaluation of the moral status of police.

13.6.1 Loss of Police Neutrality

It is a truism of policing scholarship that political neutrality is fundamental to police legitimacy. In the Hong Kong context, this would mean that members of different political camps – whether pro- or anti-establishment – would be treated impartially when police officers implement policies, enforce the law, and deliver community services. Police officers we interviewed emphasized that, as individuals, they have remained neutral while discharging their duties.[64] Recent events, however, have exacerbated longer-term trends[65] in the erosion of public confidence in police. Particularly damaging was the 'Yuen Long attack' – an incident on July 21, 2019 in which a group of at least one hundred pro-establishment, white-clad men, some of whom were local gang members, attacked protestors arriving home after a demonstration (along with civilians who happened to be there) in the Yuen Long transit station. Despite receiving hundreds of emergency calls, local police officers arrived 35 mins late and

[63] Ben Bradford, Jonathan Jackson, Mike Hough, and Stephen Farrall, "Trust and Confidence in Criminal Justice: A Review of the British Research Literature," in Anniina Jokinen, Elina Ruuskanen, Maria Yordanova, Dimitar Markov, and Miriana Ilcheva (eds.), *Review of Need: Indicators of Public Confidence in Criminal Justice* (Finland: Criminal Justice Press, 2008), 141–173.

[64] Interview 39 (senior police inspector), February 2016; interview 46 (senior police constable), December 2019; interview 48 (senior police inspector), December 2019; interviews 49 and 50 (police constables), December 2019.

[65] Hui and Au, "Police Legitimacy and Protest Policing."

made no arrests in connection with the incident.[66] Moreover, Junius Ho, a pro-establishment politician and former head of the Hong Kong Law Association was videoed shaking hands with several white-clad men in the neighborhood on the day of the attack. This event raised public suspicion of police collusion with local gangs, as one former Royal Hong Kong police officer noted,

> The Yuen Long attack, believed to have been conducted by local villagers and gangs of triad (criminal secret society) members, shocked Hong Kong and led to a wide- spread believe [*sic*] that the Police were in collusion with triads. This event turned a substantial number of the passive Hong Kong population against the Police, and many people started to label the Police as "haak ging" (黑警), or "black police."[67]

Soon after, we heard chants of "Triads! Triads!," issuing from protestors toward police at local rallies. Most police officers we interviewed were reluctant to make detailed comments about police inaction during the Yuen Long attack, but several did emphasize that they felt the conduct of the HKPF in connection with the event was shameful. For example,

> The Yuen Long [attack on] 7.21 (21 July) is something that I don't want to comment [on], I "feel shame on the HKPF" [as well].[68]
>
> Um…It's hard to comment what was happening on 7.21, I won't say it was a wrong decision, but should have a better solution.[69]
>
> The Yuen Long attack put so much shame on HKPF, it's totally ridiculous.[70]

One frontline police officer was willing to be more candid, telling us that:

> The HKPF totally lose in this point [the Yuen Long attack]. There was no police to help or save citizens when they needed [help]. It was definitely a stain. Especially [when] two uniformed police officers had arrived on the scene but then turned away—that was a real shame… my colleague and his/her team went directly from Western district to Yuen Long, attempting to control the situation. However, they received an order asking them on hold.

66 Christy Leung and Victor Ting, "Police Chief Defends 'Late' Force Response to Mob Violence in Yuen Long," *South China Morning Post* (July 22, 2019), www.scmp.com/news/hong-kong/law-and-crime/article/3019657/hong-kong-police-chief-defends-officers-arriving-35.

67 Martin Purbrick, "A Report of the 2019 Hong Kong Protest," *Asian Affairs* 50 (2019): 465–487, at 473.

68 Interview 46 (senior police constable), December 2019.

69 Interview 48 (senior police inspector), December 2019.

70 Interview 47 (senior police inspector), December 2019.

> The upper level management team mentioned that the incident [the attack] was related to the gentry,[71] [and to] let them deal with it in their own way.[72]

The HKPF's seeming tolerance toward triad attacks on protestors confirmed to many within the public that they can no longer expect to receive impartial treatment from police. This event deserves to be recognized as a turning point of the 2019 antiextradition protests, in that it was at this moment that the police themselves became central targets of the movement as a whole – even, sometimes, among police officers themselves. As an enforcement officer mentioned,

> My Facebook has around 400 to 500 friends, many of whom are officials from disciplinary forces. Before the Yuen Long attack, 30% were anti-government and 70% were pro-government. But after the Yuen Long event, 70% became "yellow" [i.e. pro-democracy and anti-government], including even enforcement officials...I saw that many of them shared information and news articles supporting social protest.[73]

13.6.2 Policing's Greater Visibility and Police Legitimacy

Before the late 1980s, the use of force by police was typically 'visible only to those most chronically policed.'[74] Recent decades, by contrast, have seen a dramatic transformation of the optical interface between police and society. The prevalence of camera phones has combined with the emergence of video-sharing platforms such as YouTube and social networking sites like Twitter and Facebook to enable populations to engage in collective projects of sousveillance ('watching from below').[75] Ericson[76] provides a useful dichotomy for conceptualizing this transformation: on the one hand, this expansion of police visibility increases police *accountability*; the extent to which police actions are subject to evaluation and judgment by

[71] The local village establishment, in which triad societies exercise considerable power.
[72] Interview 49 (police constable), December 2019.
[73] Interview 48 (senior police inspector), December 2019.
[74] Ben Brucato, "Policing Made Visible: Mobile Technologies and the Importance of Point of View," *Surveillance & Society* 13 (2015): 455–473, at 456.
[75] Andrew J Goldsmith, "Policing's New Visibility," *The British Journal of Criminology* 50 (2010): 914–934; John B Thompson, "The New Visibility," *Theory, Culture & Society* 22 (2005): 31–51.
[76] Richard V. Ericson, "The News Media and Account Ability in Criminal Justice," in Philip Stenning (ed.), *Accountability for Criminal Justice: Selected Essays* (Toronto: University of Toronto Press, 1995), 135–161.

the general public. Meanwhile, greater visibility decreases police's *account ability* – namely, the capacity of police to justify their actions and shape their public reception[77].

The existing literature on protest policing in Hong Kong attributes the erosion of police authority to a reversal of the stance, on the part of conventional media, from a pro- to an anti-establishment orientation. Chan and Lau[78] note, for example, that 'the local media, from being generally pro-establishment before 1997, had post-1997 become one of the world's most fierce critics of, even hostile to, government.' Especially in the 2010s, however, developments in non-traditional reporting, combined with visual recording technologies, have arguably made a greater contribution to the (negative) visibility of policing. Anyone in the Hong Kong community during the last half decade (and especially during the latest wave of protests) has been exposed to at times daily streams of videos, captured by protesters and shared across Facebook, YouTube, LIHKG (a reddit-like message board) and Telegram (an anonymous messaging platform). Multiple protest sites (along with multiple vantage points of single sites) are streamed together over the same collective feed, often in a three-by-three grid.[79] Instances of police brutality, illegality, and unprofessionalism are clipped and circulated widely, and the sheer volume of this material, combined with the quantity of citizen contributor-curators, dramatically overwhelms any prospect for 'account ability' on the part officers[80].

During the 2019 protests, new media practices were indeed a key vector for the spread of anger toward police, inaugurating and then exacerbating violent interactions between police and protesters. The collapse of trust in the formal legal system, along with increasing grievances among protestors, in turn led to the widespread use of *sil liu*, a term put to use by protestors to refer to settling political disputes through private, extra-judicial punishments – at times directed against police themselves. Social media forums like LIHKG and encrypted apps such as Telegram have been used to share private information about officers and their families, facilitating the use of *sil liu* to resolve grievances.

77 Ericson, "The News Media and Account Ability in Criminal Justice;" Steve Mann, Nolan Jason, and Wellman Barry, "Sousveillance," *Surveillance & Society* 1 (2003): 331–355.

78 Chan and Lau, "The Police Force," 146.

79 For an example of such formatting, see: www.youtube.com/watch?v=hRZwSkORWk0&t=7s.

80 Ericson, "The News Media and Account Ability in Criminal Justice").

In a joint symposium hosted by the HKPF and a local university in October 2016, the first author and a police superintendent had a discussion on the relationship between social media and police legitimacy. A common complaint among police officers has been that video clips of interactions between themselves and protesters are cut and framed in ways that emphasize police violence and downplay violence from protesters, prompting the author to pose a question about the possibility for a media counteroffensive:

Q: 'Why don't police officers upload photos and videos online in a timely manner…to justify police use of force and safeguard the police's image?'

A: 'Unfortunately, we cannot do that. The evidence collected from CID [Criminal Intelligence Department] officers are used only for prosecution. If we want to disclose these evidences, like photos and videos, to the public, we need to go through a special procedure…. [W]e may need neutral and non-profit-oriented groups to do this instead…but we have not found it.'[81]

As Brucato[82] has found, police agencies in many jurisdictions are indeed increasingly advocating for the use of body-cameras as a means of preempting the asymmetrical use of video evidence, whether in legal trials or the court of public opinion. Hong Kong police, however, have not adopted this practice. Thus, while the HKPF has remained tied to procedures that have their origins in the pre-social media age, protesters have been able to adapt to the new media climate, spreading and amplifying depictions of police violence. As a result, police attempts to counter new labels like 'dirty police,' 'triads,' 'black police,' 'dogs,' 'murderers,' and 'terrorists' have been feeble and ineffective.

13.7 Micro-Level: Spirals of Violent Action and Reaction

These dynamics point to the importance of the micro-interactional level for understanding the evolution of protest policing in Hong Kong. As Newburn[83] noted, 'the interactions between the police and "protestors" includes the ways both interpret the situations they find themselves in and the actions

[81] Informal interview (police superintendent), October 2016.
[82] Brucato, "Policing Made Visible."
[83] Tim Newburn, "Reflections on Why Riots Don't Happen," *Theoretical Criminology* 20 (2016): 125–144, at 137.

and reactions that both sides adopt towards each other.' This reciprocal perceptual dynamic has certainly been important in Hong Kong, where protests that are initially peaceful soon develop into an escalating spiral of invidiation and retaliation between police and the public. A key moment that sparked processes of mutual radicalization occurred during the attempted clearing of the Occupy Movement sit-ins of 2014. One interviewee recalled that a sense of comradery with fellow participants grew hand-in-hand with a developing sense that police were a key enemy on September 28, a moment when organizers announced their civil disobedience campaign and when police responded with teargas. The transformation was visceral:

> I remember it was very hard because it was very hot. We were sitting close to together in rows in raincoats, feeling sticky... I had just pulled an all-nighter, so I felt like I was on the verge of having a stroke.... However, just when I was thinking to leave, feeling hopeless about the situation, I saw suddenly... there were people standing on the footbridge at the beginning [who] would throw us bottles of water, and I witnessed the moment of people pushing through the area that was closed off. When I saw a crowd of people pushing through, Wow!—at that moment, the feeling of *someone's got your back* appeared again. I realized I was not the only one going through a tough time. There were many more coming out to support you for doing the right thing, so I shouldn't give up easily.
>
> Then it was tear gas.... Everything was so chaotic. I couldn't think.... We didn't really know what they dropped on us. There were lots of smoke and we couldn't see what or who was around us.... It was impossible to stay there as you may die. We all ran in the opposite direction of the gas.... I was angry at that time. It was fear before, but now it's anger.... I mean we were all unarmed—why did they use such violent measures in driving away civilians protesting? They treated us like mobs, but we were peaceful protesters doing something for the good of HK. So I was especially mad at the cops... My friends were all furious and shouting at the police while staring them down.... That whole process was too, too draining, for me. But I was really angry.[84]

Another interviewee's opinion of police changed dramatically after witnessing a particular encounter during a student strike that same week:

> the student told the police that he wanted to go toilet, but the police didn't allow them.... So I took a plastic bag and told the police if they he could give the plastic bag to the student. But the police threw away the plastic bag, and walked in front of the student and said 'if you want to go toilet, do it here.' I was very angry at that time, as he just wanted to go to toilet. You may forbid them to go, or you may arrest him if he committed any offense. But it wasn't

[84] Interview 17 (protester), December 2017.

> necessary to insult him. What's the purpose for him to [relieve himself] in front of many people? It's terrible. This is a scene that I will not forget, so my anger towards police would not [subside].... While clearing out, those police would spray the pepper spray between and under the shields. These acts were very dirty. When you experience these, you would then know the political power and enforcement power...the enforcers were so dirty.[85]

Moments like these point to the micro-interactional basis for opinion formation in police-protester relations. The 2019 anti-ELAB movement has provided an intensive crucible for many more such encounters: a figure generated by *The New York Times* on 18 November 2019 shows key dates and their interlinks, which is helpful for understanding the impact of government policy or police actions to the development of the social movement in its first six months.[86] Rather than engaging in the obstreperous task of providing an overview of all of these events, we choose instead to examine this history with reference to two key factors that have altered the interactional basis for police-protester encounters: 1) the influence of face masks on the use of violence and, 2) an increasing collective identification among protesters as 'police victims.'

13.7.1 Face Masks and the Use of Violence

Face masks are increasingly used by both protestors and police officers to conceal their identities and protect themselves from tear gas and Molotov cocktails. There have been significant developments in typical protester gear from the 2014 Occupy movement to the 2019 antiextradition protests, where masking and other anti-surveillance strategies have taken on a central role.

Most protestors in 2019 did not wear face masks until after 12 June 2019. On that day, police employed tear gas, rubber bullets and pepper spray to disperse demonstrations near the Legislative Council and government headquarters. The readiness to use these methods shocked demonstrators, many of whom decided to wear protective face masks, goggles, and gas masks in later protests.[87] As a local university student told Amnesty International (2019):

[85] Interview 28 (protester), January 2018.

[86] Jin Wu, K. K. Rebecca Lai, and Yuhas Alan, "Six Months of Hong Kong Protests. How Did We Get Here?" *The New York Times* (October 1, 2019), www.nytimes.com/interactive/2019/world/asia/hong-kong-protests-arc.html.

[87] Interview 46 (senior police constable), December 2019; interview 48 (senior police inspector), December 2019; interview 47 (senior police inspector), December 2019; interview 49 (police constable), December 2019; interview 51 (police constable), December 2019.

> The first time I experienced tear gas was on 12 June [2019]. It was a very, very bad day. I was trying to distribute protective gear to protesters when tear gas was suddenly deployed at our first aid station. Tears poured uncontrollably from my eyes and I could hardly breathe.

A further increase in the use of facemasks occurred, ironically, in response to a face-mask ban introduced in early October by HK Chief Executive Carrie Lam, who invoked controversial emergency powers enshrined in HK's mini-constitution.[88] Based on the authors' observations, after the ban, a vast majority of protestors started to cover their faces with black surgical-style masks in order to pointedly defy the facemask ban. As an exercise in legitimacy, therefore, the action had completely backfired: before, law-breaking elements of the protests movement were largely confined to fringe 'frontliners' who were prepared to face arrest, should they be caught. Now, by virtue of their defiance of the mask ban, tens of thousands of protesters could be counted among the movement's law-breaking constituency.

This upsurge in newly concealed identities, in turn, facilitated participation in property crime, with many protestors vandalizing public facilities, police stations, and China-linked property. As a local newspaper relayed,

> The masked mobs smashed banks, stores and bookshops associated with mainland China, trashed government buildings and started fires at the exits of several MTR [subway] stations as they continued their attack on the city's railway operator for allegedly aiding police in their clearance operations[89].

Social control theory suggests that external factors such as close relationships, cultural norms, and the cost of punishment can explain why people obey rules and conform to societal expectations for behaviour.[90] Face masks therefore seem to have a disinhibiting effect: protected from identification by family, employers, and the authorities, protesters are 'released' – within the protest context – in ways that allow for behaviour that they would not do otherwise.

The dynamics of masking have had a denaturing effect on the basis for police-public interactions in another way: while the use of masks can at

[88] Last used in 1967, the 'Emergency Regulations Ordinance' came into effect in 1922, as a measure that the colonial government could use in order to restore public order.

[89] SCMP Reporters, "Hong Kong Protests," *South China Morning Post* (October 7, 2019), www.scmp.com/news/hong-kong/politics/article/3031782/hong-kong-protests-tens-thousands-defy-mask-ban-go-rampage.

[90] Travis Hirschi, *Causes of Delinquency* (Berkeley: University of California Press, 1969).

times effectively protect individuals from arrest or being harmed by police violence, in general, their use generates the need for police officers to be more aggressive when making arrests, including chasing, tackling, and occasionally beating protesters who fight back.

A large number of police officers also have begun to hide their identities during protest events, using face masks and removing badge numbers from their uniforms.[91] This has been justified as a means of preventing personal information leakage and protecting their family members from being harassed or threatened by radical protestors ('*sil liu*,' mentioned earlier). As one constable told us, "I do not agree [to] hide identity during the duties, but I have no choice. All my colleague and senior ask me to act in this way. I can only follow the majorities."[92] Our interviewees emphasized that frontline officers in Hong Kong have been well trained to handle social protests, but they also noted that most frontline officers are young and that they lack experience with managing violent confrontations, specifically.[93] Likewise with the case of protesters, the concealment of identity seems to have had a disinhibiting effect on the use of force, and authorial observations can confirm that masked police can occasionally now be seen goading masked protesters into confrontations, beckoning them with their billy-clubs.[94] As one constable told us,

> I see that some frontline colleagues are over-use of force during the operations. I do not agree with their action. Most of the times, we could handle the situation in the better way but they chose the act in other way. For examples... kicking the protestor on street by more than seven polices is definitely not necessary...and scenes of stepping the protestor's face on ground is extremely ugly. I totally do not understand why those colleague have to do so...Maybe it's because they do not have to bear any responsibilities when doing such things.... [I]f my colleague did not hide their

91 Alvin Lum, "Identification of Hong Kong Riot Officers Using Undisclosed Codes on Helmets Is 'Unsatisfactory', Police Watchdog Says, Calling for Clarity and Accountability," *South China Morning Post* (August 23, 2019), https://amp.scmp.com/news/hong-kong/politics/article/3024160/identification-hong-kong-riot-officers-using-undisclosed.

92 Interview 51 (police constable), December 2019.

93 Interview 41 (frontline police officer), March 2016; interview 48 (senior police inspector), December 2019; interviews 49, 50, and 51 (police constables), December 2019.

94 Phila Siu, "Hong Kong Police Accused of Provoking Protesters and Failing to Wear ID during Mong Kok Chaos after Extradition Bill March," *South China Morning Post* (July 8, 2019), www.scmp.com/news/hong-kong/law-and-crime/article/3017775/hong-kong-police-accused-provoking-protesters-and.

> identity by covering their face, they [would] not dare to say 'open a champagne to celebrate Chow Tse Lok's death'[95] and 'I need to repeat the scenes of 4th June'[96] for 100% sure.[97]

The masking and/or concealment of identity – on the part of protesters and police alike – seems therefore to be an important factor in the evolution of protest policing styles in Hong Kong.

13.7.2 Collective Identity as Police Victims

Social identity theory suggests that certain circumstances can 'make a collective identity more salient and compel people to act as members of [a] group.'[98] As Newburn[99] observed in his work on the 2011 England riots, protesters can 'experience a shift in their self-definition, away from unique personal attributes towards more generalized, group-based attributes.' We have indeed observed shifts in the movement that have led to the salience of a new style of collective identification; namely, as 'police victims.'

A key moment for collective identity formation came in the wake of an event in which a young woman's right eye was seriously injured by a projectile. Demonstrators alleged it was fired by police during a protest outside a Hong Kong police station on 11 August 2019, and the image of the woman, crying in pain and with a bloodied and bandaged eye, quickly took on an iconic status within the movement. Participants began wearing their own 'bloodied eye' bandages, and covering their right eyes at events, replicating the injured-eye 'meme' across movement culture.

Several other examples exhibit this trend. On 8 November 2019, Chow Tsz-lok (mentioned above), a 22-year-old undergraduate student died at a local hospital due to a fall from a car park near an area of violent confrontation between protectors and police.[100] Demonstrators attributed

[95] A protester who had recently died (discussed in Section 13.7.2).
[96] This refers to the events in Tiananmen Square, June 4, 1989.
[97] Interview 50 (police constable), December 2019.
[98] Bert Klandermans, Jose Manuel Sabucedo, Mauro Rodriguez, and Marga de Weerd, "Identity Processes in Collective Action Participation: Farmers' Identity and Farmers' Protest in the Netherlands and Spain," *Political Psychology* 23 (2002): 235–251, at 235.
[99] Newburn, "Reflections on Why Riots Don't Happen."
[100] Alvin Lum, "Student Who Suffered Brain Injury in Car Park Fall Has Died," *South China Morning Post* (November 8, 2019), www.scmp.com/news/hong-kong/politics/article/3036833/hong-kong-student-who-suffered-severe-brain-injury-after.

Chow's death to a police dispersal operation that took place nearby[101], called Chow a 'freedom fighter,' while also calling police officers 'murderers.' One of emergent slogans, 'his name is Chow Tsz-lok, he just happens not to be your son,' serves to remind the public of Chow's death and that everyone bears the potential for victimhood at the hands of police. Makeshift shrines to alleged 'murder victims' and deaths of movement participants have become a focal point for many participants within the movement.

Collective identification as 'victims' has thus become a key organizing principle for the movement, shifting the focus away from the broader public-government interface (where demands for democratic representation had taken center stage) and onto the more specific interplay between protesters and police. The widespread acceptance and promulgation of this identity marks dramatic a change in the public reputation of the police, which routinely now attracts the worst possible appellations ('murderers' 'terrorists' 'triads'). As a result, the mere presence of police officers at public events significantly triggers protestors' law-breaking behaviors and leads to an escalation of violence. 'Softer' policing strategies, involving communication, negotiation, and facilitation have become all but impossible, and there is no real choice for the police force but to move in the direction of coercive force, increasing the use of violence amid increasingly futile attempts to maintain social order and manage protests. This forms the violent action-reaction spiral that portends dire consequences for Hong Kong in the coming years.

13.8 Conclusion

While protest-policing strategies in democratic regimes (e.g. the UK, the US and continental Europe) have attracted a great deal of scholarly attention, this article contributes data and analysis of protest policing as it exists in the hybrid regime of Hong Kong. Past research on the evolution of protest policing tends to employ a policecentric explanation that foregrounds police knowledge and understandings of external realities (e.g. political opportunities and the characteristics of social movements). In a departure from these approaches, this article deploys a 'mixed embeddedness' perspective, showing how policing tactics, strategies and styles are

[101] Iain Marlow, Josie Wong, and Natalie Lung, "Hong Kong Student Death Fuels Anger before Weekend Protests," *Bloomberg* (November 8, 2019), www.bloomberg.com/news/articles/2019-11-08/hong-kong-student-who-fell-near-protest-dies-scmp-says.

historically-, politically-, contextually- and interactionally-constituted. Officers are not atomized actors, and they are not necessarily instilled with knowledge and ability that is apposite to developing best practices for handling social protests. Instead, as our case shows, the choice of protest policing styles can be largely constrained by external factors. As a hybrid regime, Hong Kong is particularly effective for highlighting the constraint-laden context within which police choices are often embedded. This is because contradictions inherent in hybrid systems provide flashpoints that can illuminate factors – from micro- to macro-levels – that give shape to police strategy.

In the latter half of 2019, the non-viability of Hong Kong's political system has increasingly revealed itself. A growing legitimacy crisis has emerged, spurred by the government's failure to deliver 'outputs' (e.g. economic growth and public services) and its concomitant refusal to accept greater 'inputs' through democratic reform. At the cusp of the crisis is diminishing police legitimacy, resulting from a perceived lack of political neutrality and the emergence of civil-sphere moral entrepreneurship which has worked to define the police as an odious force. Amid the deterioration in police-public relationships, members of the public have become increasingly unwilling to cooperate with the police and comply with the law, leading to an action-reaction spiral that has increased violence on all sides. The use of face masks – among protesters and police alike – has allowed actors to escape normative and legal constraints that would ordinarily be in operation, and the development of social movement iconography related police brutality and victimhood has foreclosed the possibility for non-coercive and non-authoritarian styles of policing.

Developments since the initial phase of this research[102] bear this out. With the enactment and implementation of the National Security Law (NSL) in Hong Kong in June 2020, police have been empowered through the establishment of a National Security Department that is responsible for investigating offenses endangering national security. The Law criminalizes "secession," "subversion," "terrorist activities," and "collusion with a foreign country or external elements to engender national security."[103] While receiving criticism for the vagueness of its descriptions (Hernandez 2020; The Standard 2021), the new offences are understood as criminalizing many

[102] Wang, Joosse, and Cho, "The Evolution of Protest Policing in a Hybrid Regime."

[103] An English translation of the law can be found at: www.gld.gov.hk/egazette/pdf/20202448e/egn2020244872.pdf.

of the protest activities and slogans of the 2019 Anti-ELAB movement and wider pro-democracy movement, targeting both rank and file protesters and high-profile pro-democracy leaders with harsh penalties including the potential for life imprisonment. Many civil society organizations and political parties have permanently disbanded, and nearly all sympathetic Legislators in Hong Kong have resigned their seats.

Thus, owing to the law, and to the general pause on public activities amid the COVID-19 pandemic, it seems that the aforementioned violent action-reaction spiral between protestors and police officers has been effectively halted in the short term through the conclusive suppression of the 'protest side' of this dynamic. At the same time, there is worry that the current societal-political arrangement creates the very conditions that the NSL is expressly designed to prevent: increasing the appeal of clandestine organizing and violent action for some substantial subset of the Hong Kong population.[104] After all, the Law does not address the macrohistorical root causes of social instability in Hong Kong described above. In the long term, to gain legitimacy, the Hong Kong government still needs to significantly increase its capacity to promote more equitable economic growth, provide better public services, solve the city's deteriorating housing and poverty problems, and find some means of delivering acceptable levels of freedom of expression and political representation to the Hong Kong public within the 'One Country, Two Systems' framework. For its part, the HKPF needs to learn lessons from its failure to perform police neutrality during the 'Yuen Long attack', work to repair its relationship with the local community, come up with a strategy for protest policing that facilitates peaceful and lawful demonstrations, and avoid the indiscriminate use of force.

[104] Christy Leung and Clifford Lo, "Is Hong Kong Turning into a Breeding Ground for Terrorism?" *South China Morning Post* (July 8, 2021), www.scmp.com/news/hong-kong/law-and-crime/article/3140233/hong-kong-turning-breeding-ground-terrorism-how.

PART V

Conclusion

14

Authoritarian Police and Policing in East Asia

Scope, Patterns, and Paradoxes

JACQUES DELISLE

14.1 Defining Authoritarian Police and Policing in East Asia

"Authoritarian police" and "authoritarian policing," unlike "authoritarian legality,"[1] are not phrases that risk being read as oxymorons. Nonetheless, they present terminological and conceptual challenges. The Venn diagram of "authoritarian," "police," and "policing" is complex, contestable, and contested.

The police are generally – and, arguably, inherently – authoritarian organs, clearly so in authoritarian polities, but also in democratic and hybrid ones. Police forces have authoritarian structures of command and responsibility (although they vary considerably in their degree of centralization, subordination to political authorities, and accountability under law). In authoritarian polities in East Asia, police sometimes relatively closely resemble military units – and the dividing line between police and military or paramilitary can become blurred, especially where the apparatus of authoritarian rule includes "special" or "political" police, partly differentiated from "ordinary" police.

Police in authoritarian polities are in many cases an emblematic and highly visible aspect of the regime's rule. They are typically a major, and sometimes a nearly omnipresent, interface between an authoritarian state (or party-state) and the society over which it rules. The police are often a principal – and, sometimes, *the* principal – institutional manifestation of the Weberian principle of the state's monopoly over the legitimate

[1] Authoritarian legality is the subject of another book edited by the editors of this volume and with many of the same contributors examining several of the same polities. Jacques deLisle, "Authoritarian Legality: What, Why, and Whither?" in Chen Weitseng and Hualing Fu (eds.), *Authoritarian Legality in Asia: Formation, Development and Transition* (Cambridge: Cambridge University Press, 2020), 17–59.

use of coercion,[2] deployed, more or less ambitiously, to control, repress, or transform society. Tellingly, authoritarian regimes are sometimes referred to as "police states." Yet in East Asian authoritarian polities (and in East Asian democracies where police and policing sometimes show strong continuity with earlier authoritarian eras), the police also are often a daily presence, deeply embedded in society (especially at the neighborhood level in urban areas), enjoying social legitimacy and public support, and reflecting and reinforcing immanent norms – resonating with a more Durkheimian notion of police.[3]

"Policing" thus covers a range of tasks that authoritarian regimes undertake, many of them also performed by their democratic cousins – a commonality that has been the foundation for a large body of comparative work on authoritarian policing and democratic policing. Yet policing is a special focus and concern for authoritarian regimes, including in East Asia. Policing – in the forms of monitoring or controlling society, enforcing restrictions on social behavior deemed deviant or disfavored, preventing perceived or purported threats to social and political order, and implementing regime policies and goals (in some cases ambitious and transformative ones, at times through highly coercive means) – often looms large in the portfolio of authoritarian governance, and the ends that policing serves rank high on authoritarian rulers' agendas. In a telling phrase, authoritarian regimes "police" their societies. At the same time, some of the most significant roles that police play in East Asian authoritarian polities include extensive welfarist functions, depend upon deep embeddedness in, trust from, and cooperation with social groups, and blur conventional boundaries between state and society.

As the foregoing suggests, the relationship between the scope of police and policing can be complicated. Among authoritarian regimes in East Asia, police sometimes perform, or are tasked with, functions that test or transgress the limits of many definitions of policing.[4] Yet

[2] Max Weber, "Politics as a Vocation," in H. H. Gerth and C. Wright Mills (eds.), *From Max Weber: Essays in Sociology* (London: Routledge, 1948), 77–128, at 78; Jan Terpstra, "Two Theories of the Police: The Relevance of Max Weber and Emile Durkheim to the Study of Police," *International Journal of Law, Crime and Justice* 39(1) (2011): 1–11.

[3] See, for example, Nguyen, Chapter 5, Chen, Chapter 8, and Tan, Chapter 11, in this volume. See also Emile Durkheim, *The Division of Labor in Society* (New York: Free Press, 1997).

[4] See Nguyen, Chapter 5 (on the response to COVID-19), and Mobrand, Chapter 6. The neighborhood roles of the Japanese *koban* and its progeny in other East Asian authoritarian

significant aspects of policing – at least on expansive definitions – are in some cases performed by entities other than the police.[5]

"Authoritarian" is another complex concept in the context of the issues and cases of police and policing addressed in this book. Any but the simplest concept of authoritarianism sees it as multidimensional, more prevalent in some dimensions of a state or political order than in others. Police and policing can be among a state's more authoritarian features. This is especially, but not exclusively, so in the context of "high policing" to suppress political dissent or cope with perceived or asserted threats to the regime.[6] On the other hand, the widespread assignment of arguably nonpolicing welfare-related functions to police organs in East Asian authoritarian regimes can make the police – at least in some aspects of their work and in societal perceptions – less authoritarian than the regime as a whole or some of its other major instrumentalities, including special police units or the military.

What should count, more generally, as an authoritarian regime – and where to draw boundaries among authoritarian, democratic, or hybrid regimes – is a controversial question not amenable to a simple answer. The cases examined in the chapters of this book are – or, during salient periods, were – on the authoritarian side of the lines usually drawn between authoritarian and non-authoritarian political orders.[7] China and Vietnam have remained indisputably authoritarian throughout the eras following

polities is a prominent example of the phenomenon. See generally David H. Bayley, *Forces of Order: Policing in Modern Japan* (Berkeley: University of California, 1976, 1991) 11–30, 79–97.

5 A few contributors venture into broader discussions of "policing" apart from "police." For example, Chapter 12 focuses to a great extent on nonpolice institutions. Chapters 3 and 4 (on China) address the extensive vesting of policing functions and police-like authority in many state and parastatal entities that are not formally part of organs that fall within even vague and capacious definitions of "police."

6 Jean-Paul Brodeur, "High Policing and Low Policing: Remarks about the Policing of Political Activities," *Social Problems* 30(5) (1983): 507–520.

7 See The Economist Intelligence Unit, *Democracy Index 2020: In Sickness and in Health?*, table 6 (China and Vietnam authoritarian, Hong Kong hybrid regime, Singapore flawed democracy) (The Economist Intelligence Unit, 2021), www.eiu.com/n/campaigns/democracy-index-2020/; Center for Systemic Peace, "Polity IV Individual Country Regime Trends, 1946–2013," *Polity IV Project: Political Regime Characteristics and Transitions, 1800–2013*, www.systemicpeace.org/polity/polity4x.htm (China, Vietnam, Taiwan before democratic transition, and South Korea in the early to mid-1960s and from the early 1970s to the early 1980s are all classed as autocracies; Singapore as a closed anocracy; and Thailand cycles from autocracy to democracy, as does the Philippines).

the coming to power of communist party-led regimes. In the period preceding defeat in World War II and the subsequent US occupation, Japan was ruled by an unquestionably authoritarian regime. The same can be said about Korea and Taiwan for the periods preceding democratization in the 1980s. Colonial rule for Singapore, Hong Kong, Korea, and Taiwan was authoritarian rule for those subjected to it, even though the first two were colonies of a democratically ruled imperial power. Thailand and the Philippines have been at times clearly authoritarian (and at other times democratic) during the postwar era.

Postreversion Hong Kong and postindependence Singapore have had substantial elements of democracy, and arguably are "hybrid" regimes,[8] but still are credibly classed as authoritarian rather than democratic. Several developments have kept Hong Kong – increasingly clearly – on the authoritarian side of the ledger: the unfulfilled promises and expectations of democratization (including universal suffrage to choose among legislative and chief executive candidates through increasingly open nominations procedures); the long-present and, especially since 2019, sharply increased constraints and interventions from the central government in Beijing; the resort to force by local police (and the brief prospect of deploying mainland military or paramilitary units) during the 2019 protests; the arrests and prosecutions of prodemocracy or regime-criticizing leaders and activists, in some cases pursuant to the draconian new National Security Law; and the decision to delay the 2020 legislative elections and conduct them under far less democratic rules.

For taxonomists of regimes, Singapore may be the most challenging among the examples considered in this volume – and in East Asia. Its democratic features are sufficiently robust that it is arguably located in the borderlands between soft authoritarian rule and one-party-dominant democracy. Still, categorizing the city-state as authoritarian is defensible and common.[9] And, as the cases of Thailand, the Philippines, and pre-1980s South Korea – and the global democratic recession in recent years – show, transitions from authoritarian to democratic rule are not irreversible or immune from erosion.

As this brief inventory indicates, authoritarian attributes of police and policing are found in East Asian contexts that range from indisputably

[8] See Wang, Joosse, and Cho, Chapter 13 (characterizing HK as a hybrid regime).

[9] Mark Tushnet, "Authoritarian Constitutionalism," *Cornell Law Review* 100(2) (2015): 391–461; Jothie Rajah, *Authoritarian Rule of Law* (Cambridge: Cambridge University Press, 2012); see also Tan, Chapter 11, in this volume.

(but notably diverse) authoritarian regimes, to ambiguous, transitional, or hybrid systems, to fully consolidated democratic polities that have emerged from authoritarian pasts. As many of the contributors to this volume address, habits and legacies of authoritarian police and policing often persist after a regime transitions from authoritarian rule.[10] These traits and features can linger even in states that have addressed authoritarian-era police conduct through processes of transitional justice, and – as illustrated by responses to terrorism after 9/11 and kindred reactions to other perceived or purported serious threats to order or security – authoritarian features of police and policing can become resurgent even in long-established democracies.[11]

"East Asia" – like many terms that use geography as a proxy for social, political, economic, or historical commonalities and communities – is a designation with imprecise contours and contestable utility. Cultural and political-cultural explanations are notoriously fraught and vulnerable to charges of a lack of rigor, oversimplification, or casual empiricism. But such perspectives can point us to attributes that help to explain – or that, at least, appear to fit – common patterns. And attention to cultural and political-cultural factors can mitigate the risk of taking the formal legal and institutional changes – including especially those that accompany democratization – too much at face value, while underestimating the resilience of long-standing (and arguably culturally rooted) traits. And authoritarian regimes in East Asia (in this book, defined to include Southeast Asia) do mostly share some notable common features – including some that appear to matter for issues of police and policing.

Examples of familiarly "East Asian" attributes that align with observed features of authoritarian police and policing in the region include official and, perhaps, societal preferences for legal informality (at least when compared to purported Western rule-of-law ideal types);[12] an understanding of sanctioning and sanctionable behavior that looks more like a gradual slope running from social disapproval and monitoring to state-imposed criminal punishments (in contrast to a Western ideal type that resembles a cliff, with clear demarcation between what is legally permitted and what brings

10 See Kroncke, Chapter 2 (on Japan); Martin, Chapter 7 (on Taiwan); Chen, Chapter 8; Nakano, Chapter 9; and Mérieau, Chapter 10 (on Thailand).

11 See, for example, Kroncke, Chapter 2; Chen, Chapter 8; and Nakano, Chapter 9.

12 See, for example, Frank K. Upham, "Speculations on Legal Informality," *Law and Society Review* 28(2) (1994): 233–242; Philip C.C. Huang, "The Past and Present of the Chinese Civil and Criminal Justice Systems," *Modern China* 42(3) (2016): 227–272.

a person within reach of legitimate punishment by state authorities);[13] conceptions of just or proper legal outcomes that emphasize substantive justice, rather than procedural justice or procedural fairness (when measured against views apparently or purportedly held in the West);[14] notions of identity that are deeply embedded in social contexts and relationships (in contrast to Western individualistic paradigms) that – among other things – affect police behavior and authorities' ability to exert leverage over targeted individuals;[15] assertions (by rulers) and acceptance (in society) of a view that the state properly has (again, when compared to Western liberal views) an extensive or intrusive rule in managing and normatively guiding or transforming citizens and society;[16] traditions of law and governance that do not draw sharp lines among functions of government (including policing) or establish strongly functionally differentiated state institutions (including the police), especially at local or grassroots levels;[17] and norms of good government that prize benevolent rule (often by a strong, authoritarian state) over rule structured by law (which could entail greater public accountability for the state and state actors).[18]

Some commonalities across the region may reflect shared or overlapping influences from the West. In modern times, many authoritarian

[13] See Victor H. Li, "Law Without Lawyers: A Comparative View of Law in China and the United States," *Philosophy East and West* 29(2) (1979): 237–240; Xiaoming Chen, "Social and Legal Control in China: A Comparative Perspective," *International Journal of Offender Therapy and Comparative Criminology* 48(5) (2004): 523–536.

[14] See Ethan Michelson and Benjamin L. Read, "Public Attitudes toward Official Justice in Beijing and Rural China," in Margaret Y. K. Woo and Mary E. Gallagher (eds.), *Chinese Justice: Civil Dispute Resolution in Contemporary China* (Cambridge; New York: Cambridge University Press, 2011), 169–203 (reflecting survey work Beijing/Chicago); Xin He and Jing Feng, "Unfamiliarity and Procedural Justice: Litigant's Attitudes towards Civil Justice in Southern China," *Law and Society Review* 55(1) (2021): 104–138.

[15] See Fu, Chapter 3 (discussing relational repression) and Wang, Joosse, and Cho, Chapter 13 (applying the work of Mark Granovetter) in this volume; and Yanhua Deng and Kevin J. O'Brien, "Relational Repression in China: Using Social Ties to Demobilize Protesters," *China Quarterly* 215 (2013): 533–552.

[16] See Chen, "Social Control in China"; Jacques deLisle and Shen Kui, "Lessons from China's Response to COVID-19," *University of Pennsylvania Asian Law Review* 16 (2020): 66–149, 89–90, 111–112, 124–132. See also Nguyen, Chapter 5; Mobrand, Chapter 6; and Chen, Chapter 8, in this volume.

[17] See, for example, Tung-tsu Chu, *Local Government in China under the Ch'ing* (Cambridge, MA: Harvard University Press, 1962); William P. Alford, "Of Arsenic and Old Laws: Looking Anew at Criminal Justice in Late Imperial China," *California Law Review* 72(6) (1984): 1180–1256.

[18] See generally Benjamin I. Schwartz, *The World of Thought in Ancient China* (Cambridge, MA: Harvard University Press, 1985), 255–320. See also Yi-Huah Jiang, "Confucian

polities in East Asia imported and adapted basic laws (including those empowering, structuring, and constraining the police) and related legal institutions from European continental sources, primarily Germany or France, directly (for example, through conscious adaptation by Japanese or pre-People's-Republic-era Chinese reformist elites, or the effects of French colonial rule in Vietnam) or indirectly (for example, through Chinese and Vietnamese communists' imitation of Soviet – and, in Vietnam's case, PRC – models, or through Japan's colonial rule in Korea and Taiwan). Other places experienced the impact of a different part of the Western legal-political tradition: Anglo-American models, whether through British colonial rule (for example, Hong Kong and Singapore), US occupation or colonialism (postwar Japan and the Philippines), or the more diffuse influences of rule-of-law promotion efforts (law and development initiatives in the early postcolonial era or rule of law programs in the post-Cold War period).

Some East Asian cultural or political-cultural traits partly reflect diffusion within the region over long periods. Almost all of the cases considered in this volume are part of the subregion most affected by Confucianism – the Chinese mainland, other ethnically and culturally Chinese polities, and historically long-Chinese-influenced Korea and Japan. In relatively recent times as well, intraregional influences have been a source of commonality. The mechanisms have included imperial (in the case of Japan and its former dependencies), and less formal or more mediated impacts through contests over constitutional governance, democracy, and the rule of law (for example, in the case of the central Chinese state and the Hong Kong Special Administrative Region, SAR) or the persuasive power of successful foreign examples (as has been the case for Vietnam with China and China with Japan and other exemplars of the East Asian Model of development).

Foreign influences – whether extraregional or intraregional – matter most clearly for the formal legal and institutional structures of police and policing. They sometimes appear to be largely limited to those dimensions, having less effect on the more diffuse and informal aspects of police and policing in East Asian authoritarian polities. The substantive and procedural criminal law on the books, and the official place of the police in the

Political Theory in Contemporary China," *Annual Review of Political Science* 21 (2018): 155–173; Jeffrey T. Martin, "The Confucian Ethic and the Spirit of East Asian Police," *Crime, Law and Social Change* 61 (2014): 461–490.

matrix of law-related state institutions, and so on, are often quite similar across foreign model and adopting or adapting states, but – as the case studies in this book illustrate – such similarities can coexist with significant cross-national differences in practice. And those differences can be deeply rooted, conducive to patterns of police–society interactions – or mechanisms of police accountability – that prove resistant to pro-rule-of-law or democratic reforms, or that limit the reach and dilute the effects of an authoritarian regime's ambitious agendas for using the police (alongside other mechanisms) to control or transform society.[19]

Authoritarian polities in East Asia are also broadly similar in having generally – and sometimes highly – capable states, especially if we adjust for levels of economic development (which tend to correlate with state capacity). The contemporary cases almost all score relatively well in quantitative cross-national metrics (overall, and for states with similar levels of per capita income) on key measures of state or government capacity.[20] As the qualitative studies in this book, and much other scholarship on the cases considered here, reflect,[21] East Asian authoritarian regimes today and in earlier periods have achieved (and now-democratic polities in the region have retained) considerable ability to govern, control, and penetrate their societies. Such state capacity matters for patterns of police and policing: police and policing are significant components of state capacity, and effective police and policing (at least at the nationwide levels that are the principal focus of the studies in this book) are rarely achieved in weak or failed states.

Alongside these similarities, the East Asian authoritarian polities considered in this collection also exhibit considerable diversity. Politically,

[19] On the uneven and complex effects of legal transplants, see Jacques deLisle, "Lex Americana?: United States Legal Assistance, American Legal Models, and Legal Change in the Post-Communist World and Beyond," *University of Pennsylvania Journal of International Economic Law* 20(2) (1999): 179–308. See also Kroncke, Chapter 2, concerning the weakness of links between legal reform efforts and policing performance and behavior; Mobrand, Chapter 6 (on Korea), concerning social constraints on implementation of laws reflecting regime policies; and Nakano, Chapter 9, concerning the limited impact of US occupation reforms in Japan.

[20] East Asia-Pacific states that are not consolidated democracies (as well as those that are) rank 0.65 or above (on a 0 to 1 scale) in the World Justice Project's "order and security" metric and all but the Philippines are above median for their income bracket. All but Cambodia rank 0.45 or better on regulatory enforcement and above median for their income bracket.

[21] See, for example, Kjeld Erik Brodsgaard and Susan Young (eds.), *State Capacity in East Asia* (Oxford: Oxford University Press, 2000); Cristobal Kay, "Why East Asia Overtook Latin America," *Third World Quarterly* 23(6) (2002): 1073–1102.

they cover a spectrum from strongly authoritarian regimes (including the Peoples's Republic of China (PRC), and Japan, Korea, and Taiwan during predemocratization periods), to soft authoritarian, or borderline authoritarian, or arguably hybrid polities (such as contemporary Singapore, or transitional Taiwan or the Philippines during its periods of challenged democracy), to now-democratic regimes that operate partly under the shadow of superseded authoritarian predecessor regimes (including Taiwan, Korea, and Japan). Economically, they range from poor or relatively poor developing countries (such as contemporary Vietnam and the Philippines, China during the prereform era, and Korea and Taiwan in the early postwar decades) to wealthy societies (such as Singapore and Hong Kong today). In scale, they run the gamut from states with populations and territories that are among the world's largest (China) and smallest (Singapore).

Culturally, they include regimes that govern societies with strong Confucian influences (Korea, Taiwan, arguably Singapore, and – especially if a recent regime-encouraged revitalization project proceeds – China),[22] and also those where other normative megatraditions hold much sway (Buddhist Thailand or the Christianized Philippines). In terms of external relations, the polities examined in this book have had strikingly diverse experiences, including Japanese, British, French, and American colonial rule and formal occupation by – or de facto Cold War dependence on – the US; clear formal independence (almost all of the cases in this book during the contemporary period) or contested or ambiguous international status (such as Taiwan or Hong Kong); and high (in Taiwan and South Korea during the postwar period, Vietnam during the early postindependence decades, and postreversion Hong Kong) or low threats of intervention, or profound or autonomy-challenging influence from beyond the jurisdiction's boundaries.

Politics has varied significantly over time within individual country cases. Some polities – including Japan, Korea, and Taiwan – have transitioned from authoritarian rule to consolidated democratic governance – and thus can tell us much about the persistence of elements of authoritarian policing under democratic regimes (a focus for some of the contributors to this collection). Some polities have undergone qualitative political change within long periods of authoritarian governance

[22] See Jin Kai, "The Chinese Communist Party's Confucian Revival," *Diplomat*, September 30, 2014, https://thediplomat.com/2014/09/the-chinese-communist-partys-confucian-revival/; "How Did Confucianism Win Back the Chinese Communist Party?" *Economist*, June 23, 2021, www.economist.com/the-economist-explains/2021/06/23/how-did-confucianism-win-back-the-chinese-communist-party.

(in some cases interrupted by periods of fragile democracy). Examples include Korea, Taiwan, Singapore, and Hong Kong during colonial and postcolonial periods, China in the Mao era and the Reform Era (as well as within each of the two major phases in the conventional periodization of PRC history), and Thailand (which has oscillated between military rule and shaky democracy). Changes – within ongoing authoritarian rule or between authoritarian and democratic rule – have ranged from relatively smooth to jarringly disjunctive and even catastrophically violent. Diverse influences on authoritarian East Asian polities from abroad and from the past cannot but teach multiple or complex lessons – whether or not fully perceived by leaders and publics – about police and policing.

The conceptual and empirical terrain traversed in this volume is vast and varied, and – partly for those reasons – broadly illuminating. The East Asian experience with authoritarian policing partly transcends regional boundaries. This feature dates to the era of Western imperialism in the region, and it is likely to persist in this part of the world where memories of colonial rule are still relatively fresh or enduringly raw, where political and intellectual engagement with the wider world remains wide and deep, and where some of the world's most immediate and intense confrontations relevant to policing (as well as governance and politics more broadly) are likely to occur in the context of a growing ideational contest between an as-yet still-diffuse authoritarian model pressed by a more powerful and assertive China and a possibly reinvigorated (if troubled) democratic paradigm pushed by an avowedly (re)engaged US that is seeking to strengthen alignment with, and among, like-minded states in East Asia.[23]

14.2 Features and Patterns of Authoritarian Police and Policing in East Asia

As the chapters in this volume illustrate, authoritarian police and policing in East Asia have striking similarities and differences across polities and periods. Several, largely contextual, features help to make sense of the patterns.

[23] See, for example, Jacques deLisle and Avery Goldstein, "Rivalry and Security in a New Era for US-China Relations," in Jacques deLisle and Avery Goldstein (eds.), *After Engagement: Dilemmas in US–China Security Relations* (Washington, DC: Brookings, 2021), 1–47; Jacques deLisle, "The Chinese Model of Law, China's Agenda in International Law, and Implications for Democracy in Asia and Beyond," in Gilbert Rozman (ed.), *Democratization, National Identity, and Foreign Policy in Asia* (London: Routledge, 2021), 38–59; Jessica Chen Weiss, "A World Safe for Autocracy?: China's Rise and the Future of Global Politics," *Foreign Affairs* 98(4) (2019): 92–102.

Authoritarian regimes in East Asia expect police to perform a variety of functions. In nature and scope, some of these tasks would be familiar as part of policing – or low policing – anywhere, including investigating and preventing ordinary crimes, preserving public and social order against threats of unrest, or engaging in the local-level proactive measures often grouped under the label "community policing," and so on. Even in the PRC, where policework and policing have often included highly politicized and socially intrusive roles, extensive changes during the Reform Era – including developments in substantive and procedural criminal law – refocused police toward enforcing more "ordinary" criminal laws (for example, eliminating obviously political offenses such as "counter-revolutionary" crimes) and adopting a more formal approach to handling "minor" crimes (a category that, however, still does not have a clear definition in Chinese law).[24] The extent of this reorientation has waxed and waned over the last several decades, alongside shifts in the regime's views on how much to emphasize formal legality – which faded during the final years under Hu Jintao and revived, at least in some respects and with a harder authoritarian, arguably Leninist, orientation under Xi Jinping.[25]

As the PRC case also illustrates, police in East Asian authoritarian polities often undertake less conventional, and more high policing, missions, which have persisted despite the adoption in many jurisdictions of reform policies to "professionalize" police forces. These roles differ significantly across jurisdictions and over time. In Leninist-style regimes, including China, Taiwan under Kuomintang (KMT) authoritarian rule, and Vietnam, policing is, in the ruling party's conception, explicitly political work targeting the regime's enemies.[26] In East Asian authoritarian systems. police mandates (for high policing) have shifted substantially and relatively quickly in response to changes in the risks or potential challenges discerned – and the policy priorities defined – by authoritarian regimes. Contributions to this collection – and other scholarship as well – note many examples: policing cyberspace for regime-criticizing

[24] See Biddulph,Chapter 4 in this volume; also see generally Jacques deLisle, "China's Legal System," in William A. Joseph (ed.), *Politics in China* (New York: Oxford University Press, 2019), 237–273, 240–243, 251–256.

[25] See Sarah Biddulph, Elisa Nesossi, and Susan Trevaskes, "Criminal Justice Reform in the Xi Jinping Era," *Chinese Law and Society* 2(1) (2017): 63–128; Rogier Creemers and Susan Trevaskes (eds.), *Law and the Party in China* (New York: Cambridge University Press, 2020); Jacques deLisle, "The Rule of Law with Xi-Era Characteristics," *Asia Policy* 20 (2015): 23–29.

[26] See Fu, Chapter 3; Biddulph, Chapter 4; Nguyen, Chapter 5; and Chen, Chapter 8.

content in contemporary Vietnam (paralleling similar developments in China);[27] evaluating, controlling, or preempting public demonstrations – and dissenting political discourse more broadly – in China, where earlier liberalization had created space for activities that the regime later came to view with growing wariness,[28] and in Hong Kong since 2019, where police turned to hard models of policing in narrowing the once-robust space for political protests;[29] policing the media – a perennial concern in the PRC and in broadly similar regimes, particularly during periods when authoritarian rulers have seen journalism or even cultural performances as posing heightened dangers of unrest, whether at home, or from abroad, or reaching transnationally – as in the case of Hong Kong during colonial times,[30] and again, in Beijing's view, in recent years; enforcing limits on seditious speech and restricting associational freedoms to check threats that the authorities perceive from local secret societies and communist organizations in midcentury Singapore;[31] addressing criminal and other disruptive behavior that, in the eyes of the PRC regime, has posed perils for economic order and prosperity throughout much of the Reform Era;[32] suppressing prodemocracy political activism and ethnoreligious separatism in Thailand;[33] tackling the multiple purported perils of religious extremism, terrorism, separatism, and alleged efforts to undermine party rule in China in recent years; and much else.

In East Asian authoritarian contexts, police are often expected to be proactive, even preemptive, in dealing with many of these challenges. They work to penetrate and monitor society, detect and address "bad" ideas before they ripen into problematic action, maintain so thick a presence in physical space and cyberspace that collective social action (including protests) does not emerge, and (in some cases) manage – through means ranging from persuasion to cooptation to informal coercion – the sources

[27] See Nguyen, Chapter 5.

[28] See Murray Scot Tanner, "China Rethinks Unrest," *Washington Quarterly* 27(3) (2004): 137–156; Zhou Kai and Yan Xiaojun, "The Quest for Stability: Policing Popular Protest in the People's Republic of China," *Problems of Post-Communism* 61(3) (2014): 3–17. See also Fu, Chapter 3.

[29] SeeWang, Joosse, and Cho, Chapter 13.

[30] See Ng, Chapter 12.

[31] See Tan, Chapter 11.

[32] See Jacques deLisle, "States of Exception in an Exceptional State: Emergency Powers Law in China," in Victor V. Ramraj and Arun K. Thiruvengadam (eds.), *Emergency Powers in Asia* (Cambridge: Cambridge University Press, 2009), 342–390.

[33] See Mérieau, Chapter 10.

or potential roots of dissent or threats to order or the regime.[34] As the foregoing partial and selective inventory suggests, police roles often (and especially under more highly ideological regimes) are shaped by the rulers' evolving definitions of "the enemy" and high-salience threats.[35]

In Michel Foucault's terms, such actions by police extend beyond exercises of negative power, toward positive power.[36] More robustly positive power undertakings are present, and at times prominent, in police and policing in authoritarian East Asia. Some regimes have assigned the police mandates to change society, in some (but far from all) cases radically. The police in China were a key part of the party-state apparatus deployed during Mao-era campaigns to transform China's economy, social organization, politics, and, ultimately, the beliefs and inner lives of its people.[37] Alongside such radically transformative but episodic drives, the Chinese police have also been a component of more mundane systems for influencing the attitudes and orientations of individuals and targeted social groups. Especially during the PRC's early years, the police were part of a public security and criminal justice apparatus that pressed suspects not only to confess guilt but also to undergo a moral or characterological conversion to achieve reintegration into society (a society that itself was to have been remade profoundly in line with party ideology).[38] As Fu details in Chapter 3, Chinese police today use multiple methods to try to change the attitudes of human rights lawyers and other potentially troubling (for the regime) sources of dissent.

The police/public security bureau in the PRC has had a central role in operating and, later, remaining the gatekeeper to "reeducation through labor" – a form of formally noncriminal incarceration that sought to

[34] See, for example, Kroncke, Chapter 2; Fu, Chapter 3 (on coercive political persuasion targeting human rights lawyers in China); Biddulph, Chapter 4 (on the persistent view in China that much crime reflects problems of underlying political attitudes); Nguyen, Chapter 5 (on the role of police in political education of citizens in Vietnam); and Chen, Chapter 8 (on the degree of Japanese colonial police presence and penetration of society in colonial Taiwan). See also Adrian Zenz and James Leibold, "Securitizing Xinjiang: Police Recruitment, Informal Policing, and Ethnic Minority Cooptation," *China Quarterly* 242 (2020): 324–348.

[35] See, for example, Fu, Chapter 3 and Biddulph, Chapter 4.

[36] Michel Foucault, *Power/Knowledge*, ed. Colin Gordon (New York: Random House, 1986), 139.

[37] See, for example, Shao-Chuan Leng, "The Role of Law in the People's Republic of China as Reflecting Mao Zedong's Influence," *Journal of Criminal Law and Criminology* 68(3) (1977): 356–363; Franz Schurmann, *Ideology and Organization in Communist China*, 2nd ed. (Berkeley: University of California, 1968), 369–378.

[38] See generally Jerome Alan Cohen, "The Criminal Process in the People's Republic of China: An Introduction," *Harvard Law Review* 79(3) (1966): 469–533.

"reform" those subjected to it, with reform understood in a sense stronger than the goal of rehabilitation that Western criminal law discourse distinguishes from deterrence and retribution.[39] Before its formal elimination in 2013, this system focused on fluid and evolving categories of targets for "reeducation," including purported counterrevolutionaries, petty criminals, Falun Gong adherents, drug abusers, citizens who had the temerity to make trouble for local officials, activists for various social justice and political liberalization causes, and more.[40]

Other versions of police as agents of social change can be found elsewhere in authoritarian East Asia. For example, before North Vietnam's victory, the Ministry of Public Security (the Hanoi regime's principal police body) was commissioned to recruit people throughout the then-divided country to the communists' cause (and to abandon the enemy's cause), and police in contemporary Vietnam undertake political education efforts to check potential ideological threats.[41] For another example, during Korea's period of authoritarian rule with rapid economic development, police were expected to help manage the assimilation of – and keep tabs on – rural-to-urban migrants, including those who became vagrants, criminals, or sex workers in Seoul.[42]

The Korean example also illustrates how police in East Asian authoritarian regimes have filled roles that entail exercising what might be called "embedded" or "integrative" power. Police are often assigned governmental, or quasigovernmental, or social service functions that in other systems more often are performed by other institutions, such as state welfare bureaus or civil society groups, charitable organizations, and other nonstate entities. Mobrand, in Chapter 6, describes how police in authoritarian Korea provided social and related services to (and undertook management of) rural-to-urban migrants, sex workers, underemployed youth, and others. Various modes of community service provision, and the *koban*, or neighborhood police box, system in Japan and its imitation in China, are manifestations of what in the West might seem to be community policing on steroids – a public and social service role that coexists

[39] Joel Meyer, "Reflections on Some Theories of Punishment," *Journal of Criminal Law and Criminology* 59(4) (1969): 595–598.

[40] See Hualing Fu, "Reeducation through Labor in Historical Perspective," *China Quarterly* 184 (2005): 811–830; Stephen Noakes, "A Disappearing Act: The Evolution of China's Administrative Detention System," *Journal of Chinese Political Science* 23 (2018): 199–216.

[41] SeeNguyen, Chapter 5.

[42] See Mobrand, Chapter 6.

with the more repressive and intrusive side of East Asian authoritarian police forces' grassroots presence (including overseeing the household registration systems in China, Japan, and Taiwan), and their collaborative, cooptative, and sometimes mildly coercive relationship with nonstate and parastatal entities.[43] In Hong Kong's final colonial years, reforms to a once-corrupt police department included the adoption of customer service orientation toward the citizenry.[44] It is a common assessment in authoritarian or formerly authoritarian polities in East Asia that police spend much of their time in such community service and engagement and monitoring functions that lie beyond the core elements of policework

Internal institutional structures of the police are another critical factor in the character and role of police and policing in East Asian authoritarian regimes. The most prominent and widespread of these structural issues – with implications for the police's relationships with the regime and society – is relative centralization or decentralization of the police.

In small polities (such as Singapore and Hong Kong) and those under hard-authoritarian colonial rule (for example, Korea before independence), police institutions have tended to be more centralized in principle and in practice. In other contexts, decentralization of various sorts has been more prevalent. In Taiwan during the era of KMT authoritarian rule, Chen argues in Chapter 8, decentralization was the norm for the ordinary (but not the political) police, with local police deeply entangled in local politics, providing intelligence on opposition candidates and support and protection for favored ruling party candidates at the grassroots level. For much of the PRC's history, including much of the Reform Era, relative decentralization has been the de facto (but, in China's formally centralized system, not the *de jure*) norm for the police and public security bodies (as for many other state institutions), punctuated by periodic efforts to recentralize (including in recent years under Xi Jinping). Police, like other institutions in China's vast, multilayered state have been enmeshed in China's pattern of "dual rule" – with units at each level being immediately accountable to higher level organs in their own functionally specialized

[43] See Chen, Chapter 8, in this volume, and Martin, "The Confucian Ethic and the Spirit of East Asian Police" on the Taiwan case, for example. On relations with nominally nonstate entities in China, see Biddulph, Chapter 4, in this volume; Xiaohai Wang and Dennis Sing-wing Wong, "Police Social Service Work in China: Community Policing with Chinese Characteristics," *Asia Pacific Journal of Police and Criminal Justice* 9(1) (2012): 34–53; and Xiaoming Chen, "Community and Policing Strategies: A Chinese Approach to Crime Control," *Policing and Society* 12(1) (2002): 1–13.

[44] SeeWang, Joosse, and Cho, Chapter 13.

system, and to the omnicompetent party and state at the same hierarchical level in their geographic areas.[45] Political policing, Fu notes in Chapter 3, has been relatively highly centralized in China.

Centralization has been criticized from liberal and prodemocracy perspectives, for example in Hong Kong, where police behavior in responding to the Occupy Central/Umbrella Movement in 2014 was denounced as showing that the Special Administrative Region's police had become too much the instrument of the central government in Beijing. This criticism resonated still more strongly in the context of the protests of 2019–2020, when the Hong Kong police took on a larger, and more violent, role in quashing a social movement stridently condemned by Beijing, and when a National Security Law for Hong Kong adopted by the PRC's national legislature signaled that the local police – and, more clearly, a newly created special security police – were an instrument of the central government.[46]

Decentralization has been a feature of postauthoritarian reforms in some East Asian cases, for example the US occupation government's moves to dismantle the institutional underpinnings of centralized policing under the Interior Ministry in Japan, or the push for decentralization as an accompaniment to democratization in Taiwan.[47] On the other hand, Mérieau argues in Chapter 10, late 1990s democratization in Thailand prompted efforts to centralize control over the police. Kroncke argues in Chapter 2 that Japan has a mixed pattern of decentralized operation and centralized mechanisms for accountability, and that decentralization in the US may account in part for the lack of police accountability and the prevalence of abuse.

Centralization, or decentralization, affects the feasibility of some forms of police accountability and elite-led reorientation of police missions. But relative centralization or decentralization does not correlate neatly with other foci of concern in assessing police and policing – as the foregoing summary suggests. As Kroncke argues in Chapter 2, the choice between

[45] See generally Kenneth G. Lieberthal, "The Fragmented Authoritarianism Model and Its Limitations," in Kenneth G. Lieberthal and David M. Lampton (eds.), *Bureaucracy, Politics and Decision Making in Post-Mao China* (Berkeley: University of California Press, 1992), 1–32; Schurmann, *Ideology and Organization in Communist China*; see also Yuhua Wang, "Empowering the Police: How the Chinese Communist Party Manages Its Coercive Leaders," *China Quarterly* 219 (2014): 625–648 (decentralized public security system and effort to increase centralized disciplinary control over police).

[46] See Martin, Chapter 7, and Wang, Joosse, and Cho, Chapter 13; see also Jacques deLisle, "Hong Kong's Summer of Discontent," *Orbis* 63(4) (2019): 473–504.

[47] See Chen, Chapter 8, and Nakano, Chapter 9.

more top-down, centralized approaches, and more horizontal, society-including ones, to police discipline and accountability appear to make little systematic difference in addressing police violence. More broadly, decentralization may reflect high state capacity to penetrate society or high social acceptance of police (including where police pursue centrally defined missions), but it may instead reveal a weak central state unable to make its writ run among some of its most dispersed and consequential local agents (who may be more responsive to elements in the local society in which they are embedded).

Horizontal institutional contexts in which police operate – especially other organs of the state that perform policing or related functions – shape police and policing in East Asian authoritarian regimes. In some of these polities, the most evidently authoritarian and heavily political aspects of policing – surveilling, physically controlling, and suppressing perceived political opponents, or constricting spheres of privacy and autonomy in society so severely that dissent and the expression or political mobilization of heterodox views are prevented – are assigned in whole or in part to the (ordinary) police. In other systems, these roles are entrusted to specialized political or security police (or other bodies). Chapters in this volume reflect the diversity of patterns. In authoritarian Japan, Taiwan, Korea, and Vietnam, there were relatively clear distinctions between political police and ordinary police, with the former outranking the latter within the larger police hierarchy.[48] In colonial and independent Singapore, a special branch within the police focused on threats to political order and sedition – a pattern echoed and amplified in the National Security Law adopted for Hong Kong in the aftermath of thc 2019–2020 protests.[49]

In Thailand, roles of controlling and coercing dissidents and insurgents have shifted, at least at the margins, between the police and the military across many years of broader regime instability.[50] The PRC has had a large

[48] Nakano, in Chapter 9, categorizes the landscape of Japanese police organizations into "political police," "criminal police," and "administrative police." Although there was much continuity of personnel and organization despite institutional reforms under the US occupation, there was a break from the brutal secret police of the authoritarian era. In Chapter 8, Chen points to the distinction between the ordinary police, on one hand, and the secret and military police, on the other, in Taiwan. Nguyen's account of Vietnam in Chapter 5 depicts a similar division among police, public security, and strategic intelligence origins, prior to recent amendments effecting a partial institutional merger amid a professionalization drive.

[49] On Singapore, see Tan, Chapter 11.

[50] SeeMérieau, Chapter 10.

and complex array of institutions that exercise police powers, including to address threats to political and social order: the regular public security bureau police – which includes an internal domestic security protection section with responsibility for dealing with high policing matters, paramilitary People's Armed Police, urban stability-maintenance forces such as the *chengguan*, police-like officers who work for many state institutions (including, but not limited to, legal ones such as the courts and procuracy), and a parapolice auxiliary (*xiejing*).[51] The pattern in China varies both over time and by context, with different organs with various policing and other coercive powers taking different roles. In the Han heartland (especially during crisis times) and ethnoreligious minority areas (especially in times of significant unrest) – including notably Xinjiang in recent years and Tibet in years past – the more unchecked nonpolice coercive forces play a large role.

From the perspectives of rulers and citizens, the more salient issues may be the range of functions performed – and how they are performed – rather than the allocation of roles among police and other institutions. But, for the police and for policing (and sometimes for state and society as well), the differences among institutional structures can be important. Among other things, such institutional patterns of authority and behavior can have significant effects on the legitimacy of police officers and institutions in society, their relationship with higher-level powers in the authoritarian state or party-state, and their midreform or postdemocratization roles and fate (as well as the police's own institutional ethos and mindset).[52]

Another, broader, dimension of horizontal institutional context is the police's relationships with other institutions within the state or party-state. Where the police are located within complex bureaucratic and political structures, and how much the police are interpenetrated with other entities, affect the character of authoritarian policing (as well as the broader polity). Here, too, there has been variation among East Asian authoritarian polities across cases and over time. In Nakano's account in Chapter 9, high-ranking and lesser officials in authoritarian Japan's police institutions (especially the Special Higher Police) fanned out into, and influenced, the wider state bureaucracy, the military, and electoral politics and

[51] See Suzanne E. Scoggins, "Policing Modern China," *China Law and Society Review* 3(2) (2018): 79–117.

[52] See the discussion in Martin, Chapter 7 (on Taiwan and Hong Kong), and Chen, Chapter 8 (on Taiwan).

major economic actors – and they continued to do so despite postauthoritarian efforts to diminish their influence. In Taiwan, Korea, and Japan, the respective roles of police, procuracy, and courts have been a particular focus of reforms to institutional relationships. Shifts away from authoritarian rule have generally diminished the role of the police, as the crime control efficiency gains of leaving more power and discretion to the police have become less compelling, given the collateral costs to procedural justice.[53]

In China during the PRC era, relations and allocations of roles and authority among the police (public security organs), prosecutors (the procuracy), and courts have been reconfigured repeatedly. Among other shifts in the relationship among these entities, there has been movement back and forth along a spectrum from role-based professionalism, respect for procedures and legal formality, and relatively sharp distinctions among police, prosecutorial, judicial, and other functions, to close collaboration and service as coordinated parts of an integrated and relatively undifferentiated organizational weapon. So, too, there have been fluctuations from relatively expansive to relatively limited police roles – and relatively high and low levels of police power and centrality – in the criminal justice and broader sanctioning process. For example, the head of the police/public security sometimes, but not always, has been relatively dominant among the troika of police, prosecutor, and court in – and somewhat beyond – the criminal process. Shifting dynamics in relations among the Chinese Communist Party's Political-Legal Committee, the police, and other institutions related to the legal system that operate at each level in China's multitiered system of governance have meant fluctuating autonomy and clout for the police. Overall, periods within China's Reform Era of stronger regime commitment to ruling by law (if not to a full-fledged rule of law) have been associated with more restrictions on police power and discretion, and more formal and arm's-length relationships among police, procuracy, courts, and the party.[54]

53 On the Taiwan case, see Chen, Chapter 8. On Korea, see Kuk Cho, "The Unfinished 'Criminal Procedure Revolution' of Post-Democratization South Korea," *Denver Journal of International Law and Policy* 30(3) (2002): 377–394.

54 See Jerome A. Cohen, "Criminal Justice in China: From the Gang of Four to Bo Xilai," *Human Rights Watch*, July 25, 2013, www.pacificcenturyinst.org/download/media/Criminal_Justice_in_China_Jerome_Cohen.pdf; David Leheny and Sida Liu, "The Politics of Crime, Punishment, and Social Order in East Asia," *Annual Review of Law and Social Science* 6 (2010): 239–258; Dali Yang, "China's Troubled Quest for Order: Leadership, Organization and the Contradictions of the Stability Maintenance Regime," *Journal of Contemporary China* 26(103) (2017): 35–53.

Under Xi, a move to trial-centered criminal justice – and a more professional judiciary – portended narrower and more defined roles for the police. At the same time, constitutional changes to create supervision commissions that absorbed former prosecutorial powers and the CCP's internal, informal, and extralegal disciplinary system, and the reinvigoration of party control over legal institutions, have created new uncertainties about the scope and content of police – as well as other institutions' – roles, particularly in addressing the significant issue of corruption in state institutions.[55]

Vertical relations upward – connecting the police and the authoritarian regimes they serve – are another factor shaping the roles of police in East Asian authoritarian polities. One template has authoritarian rulers wielding the police as a disciplined tool to pursue ambitious regime agendas or suppress regime-identified enemies. In Leninist-style systems – including the PRC, Vietnam, and to a lesser extent KMT-ruled authoritarian Taiwan – party dominance, control, and penetration of the police are norms insisted upon by the regime, and strongly reemphasized when the leadership discerns that indiscipline in the police or too-weak political control over the police is a problem or potential problem for the regime, or more broadly when there are moves to strengthen the party's or top leader's control over the system.[56] Measures to assert such control range widely, including frequent changes to organizational structures and personnel, and ideological training and imperatives of varying levels of intensity.

Relatively subtle differences among generally similar regimes can mean different relationships of the police to political leadership (and, in turn, significant differences in police and policing), with the greater concentration of political power and tighter grounding of police agendas in the thought of the top leader in China under Mao and Xi leading to a different – closer and more controlling – relationship of regime leadership to

[55] See generally Creemers and Trevaskes (eds.), *Law and the Party in China;* Jacques deLisle, "Law in the China Model 2.0: Legality, Developmentalism and Leninism under Xi Jinping," *Journal of Contemporary China* (103) (2017): 68–84; Jamie P. Horsley, "What's So Controversial About China's New Anti-Corruption Body?" *Brookings Institution*, May 30, 2018, www.brookings.edu/opinions/whats-so-controversial-about-chinas-new-anti-corruption-body/; Li Li and Peng Wang, "From Institutional Interaction to Institutional Integration: The National Supervisory Commission and China's New Anti-Corruption Model," *China Quarterly* 240 (2019): 967–989.

[56] See Biddulph, Chapter 4 (on Xi-era insistence on party control over police and other legal institutions and use of political, legal, administrative, and personnel measures to assure control over police); Nguyen, Chapter 5 (on the Vietnamese Communist Party's

police than in Vietnam, or China at other periods. Political police or secret police in predemocratization Japan and its colonies, and during the early decades of Kuomintang rule in Taiwan, are a less ideologically charged variation on this pattern of strong regime control over parts of the police in hard-authoritarian regimes.[57]

Toward the opposite end of the spectrum are police forces that have had greater autonomy and a sense of distinctly professional and somewhat politically neutral roles, typically in softer authoritarian contexts. This is the image (and self-image) and the reality (to a significant if incomplete extent) in postindependence Singapore and in late colonial and postreversion Hong Kong (although not in Hong Kong from the mid-2010s on).[58]

But, as several chapters in this volume addressing the persistence of authoritarian policing after democratic transitions – and Kroncke's and Mérieau's skepticism, in Chapters 2 and 10 respectively, about regime type as an explanation for differences in patterns of police behavior – suggest, even differences between authoritarian and nonauthoritarian regimes (much less the more subtle distinctions *among* authoritarian regimes) do not strongly predict this, or many other, patterns of police and policing in East Asia.[59]

Vertical relations downward – connecting police and society – are another defining feature, and point of variation, among East Asian authoritarian regimes. In some cases, relations between the police and at least some segments of society are starkly adversarial and often mutually

perception of problems with the public security apparatus and the dangers that posed to the regime and broader insistence on the party's penetration of and control over the police); and Chen, Chapter 8 (on the Leninist character of the KMT and its approach to policing). See also Jacques deLisle and Guobin Yang (eds.), *The Party Leads All* (Washington, DC: Brookings, 2022).

57 For an argument that this was the case in authoritarian Korea and has led to a legacy that impedes reforms that would make the police less heavily an instrument of the ruling regime, see Byongook Moon, "The Politicization of Police in South Korea: A Critical Review," *Policing* 27(1) (2004): 128–136. See also Chen, Chapter 8, in this volume.

58 See Martin, Chapter 7, and Tan, Chapter 11; see also Michael C. Davis, *Making Hong Kong China* (New York: Columbia University Press, 2020).

59 Kroncke's endogeneity-emphasizing account in Chapter 2 concludes that the democratic/authoritarian contrast in regime type does little to explain differences in police accountability, including upward accountability. Mérieau's account of Thailand in Chapter 10 attributes the lack of change in police roles and behavior under military and democratic regimes partly to the high autonomy of the police, especially under democratic government.

violent. As many of the chapters in this book detail,[60] this tends to occur when the regime that the police serve discerns – correctly or not (and in some cases exaggeratedly or disingenuously) – serious threats from political foes in society. In authoritarian East Asia, this pattern has had a variety of foundations: national liberation movements, and sympathetic segments of the population, challenging colonial rule (as occurred, for example, in French Indochina, and as chronically concerned British authorities in Hong Kong watching waves of nationalist revolution roil mainland China); continuing resistance by supporters of a toppled predecessor (in the early days of communist regimes in China and Vietnam); threats of sedition – often from ostensibly transnationally linked and/or communist groups (as was the case in late colonial Singapore and Hong Kong); pro-democracy activists and their supporters (which are among the shifting set of groups classified as enemies of the regime in China, with analogous patterns in Thailand, predemocratic transition Taiwan and Korea, and, in recent years, postreversion Hong Kong); and ethnic or religious groups (generally different from those dominating the regime) with imputed secessionist or revolutionary agendas (as with Uyghurs and Tibetans in China, Muslim ethnic groups in Thailand and the Philippines, and elsewhere).

The role of communal cleavages can be especially complex, as, for example, in Hong Kong (where some prodemocracy Hong Kongers charged – amid heightening animosity toward relatively recent mainland immigrants – that the local police had been supplemented by mainland anti-riot officers during the conflicts of 2019–2020) and Taiwan (where the police force during authoritarian rule was drawn from the relatively small minority of the population who were "mainlanders" who arrived with the KMT government at the end of the Chinese civil war and began their rule in Taiwan with brutal suppression – including by the police – of nationalist movements backed by members of the majority Taiwanese population).

In other contexts, police relations with groups in local society are more ambivalent and intermediate. The police often seek, at the regime's behest, limited changes in social behavior but do not ride roughshod over social habits, values, and preferences, or resort to highly coercive, and alienating, methods against targeted groups. As Fu argues in Chapter 3, the Chinese police approach to human rights lawyers is to engage in various forms of

[60] See Fu, Chapter 3; Biddulph, Chapter 4; Martin, Chapter 7; Chen, Chapter 8; Tan, Chapter 11; Ng, Chapter 12; and Wang, Joosse and Cho, Chapter13, among others.

persuasion short of fully-fledged coercion, with the goal of changing the attitudes of these not-initially-strident critics or proto-opponents. More broadly, Chinese police turn to what one analyst calls "soft-line persuasive tactics" when pursuing relatively modest and not-high-priority transformative goals, including in the context of crime control.[61] In Mobrand's account of authoritarian-era Seoul in Chapter 6, Korean police sought to enforce criminal laws that would constrain the activities of criminal gangs, migrant youth, and others, and also sought such groups' cooperation and offered them partial, legally questionable accommodation. In Hong Kong, police have long played a role in the government's complex management of economic and social change in a rapidly transforming community including (in an example noted in Martin's account in Chapter 7) by implementing rules requiring changes to small-scale commercial activities. In Singapore, police have been part of the regime's complex agenda of managing the challenges of a multi-ethnic, partly immigrant society (with a Chinese majority and Malay, as well as Indian, minorities in a city-state adjacent to the much larger Malaysia).

Often, the vertical relationship of police to society lies farther along the spectrum toward cooperation and trust. In many East Asian authoritarian polities, police exhibit high levels of community engagement. They are present on the ground in neighborhoods. They proactively mediate local disputes in a community with which they are deeply familiar (as in Taiwan). They conceive of themselves as "citizen officers" or "public servants," or consciously seek to promote a positive image – often with an impetus from regime policies (as in Singapore or late colonial Hong Kong or Vietnam).[62]

Overtasked and underresourced police in such systems have incentives to develop and sustain cooperative relationships with social and nonstate groups as a means to achieving tasks that range from order maintenance to accomplishing not-radically socially transformative goals to providing regime-mandated services. As contributors to this volume detail, this type of phenomenon can be found in authoritarian Korea, China, Vietnam, Taiwan, and elsewhere. On the other side of the police–society relationship, the role of police in providing welfare goods and a variety of governmental and social services can and does build trust in and relatively

[61] See Jianhua Xu, "Authoritarian Policing with Chinese Characteristics," *Crime, Law and Social Change* 61 (2014): 439–460.

[62] See Kroncke, Chapter 2; Nguyen, Chapter 5; Tan, Chapter 11; and Wang, Joosse, and Cho, Chapter 13.

positive attitudes toward police. This pattern, too, is reflected in many of the polities addressed in the chapters in this volume, including China and Vietnam (with the role of police in COVID-19 crisis control and relief being a recent example) and authoritarian-era Korea (with job training and welfare services) and Taiwan (where the ordinary police's relationship with local society contrasted sharply with the political police's – a pattern echoed in Japan). Where a more transformation-minded regime seeks to effect unwelcome changes in society, the local police can serve – or be seen as serving – as a buffer between problematic regime policies and society, or as a hinge between society and the state, sometimes functioning as the de facto representative or protector of societal interests and preferences in interactions with higher levels of the state. Examples of this can be found across the spectrum of East Asian authoritarian regimes, from predemocratic transition Korea (where the regime agenda was relatively modest) to PRC-era China (where radical change was at times the far-from-fully-implemented mandate from on high).

In this relatively benign version of police–society relations, there may be echoes of East Asian political traditions of the omnicompetent local official and blurred state–society boundaries, cultural norms of the benevolent "father-mother official" (*fumu guan*), and inherited societal preferences for keeping the central authorities' power remote from subjects' daily lives.[63] Whatever its origins and resonances, such trust and positive relations can be fragile, vulnerable to erosion or collapse when the police act, or are required to act, as agents of a regime pressing unpopular policies at odds with established social norms. In this volume, Tan's discussion of some of the more fraught periods in Singapore's history in Chapter 11, and Martin's and Wang, Joosse, and Cho's accounts of police handling of prodemocracy protests in Hong Kong, in Chapters 7 and 13 respectively, illustrate these possibilities – in pointed contrast to the democratic-era Taiwan case, which, in Martin's assessment in Chapter 7, shows police siding with popular democratic principles against the top leadership's preferences in handling the Sunflower Movement protests (which challenged efforts to shepherd a cross-Strait economic agreement through the legislature).

External influences – from abroad and from the past – can and do affect police and policing in East Asian authoritarian polities. Past colonial and quasicolonial experiences have shaped distinctive institutions, traditions,

[63] See William P. Alford, "On the Limits of Grand Theory in Comparative Law," *Washington Law Review* 61(3) (1986): 945–956.

and trajectories. Imperial Japan replicated in its colonial outposts in Korea and Taiwan features of domestic Japanese policing and police institutions. In Singapore and Hong Kong, British colonial rule introduced different – and often less strongly or openly authoritarian – organizational structures, norms, and patterns of behavior in, and relating to, police and policing. French colonial rule in Vietnam, American colonial influence in the Philippines, and the US occupation government in Japan (with its avowed agenda of liberalization and democratization – and, to a degree, political Americanization) left their distinctive marks as well.

Foreign impacts are not limited to colonial rule or "outside-in" impositions. Reformers in many East Asian authoritarian regimes looked abroad to borrow legal techniques, including those relating to police and laws governing the police: Meiji Japan (to the West), Qing China (to the West and Japan), revolutionary Vietnam (to China and the Soviet Union), Thailand (to France and the UK, and – later, during the Cold War – the US), authoritarian Taiwan (to both Japan and pre-PRC China), and Reform-era China (to the West and East Asian neighbors). Foreign factors played still more indirect roles as well. As Ng details in Chapter 12, London and, in turn, British authorities in Hong Kong responded, with policies affecting policing, to the national security concerns of foreign governments–including those of Japan, and Qing, Republican, and Communist China, and the US. Tan argues in Chapter 11 that concern about unrest in British India (and threats from colonial Malaya) framed the development of laws that gave police greater powers to regulate and suppress politically charged speech and action in colonial Singapore.

Once received, such outside influences became part of a broader history of, and related to, police and policing. As many of the chapters in this book address, the legacy of authoritarian policing from earlier periods – often but not always rooted in foreign influence or legal transplants – can cast a long shadow. Several contributors consider the persistence of past patterns of authoritarian policing in systems – such as China, Vietnam, and Hong Kong – that have undergone significant political change while remaining authoritarian – and in some cases relapsing into harder authoritarian patterns.[64] Despite the radical changes in Chinese politics and policing during the Mao years and the Reform era, some aspects of authoritarian policing – especially low policing and basic institutional structures – have shown much continuity over much of the PRC's history.

[64] See Biddulph, Chapter 4; Nguyen, Chapter 5; Martin, Chapter 7; and Wang, Joosse, and Cho, Chapter 13, among others.

Other authors in this book address the lasting influence of authoritarian-era policing – particularly in the institutional structure, personnel, and organizational culture of police – even after a political order has transitioned to democratic rule (as in Japan, Taiwan, and Korea).[65] Kroncke's analysis in Chapter 2 also suggests a prominent role for inheritances from the past (whether or not external in origin): he finds endogeneity and path dependence likely to account for some significant aspects of police roles and behavior.

The complex and varied web of foreign influence continues today. For example, prodemocracy activists in Hong Kong in 2019–2020 (and, to a lesser extent, earlier in the postreversion era) tried to rally British, American, and other foreign pressure against the authoritarian methods of policing that the Special Administrative Region government deployed. In doing so, they have sought, in part, to counter the growing reach of PRC-style authoritarian policing into Hong Kong, including in the form of a proposed ordinance that would have permitted extradition of criminal suspects to the mainland, and a National Security Law that adopts broad definitions of sedition, subversion, and other security offenses and expands the powers of the police and other arms of the state security apparatus to quash or chill actions and views unacceptable to Beijing.

More broadly, contemporary international rule-of-law promotion efforts (primarily from North America and Western Europe) have offered legal reform advice and assistance to authoritarian states in East Asia. These efforts often seek to improve police and policing, in large part by seeking to increase accountability and professionalism but also by offering means to enhance police effectiveness. Governments and nongovernmental organizations in liberal-democratic states have sought to promote legal reforms in China to ameliorate authoritarian police behavior, including access to counsel and evidence, prohibitions on torture, limits to detention without process, privileges against self-incrimination, and presumptions of innocence. Foreign assistance programs that provide technical assistance and training for Chinese police also can make a repressive authoritarian police force more capable. As Kroncke notes in Chapter 2, there is also a robust, ostensibly politically neutral, and often technocratic transnational discourse of police professionalism that extends to authoritarian East Asia. Especially in recent years, foreign advice and efforts to

[65] See Chen, Chapter 8, and Nakano, Chapter 9.

affect police and policing in China and, perhaps, more broadly in East Asian authoritarian regimes – generally in a liberal, democratic, rule-of-law, accountability-promoting direction – appear to face diminishing prospects for influence, as China's leadership has become increasingly skeptical and wary of liberal-legalist premises underlying foreign advice or pressure, and more confident and assertive in its own illiberal model (including repressive authoritarian policing techniques) and its potential for export.[66]

The numerous and varied factors that shape and characterize authoritarian police and policing in East Asia can and do interact. Historical legacies and foreign influence may be conducive to different institutional structures within the police and institutional relations with nonpolice entities. Police who are primarily accountable upward to an authoritarian regime that exercises highly centralized political control and that pursues an agenda of radical social transformation or resolutely quashing potential dissent will have a different relationship with society than will a more decentralized police force tasked with implementing social welfare programs or managing relatively limited threats of social disorder with significant autonomy and modest resources. The factors are too numerous and the interactions among them too complex to generate consistent patterns or simple predictions.

14.3 Paradoxes and Ambivalences of Authoritarian Policing in East Asia

Several overlapping paradoxes beset authoritarian police and policing in East Asia. They pose dilemmas for those who seek to make police and policing effective (the definition of which varies considerably according to context and perspective) or to reform police and policing (generally, but not necessarily, by moving from authoritarian toward democratic).

The paradox of scope versus effectiveness confounds police and police work in East Asian authoritarian polities and gives reasons for ambivalence about the professionalism of police. Classic theories of government and management have linked functional specialization to efficiency and

[66] See generally deLisle, "Lex Americana"; Paul Tsai China Center, "Chinese Legal Reform," Yale Law School, https://law.yale.edu/china-center/programs/chinese-legal-reform; see also Sheena Chestnut Greitens, "Dealing with Demand for China's Global Surveillance Exports," *Brookings Institution*, April 2020, www.brookings.edu/wp-content/uploads/2020/04/FP_20200428_china_surveillance_greitens_v3.pdf.

effectiveness.[67] Other analyses link organizational strength to a sense of professionalism, corporate identity, and institutional purpose.[68] These concepts both suggest that police can be more effective when they have bounded and distinctively professional policing missions. As several contributors to this volume address, professionalization – generally in the service of effectiveness in performing delimited tasks – has been a recurring theme in regime policies about police and policing in authoritarian East Asia (as well as in transitions from authoritarian to democratic governance). In Vietnam and China, reforms have moved to bring formally nonstate actors performing police-like or police-adjacent functions into – or more under the control of – the state police structure.[69]

But impetuses to expand police mandates – whether from political leaders' policy choices or less purposive accretions of tasks and roles – are common, perhaps especially so in East Asian authoritarian regimes: there is a relative paucity of the features (such as constitutional rights, media scrutiny, public pressure, and judicial accountability) that sometimes limit the scope of police power and discretion in democratic, rule-of-law polities, or, arguably, in polities with more Western-style traditions of governance (with sharper differentiation of the functional roles of state institutions and officials); and local-level state officials may be viewed as omnicompetent (in the tradition of the Chinese magistrate) and the boundaries between state and society and between state-regulated and private behavior may be relatively porous.

In an obvious sense, extension of police roles beyond conventional professional or core police functions increases the power of the police. But with greater scope and reach come both immediate and more indirect risks to police effectiveness. Most simply, police may not be very well suited to perform tasks beyond their professional capabilities or that collectively exceed their capacities – a type of concern that has driven calls for reallocating various nonpolicing functions (and related resources) to social workers, mental health professionals, and others amid outrage

[67] See generally Adam Smith, "The Pin Factory," *Vocational Guidance Quarterly* 10(3) (1962): 173–174, https://onlinelibrary.wiley.com/doi/epdf/10.1002/j.2164-585X.1962.tb00147.x; Max Weber, "On Bureaucracy," in Gerth and Mills (eds.), *From Max Weber*, 196–244.

[68] See generally Schurmann, *Ideology and Organization in Communist China*; Philip Selznick, *The Organizational Weapon: A Study of Bolshevik Strategy and Tactics* (Santa Monica, CA: Rand, 1952).

[69] See Nguyen's discussion of the commune police in Vietnam in Chapter 5; Jean Christophe Mittelstaedt, "The Grid Management System in Contemporary China," *China Information* (May 2021): 1–20, https://doi.org/10.1177/0920203X211011565.

over police killings in the US in the early 2020s. Faced with expanding demands and continuing lack of strong legal restraints, police may become, in Mobrand's phrase in Chapter 6, "unrestricted but limited." In Biddulph's account in Chapter 4, the expansion of the category of minor offenses changed, and in some respects significantly increased, the large, long-standing, and often-shifting role of Chinese police in handling a wide range of sanctionable but not seriously criminal behavior.

Resource-constrained police may shirk, or be diverted from, some of their vast or growing responsibilities, including for ordinary police work, sometimes with broader deleterious effects for police and policing. As Mobrand details in Chapter 6, police in authoritarian Korea were tasked with a sprawling agenda of handling organized crime, prostitution, vagrancy, housing shortages, welfare needs, and assimilation of new and poor urbanites. Partly as a result, rather than imposing formal and substantial detention and punishment on criminal groups or targeted activists, the overstretched police engaged in sporadic widespread roundups followed by quick release of most of those detained. In Chen's account of authoritarian Taiwan in Chapter 8, the expected role of police in supporting local political machines led to reduced efficacy in more core aspects or policing and police reluctance to enforce anticorruption laws. In Vietnam (in Nguyen's account in Chapter 5) and China, directives to police to preempt or deter peaceful public assemblies, to censor traditional and new media, and to instill the regime's preferred political narratives imposed daunting demands on police forces that also shouldered significant – and sometimes deprioritized – conventional policing duties with very limited resources. Chinese police are unhappy for relatively mundane reasons of inadequate budgets, burdensome reporting requirements, and other features of their work that they see as asking too much while providing too little.[70]

Functionally broad and heavily resource-demanding mandates for police can also be conducive to pursuit by the police of "policing on the cheap." As Biddulph notes in Chapter 4, Chinese police have sought (at times with explicit support from regime policy) shortcuts from ordinary police (and, in turn, prosecutorial and judicial) procedures to reap the efficiency (in processing) gains that come with summary proceedings for vaguely defined small crimes, or informal reconciliation in criminal cases (which includes elements akin to state-facilitated private settlement and

[70] See Suzanne Scoggins and Kevin J. O'Brien, "China's Unhappy Police," *Asian Survey* 56(2) (2016): 225–242.

holds out the prospect of reducing phenomena that strain police legitimacy and resources, such as victims' discontent with the criminal justice system or resorts to socially disruptive self-help).

In China, a striking dynamic has recurred relatively frequently: already-burdened police (in a system with a low police-to-population ratio) resort to relatively short-lived campaigns that economize on resource use at the cost of consistency and order in addressing targeted behavior – to root out counterrevolutionaries (during the regime's early years) or to strike hard against crime (including economic crime and official corruption that have been among the consequences of economic reform and development), or to combat pandemics in part through controlling public behavior (as with SARS and COVID-19), or to suppress political dissent or heterodox religious activities, or other identified evils.[71] Analogized to wars or battles and pursued intensely and sometimes violently, such drives may be second-best solutions, compared with more orderly and well-resourced police (and other instruments of government policy).

Especially in the context of the campaing-style of governance that has recurred repeatedly in China during the PRC era, but also in the more quotidian roles of the police in maintaining local-level social order and management of society, the police (and other authorities) have not acted alone with only the state's or party-state's assets; they have mobilized members of society and social resources, sometimes very intensively and on a large scale. In Hong Kong during the 2010s, the de facto assignment of repressive police roles to actors outside the state took a notably violent turn, as police collaborated with triads in breaking up Occupy Central encampments and faced accusations of complicity, or worse, in gang-led assaults on protesters opposing the proposed extradition law and pushing for democratic reforms and government and police accountability.[72]

As this suggests, the quest for policing on the cheap can go well beyond methods that raise due process-type concerns and verge into brutality. In East Asian authoritarian regimes, police disregard (sometimes partly

[71] See, for example, Scoggins, "Policing Modern China"; Susan Trevaskes, "Yanda 2001: Form and Strategy in a Chinese Anti-Crime Campaign," *Australian and New Zealand Journal of Criminology* 36(3) (2003): 272–292; Peng Wang, "Politics of Crime Control: How Campaign-Style Law Enforcement Sustains Authoritarian Rule in China," *British Journal of Criminology* 60(2) (2020): 422–443; Feng Jiang and Chuanyu Xie, "Roles of Chinese Police Amidst the COVID-19 Pandemic," *Policing* 14(4) (2020): 1127–1137.

[72] See Wang, Joosse, and Cho, Chapter 13; Melinda Liu, "Hong Kong's Future: Police State or Mob State?" *Foreign Policy*, October 25, 2019, https://foreignpolicy.com/2019/10/25/hong-kong-protests-future-china-police-mob/.

owing to resource constraints) the strictures of formal procedures and rights set forth in relatively liberal laws on the books in ways that entail abusive behavior such as coerced confessions and serious punishments on questionable legal bases. China's sanctioning process often draws criticism, at home and abroad, on such grounds.[73] In the Philippines, a democratically elected but authoritarian-minded leader's impatience with (or contempt for) ordinary criminal law processes unleashed a wave of extrajudicial killings of suspected drug criminals, some of them by police. Whether or not these varied measures are effective means to achieving the regime's goals (and often they are not), they sow distrust, fear, and hatred of the police in society, which can undermine the police's ability to perform more routine functions or obtain valuable or necessary cooperation from society in addressing threats to order, stability, or regime survival.

Especially (but not only) when they have sprawling or burgeoning responsibilities, police inevitably depend on some level of cooperation from the public, and all but the most extreme police states accept or assume that the police will not stand wholly apart from the societies in which they operate. Police overstretched by expansive or expanding roles sometimes delegate functions – especially new or noncore or nonconventional ones – to nongovernmental, substate agents, and cooperators in society. Especially under Mao but with echoes today (now enhanced with high-tech tools), the police (along with other authorities) have recruited ordinary citizens as, in effect, police adjuncts to monitor and report on local residents.[74] With the growth of China's high-tech surveillance state (which took on new and broader purposes in the fight against COVID-19), and the regime's growing focus on social management and prevention and control of a vast array of perceived threats and disfavored behavior, Chinese police have had new demands piled atop more longstanding ones, sharpening imperatives to delegate to, or cooperate with, trusted members of society and formally nongovernmental grassroots organizations, including urban residents' committees and village-level organs of governance. In Nguyen's account of Vietnam in Chapter 5,

[73] See, for example, US Congressional-Executive Commission on China, *2020 Annual Report* (Washington, DC: US Government Publishing Office, 2021), 83–106; Human Rights Watch, *Tiger Chairs and Cell Bosses: Police Torture of Criminal Suspects in China* (New York: Human Rights Watch, 2015), www.hrw.org/report/2015/05/13/tiger-chairs-and-cell-bosses/police-torture-criminal-suspects-china.

[74] See, for example, John Brehm and Emerson M. S. Niou, "Police Patrol versus Self-Policing: A Comparative Analysis of the Control Systems Used in the Former Soviet Union and Communist China," *Journal of Theoretical Politics* 9(1) (1997): 107–130.

the police role in addressing COVID-19 was a more benign variation on the Chinese pattern, with police efforts to mobilize social resources being perceived as transparent and legitimate by the affected public. In authoritarian-era Korea, patterns of police interaction with local criminal organizations included reliance by police on what were ostensibly targets of police action to help maintain order and provide information, in effect supporting performance of other police functions. Aspects of this Korean experience were reprised across mid-century authoritarian East Asia, including Taiwan (as Chen discusses in Chapter 8), Hong Kong, and late-Republican China.

Such patterns of delegation and cooperation sometimes result not in cooptation but in the classic bureaucratic problem of capture – of the police by the policed – and, in turn, risks to effective performance of some assigned policing functions. This phenomenon extends to East Asian authoritarian regimes. In Mobrand's account of authoritarian Korea in Chapter 6, in pursuing some aspects of their multifaceted agenda, the police became not only dependent on cooperation with – but also vulnerable to corruption by – organized crime. In Chen's assessment of police relations with the ruling party in Chapter 8, we have an example of the potential for "capture" of the police by strongly socially embedded political actors at the local level.

East Asian authoritarian regimes also face the related paradox of legitimacy or authority of the police versus that of the regime – which fosters regime ambivalence about the institutional autonomy of the police. In several respects, the legitimacy of the police and the broader regime are symbiotic, or at least compatible. Broadly, as an integral part of the authoritarian regime – and one that interacts especially directly and intensively with society – the police as an institution is dependent on, and benefits from, the legitimacy and authority of the regime. Where the police perform their work effectively, and where the police enjoy social acceptance and trust, the regime benefits – often disproportionately, given the high visibility of the police as a manifestation of the regime and the potential for police behavior to alienate the public from its rulers.

More specifically, in authoritarian polities in East Asia, the police are often tasked with containing or preempting social or political movements that challenge regime policies or criticize the regime's failures or shortcomings in protecting public interests. This has been a major function of police in China, Vietnam, recently in Hong Kong, and beyond. In China, police have been key agents in preempting or quashing protests that have focused on issues such as property takings, gender discrimination, environmental pollution, government corruption, political reform, and foreign policy. In several cases considered in this book, and as emphasized by Nguyen in the case of Vietnam in Chapter 5 and Ng in the case of Hong Kong in Chapter 12, the regime has expected the police to control the narrative – assuring the dominance of the political leadership's view of politics, policy, and international affairs, while stamping out or choking off (including by interdicting materials coming from abroad) heterodox or ostensibly seditious thoughts and actions. Police failure at these tasks risks undermining the regime of which the police are a part.

In the largely top-down world of authoritarian politics, police legitimacy with the authoritarian leadership also affects the power and resources of police. The police's standing with the top leadership – upward-looking legitimacy – matters for police, and can be improved by police zealously and effectively doing the leadership's bidding. One vivid example of this phenomenon is the pervasive references to the thinking and views of top leader Xi Jinping in contemporary discourse on policing in China.[75] An earlier, cautionary Chinese tale is the devastating assault that Cultural Revolutionaries – inspired by the regime's top leader – undertook against the police along with other key organs of the party and state.[76]

On the other hand, the relationship between police legitimacy and regime legitimacy can be in tension, and sometimes at odds. The police can lose – or preserve – their own social legitimacy by doing – or eschewing – the regime's bidding. Perhaps most simply, where authoritarian police aggressively implement regime agendas of draconian control or radical transformation and do so coercively or against societal preferences, policework can delegitimate the police – and make the police hated – in society even as the police seek to manifest and safeguard the authority of the regime and its policy choices and prerogatives. The impact of social enmity may be greater for the police than for the regime as a whole, given the frontline, society-interfacing roles of the police

[75] See Chris Buckley, "'Drive the Blade In': Xi Shakes Up China's Law-and-Order Forces," *New York Times*, August 20, 2020, www.nytimes.com/2020/08/20/world/asia/china-xi-jinping-communist-party.html.

[76] Mao's instruction was to *zalan gong-jian-fa* (to smash police, procuracy, and courts), with a special emphasis attached to the police. See Shao-Chuan Leng, "The Role of Law in the People's Republic of China as Reflecting Mao Tse-tung's Influence," *Journal of Criminal Law and Criminology* 68(3) (1977): 356–373, at 359.

and the regime leadership's options to "point the spear downward" and blame police misconduct if the leaders seek to backtrack in response to failure or backlash.[77]

Commonplace among East Asian authoritarian regimes is the doppelganger of the pattern of broadly compatible legitimacy interests of the police and the broader regime noted above. As the Chinese case recurrently illustrates, the police/public security authorities are required – at peril to their legitimacy and reputation with the public – to preempt or stamp out potential protests against disliked regime policies and practices, including those affecting land-use rights, expressive freedoms, and political participation. Martin's and Wang, Joosse, and Cho's accounts, in Chapters 7 and 13, respectively, of the Hong Kong police in handling the Occupy Central/Umbrella Movement protests address a signal instance of this phenomenon. As Martin puts it in Chapter 7, the police had to choose between accountability up to the regime or down to democratic sentiment among much of the populace. Notwithstanding expectations or hopes that the police would side with democracy-related legal principles, the police enforced court orders – the formally lawful mandate of the state – to break up the movement, and the police's standing with some (but not all) segments of society fell. In Wang, Joosse, and Cho's characterization in Chapter 13, the Hong Kong police lost their position of perceived neutrality – which can be vital to police legitimacy.

Police in authoritarian regimes can enhance their legitimacy where there is a sense that the police are professional, functionally distinct, and institutionally autonomous, partly insulated from immediate political concerns and pressure from regime leaders. Reforms undertaken in East Asian authoritarian regimes considered in this book, and lessons drawn from the challenges facing police forces that lack these qualities, appear to recognize this phenomenon. One study of police legitimacy in contemporary China finds that police failure to follow the rules – to behave lawfully and professionally in a variety of ways – does most to sap police legitimacy with the public.[78] In Taiwan, Chen notes in Chapter 8, the regular police remained a remarkably legitimate (if residually authoritarian) institution

[77] See, for example, Yang Fan, "Report 'Scratches Surface' of Power Abuse in China," *Radio Free Asia*, December 2, 2014, www.rfa.org/english/news/china/abuse-02122014170103.html/; see also Hualing Fu, "Zhou Yongkang and the Recent Police Reform in China," *Australian and New Zealand Journal of Criminology* 38(2) (2005): 241–253, at 244–246.

[78] Ivan Y. Sun, Luye Li, Yuning Wu, and Rong Hu, "Police Legitimacy and Citizen Cooperation in China," *Asian Journal of Criminology* 13 (2018): 275–291.

after Taiwan transitioned to democratic rule in part because they had not played a large role in the more repressive facets of KMT authoritarian rule. Martin's account, in Chapter 7, of the postauthoritarian era Taiwan police's handling of the Sunflower Movement (and the contrast with Hong Kong police behavior in the context of the Umbrella Movement) resonates with this point: although politics were very much involved (including struggles among factions in the legislature and between President Ma Ying-jeou and Legislative Yuan Speaker Wang Jin-pyng), the police in Taiwan ultimately sided with the broader principles of constitutional democracy and law-governed governance that motivated the students to occupy the legislature.

The police can and do gain legitimacy through channels that do not neatly align with the regime's interest in its own legitimacy and authority. Police can gain by buffering or blunting unpopular or infeasible imperatives from above (such as near-zero-tolerance for crime, or policies demanding rapid and deep social change, or initiatives that would disrupt entrenched commercial and cultural practices). Even where cooperative relations between the police and allies and partners in society – and the ability to tap the social legitimacy and authority that the police enjoy – help to accomplish regime-designated tasks more effectively or efficiently, the leaders of the regime may have reason to be wary. Those virtues may come bundled with the vices (for the regime) of overly porous boundaries between a crucial component of the state (the police) and society, and greater downward accountability of police to constituencies and organizations in society (and, concomitantly, less disciplined upward responsiveness of police to the regime's leaders). In cooperative or trust-enhancing relations with society, the police may, in effect, help themselves, but at some cost to the regime's agenda and, ultimately, its legitimacy and authority.

Police and policing under authoritarian East Asian regimes face the paradox of law (or ambivalence about the rule of law/legality in governance): for police institutions and policing functions (and more generally), law is both constraining and empowering. Criticisms of authoritarian police and calls for reforms and democratic policing often stress the need for more and better law or the rule of law. Critics' and would-be reformers' prescriptions are often law-centered: due process-like or civil liberties-focused legal restraints on the extent and scope of the powers of police; requirements for transparency in police procedures and decision making; judicial or quasi-judicial or other formal review of police misconduct and police policies and actions more generally; monitoring by legally protected and empowered civil society organizations; internal (that is, intrapolice, sometimes strongly top-down) disciplinary mechanisms; measures to insulate police from intervention by political authority; and so on.[79]

Such legal constraints have the potential to reduce significantly the discretion, dominance, and violence of authoritarian police. In some respects, the authoritarian police's ability to "get things done" is limited by such checks on their ability to act without approval or review by other state bodies or citizen groups, or compliance with elaborate legal procedures, or subjection to probing oversight, or exposure to other modes of law-underpinned accountability. At least in a narrow or immediate sense, police gain power and effectiveness when they enjoy legally and practically unfettered opportunities to monitor, detain, or coerce citizens, or to redefine goals and change methods in response to perceived threats from below or abroad or policy directives from above.

In China, anticrime campaigns, and many other coercive or transformative drives in which the police play a major part, are a long-standing and recurring feature of authoritarian rule and a near-paradigm of weak legal constraints on the use of police (and broader party-state) power in pursuit of regime goals. As Chen and Nakano explain, in Chapters 8 and 9 respectively, the political police were notably less constrained by law – and thereby empowered to act to achieve the regime's existentially vital goals – than were the ordinary police in authoritarian Japan and Taiwan. In Singapore (as Tan addresses in Chapter 11) and in Hong Kong, special state security or anti-sedition divisions within the police were, similarly and for similar reasons, subject to weaker legal restraints than were the rest of the police.

In the East Asian context, authoritarian police and policing may interact with imperatives for legality in ways that pose a distinctive variant of the problem of the prerogative and normative states. In Ernst Fraenkel's classic formulation of this dual state, the boundaries between the law-governed normative state and the legally unconstrained and highly political prerogative state are chronically under stress in authoritarian regimes. Given their functions in such polities, the police are often at least partly in the realm of the prerogative state – and, where they exist, the special, or political, or secret police are almost inescapably so. As some notable recent

[79] See generally Graham Ellison and Nathan W. Pino, *Globalization, Police Reform and Development: Doing it the Western Way?* (New York: Palgrave Macmillan, 2021); David Bayley, *Democratizing the Police Abroad* (Washington, DC: National Institute of Justice, 2001).

scholarship on contemporary Chinese law has argued, this boundary may be especially porous and unstable – and the corrosive effect of the dynamics and logic of the prerogative state may be especially pronounced – in China (and kindred cases, especially those with deeply entwined and fused party-states), where fragile and often ambivalent projects of legal reform and development have unfolded against a very different background from the *rechtsstaat* that was the relevant past for the Nazi Germany regime that was the focus for Fraenkel.[80] More broadly, and although region-wide generalizations are problematic and interregional comparisons fraught, East Asian political traditions are, understandably, regarded as accepting of strong states but including little legality or legalism – at least when compared with the broad Western tradition.[81] To the extent that this pattern holds, strongly law-based (and often Western-derived) police and policing-relevant reforms must be planted in relatively foreign soil.

On the other hand, as leaders of authoritarian regimes in East Asia often seem to recognize, law also can be empowering for the police and the regimes they serve. A fundamental Weberian-cum-Leninist insight appears to hold in authoritarian East Asia: law and legal-rational structures create stronger organizational weapons for political authorities to wield.[82] Partly law-governed and law-structured police can be more disciplined, and responsive to political leaders, with laws strengthening the neural pathways that make the regime's hands and feet responsive to its brain. Nguyen and Chen depict, in Chapters 5 and 8 respectively, the founding rulers of authoritarian regimes in Taiwan and Vietnam as believing that legality – including for entities exercising police powers – was necessary for the effective functioning and legitimacy of their regimes. As observers of Xi-era approaches to law have noted, the Chinese leadership has turned, as its Reform-era predecessors also did to varying degrees, to

80 See Ernst Fraenkel, *The Dual State: A Contribution to the Theory of Dictatorship* (New York: Oxford University Press, 2010); Hualing Fu, "Duality and China's Struggle for Legal Autonomy," *China Perspectives* 11 (2019): 3–10; Eva Pils, "China's Dual State under Xi Jinping," UBC Community and Partner Publications, November 2, 2017, https://open.library.ubc.ca/cIRcle/collections/ubccommunityandpartnerspublicati/52387/items/1.0366867; Jacques deLisle, "The Rule of Law with Chinese Characteristics," in Barbara Faedda (ed.), *Rule of Law: Cases, Strategies, and Interpretations* (Ronzani, 2021), 103–120, at 110–111. In Chapter 10 in this volume, Mérieau argues that authoritarian Thailand exhibits similar characteristics.

81 For one recent example of this argument, see Francis Fukuyama, *Political Order and Political Decay* (New York: Farrar, Straus and Giroux, 2014), 335–385.

82 See Weber, "On Bureaucracy"; Selznick, *The Organizational Weapon.*

greater reliance on law for the police and has cast a turn to legality – most notably at the so-called Rule of Law plenum of the party's 18th Central Committee – as a means for making the police, along with other legal and law-related institutions, more effective and responsive tools or weapons of party rule.[83] As Biddulph discusses in Chapter 4, recent Chinese legal reforms have included measures to promote discipline, professionalization, fidelity to role, and vertical accountability for police.

Law (or law-like rules) conferring authority on the police and structuring police institutions and their external relationships are nearly ubiquitous features of authoritarian rule in East Asia. As many of the chapters in this book note, authoritarian police in East Asia are often governed by "police laws," which are adopted to address the changing needs, or perceived requirements, for effective policing and to provide legal bases for the use of police powers. As Biddulph notes in Chapter 4, a complex array of Chinese laws and rules have permitted – to varying degrees over PRC history – police to detain or de facto incarcerate suspected criminals and other targets without full criminal process or other significant formal constraints. For the authors who address postauthoritarian police in East Asia, democratic-era police laws appear to contribute significantly to the persistence of authoritarian policing into posttransition eras.[84]

As several chapters in this volume also address, East Asian authoritarian regimes enact laws that specifically empower the police to address perceived threats or crises, or to pursue new policy priorities. Examples include: cybersecurity and national security laws, and special provisions in the criminal law addressing terrorism and other politically charged offenses in China (some of them addressed by Fu in Chapter 3); laws providing specific legal mandates for the police to act against what the regime identified as politically motivated threats to public order in colonial Hong Kong and Singapore (discussed by Tan and Ng in Chapters 11 and 12 respectively); and the PRC's National Security Law for Hong Kong that gives expanded powers to new security-focused police units.

Although external legal accountability is generally weak for police (and for the state more generally), it is not absent in East Asian authoritarian regimes. Authorities in colonial Hong Kong empowered an independent anticorruption body to address police misbehavior that undermined

[83] See, for example, Creemers and Treavaskes (eds.), *Law and the Party*; deLisle, "Law in the China Model 2.0," and Biddulph, Chapter 4, in this volume.

[84] See, for example, Kroncke, Chapter 2; Chen, Chapter 8; Nakano, Chapter 9; and Mérieau, Chapter 10.

governing capacity and harmed the regime's image. Half a century later, Hong Kong prodemocracy voices called for legal accountability for police misconduct and abuse in handling the 2019–2020 protests that had badly damaged the public image of the police and the SAR government more broadly.[85] In the PRC, some opportunities to seek legal review of police behavior are available under the Administrative Litigation Law and less formal legal rule-invoking measures, and the Xi-era state supervision law and commissions contemplate a more law-centered (if heavily party-dominated) approach to corruption by state officers, including police. In these varied measures for legal accountability and law-based discipline of the police, there are perhaps echoes of the Legalist school of political thought in China, which argues that a potent and secure state requires strong and harsh laws governing the state's agents to incentivize them to perform their duties zealously and in accordance with the state's rules.

For authoritarian regimes in East Asia, the unappealingly constraining aspects of legality for the police may hold rule-consequentialist appeal, overriding shorter-term, act-consequentialist calculations that weigh against accepting legal constraints. Legal rules sometimes hamper or frustrate police in the immediate pursuit of their mandates (for example, by impeding torture, coerced confessions, or arbitrary detention of alleged criminals or perceived regime opponents, or by requiring higher-level or outside-the-police approval for some measures). But such legal rules and the restrictions they impose still may serve regime aims and interests – for example, by checking police indiscipline or overzealousness that can trigger public anger, distrust, or opposition toward police (and perhaps the regime) and impede the police's ability to perform tasks that are desirable, even essential, for the regime.

Finally, there is the related, broader paradox of reform, which is conducive to ambivalence in East Asian authoritarian polities about changes relevant to police and policing. In its more modest form, this paradox arises in the context of efforts at police reform. Reforms that seek to promote "better" policing – in the form of greater transparency, accountability, law-governedness, and so on – are common, explicable, and (from a

[85] See, for example, Amnesty International, "Hong Kong: Lack of Accountability for Police Violence Could Fuel Unrest," *Amnesty International*, March 5, 2020, www.amnesty.org/en/latest/news/2020/03/hong-kong-lack-accountability-police-violence-fuel-unrest/; Jesse Pang and Sarah Wu, "Hong Kong Leader Rejects Protesters' Call for Independent Police Probe," Reuters, May 16, 2020; see also Martin, Chapter 7, and Wang, Joosse, and Cho, Chapter 13, in this volume.

liberal, democratic, and rule-of-law perspective) salutary goals. In recent years, they often have been supported by foreign (largely Western) rule-of-law assistance efforts that have engaged with authoritarian regimes in East Asia. Yet such efforts can have perverse effects (and thus pose dilemmas for assistance-providers as well as some recipient-country advocates). They can make police forces in authoritarian regimes more capable – with greater technical skills and more competent organization – and thus more effective in serving the regime's political ends, including suppressing dissent and maintaining an illiberal and undemocratic political order.

Here, again, China is a prominent example. The issues resonate with the *ti-yong* discourse of the late Qing era, when reformist elites sought to learn and adapt foreign techniques – beginning with military technology but later extending to institutional design and legal reforms – in order to strengthen and preserve the existing Chinese authoritarian political order. In more recent times, the prospect that well-intentioned advice bearing on police-related issues – including administrative law, emergency powers law, and so on – would enhance the capacity of the authoritarian state has been a basis for criticism of, or skepticism toward, projects to provide law reform advice and assistance to the PRC.[86]

The paradox of reform extends to democratic reforms and transitions. For example, decentralization of police institutions is often an element of democratic policing reforms within authoritarian systems and with system-wide democratization as well. This was the case with the calls for decentralizing police administration in postwar Japan and amid democratic reform in Japan's former colonies. Yet, as contributors to this collection argue, in those cases and more generally, such decentralization can fail to produce the hoped-for results, and can reduce, or make more difficult, police accountability and transparency. It can create environments in which corruption and capture by parochial and sometimes illiberal interests can grow.[87]

More broadly and more fundamentally, democracy or democratization can fail to redress authoritarian policing and support its persistence or resurgence. As several of the chapters in this volume address, authoritarian policing practices and police structures have persisted in formerly authoritarian

[86] See generally deLisle, "Lex Americana"; Erica Marst, "Reforming Police in Post-Communist Countries," *Comparative Politics* 48(3) (2016): 333–352; Jerome A. Cohen, "Was Helping China Build Its Post-1978 Legal System a Mistake?" *Virginia Journal of International Law* 20 (2020): 1–30.

[87] See Kroncke, Chapter 2 (including comparisons with the US) and Chen, Chapter 8, among others.

but now democratic polities in East Asia. Variations of this argument can be found in Chen's account in Chapter 8 and others' assessments of Taiwan,[88] and Kroncke's and Nakano's analyses of Japan in Chapters 2 and 9 respectively (which use terms such as "democratic authoritarian police") Moreover, as contributors to this book and other scholars note, in East Asia (and elsewhere, including the US), being "tough on crime" – including through methods associated with authoritarian police and policing – can enjoy much popular (that is to say, democratic) support in democratic and postauthoritarian political systems. In Chapter 2, Kroncke points to social acceptance in Japan of few rights for suspects and few checks on police. And there was considerable support in Hong Kong – from conservative elites and from groups dubbing themselves a "silent majority" – for the unusually (by Hong Kong standards) harsh police moves against the Occupy Central/Umbrella Movement and in later protests as well.[89]

The phenomenon of popular, often nationalist or populist support for more authoritarian policing and erosion of democratic (or even nondemocratic) legal constraints on police power is likely to be all the more pronounced when severe threats to order and security arise, or are perceived or concocted. Examples addressed or noted in this book include: terrorism (most prominently in the US but extending globally, including in the Chinese regime-proffered explanations of police and other coercive state actors' roles in the massive detentions of Uyghurs in Xinjiang); drugs (in Duterte's war on drugs in the Philippines); and many allegedly foreign-backed plots to transform or destabilize authoritarian regimes (as claimed in colonial-era Hong Kong and Singapore, in China's imputation of a PRC-targeting "peaceful evolution" agenda to the US, and in contemporary Hong Kong during the Occupy Central/Umbrella Movement and the protests beginning in 2019 – which targeted, among other things, the authorization of sweeping police powers in a National Security Law for Hong Kong).

14.4 Variety and Commonality in Authoritarian Police and Policing in East Asia

Police and policing share many fundamental characteristics across contemporary and historical authoritarian regimes in East Asia. Some features are endemic to authoritarian regimes, and some extend to policing

[88] See also Liqun Cao, Lanying Huang and Ivan Sun, "From Authoritarian Policing to Democratic Policing: A Case Study of Taiwan," *Policing and Society* 26(6) (2016): 642–658.

[89] See Martin, Chapter 7; see also deLisle, "Hong Kong's Summer of Discontent."

in postauthoritarian and democratic regimes in the region, and beyond. Some features are arguably distinctly East Asian, while others appear to be shaped by more contingent common or overlapping external influences. Yet police and their roles and the functions of policing also exhibit much variation across the diverse array of East Asian authoritarian regimes. Such diversity is to be expected where the polities differ so dramatically in terms of scale, level of economic development, subtype of authoritarian regime, subtype of East Asian culture or political culture, foreign influences, and historical period.

Much of the variety and much of the uniformity stem from the multiple functions that the police perform or are expected to perform, the internal structure of police bodies, the horizontal relationships between the police and other state institutions, their vertical relationships upward with regime leadership and downward with society, and external influences from abroad and from history. Such patterns have evolved and surely will continue to do so in authoritarian polities in East Asia, and they have influenced and will continue to influence police and policing in postauthoritarian, democratic orders.

Some changes in police and policing and their roles have occurred, and will occur, without much conscious agency, but others will be, and have been, shaped – albeit often not as intended – by political and social choices. Those choices are framed, and their consequences affected, by pervasive paradoxes and resulting ambivalences of police and policing in authoritarian East Asia: expanding police duties and functions can bring perilous reductions in police efficacy, legitimacy, and responsiveness to the regime; greater legitimacy and authority for the police can be both a boon and a bane for the regime's legitimacy and authority; police-related law and legal reforms can both constrain and empower police; and reforms of a broadly rule-of-law, democratic, or liberal character to the police, or to the broader political system, can reduce some of the pathologies of authoritarian police behavior, but they may fall short and can lead to perverse results. Shared problematics thus do not portend simple convergence among East Asian authoritarian regimes' police and policing, much less inevitable progress toward what advocates of democratic or postauthoritarian police and policing may seek or expect.

INDEX

For EU product safety concerns, contact us at Calle de José Abascal, 56–1°, 28003 Madrid, Spain or eugpsr@cambridge.org.

www.ingramcontent.com/pod-product-compliance
Lightning Source LLC
Chambersburg PA
CBHW071322180926
51611CB00002B/28
* 9 7 8 1 0 0 9 0 4 5 4 2 1 *